GROPING FOR ETHICS IN JOURNALISM

H. EUGENE GOODWIN

Groping for Ethics in Journalism

IOWA STATE UNIVERSITY PRESS ● AMES

Library of Congress Cataloging in Publication Data
Goodwin, H. Eugene, 1922–
  Groping for ethics in journalism.

  1. Journalistic ethics 1. Title.
PN4756.G66 1983   174.9097   83–8566
ISBN 0–8138–0816–2
ISBN 0–8138–0817–0 (pbk.)

Composed by Typeco, Inc., Des Moines, Iowa 50309
Printed by The Iowa State University Press, Ames, Iowa 50010

First edition, 1983

C O N T E N T S

v

"Don't tell me my newspaper isn't ethical. We haven't offended anybody in this town for years."

PREFACE

WHEN I TOLD PEOPLE I was doing a book on journalism ethics, I got some interesting reactions. Like:

"What ethics?"

"Well, at least the bibliographic search will be short."

"Will it be a comic book?"

"Will the right people read it?"

I do not agree with the attitude toward journalism expressed in those only half-kidding reactions, but I understand it. Journalism is not held in high esteem by many people in this country, some of whom are journalists. Many see journalism as a tawdry calling, practiced often by unprincipled boors.

Actually journalism has gotten to be quite respectable these days. With the advent of cold type and computers, newspaper newsrooms are indistinguishable from insurance offices: rugs on the floor, no typewriters or teletypes clacking away, no glue pots, no green eyeshades, no shouts of "Hold the presses, I've got a story here that's gonna bust this town wide open!" Decorum rules. Television newsrooms tend to be more cluttered; but with makeup rooms, instant public recognition for its on-camera stars, and a five-year, $8 million contract for Dan Rather, TV journalism is nothing if not respectable. But try as it may, journalism cannot completely shake its Bohemian traditions. Hard-drinking, hard-smoking, hard-living, hard-nosed types still find news work compatible with their bad habits.

I have been observing journalists at work and play for many years. I was in what used to be called "the newspaper game" for about a dozen years; and as a teacher of journalism for more than twice that long, I have continued to watch the game being played. I like news people, scoundrels and saints alike. They do interesting things, some of which have to do with their work, and they tell interesting stories, some for public consumption. I love their irreverance and their skepticism, and admire their ability to get at the core of things in a world in which obfuscation and beating around bushes seems more highly revered.

But for a long time I have been bothered by some of the things journalists and news media proprietors do. They do not always seem to have a strong sense of morality, of what is right and wrong. Even news people I know to be honest and decent folks do wrongful things in pursuit of a story (I did the same myself and feel the shame to this day). My feelings about the occasional but serious moral lapses of journalists and of the news business as a whole began to jell when I took over the news media ethics course at Penn State that John Harrison, another newsman-turned-teacher, had taught for many years before his retirement. And as I organized my thoughts and files and dug into what had been written about the rights and wrongs of journalistic practice, I came to see a place for a book that would try to assess the current status of ethics in the field and present it in a way that might help journalists think through their ethical problems.

That is what I have tried to do with this book. It is not a philosophical book. I am not qualified by training or inclination to write a philosophical book. I did this book the only way I know how — the way I learned to report: Do your homework and then ask the questions. After reading all I could get my hands on that might be relevant. I interviewed about 150 working journalists and a few media watchers. About 100 of those I interviewed on tape are quoted in this book. I am grateful — both to those who were and those who were not quoted — for sharing their knowledge and views with me. I learned from all of them.

(Many of the journalists quoted have changed jobs since our interview, journalism being one of society's most mobile businesses. I have tried to identify them by their most current job titles in the text, but at the end of the footnotes they are identified by the jobs they held when I interviewed them.)

The journalists and observers interviewed were not scientifically selected. They were picked because I believed they would have significant things to say about journalism ethics; most did. I interviewed more big-time print and broadcast journalists than those who do their journalism in smaller communities because most (not all, but most) of the ethical problems arise in urban journalism. And frankly, most executives and journalists in the larger news organizations have thought more about and had more experiences with the questions raised in my investigation.

Another thing this book is not is a report on the ethics of all mass communicators. It does not deal with the ethics of advertising or public relations practitioners or entertainers. Their standards are important but come from different roots and have, in my opinion, less bearing on the general welfare than do those of our principal information processors.

In considering the ethics of journalistic practice in this book, my focus is on newspaper, wire service, and television journalism. That is where most journalists ply their trade. Magazine and radio journalists are a comparatively small minority. I did not try to deal specifically with cable television news, not because it lacks importance in U.S. journalism, but because — with the notable exception of Ted Turner's Cable Network News — most cable TV news comes from the wire services, newspapers, or other existing media sources. In other words, cable TV news has not — so far, anyway — added significantly to the number of journalists in this country. When you study the ethics of a profession or business, you have to study the people who are in it; the channels and technology of communication with which they deal are secondary.

In addition to the journalists and observers I interviewed, a lot of people helped me with this book. My friend, Fran Goodwin, who is also my wife, edited and typed the manuscript through its various versions and did the cartoons that make their points more tellingly than my words. She and Sally Heffentreyer dug out important articles, books, and facts for me from libraries and other sources. Colleagues on the journalism faculty at Penn State — Tom Berner, Vince Norris, John Nichols, Don Smith, Bill Dulaney, Dan Pfaff, and John Rippey — contributed valuable criticisms and suggestions. Research papers by former graduate students Jack Tobias, Robert W. Hollis, Michael Salwen, George Osgood, Neil Genzlinger, Deborah Benedetti, Kathleen Pavelko, Donald Sneed, and Martha McCoy expanded my knowledge of matters dealt with in these pages. I am also grateful to the Pennsylvania State University for the sabbatical leave that enabled me to complete research for and write this book.

Finally, I wish to dedicate this book to my wife, whose encouragement and support made the work possible and whose companionship made it fun.

H. EUGENE GOODWIN
Professor of Journalism
Pennsylvania State University

ACRONYMS

ABC	=	American Broadcasting Company
AFTRA	=	American Federation of Television and Radio Artists
AIM	=	Accuracy in Media
AP	=	Associated Press
APME	=	Associated Press Managing Editors Association
APSE	=	Associated Press Sports Editors Association
ARCO	=	Atlantic Richfield Company
ASNE	=	American Society of Newspaper Editors
BGA	=	Better Government Association
CBS	=	Columbia Broadcasting System
CIA	=	Central Intelligence Agency
FCC	=	Federal Communications Commission
GAO	=	Government Accounting Office
GNS	=	Gannett News Service
MADD	=	Minnesotans Against the Downtown Dome
NBC	=	National Broadcasting Company
NCAA	=	National Collegiate Athletic Association
NCEW	=	National Conference of Editorial Writers
NLRB	=	National Labor Relations Board
NPPA	=	National Press Photographers Association
ONO	=	Organization of Newspaper Ombudsmen
OWAA	=	Outdoor Writers Association of America
RTNDA	=	Radio Television News Directors Association
SATW	=	Society of American Travel Writers
SPJ-SDX	=	Society of Professional Journalists, Sigma Delta Chi
TI	=	Texas Instruments
UPI	=	United Press International

GROPING FOR ETHICS IN JOURNALISM

The Search for Standards

"I said they had a right to publish — but that doesn't mean I want you to read it!"

IF YOU HAVE EVER DENTED a parked car, did you leave a note?

If a clerk gives you too much change, do you give the money back?

When you are asked to give a job recommendation for an acquaintance with less than average ability, do you tell the truth?

Those are the kinds of ethical questions most of us have to face more than once in our lives. They are not in the same league with such questions as: Should Truman have authorized the dropping of atomic bombs on Japan? Should Nixon have ordered the cover-up of the Watergate burglary? Should decisions about abortions be left to the women involved and their doctors? Yet how we answer such questions, whether mundane or cosmic, determines how ethical we are as individuals and how civilized our society is.

Sometimes economic factors dictate our ethics. Remember Alfred Doolittle, the dustman in George Bernard Shaw's *Pygmallion,* who tried to get Prof. Henry Higgins to pay for the "use" of his daughter Liza? Shocked by Doolittle's effrontery, Higgins's friend Colonel Pickering asks, "Have you no morals, man?"

"Can't afford them, Governor," Doolittle replies unabashedly. "Neither could you if you was as poor as me."[1]

3

Sometimes our upbringing — what we have learned from parents, pastors, and police — guides us through our ethical thickets. But many believe the guidelines of upbringing are less influential these days, that the moral codes of society are breaking down.

"The belief in authority disintegrated in this century, particularly the latter part of the century, the sixties being the best example of that," says James Wall, editor of *Christian Century* (interview, 9 Sept. 1981).* "There's no 'sacred' anymore." Gone is "the assumption of the community, the family, and the individual that there are standards handed down to us from the authorities, the sacred holders of the Truth, or the government."

Wall believes this disintegration of authority has made codes of morals, ethics, and standards obligatory in the professions. "When there's chaos in the land, somebody's got to have some kind of order."

Whether all or most journalists in the United States see this need to establish professional ethical standards to compensate for the disintegrating morals of the larger society is uncertain, but journalists have undoubtedly become more conscious of ethics in recent years.

David Shaw, media reporter-critic for the *Los Angeles Times,* views journalism's increasing emphasis on ethics as a "positive consequence of Watergate." (Interview, 25 Nov. 1980.) He finds that "journalists have been forced to be more ethical because it is very difficult to expose politicians for lying and then turn around and lie yourself in exposing them." The combination of "the deceit that went into the Vietnam War build-up" and "the abuses of the Nixon administration culminating in Watergate . . . forced the press to clean up its act."

Any careful investigator can find plenty of evidence of what Shaw is talking about. Journalists in all our news media — newspapers, television, magazines, and radio — seem to be more conscious of ethics today than in the past. But you can also find cases that seem to show journalism has a long way to go before it can claim to be an ethical calling.

This book is a report on the state of ethics in journalism in the United States. It is based on an analysis of hundreds of interviews and discussions with print and broadcast journalists at all levels, and on the writings of ethicists, journalists, and others concerned about ethics in this vital field.

AGREEING ON GUIDING PRINCIPLES

Journalists in the United States have some major problems in coming to grips with their ethics. One has to do with their difficulty in dealing with the contrasting and often conflicting pulls of journalism the

---

*See list of interviewees following Notes.

profession and journalism the business. Unlike most lawyers and physicians, the people we think of as journalists — reporters, writers, photographers, editors, news directors, and news producers who report and interpret the news — are mostly hired hands. They are not completely in control of their own methods and products. (This problem is dealt with in Chapter 2.)

Another major problem is the strong feeling throughout American journalism that First Amendment freedom is paramount, even if it means protecting bad journalism.

The First Amendment

Congress shall make no law respecting an establishment of religion, or prohibiting the free exercise thereof; or abridging the freedom of speech, or of the press; or the right of the people peaceably to assemble, and to petition the Government for a redress of grievances.

That guarantee of freedom in the First Amendment to the U.S. Constitution, and similar guarantees in the constitutions of the fifty states, provides the legal basis for press freedom in this country. That freedom in turn has had a powerful influence on the ethics of journalists and the news media, principal beneficiaries of the First Amendment.

It must be understood that the First Amendment does not literally mean that no laws whatever can be passed abridging freedom of the press. Like all provisions of the Constitution, the free press provision has been interpreted and reinterpreted by the courts over the years, so that several restrictions on absolute freedom — libel and slander, for example — have been permitted. The courts also have granted somewhat less freedom to broadcast journalists than to print journalists, although that discrimination seems to be disappearing.

In addition to the court decisions on press freedom, the interpretations that journalists give to the First Amendment shape their attitudes toward ethics and ethical standards. Some view this freedom in absolutist terms and therefore resist efforts to impose any universal standards on journalism and the news media, whether by government or by journalism itself.

"The strength of the American press is its diversity," insists Abraham M. Rosenthal, executive editor of the *New York Times*. "There are publishers I wouldn't dirty my hands with, but I don't want a code that would exclude them." (Interview, 7 Oct. 1981.)

Jack Landau, director of the Reporters Committee for Freedom of the Press, fears that the courts will impose the "moral framework of the establishment press" on the alternative press, "all the little publications, some of which are creepy and way-out." (Interview, 24 Sept. 1981.) They will do this, he believes, through the calling of expert witnesses from the larger newspapers and by applying the codes of the larger news media and of journalistic organizations as standards for all. He contends that the smaller newspapers and broadcast stations cannot live up to the standards of the *New York Times* because they do not have the staffs and resources to be as accurate and thorough as large metropolitan newspapers can be. Besides, many of the alternative publications do not buy all of the standards of the establishment press, Landau argues. "They say, 'Why should we be fair? Fairness is your white, middle class, male, Ivy League value. We have a right to put our own views across.'" Landau does not want "courts telling these people what is right and wrong."

Because he is "an extremist about the First Amendment," Lyle Denniston, U.S. Supreme Court reporter for the Baltimore *Sun*, cannot accept a universal ethical code for journalists (interview, 5 June 1981). He believes the First Amendment states "a social value preference for an open society, in which there cannot be any governmental restraints on the communication of ideas." An industry-wide ethics code "is alien to my basic notion about the free communication of ideas: it is law or regulation in another format." Ethics for the journalist, Denniston holds, have to be individual, "based on some kind of internal moral-ethical perception."

Although they share the absolutists' fear of government interference with news media freedom, many other journalists seem to infer from the First Amendment the notion that standards and responsibility are a sort of payment for freedom. They support greater efforts by journalists, often with the help of nongovernmental outsiders, to improve the ethics and standards of the news media and to be accountable to the public for their acts.

"We vigorously oppose any government interference in the gathering and disseminating of information," says Paul Janensch, executive editor of the *Louisville Times* and *Courier-Journal*. "But we think it's wrong for the news media to wrap themselves in the First Amendment whenever someone challenges what we do and how we do it." The news media should be receptive to criticism from within and without, and "operate within written codes so that everyone involved in the news process knows what is permitted and what is out of bounds."[2]

Another who speaks for the moderate view of the First Amendment is Paul A. Poorman, editor and vice-president of the *Akron Beacon Journal* (interview, 8 Apr. 1981). "Our skirts have to be clean. We have to be above suspicion . . . if we're to, first, make money, be a profitable institution, and second, fulfill the social role guaranteed to us in the Constitution," Poorman contends. The First Amendment does not talk about confidentiality, honesty, and the many ethical problems journalists face today because its framers could not anticipate what the press has become, he adds. Poorman has compiled a list of thirty-four broad areas, including interstate commerce and labor-management relations, in which Congress has made law impinging on the absolute freedom of the press. "Anytime I hear people waving the First Amendment," he says, "I remind them of the Twenty-first Amendment — the short one that abolished prohibition and says simply that the Eighteenth Amendment is hereby repealed."

Social Responsibility. Many who have studied journalism and mass communications in America since World War II have looked to the social responsibility theory of the press as a possible basis for a system of journalism ethics. This theory was described but not labeled in the work of the so-called Hutchins Commission on Freedom of the Press and was brilliantly articulated by Theodore Peterson in *Four Theories of the Press* in 1956. Peterson, professor and former dean of the College of Communications at the University of Illinois-Urbana, wrote that the "major premise" of the social responsibility theory is that "freedom carries concomitant obligations; and the press, which enjoys a privileged position under our government, is obliged to be responsible to society for carrying out certain essential functions of mass communications in contemporary society."[3]

The social responsibility theory was seen by Peterson as replacing the traditional libertarian theory, which had guided those who established our press system when this country was founded. Libertarianism, a composite of ideas of such thinkers as John Milton, John Erskine, Thomas Jefferson, and John Stuart Mill, holds that the press and other media should be privately owned and as free as possible from government so they can pursue the truth as they see it and be a check on government. The press can be irresponsible as well as responsible, printing falsehoods as well as truth, because the citizens are rational and can separate one from the other. The important thing under libertarian theory is for there to be a free marketplace of ideas, because if all voices can be heard the truth will surely emerge.

"But somewhere along the way, faith diminished in the optimistic notion that a virtually absolute freedom and the nature of man carried built-in correctives for the press," Peterson maintained.[4]

He argued that social responsibility as a theory for the press was born out of several changes in the world. One of these was the technological and industrial revolution that changed "the American way of living," added movies, radio, and television to the media system, and encouraged concentration of media ownership in a few hands.

Another change "was a new intellectual climate in which some persons looked with suspicion on the basic assumptions of the Enlightenment," Peterson wrote. "And finally there was the development of a professional spirit as journalism attracted men of principle and education, and as the communications industries reflected the growing sense of social responsibility assumed by American business and industry generally."

Peterson did not try to build ethical standards from the theory he described. In fact, he cautioned his readers to "remember that the social responsibility theory is still chiefly a theory. But as a theory it is important because it suggests a direction in which thinking about freedom of the press is heading."

Interviewed twenty-five years after publication of *Four Theories of the Press,* Peterson points out that he never advocated anything in his chapter on social responsibility, although he is often accused of doing so (interview, 3 Sept. 1981). He believes the chapter had a great impact on schools of journalism and their curricula — "at least it introduced the notion of social responsibility" — and that may have in turn influenced the growth of a professional ethic in the practice of journalism. "But, unfortunately," he continues, "the ethic that has developed is an unreasoned ethic without a philosophical base."

Although he believes most of the media codes of ethics and standards that have emerged in this century came in response to public criticism, Peterson "has a very strong respect for the ethical behavior" of the newspaper and magazine people he knows, at least those among his generation. He maintains they have a "very strong sense of rightness."

Peterson's Illinois colleague, Clifford G. Christians, notes somewhat sadly that the social responsibility theory "has not generated seasoned ethical standards." He adds that the decreasing numbers of information channels:

> remind us that the public good may be our only valid guideline for choosing which information to transmit. And certainly social responsibility is much more compatible with public ownership of the electromagnetic spectrum. For all that, as noted, principles based on this ideology remain undefined and its ethical sophistication limited.[5]

Another academic, John L. Hulteng of Stanford University, concedes that a majority of editors and educators and many working journalists believe that in this period of shrinking numbers of channels of information "social responsibility is the only valid and acceptable guiding theory for the press." But an ethical framework does not logically evolve from that theory, Hulteng writes, arguing that "the principles and standards that are influential in the workings of the mass media today stem from many sources and a variety of theories," including the more traditional libertarian ideology and "folkways of the news business."[6]

These less than optimistic assessments of the social responsibility theory's impact on journalistic practice should not be taken to mean that the theory is dead. It has had some influence and it may have more in the future. And although the theory lacks a full-blown philosophical base for a system of ethics in journalism, its central principle that journalists are obliged to be responsible to society still has great appeal.

The Public's Right to Know. Although the social responsibility theory may not be familiar to many journalists, a slogan that came along about the same time certainly is. "The public's right to know" (or "people's right to know," if you prefer) has been a chant of American journalists in the period since World War II as they fought to expand their access to news of government, business, and other areas of the society that have found ways to hide from public scrutiny.

The phrase seems to have started with Kent Cooper, former top executive of the Associated Press (AP), and then became cemented into the conventional wisdom of journalism when Harold Cross used it as a title of a book he wrote for the American Society of Newspaper Editors (ASNE) in 1953. The general theme of his book and of the doctrine the slogan represents is that the public has a legal right to know what its government is doing and the press is the representative of the public in finding that out.[7]

From this doctrine has come a long and reasonably successful campaign by journalism to get most of the states to adopt open meetings and open records laws and to get the federal government to enact the Freedom of Information Act in 1967. None of these laws has worked to the complete satisfaction of most journalists, but they have been useful in opening up more of the activities and records of government to the news media and to the public.

There has been an ethical dimension to the public's right to know movement. It has stimulated journalists, somewhat arrogantly in some cases admittedly, to see themselves as representatives of the people. Many a reporter has sensed a special responsibility when covering some important public meeting with no members of the public present except perhaps an observer for the League of Women Voters and a couple of lawyers representing some special interest or other. The reporter in that all-too-common circumstance usually makes a special effort to report actions that might affect those absent citizens — not to sell more papers or increase his or her station's audience, but out of a sense of duty. This same sense of representing the public at large has spurred journalists as they have tried to throw light on the less obvious activities of business and other areas of the private sector in which the public has an interest.

The Baltimore *Sun's* Denniston sees a Catch 22 in Harold Cross's doctrine (interview, 5 June 1981). He does not "buy former Justice Potter

Stewart's view that the free press clause was put in the Constitution to give the press some kind of peculiar role in monitoring government. If you follow that to its logical conclusion, you end up with the concept of the press as a public utility." That notion has encouraged "the developing idea that the press is part of the government machine," Denniston believes. This means "we get access when we are necessary in the governmental process — and only when we are."

One of Denniston's ethical premises "is that you really owe your reader nothing." He tries to reach readers but that differs from being obliged to reach them, as the public's right to know doctrine implies. "I do not work for a public utility," he insists. "I don't have to pick up everybody who wants to get on my bus. I'm in the business of gathering and selling ideas. If somebody wants to buy them, fine, but don't come to me and tell me you have a right to be told."

Denniston's concern about the public's right to know doctrine may not be shared by most journalists, many of whom see the press as a public utility in the sense that it has responsibilities to the public it serves. But for some reason the slogan itself has been used less and less often by those who speak for journalism in this country. The general public, on the other hand, seems to have taken to the slogan, some treating it as if it's their natural and constitutional right to be told what they want to be told.

And journalists, too, have tried to turn the doctrine to their own ends, invoking it, for example, as justification for questionable conduct; stealing or lying to get a story is often explained away by claiming that the public's right to know had to be served.

Journalists, limited by news space and time, have to decide every day what it is that the public has a right to know. A visit to any newsroom at the end of a working day shows even the casual observer how much news is left over, unused, apparently not material the public has a right to know. The point is not to make jest of the difficult news decisions that editors have to make but to argue that what the public has a right to know is determined by editors making subjective judgments and by managers who determine how much news space and time will be available. A doctrine so imperfect can hardly justify illegal and unethical behavior by any thinking journalist.

Accuracy and Fairness. Although American journalists have a hard time agreeing on many things, virtually all of them have come to accept accuracy and fairness as the most important of their professional standards. Both of these standards, of course, are ethical as well as professional or operational.

Accuracy has been a more troublesome ideal for journalists than it might appear. For one thing, journalists have to do their work under deadlines, very demanding deadlines at times. The pressure to get the news out to the public while it is still fresh causes errors. That is why many newsrooms in an earlier day posted the old International News Service admonition, "Get It First, But First Get It Right." Fine, but every journalist soon learns that getting it first sometimes means you don't get it right, and taking the time to get it right often means you don't get it first.

A second difficulty in achieving accuracy has to do with expectations. Most people outside of journalism, and even many journalists, expect journalism to produce the "truth," forgetting what Walter Lippmann tried to tell us years ago — that news and truth are not the same thing.[8] The facts that journalists *can* produce sometimes add up to the truth, but journalists are seldom able to put sufficient facts together at a given time to be able to tell the truth about some news subject. Reporting the Vietnam War gave us a good example of this problem: the journalists who covered that confusing and complicated conflict were never able to get at the truth about that war. They could report what U.S. generals said, what a portion of U.S. and South Vietnamese troops did that day, or what a segment of Vietcong troops did that day, but those were "facts" about the war. We are only now beginning to learn the "truth" about that war. On less complex news situations, of course, journalists can get closer to the truth. But the failure on the part of both journalists and the public to see journalism as a fact business and not a truth business has caused frustration among journalists and a general misunderstanding about journalism's function in our society.

This is not to say that journalists should not be and have not been truthful in their pursuit of facts. That is what the accuracy standard really means: being truthful both in the gathering and presentation of facts and information; not lying, not plagiarizing.

Although the history of American journalism contains some colorful lapses in the accuracy standard, accuracy has been an undisputed goal of virtually all journalists in this country for at least a century.

The standard of fairness is part of and in a way an offspring of objective reporting. Depending on which history or reporting books you read, objective reporting started in the nineteenth century with the growth of cooperative news gathering through the AP, or it developed in the twentieth century as journalists imitated the scientific methods of natural science. Whichever, the idea that news should be unbiased, balanced, and fair became and remains widely accepted in the field, even though the word "objectivity" has fallen into dispute.

One reason that objectivity in reporting got into trouble was the way it was interpreted and administered by many newsroom bosses, particularly those who ran the larger wire services. Too many of them defined objectivity in very narrow terms: just report what important people say and do; don't bother about the why's and don't worry about explaining anything; let the readers figure things out for themselves.

Michael J. O'Neill, former editor of the New York *Daily News,* learned about this narrow definition of objectivity when he went out to cover a meat packers' strike in Chicago about 1950 for United Press International (UPI). The union claimed the company had scabs working inside the plant, but management denied it. O'Neill climbed over the fence, ripping his suit on the barbed wire, and discovered nonunion workers living inside the plant and sleeping on 125 cots he counted. When O'Neill got back to his office, his editor told him he could not use what he had seen unless he could quote some company official. "Well, that's stupid," O'Neill says today, "because half the truth that you develop you're never going to get anybody to announce or to officially identify with." (Interview, 8 Oct. 1981.)

Demagogues have taken advantage of journalists who insisted that news was not news until somebody in authority said it. Senator Joseph McCarthy of Wisconsin helped bring about the decline of the old narrow view of objectivity by the way he twisted it and some other conventions of journalism to his own ends. Realizing that almost anything a U.S. senator said was news, McCarthy got the press to distribute his unsubstantiated charges about the large numbers of Communists who had supposedly infiltrated the government, even the military. This was in the 1950s when a lot of people were imagining Reds under their beds as the country went through one of its periodic scares about the Communist conspiracy. McCarthy would time his speeches, press conferences, and news releases so that they would just make the deadlines of the major news media, and so there was seldom time to check any of his charges for the same day's story, even if anybody had felt inclined to do so. After McCarthy's political bubble burst in 1954 when the Senate voted sixty-seven to twenty-two to censure him for his reckless and abusive conduct, many in the press took a hard look at how they had been used by this skillful abuser of truth. And one of the shibboleths of journalism they began to question was objectivity as it had been so narrowly defined.

The notion of journalistic objectivity took a further beating during the Vietnam War and the domestic turmoil it produced through the 1960s and early 1970s. Critics blamed objectivity for journalism's failure to break out of the news management increasingly practiced by generals, presidents, and others in control of American life and institutions. Not only was it impossible for reporters to be unbiased, these critics argued, it was undesirable. And that line of criticism has persisted.

"It's stupid and dishonest for journalists to continue to insist that they are without gut feelings, values, politics, et cetera," declares Robert Scheer, a former editor of *Ramparts* and *New Times* and now a reporter for the *Los Angeles Times* (interview, 25 Nov. 1980). "And if they are, I want to know why and how did they get to be without those things and where have they been.... To me the more important question is not whether you can be neutral but how you do your job in a fair and honest way."

Objectivity also has been criticized for producing a bland, almost ignorant, kind of news reporting that gives all facts and all views equal weight to the point of distortion. Critics argue that the many complexities in the world today require not neutral observers but journalists who educate themselves in the subjects they report so that they can interpret them from a point of view; only in that way can the public make sense out of the complexities.

Because of the barrage of criticism and questioning objective reporting has been under since the 1950s, it is no longer on every journalist's list of goals and ideals. Most journalists today, even those who still profess a belief in "objectivity," see fairness as the important principle to live by. Many still insist, however, that it is desirable and possible for reporters to be reasonably unbiased and to keep their own views out of their news stories. So objectivity has not died in American news work; it simply was so abused by some of its earlier adherents that many of today's journalists prefer the simpler standard of fairness.

The record here should also show that the public has been well served as well as poorly served by objective reporting. We have been well served when reporters, most of whom are generalists expected to be able to handle all kinds of news, sensed that they were dealing with subjects better left to others to judge and tried to be neutral and fair to all sides in their reporting of such subjects. Whenever reporters are in over their heads in reporting any complicated subject, we are probably better off with a report that simply lays out whatever facts are available without having them judged or interpreted for us.

We have been poorly served, on the other hand, when reporters in their striving for objectivity produced superficial reports — a string of quotes from various sources, for example, hung across the line like Monday's wash and making very little sense to anybody. We also have been poorly served when writers refused to abandon strict objectivity in reporting something as bewildering as the Vietnam War or the American public's reaction to it, phenomena that cried out for explanation and humanistic interpretation.

The main concern of this book about accuracy and fairness, however, is what these standards have to say about journalism ethics. In the sense that accuracy means being truthful in both the gathering and reporting of facts and information, it is a significant ethical standard, just as "Don't lie" is a principal warning in the everyday codes of ethics most of us carry around in our heads. Fairness in dealing with sources and in reporting also is a significant ethical standard when it is taken by journalists to mean that they should be fair and honest in news reporting, that they should not judge others prematurely and should instead exercise a bit of compassion. Objectivity has been defined in many ways, admittedly, but the ethical implications have always been there too and have dominated the work of many journalists. Objective reporting, with all of its imperfections, has by itself been a kind of ethic for U.S. journalists. (The "dispassion" of objectivity is discussed in Chapter 10).

GROWTH OF CODES

The more formal agreement on ethical standards in journalism that has been achieved in this century has come mostly through journalism's professional organizations, such as the ASNE. In fact, adoption of a code of ethics was virtually the first action of the ASNE when it was organized in 1923.[9] Although some state press associations had by then adopted codes, the ASNE Canons of Journalism, as they were called, was the first national code of ethics and standards put forward by any organization of journalists. Since 1923, other national journalistic organizations, notably the Society of Professional Journalists, Sigma Delta Chi (SPJ-SDX), and the Radio Television News Directors Association (RTNDA), have adopted such codes, and ASNE in 1975 thoroughly revised its canons and renamed them "The Statement of Principles of the American Society of Newspaper Editors."

The canons, like all other codes of ethics and standards adopted since by other state and national organizations of journalists, were mostly statements of ideals and aspirations. The biggest common element in all such codes of national and state organizations in this field is their lack of teeth. None prescribes any procedure for punishing violators of their high-sounding strictures. Some of those early ASNE members tried to get the 1924 convention to expel at least one member and censure others for not living up to the one-year-old canons, but the majority decided against such drastic action.[10] And that's the way the ethics game has been played in U.S. journalism ever since.

The canons came at a time when there was a small explosion of concern about journalistic ethics among the major newspapers of the day, spurred perhaps by four books on that subject written by faculty members in the emerging university journalism departments.[11] The first code of ethics adopted by a journalism organization was that of the Kansas Editorial Association in 1910, and during the 1920s most of the other journalism groups existing then and most major newspaper publishers adopted similar codes.[12] Then journalism in this country seemed to lose interest in ethics until a resurgence in the 1970s.

In that decade, four large national organizations of journalists adopted or revised codes of ethics. In addition to the aforementioned revision of the Canons of Journalism by ASNE in 1975, the Associated Press Managing Editors Association (APME) agreed on a set of standards in that same year; the hard-working APME had already conducted some useful and revealing studies of newspaper ethics and continues to probe the dark corners of ethics in that medium through its highly regarded Professional Standards Committee. The Society of Professional Journalists, founded as Sigma Delta Chi on the campus of DePauw University, Greencastle, Indiana, in 1909, adopted a code of ethics in 1973. It replaced the ASNE canons the society had endorsed as its code in 1926. The SPJ-SDX code is written for all journalists, print and broadcasting, reflecting the cross-media membership of that society. The RTNDA put together a code dealing with some of the special ethical problems in broadcast news in 1966 and revised it in 1973.

The 1970s and early 1980s also saw the adoption or updating of codes by such smaller national news organizations as the Society of American Travel Writers (SATW), the Associated Press Sports Editors Association (APSE), the National Conference of Editorial Writers, and the Society of American Business and Economics Writers. Numerous state organizations of print and broadcast journalists also adopted or revised codes of ethics.

The principal author of the SPJ-SDX code, Casey Bukro, environment editor of the *Chicago Tribune,* believes that code has had a positive impact on journalism, but he wishes the society would develop some mechanism to enforce it (interview, 10 Sept. 1981). As a member of the SPJ-SDX national board for eight years after the 1973 convention adopted the code, Bukro pushed for creation by local chapters of boards to hear complaints about ethics code violations. "But there is a fear that the local chapters will go on witch hunts — which doesn't give our members much credit for intelligence," Bukro says. "Our ethical problems are going to be greater if we ignore them."

There is a "pledge" at the end of the SPJ-SDX code stating that "journalists should actively censure and try to prevent violations of these standards," but Jean Otto of the *Milwaukee Journal* conceded when she was president of the society in 1979-80 that "many of us do not believe there is anything to be gained by expelling a member who violates the code. We do believe that awareness of the code's provisions and our colleagues' adherence to the code are the most effective enforcement."[13]

Not all journalists are enthusiastic about written codes of ethics for the news media. "The journalism codes are so generalized as to be meaningless," comments Leslie H. Whitten, novelist who was senior investigator for the Jack Anderson column for twelve years (interview, 2 Sept. 1981). "The few unethical journalists I've known are really flawed people. It's not that they don't follow any codes — they're not interested in codes. They were poorly brought up and they did dishonest things." Whitten believes the news business is "full of truly good people" who got into journalism "for vanity and the desire to do good for other people." The vanity is served through the by-line, he explains. "Journalism has always been a business of ethical people," Whitten says, "because they're poorly paid and they do it because it is a good thing to do and because of the by-line."

Another prominent doubter about codes is executive editor Rosenthal of the *New York Times,* who contends that most of the journalism codes "aim at the lowest common denominator" and are "too easy." (Interview, 7 Oct. 1981.) Although he fears that national codes could be used against the press and jeopardize First Amendment freedoms, Rosenthal believes each individual newspaper has a right to adopt its own code if it wants one. He has standards for his newsroom, some of them in writing, but "we feel no necessity for gathering them together and putting them in a code," Rosenthal adds. "But if you're going to have a code, it has to be tough and it has to deal with questions of how much news, how much profit, how much space." He says that if he drew up a code of ethics for the entire newspaper business, "damned few would sign it."

Rosenthal's West Coast counterpart, William F. Thomas of the *Los Angeles Times,* concludes that "the trouble with codes of ethics is that I have yet to see one that addresses any true ethical problem of the kind we face. They are almost by definition too general; they are almost banal in their generality. To ask a grown professional man to raise his hand and swear that if he can possibly help it he will not lie, cheat, steal, etc., has always struck me as a little silly." (Interview, 2 Nov. 1981.)

Although he works for Thomas and a newspaper that has no formal code of ethics for its news staff, David Shaw, media reporter-critic for the *Los Angeles Times,* believes such codes serve a purpose (interview, 25 Nov. 1980). "Most people are honest less out of moral commitment than of fear of apprehension," Shaw says. "If you have a written code with teeth in it, people are more likely to be ethical."

Codes with Teeth. The *New York Times* and the *Los Angeles Times* do not have formal codes of ethical standards for their news staffs, but the New York *Daily News,* the *Washington Post,* the *Philadelphia Inquirer,* the *Louisville Times* and *Courier-Journal,* and the *Chicago Sun-Times* do.

The news departments of ABC, NBC, and CBS networks do; many local TV stations do not. And so on.

But the trend has been obvious and it has been toward adoption of codes or policies setting ethical standards in individual newsrooms. And unlike most of the codes of national and state journalistic groups, the codes of individual news organizations tend to be detailed and specific.

Some news staffers have been dismissed or reassigned because they violated the ethics codes or policies of their newspapers. A sports reporter for the *Philadelphia Inquirer* was taken off the local college basketball beat when editors learned that his part-time journalism teaching contract had been renewed only because the college feared reprisals in his coverage of its basketball team. He was reassigned to cover horse racing, but then it came out that he owned part interest in a race horse. He was forced to sell the horse. Shortly after that when he was assigned to cover the National Collegiate Athletic Association (NCAA) basketball tournament, it was discovered that he had written material for an NCAA brochure. All these outside activities in one way or another violated the conflict of interest section of the *Inquirer's* "Standards of Professional Conduct." The erring reporter finally had to be told, according to managing editor Gene Foreman, that "if one more conflict developed, he would be assigned to the only job left in the sports department — office clerk." (Interview, 28 May 1981.)

Joseph W. Shoquist, managing editor of the *Milwaukee Journal,* recalls having to suspend two staffers for short periods without pay for violating the code that newspaper adopted in 1973 (interview, 19 Oct. 1981). One suspension was for a reporter who took part in a political demonstration. The second was for a copy editor who surreptitiously produced campaign material for a political candidate, a close friend.

When he was managing editor of the *Democrat & Chronicle* in Rochester, New York, Richard B. Tuttle had to negotiate a resignation with a veteran copy editor who was clandestinely doing public relations work for several clients (interview, 14 Oct. 1981). The moonlighting was discovered when the editor accidentally left an opened letter from one of his clients on top of his desk. "The guy's doing very well in PR now," Tuttle notes. (Other cases of disciplinary action against journalists by their own newspapers are reported and discussed throughout this book.)

When Tuttle left Rochester to become executive editor of another Gannett Company newspaper, the *Star-Gazette* and *Sunday Telegram* in Elmira, New York, he persuaded his news staff to work with him in developing a fairly detailed code of ethics that ends with one of the strongest disciplinary clauses of any such code in the country: "Staff members violating this guideline are subject to discipline up to and including suspension without pay and dismissal."

Many of Tuttle's fellow newspaper editors reading that clause might remark: "Hell, it's easy to talk tough if you don't have the Guild!"

The Newspaper Guild. The Elmira *Star-Gazette* and about 1,575 of the 1,730 daily newspapers in the United States do *not* have contracts with the Newspaper Guild, AFL-CIO, a union representing editorial and commercial employees of newspapers, a few magazines, and wire services, including the two major ones, the AP and UPI. The Guild has contracts with only about 155 U.S. and Canadian newspapers, but they cover most of the larger dailies; Guild papers control about 31 percent of the total daily newspaper circulation in the United States and Canada.[14]

The Guild has gotten heavily involved in the ethics code movement in U.S. journalism because it opposes the imposition by management of ethics codes without their being bargained — like wages and hours — with employees. The Guild also does not like ethics codes in contracts for fear that they will be enforced like other working rules, resulting in suspension or dismissal of news workers for violating what the Guild believes should be ideals, not rules.

"Ethics codes should be advisory; they're not meant to be like criminal codes," says David J. Eisen, director of research and information for the Guild (interview, 17 Apr. 1981). Eisen and other Guild officials admit to some concern about the economic losses that occur to some news people when certain ethics code provisions are imposed. Freebies and junkets are regarded by many employees as "fringe benefits of the profession," Eisen observes. He argues that many publishers have encouraged the notion that although you have to put up with low salaries in news work, "you get free tickets to the movies and the ball game and you get to go here and there." And Guild president Charles A. Perlick, Jr., points out that an ethics code clause preventing a sports reporter from serving as a major league baseball scorer at $50 a game could remove as much as $3,500 in annual income from that reporter's family (interview, 18 Apr. 1981).

The question of whether gifts and favors to news employees are really wages, like tips received by waiters, was part of two controversial cases in which the Guild fought the imposition of ethics codes by publishers of the Madison, Wisconsin, *Capital Times* and the Pottstown, Pennsylvania, *Mercury.* In the *Capital Times* case taken to arbitration by the Guild in 1975, the first ruling in the complicated federal procedure was to the effect that freebies actually are wages, subject to collective bargaining. That decision by an administrative law judge was overturned in 1976 by the National Labor Relations Board (NLRB), which held that although an employer may put forth rules regarding free tickets, gifts, and the like, and require the reporting of outside activities that might cause conflicts of interest, that employer cannot attach penalties to such rules without first bargaining with the employees. Richard J. Ramsey, executive secretary of the Guild's national contracts committee, interpreted that NLRB decision as upholding the Guild's basic position "that an employer can have all the penalty-free guidelines it wants; but if it wants rules with penalties attached, the employer first must bargain at least about the penalty provisions."[15]

The NLRB took more or less the same position when the Guild brought the Pottstown case before it, but the board's ruling this time was appealed to the courts and the whole matter was still undecided at this writing.

The Guild's action in Madison and Pottstown was widely criticized by news executives. Probably the strongest criticism came from Norman E. Isaacs, retired editor of dailies in Indianapolis, St. Louis, and Louisville, and former editor-in-residence at the Columbia University School of Journalism, who said "the whole episode is a badge of shame" for the Guild. "I cannot fathom how it can stand apart while its locals indulge in the petty personal politics of defending free tickets, free travel, free meals, and free gifts as a matter of proper added compensation," Isaacs declared. "As with so many other facets in American life, what Heywood Broun launched as a crusade for more professional journalism has been turned into a chase for dollars and to hell with ethics."[16]

Isaacs testified against the Guild in the Madison case. "It was disgraceful to hear the Guild testimony," he contends (interview, 7 Oct. 1981). "One guy said he represented gays and the proposed code would impair his usefulness in getting things in the paper that represent gays at their best. The sports department did not want any impairment of their freebies.... The Guild people put the union movement ahead of the newspaper."

Heywood Broun, to whom Isaacs referred, was a columnist for the old *New York World* and one of the founders and the first president of the American Newspaper Guild in 1933. There was a dispute among early Guild members as to whether the organization should have a professional or a trade union orientation, but Broun, according to an authoritative study of the Guild's early days, was "a pronounced unionist." He helped lead the Guild into what it has become — essentially a trade union affiliated with the AFL-CIO.[17]

Perlik, today's Guild president, sees two principal ingredients in "the Guild's position on ethics codes whenever management takes them off the wall and attempts to transform them into office rules that can be transgressed only under penalty of dismissal":

One is that employees, through their bargaining representative, must have some input into the code; virtue is one of the few things that newspaper publishers do not have a monopoly of. Some of the codes we have seen go far beyond the normal bounds of ethical considerations and seek to deprive employees of some of the basic rights of citizenship, such as involvement in political and community activity, while imposing no such restrictions on the publishers themselves. We think this is an appropriate area for negotiation, and two NLRB judges have agreed with us.

The second main ingredient of our position is that, where a newly promulgated ethics code takes something of long standing and substantial value away from an employee, he or she should be compensated for it. Where is it written that employees should bear all the cost of a newspaper's sudden decision to be like Caesar's wife?[18]

Eisen and Ramsey (interviews, 17 Apr. 1981) note an irony in the Pottstown case. The code of ethics the now retired publisher of the *Mercury* sought to impose on the news staff is basically the SPJ-SDX Code of Ethics. There are two problems with that, they say. One is that it is virtually impossible to enforce the vague provisions of a code written as a statement more of aspirations than of specifics. The second is that SPJ-SDX itself does not try to enforce its code on its own members. They point to an "Editor's Note" in the society's magazine *Quill* in which then editor Charles Long wrote:

> Well, is ours a mandatory code? Is it to be stuffed down our throats? Are journalists to be drummed out of the corps for not following it?
>
> Of course not. Better to have no code of ethics at all if it were ever implemented as some sort of law. Such a suggestion shouldn't enter into the discussion. Enforcement of a code of ethics smacks up against the First Amendment.[19]

The Guild has its own code of ethics, adopted by the organization's second convention in 1934. Leaders of the union today hold that this 1934 code and a 1933 statement in Article I of the Guild's constitution that one of the union's purposes is "to raise the standards of journalism and ethics of the industry" is evidence that the Guild has been working for ethics since its beginning. Eisen claims that Guild officers plan to revise the code (which has been unchanged since 1934 except for editing out the sexist language) so that it will apply to publishers as well as employees.

There is also a union representing broadcast journalists, as well as others working in radio and television — the American Federation of Television and Radio Artists (AFTRA), AFL-CIO, and any journalist who is on the air has to belong, but it has not gotten enmeshed in controversy over ethics policies. In this regard it is interesting to note, in view of increasing public reliance on TV news, that of the seventy thousand full-time journalists in this country, only seven thousand or about 10 percent work for television news — local stations and networks combined. Most U.S. journalists, union or nonunion, ply their trade in the newsrooms of newspapers and wire services.[20]

WATCHING THE WATCHDOGS

A responsibility evolving out of the First Amendment that journalists these days seldom question is the obligation of the news media to be a watchdog of government. Keeping the press free from government ("Congress shall make no law. . . .") allows the press to help protect citizens from the abuses of government. In modern times this watchdog role has been extended by most journalists to business, education, sports, and other important institutions of American life.

Many observers believe that the news media also need scrutiny — some watchdog of the watchdogs. Journalism is too important to all of us to be left entirely to journalists. It needs independent and critical monitoring. But journalists (fewer today, fortunately, than in the past) have resisted such appraisals on any systematic basis, mostly out of concern that they might diminish press freedom. So the history of the U.S. journalism in this century has been only lightly spotted with examples of continuing reviews of journalism's performance.

One appraisal method that has had great appeal in this country as well as in Great Britain, Sweden, and other European countries is the news council, a body charged with monitoring the suppliers of news to the public. The idea was first put forth seriously in the United States by the Commission on Freedom of the Press (the "Hutchins Commission"), which recommended in its 1947 report "the establishment of a new and independent agency to appraise and report annually upon the performance of the press." Although the agency proposed was to be nongovernmental, many journalists at the time read veiled threats in the commission's report because of language such as this: "Freedom of the press for the coming period can only continue as an accountable freedom. Its moral right will be conditioned on its acceptance of this accountability. Its legal right will stand unaltered as its moral duty is performed."[21]

The press council recommendation, along with others the commission made, was widely attacked by the press at the time. Many of its critics honed in on the absence of any journalists on the commission — "11 professors, a banker-merchant and a poet-librarian," as the trade magazine *Editor & Publisher* labeled them.[22] This sort of criticism, of course, had to ignore the fact that among the 225 people interviewed by the commission in its study from 1943 through 1945 were 58 journalists.

The study was financed by grants of some $200,000 from Time, Inc., and $15,000 from the Encyclopaedia Britannica, Inc. The commission was headed by Robert M. Hutchins, then chancellor of the University of Chicago, who initiated the inquiry into the state of the nation's press at the urging of Henry R. Luce, founder of *Time* magazine and head of Time, Inc. Its membership included ten distinguished faculty members from Harvard, Columbia, Yale, Chicago, University of Pennsylvania, Hunter College, and the Union Theological Seminary, as well as Beardsley Ruml (chairman of the Federal Reserve Bank, New York), and Archibald MacLeish (poet, librarian of the Library of Congress, and former assistant secretary of state).

Although the commission's press council proposal was not immediately cheered by the press, the idea survived. Its supporters were encouraged by the establishment of the British Press Council in 1953. A handful of American publishers and editors began to experiment with local councils made up of representative members of their communities who appraised their local newspapers. In the late 1960s the Mellett Fund for a Free and Responsible Press financed four local press council experiments in California, Oregon, Missouri, and Illinois. The press of Minnesota set up a statewide press council in 1971, now called the Minnesota News Council, to indicate its concern with broadcast as well as print media. These local and state councils reflected the thinking of many news media appraisal advocates that in a country as vast as the United States with its complicated media system, a national monitoring body would face a virtually impossible task. The more effective way to investigate failures in the news media and improve journalistic performance is through a monitoring system closer to home, they argued.

There were still those, nevertheless, who believed in a national monitoring agency and their thinking dominated a task force put together by the Twentieth Century Fund in the early 1970s. Out of this study came the formation of the National News Council in 1973. Remembering the attacks on the Hutchins Commission, the Twentieth Century Fund put some journalism executives on its task force that recommended "an independent and private national news council be established to receive, to examine and to report on complaints concerning the accuracy and fairness of news reporting in the United States, as well as to initiate studies and report on issues involving freedom of the press."[23]

In its first eight years, the National News Council investigated about two hundred of some eight hundred fifty complaints it received. (Most complaints were settled, withdrawn, dismissed, or rejected as outside the council's purview before any formal investigation was made.) It also responded to hundreds of inquiries and investigated and published some reports on journalistic problems, such as news media cooperation with police. It has no enforcement powers, other than the force of public opinion that might result from its findings. In 1983 the council had seventeen members, six of whom had clear media connections, eight of whom seemed clearly to be representatives of the public at large, and three of whom had had lengthy media experience but were not working journalists at the time. So the news media were well represented, at least in numbers, on the council. A small executive staff that does most of the investigative work is headed by William B. Arthur, a distinguished former journalist who was editor of *Look* magazine before it folded in 1971.

Norman Isaacs, a retired but not retiring veteran of forty-seven years in newspaper journalism and nine years as a journalism faculty member at Columbia, chaired the National News Council from 1977 to 1982. Isaacs believes that journalists are slowly coming to accept the council, that "all ideas of this kind are way ahead of their time." (Interview, 7 Oct. 1981.) He suggests that the council was handicapped at first by "some serious errors in the original construction that came out of the Twentieth Century Fund task force" — particularly limiting the council's purview to "national suppliers of news." Lifting that limitation and correcting other errors has put the council on the way toward complete acceptance by journalists as well as the public by 1995 or so, in Isaacs's view. "Our first few years were fumbling years," Isaacs concedes. "We had a judge as chairman and the press was scared to death.... A lot of the early grievances the council investigated were literally chickenshit. But we're over that now. Now most of the cases are of substance, and we can start focusing on deeper issues."

Arthur makes no large claim of accomplishment for the council's first eight years, but he believes its work has helped bring a "greater awareness of the need for accuracy and fairness" in the news media and the need for "a response to the public" when journalists have been inaccurate or unfair (interview, 5 Oct. 1981). Both he and Isaacs say they are pleased with the financial support they are getting from news organizations. Foundations continued to kick in the largest share in 1981, providing 56 percent of all contributions to the council that year, but media contributions had risen to 26 percent of the total. Corporations contributed 15 percent and 3 percent came from individuals, including Isaacs.[24]

Among those notably missing from the list of contributors is the *New York Times*. It has opposed the council since its formation, even though its former assistant editorial page editor, A. H. Raskin, is one of the council's associate directors. When the council was formed, the *New York Times* and other news organizations, chiefly the Knight Newspapers (now

Knight-Ridder), said they would not cooperate if the council investigated a complaint against them. The *Times* stuck to its resolve through the first eight years of the council's existence, but many of the other early critics mellowed as the council began to build a record.

Executive editor Rosenthal of the *New York Times* calls the council "a figment of the imagination of its founders," in that it does not exist except by the attention people pay to it (interview, 7 Oct. 1981). He concedes that the council is not evil but he fears its decisions will be picked up by judges and used against the press in ways not envisioned by the First Amendment. "I'm as close to an absolutist on the First Amendment as you can get," Rosenthal declares.

He argues that no monitoring agency can make publishers spend more money on news, which he sees as the real problem in journalism. "The American press needs more professionalism, more space, more and better editors and reporters, not more press critics," Rosenthal says.

Another top editor who questions the worth of the National News Council is Eugene L. Roberts, executive editor of the *Philadelphia Inquirer.* He holds that the council, because it spends most of its time investigating complaints against the major (and particularly the more active and aggressive) news media, emphasizes the "sins of commission," when the real sins of the press are those of omission (interviews, 28 May and 15 Sept. 1981). "It set my teeth on edge to hear editors of lethargic operations condemn the *Washington Post* after the Janet Cooke affair," Roberts says.[25] "You're damned right they won't get into that kind of trouble — because they don't do anything."

Roberts believes that had a news council investigated the *Washington Post* in the early stages of that paper's investigation of the Watergate fiasco, it would have gone against the *Post* because 90 percent of the American press thought the *Post* was wrong at that time. "The National News Council scares me as the judge and jury on whether or not a journalistic act was responsible," he contends.

Arthur's response to Roberts is that the council "can't get into the business of telling editors what to publish. We can only look at those stories that are published or broadcast." (Interview, 5 Oct. 1981.) He concedes, however, that the sins of omission worrying Roberts might get more attention in the increasing number of individual in-depth studies and booklets the council plans in the future.

Isaacs finds validity in the charge that the council has ignored journalism's sins of omission, but he believes that will change (interview, 7 Oct. 1981). "We are in the process now of altering our central thrust," he explains. "The lightning rod function has to continue, but the accountability function will become more and more urgent. As we move along, we have to get into the underpinnings of journalism, such as omission. We ought to do a study of what it is the public is deprived of."

Isaacs rejects the notion that the council threatens press freedom. "The only threat to press freedom is from the government and the courts," he says. "We're not a threat. We're a natural buffer." He notes that the council requires complainants to sign a waiver of their right to sue the medium or journalists they are complaining about, and the courts have upheld the validity of the waiver in the one case in which it has been tested. As for Rosenthal's fear that judges will pick up council findings, Isaacs claims that the council is prepared to go into the courts as an amicus curiae to prevent its findings from being applied as standards for all of journalism.

One of the council's early opponents who has softened is William F. Thomas, editor of the *Los Angeles Times*. When the council was formed, Thomas's paper saw it as an intimidating force that might improperly try to tell individual newspapers what to publish or not publish. His study of the council's proceedings and reports, however, has convinced Thomas that the council "has been careful and has done a pretty good job." (Interview, 2 Nov. 1981.) Although no complaints against the *Times* were investigated by the council in its first eight years, Thomas says he would cooperate if one occurs. One view he holds of news councils has not changed. He still believes smaller, local councils can be more effective than a national council, but "even the LA area is too big" for the kind of local council he views as "invaluable and worth support."

An editor who has supported the news council since its inception, Ralph Otwell of the *Chicago Sun-Times,* has "never been able to understand why this straightforward mechanism for people to vent their gripes is feared, dreaded, and considered to be antithetical to the best interests of the news media." (Interview, 9 Sept. 1981.) Otwell, who served on the council for most of its first eight years, says the type of media monitoring journalists should rightfully dread is that being done by the ideological Accuracy in Media (AIM) organization and by fundamental Christian groups like the Moral Majority. The news council, he believes, presents "a reasonable and viable" alternative to such vested interest monitoring. "It's a safety valve that in time the public will recognize as very crucial," Otwell predicts.

Giving Readers a Voice. Another instrument for making journalists more accountable to the public is the newspaper ombudsman — an idea adapted from Sweden. About 35 of the some 1,730 daily newspapers in the United States have added such functionaries to their staffs in recent years to handle readers' complaints and to serve as in-house critics. Most

are called ombudsmen, the Swedish word, but some are known as reader
representatives or some other similar and more understandable term.
There's even an Organization of Newspaper Ombudsmen (ONO), which
they like to call by its initials, "Oh, no!", said to describe the ombudsman's
typical reaction to the paper's latest goof.

The first newspaper ombudsman in this country was on the
Louisville Times and *Courier-Journal*. He was appointed in 1967 by
Norman Isaacs, then executive editor of those two Bingham family-
owned newspapers. Isaacs got the idea from an article he read in the *New
York Times* of 11 June 1967, written by A. H. Raskin, then assistant
editorial page editor, who became associate director of the news council
after retiring from the *Times.*

Other newspapers followed Isaacs's lead and established their own
ombudsmen (ombudspersons?). These included the *Washington Post,* the
now defunct *Washington Star,* the *Boston Globe,* the *Sacramento Bee,* the
St. Petersburg Times, the *Wilmington Journal,* the *Milwaukee Journal,*
the *Minneapolis Tribune,* the *San Diego Union,* the *Cincinnati Enquirer,*
the *Seattle Times,* the *Camden Courier-Post,* the *St. Louis Post-Dispatch,*
the *Kansas City Star* and *Times,* and the *Florida Times-Union.*

The *St. Petersburg Times* later abandoned the idea and its executive
editor, Robert Haiman, became a leading critic of newspaper ombudsmen.
The press certainly needs criticism, Haiman has argued, but it needs it
from outside, not from an employee of the newspaper. "We should not
want the press as our principal critic of newspaper performance any more
than we want the State Department as our principal critic of foreign
policy."[26]

Another problem Haiman sees with newspaper ombudsmen as they
have evolved in this country is that they work after the fact. They
investigate alleged failures in their newspaper's performance after they
have occurred and do not try to prevent the failures from occurring in the
first place. He compares ombudsmen with coroners, whose job it is "to do
the post-mortem on a disaster, to pick through the tatters of flesh after a
terrible crash." The credibility of newspapers would be better improved,
he said, if ombudsmen "would have more to do with trying to keep the
plane flying, with monitoring the captain and crew who fly it, and with
trying to avoid the crash in the first place."[27]

Haiman's criticism aroused Paul Janensch, the latest of Isaacs's
successors as executive editor of the Louisville newpapers, to comment: "I
think the American newspaper business would be better off if we had
fewer executive editors and more ombudsmen."[28]

Janensch says his papers' third news ombudsman, Robert Crumpler,
a former assistant managing editor of the *Louisville Times* with thirty
years of experience on the two Louisville dailies, receives about one

hundred phone calls and several letters each week. His name and phone number are published in both papers every day. "The ombudsman reports to the executive editor, but he really works for the readers," Janensch says. "He has the authority to go directly to any editor or staffer with a reader's beef. If we erred, he sees that appropriate action is taken." Janensch believes the ombudsman "has made our newspapers more accurate and more fair and has increased our credibility with the readers."[29]

The Louisville ombudsman does not "go public" with a regular column commenting on the paper's foibles or those of the news media in general, but many ombudsmen, including the one at the *Washington Post,* have that as part of their regular assignment.

The addition of the column-writing role is one of the reasons that Isaacs, who started it all, is disenchanted with the way newspaper ombudsmen have turned out. He believes writing a regular column of media criticism gets in the way of the other more important job of responding to readers' complaints and criticizing the newspaper internally. "You can have a media critic and an ombudsman, but you can't have both in the same person," Isaacs contends (interview, 7 Oct. 1981). Another reason he has soured on the movement he started is that "in too many cases, the ombudsman is an old, battle-scarred veteran who would have been assigned to the library if he hadn't been named ombudsman. And some of them are purely cosmetic; some guy writing a media column in which all he does is explain the virtues of the newspaper is not answering the need."

Isaacs sees two reasons more newspapers have not appointed ombudsmen. The first is money. He estimates that it would take about $100,000 a year to set up an ombudsman today, counting office space and equipment, a secretary, and all the trappings. Many editors would rather put that kind of money into new reporting positions. A second reason, he believes, is that most news staffs simply do not want an in-house critic looking over their shoulders. "You don't establish an ombudsman with staff consent," Isaacs adds. "You impose it." And that requires an authoritarianism many news executives shy away from.

Two of the nation's most prestigious newspapers, the *New York Times* and the *Los Angeles Times,* have done just that — shied away from appointing ombudsmen. Executive editor Rosenthal of the *New York Times* believes that newspaper ombudsmen are "a gimmick" and "a cop-out." He maintains that editors have to be responsible for the content of their newspapers and the conduct of their staffs (interview, 7 Oct. 1981). A less adamant position is taken by editor Thomas of the *Los Angeles Times.* Thomas considered establishing an ombudsman — "some ombudsmen are very good" — but he opted for a full-time reporter covering the news business, about which more will be said later in this chapter (interview, 2 Nov. 1981). Thomas believes that his reporter's articles, published in the news columns and often starting on page one, have much greater impact than an ombudsman's column "speaking solely for himself and run on a page marked 'opinion.' "

One of the more highly regarded ombudsmen, Art Nauman of the *Sacramento Bee,* does write a regular Sunday column, but he talks about his job in some of the same terms Isaacs uses (interview, 2 Nov. 1981). Nauman sees himself as the person who makes his paper accountable to its readers, "answering some of their questions and responding to their legitimate complaints." He tries to give readers some voice in the decisions about what gets published and how. "Most of the time we have not been willing to tell our customers how we reach these decisions that have such a terrific impact on so many lives."

Nauman, who became the *Bee's* ombudsman after ten years on the paper as investigative reporter, chief of the state capital bureau, and city editor, has been deeply affected by his experience digging into and trying to explain his paper's performance. "As ombudsman, I look out at this craft I love so much and I realize, God, what a shallow job we are doing. And I just don't know whether I could ever return to that work." He explains that he is considering switching to college teaching or to magazine work when his stint as ombudsman comes to an end.

Reporting on Yourself. One kind of accountability is provided when the news media turn their spotlights on themselves, report on themselves in the same way they do other important institutions and activities. Many newspapers and a few broadcast stations run occasional pieces on the news business or about some particular incident involving journalists and how they do their work. The coverage that was given to the way the news media reported the Atlanta child murders in 1981 is an example. But only a few news organizations have turned the news business into a regular beat, a full-time assignment for some reporter or critic.

The name that comes to mind whenever coverage of the news business is discussed by people in the business is David Shaw, media reporter and critic for the *Los Angeles Times* since 1974. Shaw reports directly to Thomas, the paper's top editor. That way his reports cannot be kept out or buried in the back of his paper by subeditors upset at what he has written. Shaw often writes about the *Los Angeles Times* when he does an investigation of some national journalistic problem or issue. "If he's going to explain newspaper behavior, he can't leave us out," Thomas observes (interview, 2 Nov. 1981). Shaw's work evoked a negative reaction in his own newsroom at first, Thomas adds, but "they have accepted him now."

The *New York Times* has a full-time reporter assigned to cover the news media. The *Wall Street Journal* and *Newsday* report regularly on the news business, as do the two leading news magazines, *Time* and *Newsweek*.

Broadcasting has not done much regular reporting on itself and other media, and media criticism is even scarcer. The Public Broadcasting Service started a regular media criticism program called "Inside Story" in 1981. Anchored by Hodding Carter III, the show had few precedents to guide it, since regularly scheduled media criticism on television was a primitive art form. The *Washington Post*-owned TV station in Detroit, WWJ-TV, had done some, but that was about it.

One forum of media criticism that has evolved in recent years is the journalism review — a periodical devoted to reporting on and criticizing the news media. Chief among them has been the *Columbia Journalism Review,* published by the Columbia University School of Journalism since 1961. Its raison d'étre is "to assess the performance of journalism in all its forms, to call attention to its shortcomings and strengths, and to help define — or redefine — standards of honest responsible service . . . to help stimulate continuing improvement in the profession and to speak out for what is right, fair, and decent."[30]

A more recently founded review striving for the same kind of national circulation as the *Columbia Journalism Review* is the *Washington Journalism Review,* published under private ownership out of Washington, D.C. Some regional or local reviews — particularly *Feed/back,* a California journalism review published by a nonprofit corporation with the help of the Journalism Department of San Francisco State University — have had an influence in their areas.

These reviews, of course, are read mostly by people in news work, so the impact of their explanations and criticisms extends to the public at large only through the journalists who take them seriously.

Most journalists interviewed for this book do not seem to believe that journalism does a very good job of reporting on itself to the public. Ombudsman Nauman of the *Sacramento Bee* puts it more strongly. "The press does an abysmal job of explaining itself," he charges (interview, 2 Nov. 1981). "We've gotten very big and arrogant; we don't listen to anybody; we don't like dissenting views; we're always right and unwilling to admit our mistakes."

Some, however, question whether the public is all that interested in the news business. Julius Duscha, director of the Washington Journalism Center, agrees that news media do not cover themselves nearly as well as they cover other comparable businesses and activities. But although he feels there is considerable public interest in television, he questions how much people want to know about newspapers (interview, 5 June 1981).

"They certainly want to know about the television stars," he remarks. "You can't write enough about Dan Rather and the local anchor man." He notes that even at National Press Club luncheons, the journalists present are more interested in the TV photographers taking their cut-in shots of audience reaction than they are in the speaker of the day.

Covering yourself is not easy, of course. Many important stories about the news business are embarrassing and reflect negatively on some news organization or executive. That is why, Duscha explains, you did not read much in the *Washington Post* about the many changes in publishers that paper went through at one period; or in the *Chicago Tribune* about the troubles of the paper the Tribune Company owns in New York, the *Daily News;* or in *Time* magazine about the problems of the *Washington Star,* the newspaper it owned and closed in 1981.

"How do we cover ourselves?" asks editor Poorman of the *Akron Beacon Journal.* "Like porcupines making love: tenderly, very tenderly." (Interview, 8 Apr. 1981.)

Business or Profession?

"If they're giving us eight papers in one, you'd think they could at least run Blondie."

SOMEONE ONCE DESCRIBED JOURNALISM as a profession grafted to a business. Leaving aside for a moment the question of whether journalism truly qualifies as a profession, that description accurately reflects the employee status of all but a handful of journalists. There are a few free-lancers around, but most journalists ply their trade in the employ of others, mostly private companies that have to succeed in the marketplace just like other American businesses, seeking security and survival through profits.

No discussion of ethics in the journalism of this country can proceed very far without an understanding of how business considerations of the news media affect the journalism they present. Unlike most businesses, the media get most of their profits not directly from the consumer or the public, but indirectly through advertising, which contributes 60 to 100 percent of the revenue of most U.S. media. The consumer gets nothing free, of course, despite the absence of any direct payment for most television and radio programs and for some publications. You pay through your purchase of advertised goods and services, whose prices include the cost of advertising. It's like sales taxes, which you're not supposed to notice very much because you pay them in small amounts every time you buy things.

The secret of success in the news business is to gather an audience that at least some advertisers want or need to reach. It is not necessary or even desirable often to reach every person or household in a given community, region, or nation. If you have an audience of some sort that certain advertisers are willing to pay for access to, you can make a go of it in the news business. A larger audience may not be desirable if the additional members are people advertisers are unwilling to pay to reach.

So we have media, such as television networks, that try to be seen by or at least be available to almost everybody in the country. Newspapers and magazines tend to be more selective in the audiences they seek — newspapers in a geographic sense and magazines demographically. These are generalizations, of course. Local TV stations have local audiences, too, and they are limited to the area covered by the station's signal. Some magazines try to appeal more to a mass audience than a selective one, and some even try to do both. Some newspapers are abandoning their democratic traditions of trying to appeal to everyone in a given community or region and are seeking more affluent audiences better able to respond to advertising.

The facts of life about balancing audiences and advertisers have a lot to say about the kind of media we get in our system. And the kind of journalism we get.

BUSINESSES FIRST

Claude Sitton, editorial director and vice-president of the News Observer Publishing Company, Raleigh, North Carolina, contends that the decision about how much of the newspaper's budget should go to the news and editorial department "is not a simple matter. It's a hard balance to strike." If a newspaper is not doing well as a business, "it becomes weak and vulnerable to those people who would use the newspaper for their own purposes." (Interview, 4 Nov. 1981.)*

Otis Chandler, editor in chief of the Times Mirror Company, Los Angeles, believes that "successful newspapers do not have to let the business side into the editorial arena. They have the luxury of letting the editorial department be completely independent to cover the news as it sees it." (Interview, 25 Nov. 1980.) Chandler recalls working for a paper that was not successful financially, the old *Los Angeles Mirror-News*, which his corporation eventually folded. "Every line of advertising was so

---

*See list of interviewees following Notes.

important," he says. "We really killed some news stories because we were trying to get the major department stores to advertise and we did not want to rock any boats."

Another who believes that a newspaper has to succeed as a business in order to provide quality journalism is Donald Graham, publisher of the *Washington Post* (interview, 4 June 1981). He sees the *Post* as testimony of that fact. "In the early 1950s," he recalls, "the *Post* aspired to be a world-class newspaper; its heart was in the right place, but it just didn't have any money. There's an old joke around the *Post* that in those days we could cover any international conference as long as it was in the first taxi zone." Noting with pride that although the *Post* had no foreign correspondents before 1960, it has bureaus all over the world today, Graham concludes, "Profits are not inconsistent with good journalism."

Because the news media are businesses — and big ones at that — they are influenced by the same forces that bear on all American business enterprises. There is nothing intrinsically wrong or illegal about the media following the same economic Pied Pipers that motivate K-Mart, Mobile, United Technologies, IBM, and Crazy Joe's Used Cars, but news businesses differ from other businesses in one important way. Their constitutionally protected freedom is interpreted by most people to mean that they are a semipublic service as well as being private profit-seeking businesses. As James C. Thomson, Jr., curator of the Nieman Foundation, tells us, news organizations have to operate "both To Make Money (or at least not to lose it) *and* To Do Good (or to expose iniquity, and thereby improve society.)" Because of this tension "between greed and idealism," Thomson believes every news organization has "two cultures, or at least outlooks, that are often at odds with each other: on the one hand, reporters and editors, who traditionally see their role as uncovering and disseminating the truth (or some approximation thereof); and on the other hand, owners, publishers, 'management,' who seek to stay in business and make a tidy profit."[1]

Although most news businesses are highly secretive about how much money they make, they make plenty. A. Kent MacDougall, in his prize-winning series on "Business and the Media" in the *Los Angeles Times,* tells us that the news business "is near the top of all industries in profitability." He maintains that "daily newspapers keep up to a quarter of every dollar they take in, even after taxes. *Time* and *Newsweek* are gold mines. And television, which has been likened to 'a license to print money,' is so lucrative that it bestows corporate presidents' salaries on many of its journalists." MacDougall points out that the *Los Angeles Times, New York Times, Wall Street Journal,* and *Des Moines Register* are exceptions to the general news media custom of not reporting how much money they make.[2]

Ownership Trends. The most obvious indication of the business nature of the news media in recent years has been their tendency to be purchased and owned by groups and conglomerates. Just as small, independent grocery stores have all but disappeared from the American scene, the independent, family-owned newspaper has become the exception — only about 540 of the 1,730 daily newspapers were still in independent ownership in 1982. The others were owned by about 160 groups (also called chains when they get big enough), which gobbled up independent papers at the rate of about 50 per year in the late 1970s before the acquisition pace began to slow.[3]

Although almost ninety of the newspaper groups (defined as two or more dailies in different cities, under the same ownership) publish four or fewer newspapers, group newspapers control about 74 percent of the total daily U.S. circulation of about sixty-two million. And some groups are very large by any measure. If you look at total daily and Sunday circulation, Gannett Company and Knight-Ridder Newspapers are the largest. If you use numbers of papers as your measure, Gannett with eighty-five and Thomson Newspapers with seventy-seven in the United States are the largest (See Table 2.1).

TABLE 2.1. **The twenty largest U.S. newspaper companies (as of March 1982, ranked by daily circulation)**

	Daily Circulation	Number of Dailies	Sunday Circulation	Number of Sunday Editions
Gannett Co. Inc.	3,621,800	85	3,523,800	55
Knight-Ridder Newspapers Inc.	3,458,400	33	4,049,200	21
Newhouse Newspapers	3,133,500	29	3,768,100	21
Tribune Co.	2,806,600	8	3,552,800	6
Dow Jones & Co. Inc.	2,433,400	21	346,000	9
Times Mirror Co.	2,315,500	8	2,867,600	8
Scripps-Howard Newspapers	1,518,800	16	1,559,300	7
Hearst Newspapers	1,362,300	15	2,098,200	9
Thomson Newspapers Inc. (U.S.)	1,219,600	77	713,500	34
Cox Enterprises Inc.	1,165,100	18	1,245,600	13
The New York Times Co.	1,137,000	12	1,677,700	7
Cowles Newspapers	953,900	10	1,141,600	7
News America Publishing Inc.	917,600	3	185,479	1
Capital Cities Communications Inc.	900,500	7	774,100	4
Freedom Newspapers Inc.	798,400	31	740,000	20
Central Newspapers Inc.	774,600	7	792,174	4
The Washington Post Co.	696,200	2	926,700	2
Evening News Association	678,900	5	823,500	1
The Copley Press Inc.	635,000	9	626,000	6
Harte-Hanks Communications Inc.	584,200	28	582,300	21

Source: Reprinted with permission from "Facts about Newspapers '82, A Statistical Summary of the Newspaper Business Published by the American Newspaper Publishers Association," based on research by Morton Research, Lynch, Jones & Ryan.

Some of the newspaper ownership groups have expanded into other media, particularly radio, television, and cable TV, and even into some enterprises completely outside the news business — the company that owns the *Chicago Tribune* buying the Chicago Cubs baseball team, for example. The Gannett Company in recent years has added seven TV stations, eight radio stations, several outdoor advertising companies, and the Harris Research firm to its holdings. The Los Angeles-based Times Mirror Company is widely known as the owner of the *Los Angeles Times,* but it also owns seven other newspapers, seven book publishing firms, two television stations, four magazines, cable television systems in thirteen states, paper mills and timberlands, half of the *Washington Post-Los Angeles Times* News Service, and firms publishing informational materials for engineers, draftsmen, and aviators. And the list could go on and on of media and nonmedia additions to what used to be primarily newspaper companies.

A more alarming development to most media watchers has been the acquisition in recent years of news media by conglomerates from outside. The Charter Company, which had concentrated pretty much on oil refineries and insurance, decided in the 1970s to get into the media by buying the ailing Philadelphia *Bulletin,* three magazines, and five radio stations. In that same decade, Blue Chips Stamps — which also owns some candy stores — added the *Buffalo Evening News* to its holdings. And the Atlantic Richfield Company (ARCO) bought the London *Observer.* (Both Charter and ARCO later sold their media properties.)

Otis Chandler of the Times Mirror Company has often warned against foreign interests buying up U.S. news businesses (interview, 25 Nov. 1980). His fear, he declares, is that some of the large energy companies "with their enormous cash flow might look at media businesses as a good investment and a good thing to get into because they bring prestige, power, and clout." He points out that "a foreign oil company could not buy Times Mirror without making some arrangement to sell our TV stations because there is a Federal Communications Commission [FCC] rule against foreigners owning U.S. TV and radio stations. But that's not much of an inhibition."

The FCC, which regulates broadcasting in this country, has inhibited the kind of grouping up of broadcast media that we have seen in the newspaper business, which has no FCC to answer to. Broadcast stations have had conglomerate owners since their beginnings in this country in the 1920s, with Westinghouse, General Electric, and RCA being just a few of the owners of television and radio stations or networks who also own other types of business. But the FCC has restricted the number of broadcast stations any one owner could own. That limit stood at twenty-one in 1983, and within the twenty-one, no single person or company could own more than seven of the more powerful AM radio stations, seven FM radio stations, or seven television stations (with no more than five of the television stations being in the more desirable VHF category).

Media ownership has been affected by another kind of FCC interference in recent years. Its rules against a single person or firm owning TV stations and newspapers in the same city or market forced many newspapers to sell or trade their TV properties. The owners of the *Washington Post* and the *Detroit News* gave us an example of this when they simply swapped the TV stations each had owned in its own city. And most of the TV stations sold by newspaper firms under FCC pressure were acquired by other newspaper firms; so, the Times Mirror Company of Los Angeles now owns five TV stations Newhouse had to unload in St. Louis, Birmingham, Elmira, Harrisburg, and Syracuse because they were in communities where Newhouse also owned newspapers or radio stations.[4]

Going Public. Chandler's fear that some morning we may wake up to find an oil-rich sheik atop the Gannett empire of newspapers and broadcast stations is plausible because of another business trend that media companies have joined. Most of the large media groups and conglomerates are public corporations whose shares of ownership are available for purchase in the stock market. Although families like the Sulzbergers of the *New York Times* and the Grahams of the *Washington Post* control and are not likely to sell the dominant shares of ownership in their news companies, many media companies are more vulnerable to the kind of acquisition Chandler fears.

Of more immediate concern, however, is the pressure from their stockholders for greater and greater profits and dividends that many public corporations experience. Treating a newspaper as just one more unit of production can be devastating to the quality of journalism in that newspaper. William B. Arthur, executive director of the National News Council, believes groups such as Gannett, Knight-Ridder, and Times Mirror have improved the papers they have acquired (interview, 5 Oct. 1981). He is concerned, however, about newspaper conglomerates being run not by journalists but by "business school types" whose emphasis on the bottom line could damage journalism.

When news organizations are owned by public companies, they get scrutinized by those "business school types" in the stock market. What E. F. Hutton says about your company can make a difference in how many investors you attract, and the E. F. Huttons look at media companies in a way that indicates little if any interest in quality journalism or public service. Read, for example, this "research comment" on the Times Mirror Company by a Merrill Lynch analyst:

Times Mirror's newspaper markets appear to be among the strongest for the major city dailies. We also believe that the company's participation in cable and broadcasting put it among the well-situated media companies.... Times Mirror's key newspapers — The *Los Angeles Times, Newsday,* the *Dallas Times Herald,* and the *Hartford Courant* — are well-run, profitable, and situated in attractive markets. The *Denver Post,* acquired at the end of 1980, has been marginally profitable. Denver is a competitive market but appears to have good growth potential. Times Mirror's management has demonstrated its ability to do well in such an environment. We expect solid improvement in profitability of the *Denver Post* during the next few years. For the newspaper group as a whole, we expect operating earning to grow at a rate of about 15 percent a year for the next five years.[5]

Times Mirror's Chandler believes group or conglomerate ownership can give individual newspapers "a deeper pocket to draw from." (Interview, 25 Nov. 1980.) This benefit depends, of course, on group owners who "are willing to invest more to make their newspapers better, more credible products," Chandler contends. "To make newspapers ultimately profitable, you have to assure that the editorial departments have their independence and credibility."

Robert Giles is in the perhaps unenviable position of editing the two Gannett newspapers that Gannett president Al Neuharth and other Gannett top brass are apt to read every day. But as editor of the *Times-Union* and *Democrat & Chronicle* in Rochester, New York, Gannett's corporate headquarters, Giles feels he has complete freedom to run those newspapers as he sees fit (interview, 15 Oct. 1981). He reports to his publisher, who "gives me a free hand in how I handle the news every day, how we select people for the key jobs, and all of the things that go into putting out a newspaper." John Quinn, who as Gannett's vice-president for news is Giles's corporate supervisor, has supported the editor's attempts to change and improve the two Rochester papers. "But John Quinn doesn't call me to complain about an editorial, or comment on a news story," Giles says. "In my four years as editor, I probably have had six memos from John Quinn about something that appeared in the paper, and he does it in a very gentle and professional way."

But Gannett influences Giles's job in other ways. "The bottom line requirements limit what we want to do," Giles observes.

The Gannett Company has very aggressive and ambitious profit goals. Anybody who wants to work for Gannett and be comfortable ought to understand that. Al Neuharth [chairman and president, Gannett Co.] clearly sets the pace, and the standard is that our profits

will be 15 percent better this year than they were last year.
Everybody in the group, for the most part, is expected to contribute to
that, which means that the kind of news hole I think we require here
to put out absolutely first-rate newspapers is not available to me.
That's a frustration because of my own standards for good newspapers and the standards of many of the people I've hired or promoted
here.

Giles believes that Gannett has taken over many family-owned
newspapers and "improved them enormously," but on very good independent newspapers, such as those in Louisville and St. Petersburg, "the
resources made available to their editors by those families are superior to
what I have to work with in Rochester." Giles contends that Gannett
wants to have it both ways — "put out good newspapers and continue to
make a lot of money, and you can't always do that."

The frustration Giles feels is shared by other editors of group- or
conglomerate-owned newspapers. Group executives set profit goals that
often mean less space for news, more advertising, and tighter budgets.
Local publishers and editors who fail to meet those goals do not last long.
The group accountants hold all the trump aces.

No one knows this better than Eugene L. Roberts, Jr., executive
editor of the *Philadelphia Inquirer,* who has had a tough fight turning a
once disreputable newspaper into a successful one, both journalistically
and financially. Most people in journalism believe Roberts has succeeded
spectacularly in the area of his prime responsibility — the news and
editorial department. His staff in recent years has won all the top
journalism awards: photographs in his crowded newsroom of the traditional champagne popping after Pulitzer Prizes are announced have
become commonplace. But financially even Roberts's admirers wondered
aloud whether Knight-Ridder didn't regret that it ever came into
Philadelphia to run the *Inquirer* and the tabloid *Daily News,* two of the
city's three dailies then.

Roberts's own analysis of the *Inquirer*'s financial status is that
although the newspaper was not an immediately pleasing investment,
Knight-Ridder knew "right from the beginning that it was buying a sick
newspaper that could be fixed." Roberts believes the *Inquirer* will end up
being one of the better investments Knight-Ridder has ever made
(interviews, 28 May and 15 Sept. 1981). Knight-Ridder "has never been
greedy about quick profits but it has never been tolerant of losses."
Roberts claims the *Inquirer* stopped losing money for its owners after
1976, but it was tough going before that. In his first three or four years
after joining the paper in 1972, he recalls that there were nine separate
work stoppages by *Inquirer* unions.

Roberts does not complain about any pressure he might have been under to get the *Inquirer* into the black. Although Knight-Ridder "doesn't understand losing money" and "goes berserk with red ink," he feels the group "wants the *Inquirer* to be accurate, reliable, fair, and aggressive." In general, Roberts believes that "good journalism is amicable with good business."

Knight-Ridder Newspapers and Times Mirror were most often mentioned by journalists interviewed for this book as companies that push for quality journalism in the news media they own. Gannett also got praise for improving the papers it buys. (Conversely, Thomson Newspapers comes in for the most criticism. Norman E. Isaacs, senior adviser to the National News Council [interview, 7 Oct. 1981], calls the Thomson operation "a commercial printing establishment.")

It is true that many family-owned newspapers, limping along under the lethargic management of third-generation sons or nephews who would rather be entomologists or merchant seamen, have been greatly improved after their sale by the imported skills of group executives. And many if not most of the dailies on anybody's "Ten Best" list are group-owned papers, such as the *Wall Street Journal,* the *New York Times,* the *Washington Post,* the *Los Angeles Times,* the *Philadelphia Inquirer,* and *Newsday.* So it would be foolish to argue that group or conglomerate ownership results in bad journalism. Sometimes it does, but very often it does not.

A family-owned newspaper that also appears on those "Ten Best" lists is the Louisville *Courier-Journal.* Its executive editor, Paul Janensch, observes that although his newspapers (he also edits the *Louisville Times*) are "financially healthy," they do not make the profits that most other daily newspapers make (interview, 19 Oct. 1981). He says one of the first things that would go if the Louisville papers were bought by one of the groups is the circulation in Kentucky outside of the Louisville metropolitan area. That circulation costs the papers $1 million net a year, and groups usually chop off fringe subscribers who do not pay enough to justify delivery costs. The Louisville papers keep serving those faraway subscribers "as a public service," Janensch says. "There's a saying in Kentucky that three things hold the state together: the state government, the University of Kentucky, and the goddamned *Courier-Journal.* The state would be devastated if we pulled in our circulation." Janensch believes that most newspaper chains operate on short-range goals and do not put enough money into news.

Some other journalists decry the loss of eccentricity and sacred cows they believe were more common when most newspapers were family owned. Norman C. Miller, Washington bureau chief for the *Wall Street Journal,* holds that "eccentricity is a healthy thing" in the news business (interview, 29 Oct. 1981). "It tends to come from owner or independent editors," he contends. "Chains don't encourage that sort of thing. They encourage a certain conformity and mediocrity, a profit-line mentality, a shrinking from controversy." He concedes that some chains improve the newspapers they buy, such as Knight-Ridder did with the *Philadelphia Inquirer,* but other chains "are run by people for whom it doesn't make that much difference whether they're manufacturing shoes or newspapers."

"Group editors may be given local autonomy," says Curt Matthews, Washington correspondent for the Baltimore *Sun,* "but they are in greater fear of making a mistake." He believes that many of the old newspaper-owning families were interested in and had a sense of outrage about certain issues (interview, 3 June 1981). "Memos would come down asking, 'Why hasn't the trash been picked up along Fourteenth Street?' Some guy sitting in New York doesn't even know the trash hasn't been picked up on Fourteenth Street!" Recalling his early newspaper days with the *St. Louis Post-Dispatch,* owned by the Pulitzer family, Matthews argues that every newspaper "ought to have three or four sacred cows," special issues the staff overcover because the owners are concerned about them. Most of the chains he is familiar with "are sensitive to the criticism of managing the news from on high, and bend over backward to give their local publishers and editors autonomy." It would be better, Matthews believes, if chain owners got more involved, "if they spent enough time in their communities to say, 'For chrissake, why is St. Louis dying? Let's do something about it.' "

The Newspaper Auction. In the four years from 1977 to 1981, about two hundred independent daily newspapers were sold, most of them to groups or conglomerates. Prices were high. Capital Cities Communications paid $125 million for the *Kansas City Star* and *Times* in 1977, for example. Gannett laid out $60 million in 1978 for the News-Journal Company in Wilmington, Delaware. In 1979, Times Mirror bought the Hartford (Connecticut) Courant Company for $106 million.

Two economic forces stimulated the high number of newspaper sales in recent years and the high prices paid for them. The groups and conglomerates were encouraged by federal tax penalties to keep reinvesting their accumulated earnings; also, they like to show earnings growth to attract investors.[6] Federal estate taxes encourage many families to sell their newspapers when the principal owner dies. J. Hart Clinton, publisher of the family-owned *San Mateo* (California) *Times*, explains that the bidding for independent newspapers by the chains drives up their values. When the major owner dies, the survivors are faced with a federal estate tax based on the market value of the paper that is so high they sell, and usually the best price is offered by a chain. "Considering that the federal estate taxes take 70 percent of an estate after the $5 million value is reached, and that newspapers in northern California have been selling for amounts in excess of $25 million," Clinton noted, "it is easy to understand why the owners have felt the only escape open to them is to sell to the highest bidder."[7]

Going back to 1900 and to 1940 gives us a picture of how newspaper ownership has changed. In 1900, 8 groups owned 27 of the some 2,200 daily newspapers in the United States, slightly more than 1 percent. In 1940, 60 groups owned 319 of the 1,878 dailies, or 17 percent.[8] In 1982, about 160 groups owned almost 1,200 of the 1,730 dailies, or about 69 percent.[9] (The downward trend in the total number of dailies leveled off after World War II. The total stood at about 1,750 from 1945 through 1980 when it began a new although slight downward trend.)

Group ownership has encouraged a trend toward monoplies that has left many cities without real newspaper competition. And recently two important cities — Washington, D.C., and Philadelphia — were added to that list, not by some group gobbling up the newspaper properties there, but by old-fashioned economic failure. The *Washington Star* ceased publication in August 1981 when its owner — Time, Inc. — decided it could no longer afford to add to the $85 million it had poured into the *Star* in three and one-half years. ("Time has run out on the Star," the T-shirts soon said.) That left the nation's capital with only one daily, the morning *Post*, until the Rev. Sun Myung Moon's Unification Church started a new daily, the *Washington Times,* in the spring of 1982. Charter Company, a Florida-based oil and insurance conglomerate, closed the 134-year-old Philadelphia *Bulletin* in January 1982; at the time, it was losing $60,000 a day. The *Bulletin's* disappearance left Philadelphia with two dailies, the *Inquirer* and the *Daily News,* both owned by Knight-Ridder and published out of the same plant. For a period just before the *Bulletin* closed, Philadelphia had four dailies — more than any U.S. city — but the *Philadelphia Journal,* a sort of local *National Enquirer* that emphasized sports and sex, bit the dust in late 1981.

Owners of both the *Star* and the *Bulletin* tried to sell their papers and keep them alive, but no buyer was interested in bucking the malaise that has come over many big-city afternoon newspapers in modern times. Morning papers have always had a better break on the news (most of which tends to occur during daytime hours) and on delivery (having all night to get their papers out to the customers). But readers, until recent years, seemed to prefer evening newspapers, so the big afternoon dailies kept moving their deadlines forward to allow their traffic-slowed trucks more time to deliver their wares to customers who kept moving farther and farther out into the suburbs. Then people began to turn away from afternoon papers — or lots of them did anyway — preferring to get their evening news from television. In addition, many former metropolitan afternoon newspaper readers in the suburbs have switched to the dailies and weeklies that serve their suburban communities. Not all big-city afternoon papers are in trouble, but economic forces and changing life-styles of readers do appear to be ganging up on them.

Before she became managing editor-news of *USA Today*, Nancy Woodhull served at different times as managing editor of both Gannett dailies in Rochester, New York — the morning *Democrat & Chronicle* and the afternoon *Times-Union*. She believes morning papers have an advantage over afternoon papers today because of the way most readers live (interview, 16 Oct. 1981). "You feel you have to read a morning paper because you're in a certain business and you don't want to look like an asshole; you want to know what's going on." The afternoon papers, on the other hand, "don't have the latest news because it takes so long to get them to your house," she adds. "And TV is so easy, you can chop wood and still listen to it."

Rochester, with two Gannett dailies operating out of the same plant, is one of a number of cities in the United States with two jointly owned daily newspapers. Woodhull claims the competition between the *Times-Union* and the *Democrat & Chronicle* "is very serious," and that seems to be the case in other cities where both dailies are under the same ownership. But there has been a disturbing trend in such cities for owners to cut costs by consolidating their two "competing" dailies, as has happened in Minneapolis and Duluth, Minnesota; Allentown, Pennsylvania; Salem and Portland, Oregon; Des Moines, Iowa; and New Orleans, Louisiana, to mention just a few. (For a while at least, readers in New Orleans could subscribe to the morning or afternoon editions of a paper with the mouthful title of New Orleans *Times-Picayune/States-Item*.) There are about twenty-five cities with two separately owned dailies that have merged all but their news and editorial departments under a special federal law called the Newspaper Preservation Act. Most readers have difficulty finding any major differences between two dailies in one city produced by the same company and two privately owned dailies under a joint operating arrangement being produced out of the same plant with shared business, advertising, circulation, and printing departments.

There are still about thirty cities in the country — like New York, Boston, Chicago, and Detroit — that have at least two separately owned competing daily newspapers. That is quite a comedown from 1923 when there were about five hundred such U.S. cities. And New York at one time had twenty-three dailies; Chicago had eight, and Los Angeles, seven.[10]

The number of weekly papers has also declined, but less dramatically than did the dailies between 1900 and 1940. There were 7,666 weekly newspapers being published in the United States in 1981, with a total weekly circulation of more than 45 million. In 1960, the country had 8,138 weeklies but total circulation was only 21.3 million.[11]

Although the pace of newspaper sales slowed in 1981, partially because many of the major groups began investing heavily in cable television systems, the trend does not seem reversible. It is possible that no independent or family-owned daily newspaper will be left in the United States by the year 2000. A company like Gannett might own as many as 150.

"A tremendous amount of what happens to a community is in the hands of those family publishers when they decide to sell," *Washington Post* publisher Donald Graham comments (interview, 4 June 1981). "It's not just a question of who you sell to but at what price. Invariably if you auction off a newspaper like a side of beef, the highest bidder is likely to be a person who wants to take the most money out of the paper."

THE ROLE OF ADVERTISING

The heavy dependence on advertising as the financial base of our media system can also affect the quality of journalism we get. This is not to say that advertisers are allowed to dictate what goes into news columns or newscasts, although unfortunately this does sometimes happen, particularly on smaller or competitively inferior newspapers or broadcast stations. But advertising has a more subtle and indirect effect on the nonadvertising content of our news media. Take the matter of space and time that journalists have for their news and commentary.

Open, adless pages are rare on most U.S. newspapers (the *New York Times* even allows advertisers on its front page, although it restricts them to extraordinarily small type at the bottom of news columns). Editors often have to treat news as fillers to stuff around the ads. Newspaper pages with ads occupying three-quarters to five-sixths of the space, quite common proportions, leave editors with virtually no opportunity for displaying news in an appealing way or for illustrating news with photographs or other graphics. And many Sunday newspapers are so crammed with ads and so stuffed with advertising supplements (preprints is what the industry calls these inserts that used to come to us as "junk" mail) that they almost have to be forklifted off the porch. Publishers usually impose a formula for how much advertising the average day's newspaper should carry, and the proportion of ads to nonads has been growing. It used to be close to 55 percent ads, 45 percent nonads in the late 1940s; today the ratio is more like 65 percent ads, 35 percent news on the average.[12] What happens most days on most U.S. newspapers is that the advertising department lays out its ads on the pages available and the news department gets what's left. The size of the paper most days depends not on that day's news but on that day's advertising.

In broadcast news, editors also have to shape their newscasts around the commercials, so there is always a limit on how much continuous time can be devoted to a single story or piece of audio or video tape. The average 30-minute newscast on network or local TV is divided into four or five chunks, never adding up to more than twenty-four minutes of news.

Soft News Sells. At the same time that the proportion of advertising to nonadvertising has been going up in most American newspapers, an increasing share of that nonadvertising space has been turned over to "soft news" or features. Most newspapers today run special sections devoted to such subjects as food, homes, education, life-styles, people, and recreation. Although the subject matter varies from paper to paper, these new and emerging sections have in common content that is designed to appeal not only to special segments of the audience, but to advertisers interested in reaching people with such interests. That same marriage of interests was seen, of course, in more traditional sections dealing with travel, real estate, and business. It is just that today's daily newspaper is devoting a much greater share of nonadvertising space to what people in the news business call "features."

Are these new specialized sections new evidence of advertiser influences on news? Many editors, particularly those atop newspapers that have gone in for the new sections, would defend them as legitimate journalism. Although he concedes that the *New York Times* started its special sections in the late 1970s for commercial rather than journalistic reasons (to attract more readers and advertisers), executive editor Abe Rosenthal is proud of them because "they have strengthened the paper, have made it more interesting." (Interview, 7 Oct. 1981.) His newspaper in 1976 was just barely out of the red. "We wanted to keep the *Times* as it was, but to stay the same we had to change," Rosenthal explains.

In his history of the *New York Times*, Harrison E. Salisbury writes that Rosenthal stole the idea for the special sections from the old *New York* magazine that editor Clay Felker had developed. Salisbury quotes Rosenthal as saying, "I'll steal any idea from anybody as long as it's not nailed down." His cannibalized special sections did not go down well with all *Times* readers, Salisbury tells us:

> And there were those who criticized the new incarnation saying that
> *The Times* must now invent another section and label it "News." To
> this Abe's answer was that the new sections had given the paper a
> financial floor that made its position virtually unassailable, and this
> at a moment when the *News* and the *Post* [the *Times*'s two New York

competitors] were foundering. Now, unlike any other paper in the country, *The Times* could and did throw $30,000 a month, maybe $50,000 a month, over and above salaries and staff into covering the fall of Iran, the money was there, no strain. Abe could maintain forty correspondents in Europe without looking over his shoulder at the auditors.[13]

Some media watchers criticize the special feature sections for directing the energies and talents of journalists just to subjects that attract the kind of readers advertisers want. You don't see special sections appearing each week with labels like "Poverty," "Ghetto Life," "Hard Times," "Living Off The Land," or "Making It On Welfare." Nothing personal, but advertisers don't find poor folks very interesting.

Another extending of the definition of journalism to attract more or special kinds of readers and perhaps sell more advertising is apparent in the increasing chunks of space and time devoted to what one editor has called "celebrity journalism." Eugene Patterson, editor and publisher of the *St. Petersburg Times*, has said that the press has gotten so involved with celebrities he can no longer tell it from show business.[14]

Even gossip, the long-lasting antithesis of news, has wormed its way into the respectable columns of some of our leading papers. A lot of the regular features of the old *Washington Star* died with that paper when it folded in 1981, but one the *Post* felt it had to continue was a popular gossip column called "Ear." Some media critics expressed dismay that the *Post* would add such a feature to a "serious newspaper," but Charles Seib, who frequently and severely criticized the *Post* when he was the paper's ombudsman, sees no harm in the "Ear." He says it does not upset him any more than the horoscope columns many newspapers run (interview, 9 Nov. 1981).

Tabs. Another example of advertising's subtle influence on the news content of newspapers is the special theme supplement common in most medium and small daily newspapers. Often called "tabs" because they are printed tabloid size, these special sections are built around some theme like cars, brides, house and lawn care, football, business progress, restaurants, or some holiday. They are loaded with ads but they also contain what looks like news and informational material. Some of it is legitimate and useful information, but lots of it is simply puffery to wrap around the ads. The ideas for these tabs usually originate in the newspaper's advertising department, but the news department usually has to write or edit the nonadvertising material and lay out the pages. This irks many editors and reporters because it takes time away from covering and processing serious news they feel would be more useful to the readers than the advertising-support material found in most tabs.

The *Philadelphia Inquirer*'s Roberts cancelled such tabs whenever they were proposed after he joined that paper in 1972 (interviews, 28 May and 15 Sept. 1981). But he recalls letting one on savings and loan institutions survive because he feared that the advertising department was getting fed up with what must have seemed like an antiadvertising attitude. Then he discovered the reporter who traditionally had done this particular tab was working with the ad salesman to the extent of promising each potential advertiser that such and such a story would accompany each ad. Another *Inquirer* tab went down the drain.

Editors of smaller dailies have to put up with the creatures. James A. Dunlap, editor of the *Herald* in Sharon, Pennsylvania, has had to tolerate such supplements since his paper became part of the Ottaway group a few years ago (interview, 28 Oct. 1981). "We object to news theme tabs . . . but they're a fact of life of newspapers." Ottaway is a good group with high editorial standards, he adds, but "they want revenue and this is a way of getting some ad linage." Dunlap wishes, however, that the paper did not publish tabs "because of the junk that's run as news and of the time it takes" overworked news people to produce them.

An executive editor of a group of two dailies, six paid weeklies, and six free weeklies in the Philadelphia suburbs believes he has a solution to the tab problem. Fred Behringer, vice-president of the Montgomery Publishing Company in Fort Washington, Pennsylvania, reports that when a proposed tab does not meet their editorial standards, it is produced by the advertising department and "labeled 'advertising supplement' to make the reader realize that it's all advertising." His staff does produce tabs that contain legitimate news content, such as one about the U.S. Open golf tournament when it was held in the Philadelphia area (interview, 26 May 1981).

Newspapers have always published a lot of soft news — information of less than life-and-death importance but interesting to many or at least some readers. What is a more recent development is the addition of special sections, tabs, and features, not out of editors' beliefs that the readers need this additional information but because the supplements might attract a new audience to sell to advertisers.

More Direct Pressures. Some advertisers seek preferential treatment in the news media in which they buy advertising space and time. Sometimes they buy ads to be run during certain radio and TV programs and in some cases advertisers sponsor and are identified with entire programs ("GE Theatre," "This second half of the Tampa Bay-Atlanta football game is brought to you by . . . ," and the like). Sometimes they want their ads in certain places in the newspaper, and a recent Newspaper Advertising

Bureau survey shows that about 80 percent of U.S. dailies are willing to grant such requests.[15]

Nobody gets too excited about advertisers attempting to position their ads in certain parts of the newspaper or magazine, or at certain times of the broadcast day. But what does disturb journalists and observers is allowing advertisers to dictate or influence what passes for untainted news. The news columns and newscasts are not supposed to be for sale. And, generally speaking, they aren't.

But some advertisers have found ways to invade the news columns, as R. J. Reynolds Industries has done with its "Camel Scoreboard." Reynolds asked 600 daily newspapers if they would be willing to sell a full sports page each week to be filled by the sports department with scores, results, and other statistical material of interest to sports buffs. The sports statistics were to be stuffed within borders designed to resemble a pack of Camel Light cigarettes. About half of the papers that received Reynolds's inquiry said they would accept the proposal if offered, and the company inaugurated the weekly scoreboard in 1982 by purchasing full pages in about seventy-five dailies.[16]

Xerox Corporation got its camel into the editorial tent of *Esquire* magazine a few years back, but cancelled plans for further excursions into "sponsored journalism" after a scolding from essayist E. B. White, living in retirement in North Brooklin, Maine. When the former *New Yorker* magazine writer heard that Xerox had paid $55,000 in fees and expenses to Harrison Salisbury for a twenty-three page article (evaluating the state of the country in its bicentennial year) and $115,000 in advertising to *Esquire*, which published the article in its February 1976 issue, he wrote a critical letter to his hometown newspaper, the *Ellsworth American*. A fascinating exchange of letters between White and W. B. Jones, director of communications operations for Xerox, ensued. Jones explained that Xerox merely wanted to extend what it had been doing for years on television — "sponsoring programs of substance that might not otherwise have gotten on the air." But White saw it as "sponsorship" that was "an invitation to corruption and abuse." He argued:

> A funded article is a tempting morsel for any publication — particularly one that is having a hard time making ends meet. A funded assignment is a tempting dish for a writer, who may pocket a much larger fee than he is accustomed to getting. And sponsorship is attractive to the sponsor himself, who, for one reason or another, feels an urge to penetrate the editorial columns after being so long pent up in the advertising pages. These temptations are real, and if the barriers were to be let down, I believe corruption and abuse would soon follow. ... Buying and selling space in news columns could

become a serious disease of the press. . . . I don't want IBM or the National Rifle Association providing me with a funded spectacular when I open my paper. I want to read what the editor and the publisher have managed to dig up on their own — and paid for out of the till.[17]

Two letters later, Jones wrote to White that Xerox had aborted two other *Esquire*-like projects "and although that process involved some discomfort, we now feel better for it. Your correspondence was a primary factor in our reconsideration, and we do appreciate your help in reaching what I am convinced is the right decision."[18]

Advertisers less thoughtful than Xerox still try to influence the selection and play of news, not by buying their way into the news columns, but by threatening to cancel or actually cancelling their ads. Car dealers in Trenton, New Jersey, pulled their ads from the *Trenton Times* a few years back (just after the paper had been purchased by the *Washington Post*) to protest a local columnist who wrote that the high price of a new car made him keep his clunker. Richard Harwood, the editor the *Post* sent to Trenton to edit the *Times*, refused to censure the columnist, telling the car dealers, "This paper is not for sale."[19] But the *Trenton Times* started whistling a different tune after Joseph Allbritton bought the paper from the *Post* in 1981 and almost immediately dismissed twenty-four people from a news staff of eighty. Fourteen other news staffers soon left the paper, complaining that the business office was taking over the newsroom and catering to advertisers. One who left, business editor Perri Foster-Pegg, said she had been told to include in an annual business supplement some flattering articles submitted by advertisers in the section. The advertisers complained after Foster-Pegg shortened or rewrote their news releases, unlike the rival *Trentonian*, which had published them as submitted. Shortly after that incident, which prompted Foster-Pegg to flee to a public relations job, the *Times* fired a new young business section reporter who added some clarifying information to a news release from an advertiser after he had been told by his editor to type it verbatim into the paper's computer system.[20] Allbritton, Texas financier who owns five other newspapers and owned the old *Washington Star* from 1974 to 1978, claimed in a signed editorial in the *Times* that it was not the policy of "Allbritton Communications to allow the interests of our advertisers to influence the news." He said the management of the *Times* had erred when it ordered the news release to be used verbatim, but the dismissed reporter also had been wrong in defying the orders of his editor. Rem Reider, who was forced out as managing editor of the *Times* after the Allbritton takeover and who became associate news editor of the *Miami Herald*, said the new management Allbritton installed had "great sensitivity" about "pleasing the advertisers."[21]

Editor Dunlap of the Sharon, Pennsylvania, *Herald* has experienced advertisers who have withdrawn ads because of news stories that reflected adversely on them in some way, but that has not changed his policy of not allowing advertisers to influence news. He does not believe, however, that his news staff should go out of its way to offend advertisers (interview, 28 Oct. 1981). He objected, for example, to a travel feature in his paper that "played up one bus company that doesn't advertise and ignored another that does, that mentioned three travel agencies but omitted one that is an advertiser." If a story needs to be illustrated with local examples, Dunlap says, "our policy is to use the ones who advertise. I don't think that's compromising anything. ... If you're going to pick only a few people to talk to, pick the ones who spend money with us."

Sometimes reporters and editors can buck when they get assignments that cater to advertisers. Ellen R. Findley of the *Sacramento Bee* recalls that when she worked as a special projects reporter on the Baton Rouge, Louisiana, *Morning Advocate*, another reporter was told to do a story on National Insurance Week to accompany ads the advertising department had sold with the promise of a big article that would appear in the same edition. The managing editor had gone along with the ad department's request for this special story because he had developed a cooperative arrangement with the advertising director in order to obtain extra news space occasionally for lengthy articles and special features. Although the city editor and two assistant city editors balked at assigning the story, the managing editor insisted. The reporter who got the assignment eventually turned in a story based on complaints about insurance companies to the state insurance commission — a sort of antiinsurance story, Findley reports. The angry managing editor almost fired the city editor and edited the story so heavily that it made little sense, she adds (interview, 15 Feb. 1981).

Some large advertisers still try to influence news policy, in the opinion of executive editor Behringer (interview, 26 May 1981). He tells a story about one such advertiser who insisted that Behringer's staff do a story about his business. "We questioned him about it, searching for some news peg, and finally asked him why he should get a special news story. He said he owed the paper a lot of money for advertising and if we didn't do something to promote his business, he was going to go bankrupt and couldn't afford to pay our bill." The request was denied, Behringer reports.

Sometimes the news content affects what is in the ads. What do you do, for example, when your news staff comes up with a story that contradicts what some of your advertisers are saying in their ads? Many publishers would simply look the other way, and run both. The *Chicago Sun-Times* had such a problem recently when its investigative reporting team came up with a major series on abuses and profiteering in abortion clinics. Pamela Zekman, who headed the team that produced the series, recalls that a week before the articles were to appear she pointed out to her editors that "people were coming into those clinics on the basis of ads we were running." (Interview, 8 Sept. 1981.) She claims that "without a moment's hesitation," the paper cancelled contracts with the clinics that were worth $600,000 a year in advertising revenue.

PROFESSION, TRADE, CRAFT?

What is this thing called journalism? A lot of people in it refer to it as a business. And it certainly is a business, as this chapter has tried to argue. But it's more than that. Some journalists say it's a profession; others prefer words like trade or craft.

Journalism is not a profession under the traditional definition of that word, the definition that is used in the National Labor Relations Act. And in a recent test of that definition applied to journalists, the NLRB ruled three to one that news department employees of the *San Antonio* (Texas) *Express and News* were not "professional employees" as defined in Section 2(12) of the act, which states:

> The term "professional employee" means —
> (a) any employee engaged in work (i) predominantly intellectual and varied in character as opposed to routine mental, manual, mechanical or physical work; (ii) involving the consistent exercise of discretion and judgment in its performance; (iii) of such character that the output produced or the result accomplished cannot be standardized in relation to a given period of time; (iv) requiring knowledge of an advanced type in a field of science or learning customarily acquired by a prolonged course of specialized intellectual instruction and study in an institution of higher learning or a hospital, as distinguished from a general academic education or from an apprenticeship or from training in the performance of routine mental, manual, or physical processes; or
> (b) any employee, who (i) has completed the courses of specialized intellectual instruction and study described in clause (iv) of pararaph (a), and (ii) is performing related work under the supervision of a professional person to qualify himself to become a professional employee as defined in paragraph (a).

While not questioning the "intellectual demand" of being a journalist and conceding that such work requires "superior writing skills," the majority of the NLRB held that journalism does not conform to the definition of a profession in the law because journalists are not required to meet the fourth criterion, "knowledge of an advanced type."[22]

The Newspaper Guild would be horrendously if not fatally disrupted if the NLRB had decided the other way and made all news and editorial department employees ineligible as "professionals" to collectively bargain for themselves through labor unions. That is why it supported the International Typographical Union, which brought the San Antonio case to NLRB, and fought for the same cause in a more recent case it initiated in Philadelphia. Although the Philadelphia case never came to decision, testimony was taken and among those who testified that journalism is a craft, not a profession, were Russell Baker, *New York Times* columnist; Curtis MacDougall, retired Northwestern University professor of journalism; and William Rivers, professor of communications at Stanford University.

Norman E. Isaacs, senior advisor to the National News Council who fought the Guild in the old days as a newspaper executive and more recently when the Guild opposed imposition of ethics codes, finds himself in the same corner with the Guild on whether journalism is or is not a profession (interview, 7 Oct. 1981). "It can't be a profession," Isaacs declares, "unless we accept licensing, which is abhorrent to us."

The fear journalists have of being licensed by government or by an organization of peers in the way that lawyers and physicians are seems to be the major objection to professional status in the minds of most journalists. "We should admit to ourselves and to others that we are not professionals in the sense that doctors, lawyers and accountants are professionals," says John Seigenthaler, president, editor, and publisher of the Nashville *Tennessean*.

> We do not license. We do not disbar or defrock as a profession. Candidly, we must acknowledge that to try to do so would offend the basic and precious constitutional concept of free expression. Journalists, editors and publishers who bear and share the responsibility for presenting the news must never surrender their understanding of their ultimate responsibility to other judgments.[23]

Lyle Denniston of the Baltimore *Sun* contends that journalism cannot be a profession "because a profession has common universally-accepted ethical laws and a system of sanctions to enforce them — like law, medicine, architecture and accounting. . . . We are communicating ideas for sale, and so the ultimate restraint on us is the commercial one: will it sell? I don't apologize for working for a profit-making organization." (Interview, 5 June 1981.)

On the other hand, some journalists believe they are working in a profession. One of these is William E. Deibler, managing editor of the

Pittsburgh Post-Gazette, who maintains he is not worried about journalists having to be licensed "because, unlike other professionals, we have a constitutional protection in the First Amendment." (Interview, 22 Oct. 1981.)

And Ralph Otwell, editor of the *Chicago Sun-Times*, believes you cannot mandate that journalism will be a profession and he hopes "there will never be a licensing requirement that will professionalize us in the way that medicine, law, and some other fields have been professionalized." (Interview, 9 Sept. 1981.) But he thinks of journalism as a profession, which to him means that "in your job you have an obligation to the public that transcends mere business, commerce, or trade." Unfortunately, according to Otwell, journalism is not widely perceived as a profession by the public or by "a lot of people who are in it."

A recent Gallup Poll asked people to rank members of twenty-four professions and occupations for honesty and ethical standards. Journalists ranked ninth and tenth. The rankings, in order from the most honest and ethical to the least, were: ministers, pharmacists, dentists, M.D.'s, engineers, college teachers, policemen, bankers, TV reporters and commentators, newspaper reporters, funeral directors, lawyers, stockbrokers, senators, business executives, building contractors, congressmen, local officeholders, realtors, union leaders, state officeholders, insurance salesmen, advertising practitioners, and auto salesmen.[24]

Gallup's list includes occupations besides journalism (such as college teachers, union leaders, and advertising practitioners) that have no licensing requirements. Yet that remains a major fear of professionalism in the minds of many journalists, even those like Paul Janensch and Joseph Shoquist who believe journalists should act like professionals. "We should try to be a profession," says Janensch, executive editor of the *Louisville Times* and *Courier-Journal,* "but the problem is the threat of licensing." (Interview, 19 Oct. 1981.) Shoquist, managing editor of the *Milwaukee Journal*, sees journalism as being a profession "philosophically but not literally so." (Interview, 19 Oct. 1981.) It is not "an occupation that is licensed like medicine and law, and we don't want to be a profession in that sense," Shoquist contends. "But we have the ethics and ideals of a profession and we are more ethical than law or medicine."

James W. Carey, dean of the College of Communications at the University of Illinois-Urbana, calls journalism "a profession by fiat." He believes journalism has been made a profession "without meeting the historic canons by which professions are identified" because of the "status and prestige" it has achieved "as the media have become more central and more centrally visible in the life of society." Carey is not cheered by the growth of professionalism in journalism and other fields:

The principal effect of professionalism is to erode the moral basis of society. It does this because the professions insist that each inhabits a particular moral universe, peculiar unto itself, in which the standards and judgments exercised are those not of the general society and its moral point of view, but of a distinctive code. The professions divide up the moral universe in highly self-conscious ways, reorganize it through the explicit formulation of codes of ethics, and prosecute their distinctive moral claims with judicial, financial and authoritative power. . . . Moreover, the narrowness of the moral claims asserted by the professions have two confounding results. First, it means that professionals are privileged to live in a morally less ambiguous universe than the rest of us; they are able to treat as matters of principle what most of us must struggle with situationally and in terms of fine gradations of ethical judgment. Professionals are so busy standing on principle that there is no room left for the rest of us to stand. Secondly, the professions regularly conflate their own moral claims into principles that are binding upon the society for the welfare of everyone independent of their concrete relevance to particular situations. For example, the professions, and journalism is a leading case, often treat the Constitution as a suicide pact, as if it were written on Masada and not in Philadelphia, as if the entire social world must hinge on the sanctity of professional privilege.[25]

Journalism Education. The founders and organizers of the nation's journalism schools, which began in American universities shortly after the turn of the century, were boosters of professionalism. They hoped to provide the educational prerequisite for professional status. Elevating newspaper work to the level of a profession also added suppport and justification for having journalism courses and faculty in the first place. But acceptance by news media employers of a university journalism degree as the best preparation for work in journalism has been slow in coming. Only in recent years have newsrooms begun to be dominated by journalism school graduates, and most of these graduates have completed only a baccalaureate program. Graduate degrees in journalism or communications, or in subjects important to the understanding of news and people — such as history, political science, economics, literature, philosophy, science, or sociology — are rare in U.S. newsrooms. And on the other side of the coin, it is still possible to begin in news work with no college degree: even the prestigious *Wall Street Journal* does not require one. So journalism appears to be a long way from meeting the educational criterion of the traditional definition of a profession.

Explanations for the slow retreat by U.S. news executives from what must strike most outsiders as an idiotic prejudice against an educational program designed to serve them are not easy to come by. One explanation must be in the inability of news executives to agree on what kind of education they want their prospective employees to have, so that disparate signals are sent to the universities. Some of the smaller newspapers and broadcast stations want people who can come in and go to work with little if any instruction. They want technicians. Yet it is obvious to most journalists, and even to journalism students who clamor for more and more instruction in technical skills so they can get and hold those beginning jobs, that a broad and general education is what is needed for success over the long haul. Journalism schools try to give their students both a technical and a general education to serve both their short-range and long-range interests, but that is not a simple task, and to most thoughtful journalism educators four years hardly seems enough time. Yet requiring advanced degrees for news work does not have widespread support among journalism employers, some of whom must realize that more and more educational prerequisites would mean that the news media would have to do something about their generally low beginning salaries.

It is true that the stars of journalism — TV anchors for network and metropolitan station newscasts; top writers, reporters, and editors of the large newspapers; executives of *Time* and *Newsweek* — are well paid. But beginning salaries in the field have been disgraceful. Maybe it is because journalism has always appealed to people who were willing to work without pay, as many newspaper and broadcast interns do today. Jack McKinney thought he was working for pay when at the age of 20 he talked the *Philadelphia Daily News* into letting him submit some music reviews. Now a columnist for that paper, McKinney recently wrote about how gratified he had been that most of his reviews were published but how bewildered he was when after his first two months as "music critic" he still had not been paid. One night he screwed up enough courage to awaken the managing editor, Dean McCullough, who was napping curled up in his roll top desk:

> The slats rolled up and there, lying on his side all tucked up in a fetal position with a dead cigar in his mouth, was McCullough.
> "Yeah, what is it?" he demanded, blinking.
> "I guess you don't remember me, sir, " I said. "I'm Jack McKinney. . . ."
> "Oh, yeah," said McCullough. "Good stuff, kid. Reads real good. Keep it coming."
> Feeling more confident now, I told him I was sorry to disturb him but I thought something must have gone awry in the *Daily News* accounting system.
> "Why do you say that?" McCullough asked.
> "Because I haven't been paid yet for any of my reviews," I told him.

"No kidding!" he roared, swinging his short legs around to sit up in the desk. "Who hasn't been paying you?"

"Why, uh, the *Daily News* hasn't been," I said.

McCullough laughed heartily at this.

"You don't understand, kid," he said. "You're supposed to get the money from them."

Puzzled, I asked him who he meant by "them."

"The people you write the reviews about," the managing editor explained.

"But, sir," I protested. "That wouldn't be ethical."

"Well, if that's the way you feel about it, suit yourself," said McCullough, returning to the fetal position and reaching up for the roll-top slats. "At least you're getting in to hear all that stuff for free."[26]

Pay is better for beginners now, but not much. A survey conducted by Warren W. Schwed with the help of the Newspaper Fund in 1981 showed that beginning pay in newspaper newsrooms was $204.95 a week, or $10,657.40 a year.[27] The median entry level salary in news departments of U.S. radio and television stations in mid-1981 was $200 a week, or $10,400 a year, according to a similar study done by Vernon A. Stone for the RTNDA.[28] As these surveys were being done, the U.S. Postal Service was advertising in Washington newspapers for clerk carrier trainees at $9.50 per hour, which amounts to $380 a week for a 40-hour week, or $19,760 a year. So much for the rewards of professionalism.

Conflicts of Interest

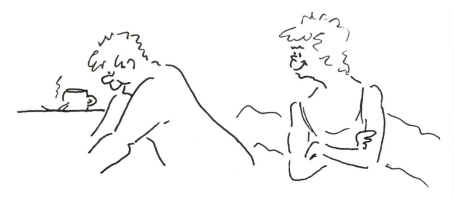

"You know I'd marry you if I could, Suzie, but my editor says it would create a terrible conflict of interest."

SUPPOSE YOU LIVE in this progressive city, which has a national reputation for its cultural, educational, and entertainment advantages. As an alert citizen who keeps up with what is going on, you are aware that the owner of your city's daily newspaper is very active in the community. Not only has he put his company's money into your city's art gallery, symphony orchestra hall, theater, and sports stadium; he has been a leader in fighting for such projects. His most recent involvement — getting a new domed sports stadium for two professional teams in your city — has aroused controversy in the community, controversy that is fully reported in his newspaper. At one time, in fact, you notice a large advertisement in the paper signed by forty-five members of the news staff and stating that although the owner has not tried to influence coverage of the stadium issue, "we believe management should avoid a leadership role in sensitive political and economic issues." Later, the paper publishes a series of articles alleging that its owner and other corporate executives in a consortium stand to profit more than they had promised the city in redeveloping the land around the stadium. In a subsequent column, the paper's executive editor scolds the owner for his involvement in the stadium project.

Do you agree with the editor and staff that the proprietor of your city's only daily newspaper should not have involved himself in community activities as he has? Hasn't the community benefited from his projects? Do you believe the owner tries not to influence the reporting of those activities in the paper he owns? Do you believe editors and reporters are independent and secure enough to report fairly on community projects in which their owner is involved, even if such reporting makes the owner look bad? In other words, do you feel that what you have been reading in your newspaper about the owner and his projects would be any different if he had stayed out of them as the news staff apparently wants him to?

Those are some of the questions that thoughtful readers of the *Minneapolis Star* and *Tribune,* now merged into one newspaper, must have asked themselves not too long ago. To many of the journalists on those two papers and to many journalists elsewhere, what the president of Cowles Media Company had done constituted a conflict of interest. Whether the readers also saw it that way is an interesting question this study cannot answer.

The kind of civic activities that John Cowles, Jr., got involved in probably would have earned him praise and esteem, especially from his own employees, if he had been any kind of president except the president of a newspaper publishing company. He put his energies and his company's money into building the famous Guthrie Theater, the Walker Art Center, and the orchestra hall for the Minnesota Symphony. During the racially tense sixties, he led the formation of a coalition of business leaders and public officials to provide communication with blacks and other minorities.

His father had been principal purchaser of the bonds floated to build the stadium in suburban Bloomington used by the professional football and baseball teams in that area. When the two teams, the Vikings and the Twins, threatened to leave the Minneapolis area if they did not have a larger, weather-protected facility, John Cowles, Jr., set out to give them what they required to stay, the new domed stadium in downtown Minneapolis that opened in 1982.

Cowles explains that he involved himself in these projects to improve the economic health of the community (interview, 15 Mar. 1982).* "I didn't regard these things as charities in the old-fashioned sense — like Lady Bountiful leaving baskets on doorsteps at Thanksgiving," Cowles says. "I saw my actions as long-range enlightened self-interest."

Building the new stadium, however, turned out to be more controversial for Cowles than his previous civic projects. For one thing, he

_____
*See list of interviewees following Notes.

encountered opposition in the community from, among others, a group that called itself Minnesotans Against the Downtown Dome (MADD). For another, he ran smack up against a growing sensitivity in journalism about outside activities that create or appear to create conflicts of interest.

What Cowles did to promote a new domed stadium in downtown Minneapolis was to take the lead in raising funds, in lobbying necessary legislation through the state legislature, and in negotiating with the city government. Cowles contributed "something like $4.9 million in cash and land to make it happen," according to Stephen D. Isaacs, CBS News producer, then editor and senior vice-president of the now defunct *Minneapolis Star* (interview, 12 Nov. 1981). The deal that was finally made with the city allowed the principal donors certain rights to develop the land around the new stadium. To accomplish this, Cowles and other business leaders formed Industry Square Development Corporation and "limited themselves to a 6½ percent profit," Isaacs reports.

Few outside the two newspapers understood how independent the *Star* and *Tribune* were under Cowles, Jr., before company directors forced him out of the presidency in 1983. He had given up the title of editor of the two papers more than a decade ago, and more recently he had moved the corporate headquarters out of the newspaper building. He appointed a publisher to supervise the two Minneapolis newspapers.

But many of the news people on Cowles's Minneapolis papers believed that the appearance of conflict of interest could be just as damaging to their credibility as a real conflict. Forty-five news staff members of the morning *Tribune,* including a city editor, a state editor, and some assistant editors, signed an ad they purchased in their own newspaper to say:

> As journalists, our responsibility is to be dispassionate and fair in covering public issues. Our role is to report, not to participate in these issues. Because we work for the *Minneapolis Tribune,* we recognize some people may question our fidelity to that principle when John Cowles, Jr., chairman of the board of the Star and Tribune Company, is a leading advocate in the debate over whether and where the sports stadium should be built. We bought this advertisement to assure our readers that our professional principles have not been undermined by Cowles' involvement in the stadium issue. We neither advocate nor oppose building a stadium, domed or un-domed, at any location. Furthermore, neither Cowles nor any other company executive has tried to influence the *Tribune's* coverage of this issue. But to prevent even an appearance of such a conflict of interest, we believe management should avoid a leadership role in sensitive political and economic issues.[1]

Cowles met with the *Tribune* news staff after the ad appeared, but "he did not budge from his position, which is that this kind of community involvement can be very essential and does not necessarily affect the credibility of the newspapers," *Tribune* managing editor Frank Wright told the national convention of the SPJ-SDX. Wright said Cowles told the staff that he maintains a "functional distance" from the two papers and that he does not interfere in the newsroom. "And he does *not* mess in the newsroom," Wright added.

Wright, however, rejected the principle of "functional distance." He said the readers "know he owns the newspapers and they assume he runs them." Wright saw the stadium controversy as one more argument against the long-standing policy of his company of encouraging community activity by people in the front office. He recalled that some years back private investors were asked to finance an expansion of the old stadium to attract professional teams but were not willing to do so unless public tax money was promised to back up the investments. Wright said when he, as city hall reporter, sent in stories about this matter, all references to the possible use of tax money were edited out. As a result, a "summit meeting" with the *Tribune's* executive editor at that time was held. Wright said he will never forget the editor telling him at that meeting, "Well, at some point you have to decide whether you want a news story or a major league baseball team."[2]

Wright declared that newspaper publishers and proprietors "ought to ask themselves what effect their involvements will have on the newspaper's believability and . . . on its professional arm's length relationship with the community." If a newspaper's credibility is eroded, Wright argued, it makes no difference whether the news staff is accurate and fair because "the readers will eventually come to doubt whatever we print."

The Minnesota News Council looked into the coverage of the stadium controversy by the two Minneapolis dailies after MADD complained that the reporting was biased. Backing away from outright condemnation of Cowles for his leadership role in the stadium project, the council concluded that readers of the *Star* and *Tribune* received "a reasonably fair, accurate and balanced report of events surrounding the stadium decision." The council said it found no evidence that Cowles had "attempted to influence coverage," nor that reporters and editors had "experienced subtle pressure to inhibit aggressive coverage of the stadium issue as a result of Cowles' involvement."

In an interesting "partial dissenting opinion," news council member Robert M. Shaw, manager at that time of the Minnesota Newspaper Association, said the council sidestepped the most important ethical issue in the case: "Is it ethical in the *first* place for a publisher of a dominant metropolitan newspaper organization, or any newspaper organization, to take actions which will surely reduce the credibility of his newspaper or newspapers and place an unfair professional burden on his staff?" Shaw contended that "no publisher should ever put his newspaper's credibility in the position which Mr. Cowles has done." He said the loss of a newspaper's credibility, "the only thing that really matters," may be "hastened by the extrajournalistic activities of the man at the top. The best way to avoid conflict of interest is to stay out of it in the first place."[3]

As the new domed stadium was nearing completion, the *Star* stoked the controversy anew with articles published after fourteen months of investigation that raised new questions about the consortium of business executives to which the city had granted redevelopment rights in a fifty-block area around the stadium. Cowles, of course, was a part of that consortium. The articles attracted several newspaper pages of letters to the editor, including one from the consortium.

But to *Star* editor Isaacs, most of these letters "missed the point of what an extraordinary newspaper company this is that would talk about these sorts of things openly." (Interview, 12 Nov. 1981.) Isaacs confesses he is "astonished that so many people take for granted what John Cowles, Jr., allows his newspapers to be, when it is unprecedented to my knowledge in the history of journalism. And that really is a question of John's integrity and sense of ethics that these kinds of things are properly debated in the columns of his newspaper." Isaacs points out that the stadium area redevelopment articles, an assignment that originated with him, were not shown in advance to Cowles or any other corporate officers or even to Donald R. Dwight, publisher of the *Star* at that time.

But Isaacs is not happy that his corporate owner involved himself in the stadium fight the way he did. "John didn't just contribute to the cause ..." Isaacs says. "He was the principal negotiator with our city government: he was not *a* player, he was *the* player." Isaacs recalls that his staff had to overcover Cowles, had to lean over backwards to show "that we were not in fact distorting our coverage because of John's involvement."

"The greatest contribution an owner can make to his community is by putting out a quality newspaper that has a high standard of integrity and ethics," Isaacs argues. "The claim of owners that they need to put something back into the community is hypocritical and a lie. If they wanted to make a generous contribution, they could put it in a noncontrolled trust and turn over all the revenues they wanted to some kind of institution that would use them in an honorable way. . . . But I don't know a single owner who would do this, because what they're really after is power." Newspaper publishers and owners getting involved in community affairs is counter to their most important commodity — credibility — and therefore counter "to the essence of their business," Isaacs maintains.

Cowles, of course, disagrees with Wright and Isaacs (interview, 15 Mar. 1982). He believes "publishers have a positive obligation to engage in the important activities of the community." He believes the "whole notion that newspaper publishers and owners, as well as newspaper editors and reporters, should isolate themselves, sanitize themselves, from the community is a kind of recent idea, developed mostly by the biggest papers in communities so large that is is not clear and easy to see how an individual publisher can make a lot of difference." Cowles is sympathetic to the developing view that newspapers have to be "neutral bystanders," but he maintains that such neutrality should apply only to the news departments. "Publishers should be able to express their views not just through their editorial pages but through their efforts and work in the community," he contends. In most places in America, it is not seen as "improper behavior" for a publisher to lead a fund-raising drive for a new hospital, or similar projects, he adds.

Cowles does draw the line at newspaper proprietors and publishers running for partisan political office "because that makes life more difficult for their reporters and editors." But he sees nothing wrong in a publisher running for nonpartisan office, such as the school, park, or library board. Nor does he see any reason for publishers to refrain from making personal financial contributions to political campaigns. But "generally, high-profile politically partisan activities should be avoided in the city where you publish your paper," he concludes.

THE ACTIVIST TRADITION

Cowles is neither the first nor the only news media proprietor or executive to play an active role in community, state, or national affairs. His involvement in extrajournalistic matters is mild if you compare it, for example, with:

1. Walter Lippmann. During his long career as a magazine and newspaper editor and columnist, Lippmann often got involved in national politics, not merely as an observer and commentator, but as a participant and political manipulator. As a young editor of the *New Republic,* Lippmann not only wrote speeches for President Woodrow Wilson in his 1916 campaign for reelection; he delivered them from the back of a trailer truck in upstate New York. Still with the *New Republic* in 1920, Lippmann tried unsuccessfully in personal conferences and in editorials in his magazine to get Herbert Hoover to run for president. In 1928, by that time editorial page editor of the old *New York World,* Lippmann worked behind the scenes to get the Democratic party to nominate Al Smith for president; then he traveled to Albany on Governor Smith's private railway car to advise the candidate on strategy and on foreign policy issues. In 1940, trying through his respected newspaper

column to sell America the idea of providing destroyers to Great Britain just before World War II, Lippmann persuaded General George Pershing, the hero of World War I, to endorse the move. When Pershing agreed, Lippmann helped him write his speech hailing Lippmann's idea for an exchange of American destroyers for British bases in the Western Hemisphere. Lippmann became a sort of government emissary for President Kennedy after the Cuban missile base crisis in 1962. The president persuaded the columnist to present the administration's argument for an American nuclear monopoly in a talk to a group of European and American journalists in Paris. Lippmann got himself briefed by a top Kennedy aide before delivering the speech and apparently had no qualms about serving as Kennedy's messenger.[4]

2. Warren G. Harding. Harding used the *Marion* (Ohio) *Daily Star,* of which he was editor and publisher, to launch a political career that took him all the way to the White House. On his way to the presidency, to which he was elected in 1920, Harding held political jobs as county auditor, Ohio state senator, lieutenant governor of Ohio, and United States senator from Ohio. Harding apparently enjoyed being a newspaperman, but he had little time for his paper after he began his rise in politics. He thought about selling it, not because he saw it as a conflict of interest but because he wanted the money. Reminiscing with William Allen White, Harding confessed that back in Marion when the county printing contract was put up for bids, all the printshop owners would get together, choose a low bidder, and then add enough "to give us all a little slice of the profits above his low bid." Harding died in office in 1923, disgraced by the Teapot Dome scandal, his Watergate.[5]

3. Philip L. Graham. While publisher of the *Washington Post,* Phil Graham became a counselor and political operator for Senate Majority Leader Lyndon B. Johnson, even to the extent of helping to lobby Johnson's compromise voting rights bill through Congress in 1957. Graham also worked to get the Democrats to nominate Johnson for president in 1960, and when the convention nominated Senator John F. Kennedy instead, Graham became the go-between in negotiating the vice-presidential nomination for his friend Johnson. Graham also employed his political skills to improve his city, and when no local entrepreneur would tackle the huge southwest Washington redevelopment project, Graham persuaded New York developer William Zeckendorf to come in and direct the federally funded rebuilding.[6]

4. William F. Knowland. Active in Republican politics all his adult life, Knowland was also publisher of the *Oakland* (California) *Tribune,* a paper he inherited from his politically active father. In 1933, the same year his father named him assistant publisher, Knowland became at the age of twenty-five the youngest member of the California State Legisla-

ture. Later he served in the state senate and the U.S. Senate. He was a U.S. senator for thirteen years. During all his political career and until his death at the age of sixty-five, he was also assistant publisher or publisher of the *Oakland Tribune*.[7]

5. Even William Allen White, editor and publisher of the *Emporia* (Kansas) *Gazette* in the early part of this century, surprised his friends when he ran for governor of Kansas in 1924. He did it, though, not to get elected, but in an attempt to shake the two major party candidates from their position of failing to repudiate the Ku Klux Klan.[8] White is better remembered today as the progressive publisher from the prairie who warned the press against conflicts of interest when he wrote:

> The American Press is afflicted with the country club mind. It doesn't make much difference how much of a crusading young Galahad the young publisher may be when he starts; by the time he starts to put his paper across, he is taken up by the country club crowd, and when that happens, he is lost. He joins the country club, for that is our American badge of success. And, before he knows it, he sees his community from the perspective of the country club porch and edits his paper to please the men who gather with him in the country club locker room.[9]

Pros and Cons of Involvement. In an earlier day, it was common for newspaper owners, publishers, and editors to take part in community activities, even political activities. Some, like Warren Harding, ran for and were elected to political office. Others who may have shunned political office accepted others kinds of community leadership roles in the style of John Cowles, Jr. Still others worked behind the scenes as part of the power bloc in their communities and regions. If such activities caused concern about conflicts of interest among newspaper employees or the public, it does not show up as a major ethical problem in most of the early literature about journalism ethics. Early press critics — such as Will Irwin, George Seldes, and Upton Sinclair — sounded alarms about possible control of newspapers by outside vested interests, but few listened.

Only in recent years do conflicts of interest caused by the outside activities of the top brass appear to be matters of great critical interest both in and out of journalism. Most newspaper editors these days avoid any outside activity that could in any way put them in a position where it seems that they are favoring or disfavoring some group or groups in their news decisions. The few editors who still involve themselves in community activities, at least to a degree, appear to be editors in smaller towns. Owners, publishers, and executives responsible for the business side of the news media, regardless of size, feel less restricted in their outside activities. Most do not get as involved as John Cowles, Jr., did in Minneapolis, but many feel they have to pitch in to do their share as heads of major businesses in their communities.

Perhaps the modern concern about the extrajournalistic projects of news media owners and managers has something to do with the decline since World War II in competitive newspaper markets and in locally controlled, family-owned news organizations. The big, less personal corporations that own most of our news media today seem more threatening, less susceptible to local influence, less sensitive to local needs. And in Lippmann's time community and political activism was more acceptable because there was always a competing voice offering an alternative view.

Donald Graham, who sits in the publisher's chair at the *Washington Post* that was occupied before him by his grandfather, his father, and his mother, maintains that the "whole conception of what a publisher should do has changed." (Interview, 4 June 1981.) He believes the basic responsibility of a newspaper owner "is reporting the news rather than making it." While he hesitates to condemn what other newspapers do, because "the health of a given community is of vital importance to the newspaper," Graham says that like his mother, Katharine Graham, now chief executive of the Washington Post Company, he chooses to do his job as a newspaper person, staying out of politics "or any action that could be said to be political."

Julius Duscha, director of the Washington Journalism Center, covered politics for the *Post* when Donald Graham's father, Philip Graham, was publisher and later when Katharine Graham held that position. Although he was aware of Phil Graham's interest in politics, Duscha believes it did not affect his reporting of such presidential candidates as John F. Kennedy (interview, 5 June 1981). "It's probably harder for reporters to cover things when their owners or publishers are involved, but it's still possible to do a fair job," Duscha says. He believes a newspaper publisher should be "on the scene and involved in his town, not antiseptic, but willing to accept the presidency of the chamber of commerce one year, and be on the redevelopment committee, the new city committee, or whatever."

Charles Seib, retired ombudsman of the *Washington Post* and former managing editor of the old *Washington Star,* sees considerable pressure on publishers — especially in smaller communities — to be active (interview, 9 Nov. 1981). Although it might be all right for publishers in these smaller communities "to get involved in some outside activities," Seib concedes, "editors and reporters must avoid any significant outside involvements."

That distinction between publishers, who reign over the newspaper as an important business in the community, and the editors and reporters, who do the daily work of reporting and commenting on the news, is commonly made by those concerned about conflicts of interest. Phil Currie, vice-president/news staff development for Gannett Company, believes reporters and editors should avoid even registering to vote as Democrats or Republicans, but "publishers have to represent the newspaper in the community," even if that sometimes puts the newsroom in an awkward position (interview, 22 Oct. 1981).

Even such an innocuous outside activity as the United Way can boomerang. News media proprietors across the land, including those on the *Washington Post,* have commonly supported and headed up fund drives for this umbrella charitable organization, seen as nonpolitical and noncontroversial in most communities. Joseph W. Shoquist, managing editor of the *Milwaukee Journal,* who believes that publishers and corporate executives need to be involved in some community activities such as United Way, tells of an exposé his paper did on United Way (interview, 19 Oct. 1981). "We reported that the paid executive and top officers of United Way were living high on the hog with the agency's money, routinely entertaining each other at fancy restaurants and holding meetings at places like the Playboy Club at Lake Geneva," Shoquist recalls. His newspaper company is a vigorous supporter of United Way, the editor reports, and the president of his company was named as one who attended the Playboy Club meeting.

A newspaper that still encourages nonpolitical community involvement, even for reporters and editors, is the Sharon, Pennsylvania, *Herald.* "We're still a part of the community and have community responsibilities," observes *Herald* editor James Dunlap (interview, 28 Oct. 1981). "You cannot be part of your community and know what's going on in your town unless you are involved. You learn about things a reporter or editor would have no way of knowing without that contact with the power faction in the community." Dunlap notes that his publisher belongs to the country club, one news executive is on the board of the chamber of commerce, another is on the board of United Way, and still another is on the local hospital board. Dunlap is active in Rotary and the Boy Scouts; other members of the staff are involved in other service organizations. "These are basically noncontroversial organizations that rarely make the news in any significant way," Dunlap maintains, "but if there was a scandal or something in United Way, we'd report it."

Although he has no outside activities, Paul A. Poorman, editor and vice-president of the *Akron Beacon Journal,* believes "the newspaper is a corporate member of the community and has to do its share." (Interview, 8 Apr. 1981). He explains that Knight-Ridder Newspapers, owner of the *Beacon Journal,* approves of "civic endeavors beyond suspicion" for publishers and general managers but does not want its editors involved in any outside activities.

Poorman says he disagreed with Knight-Ridder's participation in a recent Florida controversy over legalized gambling that presents us with another important illustration of the divisions in journalism about conflicts of interest, as well as an unprecedented example of the press ganging up on an issue.

The Florida Lock Step. Should a newspaper or television station contribute money to one side or the other in an election? That was the central question raised by the decision of several news organizations in Florida to kick in $180,000 to fight legalization of casino gambling in Miami Beach and other nearby resorts. A related conflict of interest question was raised by the leadership of the anticasino forces by the governor of the state, Reubin Askew, who personally solicited the contributions from many of the media companies. Florida voters eventually rejected legal casinos in 1978 by a margin of 72 to 28 percent.

Almost every major media company in the state responded favorably to the governor's plea to help him stop what he saw as a disaster for Florida. He raised a total of $1.7 million. Hotel owners in the Miami Beach area, who were pushing for legal casinos, raised $600,000 to underwrite the petition drive that resulted in 420,000 signatures and put the issue on the ballot, and they ended up contributing almost 90 percent of the $2.9 million collected by the procasino side. The casino backers also hired Sanford Weiner of San Francisco, who organized the successful campaign that brought legal casinos to Atlantic City, New Jersey.

Among the media company contributors to the anticasino campaign were the *Miami Herald,* principal newspaper of the Knight-Ridder group, and three other Knight-Ridder dailies in Florida; Cox Newspapers, publishers of the *Miami News* and *Palm Beach Post-Times;* the *St. Petersburg Times;* Wometco Enterprises, parent company of WTVJ in Miami; the *Orlando Sentinel-Star,* owned by the Chicago Tribune Company; the *Tampa Tribune;* the *Florida Times-Union* of Jacksonville; and the *Fort Lauderdale News.* Two Knight-Ridder executives gave almost $20,000 in personal funds. (Notably missing from the list of contributors was the New York Times Company, which then owned eight dailies and one weekly in Florida, and Gannett, which had four dailies and two weeklies in the state.) The only media company that gave money to the casino side was the Miami Beach *Sun Reporter,* which contributed $5,000 to underwrite a feasibility study.

The National News Council investigated the *Miami Herald's* involvement and coverage of the casino fight after receiving a complaint from Jim Bishop, author and syndicated columnist. Apparently unconcerned about his own conflict of interest, Bishop chaired the statewide steering committee of "Let's Help Florida," the group that put the issue on the ballot through petition, and fought for legalizing casinos along Florida's so-called Gold Coast. Bishop, whose column appeared in the *Herald,* among other newspapers, challenged the news council to determine if financial contributions from the *Miami Herald* and solicitation of other contributions from other publishers by its president, Alvah H. Chapman, did not constitute, when linked to its hostile editorial stance, "an unprecedented influence of the media in a people's referendum campaign." Bishop also raised questions about the objectivity of the news coverage by media whose corporate owners had put money in the campaign.[10]

The council found no evidence of unfairness in the way the *Miami Herald* reported the referendum battle. In fact, the council concluded that "the Herald acquitted itself with distinction." Although the financial contributions by Chapman put the reporters and editors assigned to this story in an uncomfortable spot, "they decided, in the best tradition of journalism, that the only response they could in conscience make was to strive even harder than they normally did to be fair," the council said. "They succeeded admirably in that effort." The council did not examine coverage of the issue in other Florida media.

On the appropriateness of the media company contributions, the news council did not specifically condemn what the Florida media executives had done, but it warned other news organizations that the Florida example may not be a good one to follow. Media executives who "decide that the business interests" of their organizations require similar financial contributions in public policy issues up for decision by voters face three serious risks, the council concluded:

1. "First, they run the risk of undermining public confidence in the fairness of their news columns." It noted that a *Herald* poll during the campaign showed that a majority both of those favoring casinos and those opposed believed that newspapers contributing financially to the referendum could not be fair in their news columns. Among the anticasino respondents, 59 percent said financially contributing papers could not be fair, as against 25 percent who felt they could be fair, and 16 percent who said they did not know. In the procasino group, 58 percent said they thought such papers could not be fair, 33 percent thought they could, and 9 percent were on the fence. (Of the 701 persons in the sample, roughly two-thirds were anticasino.)

2. A second danger lies in the possible "blurring [of] the line of separation that should properly exist between the state and the media." Here the council referred to Chapman's conduct "as chief fund raiser for

the governor . . . in a campaign that becomes the overriding preoccupation of both men" and in soliciting funds from bankers and other business leaders outside the media. Such behavior could raise questions in readers' minds "about how detached the press can be in covering news or making editorial judgments affecting the business community."

3. Another risk is created by the justification that proprietors often give when they get involved financially in extrajournalistic activities — the argument that they do it for the financial health of their own news organizations. "They may find themselves reinforcing the argument of those who contend that the assertiveness of the trend toward conglomerate ownership has made newspapers and other media corporations just another form of big business, indistinguishable from other large corporations in their right to claim special protection under the Constitution."

In one of two dissenting opinions from the council majority, council member William A. Rusher, publisher of *National Review*, disagreed that journalists face risks "if they participate, as citizens or civic-minded corporations, in forms of political activity that would be regarded as downright praiseworthy if engaged in by a non-journalist." Rusher said "the American people fortunately do not share the perception of journalists as priests." He argued that each journalist should be allowed to "be a fully rounded human being: faithful to his God if he has one, and loyal to whatever political creed attracts him. And if he cares enough to contribute financially to some cause he deeply believes in, most people won't think less of him for it, but more."

The news council staff's report on the Florida case included some statements from the principals. One of these was Eugene C. Patterson, editor and president of the *St. Petersburg Times*, which made a $25,000 contribution to the anticasino drive. "This was our first venture in contributing financially to support our editorial view on a public vote and I would expect it to be our last, since a question that would change the fundamental nature of a society rarely presents itself," Patterson observed. He saw the casino fight as one such question. "I would hate to think newspapers are neutered as citizens by a pacifist mentality when rape is threatened. . . ." Patterson added. "The magnitude of the gamblers' financing convinced me this was no time to be spooked by the hobgoblins of little minds. Advertisement of our own virginity scarcely responded to the threat. Wearing a chastity belt presupposes we'll resist the lock pickers."

The executive who made the decision not to put any *New York Times* money into the anticasino pot, John R. Harrison, said he got two personal pleas to do so from Governor Askew. Harrison, who as vice-president of the New York Times Corporation was in charge of its Florida papers, feared that financial involvement would compromise reader confidence.

Allen H. Neuharth, chief executive of the Gannett chain, the other major media company that did not contribute money to the anticasino fight, said the decision was made by the local managers of the Gannett papers in Florida, but he applauded it. "The whole question of press credibility is such a sticky one," Neuharth told council investigators, "that those of us who own media and identify ourselves financially with one side of a controversial issue, no matter how objective our reporting is, will be suspect."

Other Activist Owners. Readers of the Allentown, Pennsylvania, *Call-Chronicle* learned a decade after the fact that their only daily newspaper had skewed its reporting of an important controversy about local hospitals because the bias of the paper's owners had permeated the newsroom. A Mellett Award-winning series by Walt Harrington told how the newspaper had been a cheerleader rather than an observer in reporting Allentown's efforts to provide better hospital care in the late 1960s. In its coverage, the paper reflected the views of its owners (the Miller family) that what the community needed was a merger of the community's two existing hospitals into a new hospital. However, one of the existing hospitals, Catholic-run Sacred Heart, opposed the merger and later claimed its opposition was not given a fair hearing in the paper. The reporter who covered the fund drive for the new hospital, to which the newspaper contributed $100,000, was assigned by his editor to actually sit as a member of the campaign's public relations committee. The paper's publisher, Donald Miller, was vice-chairman of the special gifts division of the campaign. His father, David A. Miller, the founding publisher of the Allentown paper, had also helped found Allentown Hospital and had served on its board. No wonder that reporter Dan Pearson felt the importance his management attached to the campaign. "At no time did I slant what I wrote or was I pressured," Pearson recalled. "But I knew my company's interests." He did not cover up news, he claimed, but he selected stories he knew would be looked on favorably by his bosses. "I wasn't nosing around like an anteater," he added.[11]

Edward D. Miller, the third generation of the owning family, stepped in as executive editor in 1969 as the coverage of the hospital campaign was winding down. Harrington, in his 1979 series, quotes Ed Miller as saying that he now believes the paper's coverage was "unfair" and "biased." Newspaper executives were active participants in their communities in the old days, Miller said. He compared newspapers with drug stores and ball teams that grew with their communities. But by the mid 1970s, young Miller no longer viewed his newspaper as a place where the ideas of the community's influential men should be sold to the public after they had been hammered out in back rooms or at country club dinner tables. Rather than be a consensus-building organ of the power bloc, the newspaper should be an outside mediator between various groups, contributing to the decision making through its coverage of onstage and offstage news, Miller contended. (Miller resigned from the *Call-Chronicle* in 1981.)

The Tribune Company, publishers of the *Chicago Tribune*, raised some possible conflicts of interest for its journalist employees when it purchased the Chicago Cubs, one of major league baseball's least successful franchises. The *Tribune* editor who would feel the most pressure if the owners insisted on anything special for the Cubs, sports editor George Langford, was confident that the independence of his sports staff would not be compromised (interview, 8 Sept. 1981). He recalls that when his reporters were investigating the pending sale of the Cubs, the people who were trying to arrange the deal appealed to the *Tribune* publisher to intervene, "but the publisher simply kept his hands off." Langford expects that policy will continue. He believes, however, that readers will be suspicious of anything his staff writes about the Cubs "until we establish a performance record beyond reproach.... Maybe then they'll get the idea that we are independent." What most readers don't know, Langford suspects, is that his staff for years has been covering two other professional franchises in town — the Black Hawks and the Bulls — that are owned by two members of the Tribune Company board of directors.

Even journalism reviews, unofficial watchdogs of journalistic foibles and failures, are not exempt from conflicts of interest. The eyebrows of media watchers were raised when a politically active couple — Henry Catto, Jr., and Jessica Catto — purchased the *Washington Journalism Review* in 1979. Henry Catto had been ambassador to El Salvador and U.S. chief of protocol in the Nixon and Ford administrations. Jessica Catto is a member of the Hobby family of Texas: her father William Hobby was once governor; her mother Oveda Culp Hobby was the first U.S. Secretary of Health, Education, and Welfare; her brother William Hobby, Jr., was then lieutenant governor of Texas and also president of the *Houston Post*. The eyebrows went even higher when Henry Catto jumped back into the political arena in 1981, becoming assistant secretary of defense for public affairs under President Reagan.[12] Only Jessica Catto's name appears on the masthead of *WJR* as president of Washington Communications Corporation, the magazine's publisher, but observers wonder how trustworthy *WJR* can be on issues close to the Cattos.

WORKING JOURNALISTS' CONFLICTS

Rod Nordland got more respectable when he became a foreign

correspondent and the *Philadelphia Inquirer* sent him off to report on the Far East. But back in the days when his specialty was covering and evading motorcycle gangs, he came into the presidency of a rejuvenated drinking and social organization in Philadelphia known as the Pen and Pencil Club. One of his first irreverent acts as leader of that group was to establish the Harry J. Karafin Award to memorialize that city's worst journalist. Harry who? Karafin, Harry Karafin. He was a reporter who was fired by the *Philadelphia Inquirer* in 1967 after *Philadelphia Magazine* exposed how he used sources and his access to the news columns of the *Inquirer* to build up his public relations business sideline. Karafin would prey on shady businesses under investigation by some legal agency or other and get them to buy his public relations services. Then he would turn the publicity faucets on and off in the *Inquirer* to suit his clients. He died while serving time in prison for blackmail. It is interesting that his unethical career was exposed by *Philadelphia Magazine*, not by his own newspaper (then owned by Walter Annenberg) nor by the town's leading paper at that time, the since deceased *Bulletin*.[13]

Eleven years later, however, the *Inquirer*, now under the new management of the Knight-Ridder chain, broke the news when it had to reassign its nightlife columnist because of a conflict of interest.[14] The columnist, Bill Curry, left the paper. Gene Foreman, managing editor of the *Inquirer*, reports that Curry had "disturbed us by business investments that were close to a conflict of interest, but when he went into business with a restaurant he had promoted in his column, a resignation was negotiated." (Interview, 28 May 1981.)

Another case of a working journalist trying to use his position or special knowledge for profit turned up in Milwaukee in the mid 1970s. The reporter was discharged from the *Journal*, managing editor Joseph W. Shoquist relates, after investigative articles he wrote almost drove a local bank into bankruptcy and eventually helped send some of its officers to jail (interview, 19 Oct. 1981). That was good journalism, but the reporter ran afoul of the *Journal's* tough ethics code when he went to a distress auction in Chicago one day and bought several thousand shares of that bank's stocks, sharply depressed in value because of the reporter's articles. "We found that utterly unacceptable," Shoquist says.

Those are just three examples that illustrate how the conflict of interest problem in journalism is not confined to the owner-executive level. Most conflicts are not as blatant as the preceding examples, but some reporters and editors do get involved outside their newsrooms with friends, causes, organizations, activities, and sidelines that constitute possible or real conflicts of interest.

Outside Jobs. Moonlighting, or holding down a second full- or part-time job, has become common in acquisitive modern society. Other than possible damage to health, moonlighting seems to present few serious problems to its participants. But if you are a young reporter making less money than your moonlighting neighbor, a store clerk who drives a cab on the side, you risk your job and your reputation unless you choose your second occupation with great care. Writing a book is fine. It might make you some money and bring credit to you and your news organization. Writing a promotion booklet for a local developer can get you fired. Doing an article for a national magazine is permissible. Doing an article for another newspaper in your area can get you fired. Doing a piece for a program put out by a professional team you cover can get you in trouble.

Selling your writing skills to the highest bidder may not be wise if you wish to survive as a reporter. Increasingly, U.S. news organizations have taken a dim view of outside jobs and activities that might cause the public to smell a conflict of interest — a situation in which you find that one of your jobs, interests, activities, or duties can be advanced only at the expense of another of your jobs, interests, activities, or duties.

Many of the contracts that the Newspaper Guild has with newspapers include so-called outside activities clauses, restricting what news department employees can do with their off duty hours. David J. Eisen, director of research and information for the Guild, claims that these clauses are "not ethical provisions: the public doesn't give a damn about them. They're publishers' interest provisions" that serve the economic interests of the employers (interview, 17 Apr. 1981). Eisen and other officers of the union obviously believe that newspaper managers have used conflict of interest as a justification for extending their authority over their employees. And this restricts reporters and editors from obtaining maximum economic benefit from their skills and talents.

The Guild went to arbitration when the Rochester, New York, *Times-Union* and *Democrat & Chronicle* refused permission for one of their photographers to work for a short period for the Lake Placid Olympic Organizing Committee. Executive editor Robert H. Giles said that working for a news source while employed by his newspapers was a conflict of interest, even if photographer Talis Bergmanis took vacation or leave to do it. (The Olympic Committee invited Bergmanis and nine other photographers to illustrate a proposed book on how to organize a winter olympics and also to provide news photos to smaller papers unable to staff the 1980 competition at Lake Placid, New York. Most of the invited photographers were free-lancers, but some were newspaper photographers, and one of those who accepted was Joe Traver, who got permission from the Buffalo *Courier Express* to do so.) After two hearings, the arbitrator, Joseph Shister of Buffalo, ruled in essence that the company had not proved a real conflict of interest. He made the company pay

Bergmanis a total of $1,850 — the $600 he would have been paid by the Olympic Committee (twelve days at $50 per day) and $1,250 for the free-lance photographs he might have sold if he had been allowed to work the olympics for the committee.[15] Bergmanis left the Rochester papers after winning his grievance.

Giles believes his organization was "the victim of an arbitrator who does not understand the newspaper business." (Interview, 15 Oct. 1981.) He explains that his newspapers did not appeal to the NLRB because the decision did not set a precedent and arbitrator's decisions are usually upheld by the NLRB and the courts.

Giles made it clear to the news staffs of his two newspapers that the arbitrator's decision had not changed the editor's attitude about conflicts of interest. "Our readers must have absolute trust in the independence and the integrity of our newspapers and the journalists who work for them," Giles stated in a staff memo. "We must avoid activities that can cause suspicion among readers about our ability to report the news in a fair and balanced way. Our relationships with news sources, promoters, advertisers and public relations people must be kept at arm's length." He said the Olympic Committee that wanted to hire Bergmanis "was, at once, a news source, a sports promoter, an advertiser, a fund raiser, and a public relations organization. Part of its mission was to influence the news." Giles wrote:

> The idea that potential conflicts of interest should be avoided is not intended to prevent members of our news staffs from doing volunteer work in the community or pursuing leisure activities or even some work related to their professional lives. The test is whether the readers of our newspapers could reasonably assume that there was a conflict. In some cases, the presence of a conflict is clear. In others, it might be a close call. Responsibility for making those calls is mine. The arbitrator's ruling has not changed the rules here. They require that any outside activities have the advance approval of the executive editor.[16]

Editors may differ on what constitutes a conflict of interest for their staffs — and some have them written down and some have not — but the requirement of advance approval for outside activities is approaching universality in U.S. newsrooms. Working for a competing news medium, usually defined as one aimed almost exclusively at the same or part of the same audience as that of the employing medium, is on almost every editor's taboo list. So is working for any public relations firm or department, or for any political or governmental agency. Free-lancing on your own time that results in a book, an article in a national magazine, or an exhibition of photographs is usually not considered a conflict. In fact, such activities often bring prestige to the employer as well as the

employee. Teaching part-time at a university or other respectable school
is usually no problem if the schedule can be arranged. Investing in stocks
and bonds or in business is usually approved unless the investments are
tied too closely to your regular assignment or to something you have
published or broadcast or intend to. Volunteer or unpaid work is also
generally verboten if it links the journalist too closely with news sources
and subjects: writing speeches, news releases, or ads for political
candidates; taking part in a controversial demonstration; holding office
in a political party or an unpaid position in government; heading a local
pro- or antiabortion group. Editors usually do not object to staff members
affiliating with conventional churches and other reasonably noncontroversial organizations (Girl Scouts, Kiwanis, Rotary, and the like), but
they might prevent staff members from holding office in those organizations, especially those involving any responsibility for publicity or public
relations. Registering with one of the major parties in order to vote in
primaries is not taboo, but many reporters and editors still choose to
register as independents.

The extrajournalistic opportunities available to photographers have
brought about some special policies on many newspapers. Most editors do
not allow their photographers to sell any photos taken for their
newspapers for fear that some photographers might be tempted to put
marketability above journalistic value in the pictures they take. Some
newspapers give away prints of the photos that have been published if
family members or others ask for them. More newspapers, however, seem
to be charging for such prints, and the *Philadelphia Inquirer* shares the
revenue from such sales with its photographers. Photographers who want
to free-lance or take photographs for pay during off-duty hours are
usually subject to the same advance permission and other restrictions
applied to writers.

Newspaper and magazine journalists usually avoid anything to do
with advertising in deference to long-standing rules about keeping news
and advertising separate. But radio and television news people, particularly but not exclusively at the local level, feel less constrained. Making
commercials, even testimonial commercials, seems to be part of the job in
the news departments at some radio and TV stations. This may add to the
income of newscasters who do commercials, but it certainly detracts from
their credibility as reporters and presenters of news. A news director
whose testimonial for a local tire dealer ("These tires get me where I need
to go in my job as news director at WJAC") is inserted in his station's
evening newscast is begging for the public to lose its trust in him and his
staff. And Gene Shalit's credibility as the theater-movie critic on NBC's
Today show is not enhanced when he all but drools over a dog food.

Sometimes it's difficult to anticipate the kind of outside work and activities by news staffers that might cause a loss of public trust. Paul A. Poorman, editor of the *Akron Beacon Journal*, recalls that one of his reporters was arrested as a client in a police sweep of prostitutes in that city (interview, 8 Apr. 1981). The reporter told police he was on assignment. He wasn't. Poorman could not fire the reporter for his false claim at that point, but the Guild later agreed to make such lying a dismissable offense. When Eugene L. Roberts, Jr., first came to the *Philadelphia Inquirer* as executive editor in 1972, he heard sirens and screeching tires in the paper's parking lot late one night (interviews, 28 May, 15 Sept. 1981). He looked out the window to see police arresting a make-up editor and two other men for passing football parlay cards for gambling — cards that the editor was having printed on *Inquirer* equipment. "He took the opportunity to resign," Roberts recalls.

Many newspapers come down hard on Congress whenever it raises or eliminates the limit on what members may acquire in outside income. (Late in the 1982 session, the Senate eliminated its previous $25,000 limit and the House raised its to $23,267 a year.) But many of the stars of journalism make plenty of extra bucks the same way senators and Congress members do — on the lecture circuit. Art Buchwald commands $12,500 per speech, and some top TV news people have been paid as high as $10,000, but $500 to $5,000 per speech is more common. These speaking engagements usually cause no problems for either the journalists or their news organizations — except for the envy of less star-worthy staff members whose speaking invitations are limited to high school journalism classes and Cub Scout dens. But many, like David R. Jones, national editor of the *New York Times*, are bothered by the high fees and the possible conflicts of interest posed by the sources of the checks. He recalls advising a fellow editor against speaking at some university (which would ordinarily be acceptable) because the talk was to be paid for by Exxon (interview, 7 Oct. 1981).

The Special Taboo of Politics. Of all the outside activities of journalists, politics seems to offer the greatest ethical pitfalls. Perhaps it is because of the vigilant attention news organizations pay to politics and government. Although this taboo gets broken every year — especially in the smaller communities around the country — it is inconceivable that a major journalist today would get involved in politics in the way that Warren G. Harding did. Even if some journalist of the stature of Walter Cronkite were to be tempted into seeking public office, most feel he would do so only after retiring or disassociating himself from active journalism.

Often journalists lose their jobs or are disciplined when they cross the line from observer of the political arena to participant. Julianne Agnew was dismissed as editor of the Today's Living section of the

Knight-Ridder papers in Duluth, Minnesota, when she filed to run for the City Council. John McMillion, publisher of the *Herald* and the *News-Tribune*, told her she had violated the conflict of interest policy that Knight-Ridder applies to its publishers and editors. Agnew lost her job and the election.[17]

Susan O'Brien, a reporter who handled the action line column for the *Troy* (New York) *Times Record*, was fired when she refused to resign as an alternate delegate to the 1980 Democratic National Convention. O'Brien had been with the paper for only about three months and said she was not aware of any policy against being a delegate to a political convention. "I had absolutely no dealings with any political figures in my position at the paper," she said. "I wrote a three-times-a-week hot line column, typed up bowling scores, put together a weekend calendar, and sat in for the receptionist when she went to lunch." Executive editor Roland Blais replied, in defense of the dismissal, that "politics gets involved in every beat. We told her she had a by-line and this identified her with the paper."[18]

Eugene Patterson, editor and president of the *St. Petersburg Times*, was once asked by one of his news staffers if she could work publicly in George McGovern's 1972 campaign for president. "I told her and the staff I could not infringe on their civil right as citizens to participate freely in politics," Patterson says. "But I appealed to their professionalism, as bearers of a special constitutional right, in expressing my hope that they would voluntarily forego partisan political activity in public. Staffers must have thought it a fair request because not one has embarrassed the *Times*, then or since."[19]

Conflicts in Sports. The sports departments of daily newspapers run into some conflicts of interest by their very nature. In the first place they have a hard time deciding whether they are covering entertainment, business, or athletic wins and losses. Most days they do all three. But their major conflict of interest comes mostly from another schizophrenia — whether to promote sports or cover them.

Most sports pages until recent years seemed to be more interested in promoting sports, being cheerleaders for the coaches and players, often to the detriment of the facts and the readers. That is still the case on many smaller and medium-sized dailies and in many of the newspapers published in university communities. Rick Starr, sports editor of the *Valley News Dispatch* in New Kensington, Pennsylvania, admits that he and his small staff do not do much critical reporting (interview, 14 Nov. 1981). For example, they gave routine coverage to three separate incidents in his area of high school football players who broke their necks and were paralyzed for life. "We should have investigated these incidents more thoroughly," Starr now believes. "We should have tried to find out why these things happen and what the coaches were doing that might have caused them to happen." Another example, he says, is in the way high school sports is reported, with the emphasis on the home team, and little if any critical material. The ideal, Starr believes, is to be entertaining and cover sports as entertainment, "but also be able to put the toys away when necessary and go after the substance."

Bill Lyon, sports reporter and columnist for the *Philadelphia Inquirer*, believes that twenty-five years ago every newspaper sports department in the country "was a 'homer' — an arm of the local team's public relations staff." (Interview, 28 May 1981.) But sports reporting has improved, he argues. "If Babe Ruth played today, you'd know he was a heavy drinker and a womanizer."

The maturing of sports journalism has been hard on some club owners, coaches, and players who really want scrapbook material and have been conditioned in many cases to get it. Alan Robinson, sports editor of the AP in Charleston, West Virginia, was rudely awakened to this attitude when he wrote a story quoting a college basketball player who had become so disillusioned with the University of West Virginia's athletic program that he was considering going into the hardship draft. A West Virginia coach threatened to cancel Robinson's press credentials, charged that the editor was trying to hurt the school's athletic program, and told a television audience that Robinson was angry at the university because he had flunked out of journalism school. Actually, Robinson had transferred from West Virginia after making straight A's in his journalism courses. Relating this incident to the 1979 convention of the APSE, Wick Temple, AP managing editor, charged that the coach "was trying to intimidate the reporter and make him a cheerleader for the basketball program." Temple urged sports editors not to be discouraged by news sources who get upset, "and while we don't want to pick fights, we must make the sports establishment understand that at long last it is going to be covered — really covered — by the press."[20]

Sports editor Langford of the *Chicago Tribune* sees sports pages today as being a combination of news and entertainment (interview, 8 Sept. 1981). Langford's paper is one of the few in the country with an investigative reporting team in sports, digging into such matters as the academic machinations that otherwise respectable universities go through to make or keep athletes eligible to play. He believes newspaper sports departments have to be watchdogs over the sports establishment. "TV and radio won't do it," Langford feels. "The Cubs and the White Sox, like most professional teams, hire the announcers. They're not journalists — most of them are just shilling for the franchise." He is referring here to the veto power most professional teams and many college teams have over the play-by-play and color announcers who cover games for radio and TV, so that the coverage is almost always positive for the image of the clubs being covered. But even radio and TV sports reporters not tied so closely to the teams seldom do any critical reporting of the sort you associate with news coverage of government, by either print or broadcast journalists. Boosterism still exists on newspaper sports pages, but it is a much greater problem — almost an incurable disease — in broadcast sports reporting.

A more direct conflict of interest in sports journalism has been the fifty-year-old custom of having newspaper baseball writers in major and minor league cities serve as official scorers at home games. After the *Milwaukee Journal* decided in 1962 that its baseball writers should no longer serve as official scorers, daily newspapers in major and minor league cities have increasingly prohibited the practice as a conflict of interest because: (1) the scorers get paid by the leagues, $50 a game in the two major leagues, making it possible for a writer to get as much as $3,000 to $4,000 in extra income from the sport he or she covers; and (2) scorers make decisions that affect statistics of individual players, such as whether a batter got on base as the result of a hit or an error, and that sometimes upsets the players to the point that the scorer has a more difficult time doing the job of reporting the game. Just one example from the 1979 season serves to illustrate the second conflict problem: *Pittsburgh Press* sports reporter Dan Donovan, serving as a scorer, ruled a ball a hit and cost pitcher Bruce Kison a no-hitter. When Donovan went to the Pittsburgh Pirates' locker room after the game to talk to players for his story, Kison berated him. The *Press* decided to join the lengthening list of papers pulling their writers out of the scorer's seat.[21]

Because more newspapers are prohibiting their baseball writers from serving as official scorers in major and minor league cities, the leagues often turn to sports reporters from suburban and nearby city newspapers to do their scoring. So in some cities, even though all of the daily newspapers published there have withdrawn their writers from scoring, active baseball writers from elsewhere are still doing the job and the conflicts of interest continue.

In some cases newspapers have given a compensating salary increase to sports writers who suffered a loss of income from the decision to prohibit them from scoring, but most papers apparently have not done so. The APME Professional Standards Committee surveyed forty-two daily newspapers in major league cities in 1980 and found that of the twenty-nine that responded, twenty-four did not permit their writers to serve as scorers and five did. Of the twenty-four that had eliminated the practice, twelve said they did not increase their writers' compensation, eight said they did, and four ducked the question.[22]

Contests. It seemed like a good idea at the time. Hold a little contest for reporting or editorial writing. Then get some respected editors to judge them. And the winners can be models for everybody, thus improving the breed.

That was years ago. Today U.S. journalists have more than 400 contests they can enter, and leaders of the field are wondering aloud whether a good idea has not been carried too far. Three main problems result from the proliferation of journalistic awards: The first is that there are so many of them that all but a handful have lost significance as improvers of the breed. Second, the competition for the few prestigious journalism awards, such as the Pulitzer Prizes, is often so intense that journalists have been known to hype their articles in hopes of winning one of the big prizes. A third problem arises from a growing minority of the contests that are sponsored by vested interests who seem to be trying to get the news media to present material that might not otherwise get in print or on the air and to reflect a slant favored by the sponsor. The National Association of Realtors, for example, offers $4,000 in prizes for "articles dealing with real estate development, property tax relief, etc." Here are some other examples of vested interest journalism contests, from *Editor & Publisher* magazine, which publishes a directory of journalism contests each year:

Outdoor writers may not be high on journalism's pecking order, but they have more specialized contests to enter than most of their colleagues. There are the Deep Woods Awards amounting to $5,000 sponsored by Johnson Wax and open to members of the Outdoor Writers Association of America (OWAA); the $2,000 Evinrude award for OWAA members who excel in "reporting on the sport of boating and preservation of the waterways"; the $1,000 award from the National Association of Engine & Boat Manufacturers for writing about boating and water sports; and OWAA's own competition for outdoors writing, with $8,000 in prizes donated by McCulloch, Evinrude, Buck Knives, and Bowhunters.

The National Coal Association offers a $2,000 prize for "stories and commentary about the U.S. coal industry." And the American Association of Petroleum Landmen offers $250 "for reporting oil and gas company information in stories, cartoons and programs." You can win $5,000 from the International Association of Fire Fighters for "stories and pictures . . . depicting fire losses and professionalism by fire fighters," $600 from the National Association of Bank Women "for articles about women in the banking force," and a silver-plated typewriter from the U.S. Ski Association "for articles about skiing."

Travel writers can outdo the outdoors writers. They can win $6,000, plus trips and art objects, from American Express Canada for "articles and programs that encourage people to travel in Canada"; $500 from the

Greater Las Vegas Chamber of Commerce for stories about that entertainment and gambling center; $500 from South Carolina "for articles promoting travel in South Carolina"; $1,000 from the Travel Industry Association of America "for articles relating to the economic impact of travel to and within the United States"; and the La Pluma de Plata Mexicana Awards, $2,750, plus silver trophies and trips, from the Mexican National Tourist Council for articles "that promote travel to Mexico."

"I doubt if a story on how to deal with Montezuma's revenge would win the La Pluma de Plata award," says editor Poorman of the *Akron Beacon Journal,* expressing the reservations that he and many journalists have about vested interest contests (interview, 8 Apr. 1981). "Nor is an exposé of the guy who put too much sand in the concrete when he built Interstate 90 around Erie apt to win the lucrative cash award for best writing about highways and highway problems sponsored by the National Highway Contractors' Association and the Cement Institute."

Spouses. Sometimes conflicts of interest in journalism, real or apparent, are caused by the activities or jobs of the wives or husbands of journalists. Al McCready can tell you about that. He was managing editor of the *Portland Oregonian* during most of the fourteen years that his wife, Connie, was in politics. For much of that time she held office as a state legislator, as a member of city council, and as acting mayor. McCready said his policy while his wife was in office was for some other editor to handle news about her or the part of government in which she served. No serious questions about a conflict of interest were raised, he noted, until Connie McCready announced in 1980 that she would run for mayor. At that point publisher Fred Stickel started getting flak from substantial people in the community concerned about whether Connie McCready's opponent could get a fair shake in the *Oregonian*'s news columns. So Al McCready volunteered to give us his managing editorship during the rest of the campaign. Stickel and editor J. Richard Nokes agreed that he should be reassigned to serve as consultant to Stickel on personnel and finance. This was announced in the paper, but McCready said "it didn't do any good" because "the campaign to discredit the *Oregonian*'s news coverage of the mayoral election continued." Connie McCready lost her election and her husband went back to being managing editor. Nokes said that would have happened even if Connie McCready had been elected mayor.[23]

The *Milwaukee Journal* reassigned an editorial writer to the Sunday magazine because of a conflict of interest caused by his activist wife. Managing editor Joseph W. Shoquist explains that the wife was very active in civil rights demonstrations, once chaining herself to a school bus and even leading a protest group through the *Journal* newsroom (interview, 19 Oct. 1981).

Mike Wallace of the CBS "60 Minutes" show, one of television's most aggressive reporters, tried to kill an update on conditions in Haiti because of pressure from his wife, Lorraine. Wallace had done a tough report on the Caribbean island in 1972 that caused, he claimed, "an infinite amount of distress" to his wife's relatives in Haiti. "They asked me, candidly, please not to do another story." So when Morley Safer, fellow star of "60 Minutes," proposed to take another look at the poverty-stricken dictatorship of that small country in 1981, Wallace asked Safer not to do it — for his wife's family's sake — and Safer agreed. But columnist Jack Anderson broke the story, which put "60 Minutes" on the spot. Executives of the show announced that the Haiti report would be done after all.[24]

Most news executives agree they have no legal right to influence the activities of spouses. So when a conflict of interest does arise because of a spouse, all the news organization can do is reassign the journalist if the conflict is serious enough or assure in some other way that this journalist does not handle any news involving the spouse. "Journalists have to be mindful of the problems their spouses can cause," says Gannett's Currie, "but we have to let each person live his or her own life." (Interview, 22 Oct. 1981.)

Most journalists and their spouses handle the conflict of interest problem themselves, without a lot of fuss. When Nancy Woodhull was managing editor of the *Democrat & Chronicle* in Rochester, New York, her husband was public relations director for a Rochester company regularly covered by her paper. She claims they had an understanding that they would not discuss one another's jobs. "So Bill would not say, 'Oh, you wouldn't believe what happened at work today,' because he knew it would be a front-page story in my newspaper the next day." (Interview, 16 Oct. 1981.)

Lynn Ludlow, *San Francisco Examiner* reporter whose lawyer wife is a deputy attorney general for the state, says they keep their confidences, and then he quips, "We have a deal. I don't write any briefs, and she doesn't write any stories." (Interview. 29 Nov. 1980.)

CODES AND CORPORATE PLEDGES

The phrase "conflict of interest" does not appear in the early codes of ethics adopted by the ASNE, various state press associations, and individual newspapers in the period just before and during the 1920s. Today it is a standard item in such codes. Some of the early codes — particularly that of the Kansas Editorial Association, adopted in 1910

and apparently the first such code in this country — expressed concern
about undue influence on the press by outsiders who owned newspaper
stock or who made loans to publishing companies, and a few of the early
ethical statements warned against news people holding office or accepting side jobs that might affect the news.[25] But today's codes are much
more explicit on this issue, reflecting the growing and general apprehension throughout American society about conflicts of interest in business,
government, education, science, and virtually all aspects of modern life.

The journalism codes adopted by national organizations deal with
the conflict problem in their typically more general language. The 1975
Statement of Principles of the ASNE, for example, states: "Journalists
must avoid impropriety and the appearance of impropriety as well as any
conflict of interest or the appearance of conflict. They should neither
accept anything nor pursue any activity that might compromise or seem
to compromise their integrity." Equally brief is the statement in the
RTNDA Code of Broadcast Ethics: "Broadcast journalists shall govern
their personal lives and such nonprofessional associations as may
impinge on their professional activities in a manner that will protect
them from conflict of interest, real or apparent."

A bit more explicit is the reference in the Code of Ethics of SPJ-SDX:

> ETHICS: Journalists must be free of obligation to any interest
> other than the public's right to know the truth. . . . Secondary
> employment, political involvement, holding public office, and service
> in community organizations should be avoided if it compromises the
> integrity of journalists and their employers. Journalists and their
> employers should conduct their personal lives in a manner which
> protects them from conflict of interest, real or apparent. Their
> responsibilities to the public are paramount. That is the nature of
> their profession.

The APME Code of Ethics declares:

> The newspaper and its staff should make every effort to be free
> of obligations to news sources and special interests. . . . The news-
> paper should avoid even the appearance of obligation or conflict of
> interest. . . .
> Active involvement in such things as politics, community affairs,
> demonstrations and social causes may compromise the ability to
> report and edit without prejudice. . . .
> Outside employment that conflicts with news interests should be
> avoided. Secondary employment by news sources is an obvious
> conflict.
> Investments by staff members — especially financial writers —
> in stocks and bonds, or other outside business interests that could

conflict with the newspaper's ability to report the news or that would create the impression of conflict should be avoided.

Stories should not be written or edited primarily for the purpose of winning awards and prizes. Blatantly commercial journalism contests, or others that reflect unfavorably on the newspaper or the profession, should be avoided.

The Ethical Guidelines of the budding APSE organization deal with some of the special conflicts in sports journalism:

II. Participation. Writers should avoid involvement in outside activities that would create a conflict of interest or give the impression of one....

Some papers and some sports editors have been prime movers in lining up potential franchises in cities. Our job is reporting developments, not serving on committees or getting involved in bringing in franchises or building stadiums or arenas.

It is in the best interest of journalism that there come an end to writers serving as official scorers....It is not the fee attached to scoring which is at issue; it is the involvement of the reporter in an official role....If the scoring function does not affect a journalist's ethical standards, it most certainly does create a question about his credibility as an independent sports analyst....

Writers should not write for game programs or other league or team publications produced by teams or leagues the writers are responsible for covering.

Specifically, writers should not take pay from the sport they cover....

VIII. Outside employment. In an era where various types of "moonlighting" have become prevalent,...frequently...staffers are offered outside employment during off-duty hours. Wherever such outside jobs affect anything the newspaper is covering, the sports editor should insist that his staffers not accept such positions. We face the age-old problem that financial involvement cannot help but affect news treatment and even the seemingly innocuous role of doing statistics for a baseball team carries with it the seed of inside-the-office pressure for favored treatment.

Conflicts of interest guidelines that have been adopted by some news media chains, by the CBS, ABC, and NBC broadcast networks, and by individual newspapers are more detailed and specific than those described above. Some of the larger news media companies — such as CBS, Gannett, Knight-Ridder, and the Louisville newspapers — require their executives to sign what amounts to pledges of conformance with company policies on avoiding conflicts of interest. But as this chapter has tried to make clear, there is still troubling disagreement among journalists as to what constitutes conflicts of interest and who is expected to avoid them.

It can easily be argued that conflicts of interest are unavoidable in modern society and that journalists, of all people, need to be part of — not aloof from — the main currents of life. And if that contention is reasonable, perhaps journalists need to insist not so much on avoiding many activities now regarded as conflicts of interest but on candidly disclosing their possible conflicts to the public.

The Seducers: Freebies, Junkets, and Perks

"So this is what they mean by a free press."

WHAT IF YOU ARE THE CHIEF EDITOR of a metropolitan newspaper in mid-America and you get an anonymous letter, apparently from a Jeep dealer in town, charging that your popular outdoor editor has free use of an International Harvester Scout. The letter, which seems authentic, also charges that your editor mentions Scouts but never other brands of four-wheel-drive vehicles in his writings. You confront your outdoor editor and he admits that for almost a year he has been using a $10,000 Scout free of charge. Although accepting such a "gift" is prohibited in your paper's code of ethics, the outdoor editor, who to your knowledge has no blemish on his sixteen-year record with the paper, argues that he has done nothing wrong and that use of the free vehicle has not influenced what he has written. What do you do? Do you take him at his word and give him another chance? Do you throw him out of your office?

In Kansas City, Missouri, where this happened, Michael J. Davies, who was editor of the *Star* and *Times* newspapers, gave the outdoor editor another chance, but then fired him about a week later (interview,

23 Oct. 1981).* Davies explains that he first decided to let the outdoor editor off with a stern warning, despite advice from supervising editors that the man should be dismissed, because he was new in the top editor's job at the *Star* and *Times* and uncertain about how strongly his predecessors had enforced the organization's ethics code. (Davies had only recently left the managing editorship of the Louisville, Kentucky, *Courier-Journal* to join the *Star* and *Times.*) So after warning the outdoor editor that he "was on the thinest of thin ice," Davies posted notes on newsroom bulletin boards declaring "amnesty week" for all to come forward and be forgiven for past violations of the ethics code so that a fresh start could be made on Monday. Davies then discovered that the outdoor editor not only had held back part of the truth about the four-wheel-drive gift; he also failed to come clean about "a couple of other goodies." Davies, who has since been promoted to president of the Kansas City Star Company, fired the offending editor on the spot and assigned two reporters to look into the ethics of outdoor writers across the country. The dismissed editor sued the newspaper company for $10 million, a suit still pending as this is written.

The two articles the *Star* and *Times* published on outdoor writers painted an ethically ugly picture. Reporters Rick Alm and Bill Norton interviewed about two dozen outdoor writers and editors, some other journalists, and some manufacturers of outdoor equipment. They found: widespread acceptance by outdoor writers of manufacturers' discounts of up to 50 percent; some acceptance of free goods (one fishing equipment company was giving away about $35,000 a year in free equipment to outdoor writers); and some acceptance by outdoor writers of boats and recreational vehicles on long-term loans from the manufacturers. Some outdoor writers were doing publicity for the same hunting lodges and fishing clubs they covered in their news columns. The ethics code of the Outdoor Writers Association of America (OWAA), which has manufacturers as "supporting members," states that loans, gifts, and discounts are "commonly accepted practices" in the trade but cautions that writers should not accept such favors for anything other than journalistic pursuits. The code also advises against accepting free room and board unless a salable story can be produced.

Alm and Norton reported that at least three newspapers had bought big equipment for their outdoor writers: the *St. Louis Post-Dispatch* provided its writer with a camper-truck and a fishing boat with trailer and motor; the *St. Louis Globe-Democrat* furnished a bass boat, motor, and trailer; the *Denver Post* provided each of its outdoor writers with a four-wheel-drive vehicle. Norton reported that the outdoor editor whom

*See list of interviewees following Notes.

Davies fired for accepting a free four-wheel-drive vehicle had tried to get the *Star* and *Times* to buy him such a vehicle for his work but had been turned down. So he struck a deal with a friend at a local International Harvester factory outlet to get himself a free Scout, but insisted that he made no promise of free publicity. The Norton article revealed that the outdoor editor had an annual travel budget from the newspaper organization of $12,000, about $1,200 of which was set aside for equipment. The dismissed outdoor editor is quoted as saying that since his budget did not provide for major expenses, he had to "beg people" because he could not personally afford a boat, a motor, a trailer, or a vehicle. Alm in his article said manufacturers freely admitted that they gave discounts, favors, and freebies to outdoor writers in return for favorable publicity.[1]

The provision in the *Star* and *Times* ethics code that cost the outdoor editor his job states that "gifts of merchandise which might be construed as a reward for past coverage or an inducement to future coverage . . . are to be rejected." Virtually all news media ethics codes have similar provisions designed to combat the attempts by outside interests to buy favorable publicity through favors to journalists. These favors come in all sorts of packages — from free lunches to fur coats, from bottles of liquor at Christmas to free trips to Tahiti. Regardless of the value of the gifts, it is the motives of the givers that bother thoughtful journalists.

FREEBIES

The freebie — something given without charge or cost — was at one time commonly accepted in the newsrooms of America. Many journalists accepted Christmas presents from the people they covered. Taking free tickets to the theater, the circus, or the baseball game was a common occurrence. Traveling free of charge on the train or airplane with the political candidate or sports team you were covering was encouraged. Letting news sources pick up the tab for your drinks or meals was often done. Freebies went with the job, perquisites of a trade notorious for underpaying its apprentices. There was "a tradition in journalism of take what you could get," says Richard B. Tuttle, executive editor of the Elmira, New York, *Star-Gazette* (interview, 14 Oct. 1981).

Freebies are still being accepted by journalists today, and the outside interests are still working hard to buy their way into the news columns with favors, but the practice is widely condemned in the field and may disappear entirely. As this chapter hopes to show, the freebie problem is greater on the smaller newspapers and broadcast stations and in some specialized areas of journalism, such as outdoor writing, travel, real estate, food, and sports.

Goodbye, Free Lunch. Efforts by public officials, politicians, and other VIPs to influence or at least gain favor with journalists through the "gifts" of free food and drink continue to be a problem.

Some news sources insist on picking up the tab whenever they have lunch or drinks with reporters; some like to wine and dine journalists at parties. They may not expect anything in return for such favors, but again they may. Most journalists these days insist on at least paying for their own meals and drinks, and some who work for big media often buy meals and drinks for their news sources.

David Shaw, media reporter-critic for the *Los Angeles Times*, started paying for lunches with news sources when he got his first full-time newspaper job on a small California daily in 1963 and was making $79.21 a week (interview, 25 Nov. 1980). "Other reporters couldn't believe I was doing it," Shaw recalls. "No one on my paper did that then." Shaw believes "the easiest way is to draw the line and take nothing from anybody, and as a result my expense accounts are enormous."

Jack Nelson, chief of the *Los Angeles Times* Washington bureau, says it is common for his reporters to take their news sources to lunch (interview, 2 June 1981). His bureau also regularly invites government officials and other news makers in for on-the-record, taped breakfast discussions that result in news stories.

A reporter for the less affluent *San Francisco Examiner*, Lynn Ludlow, says he would rather pay $10 not to have meals with 90 percent of the people his job forces him to have meals with (interview, 29 Nov. 1981). "If somebody insists on picking up the tab, I'm not going to make a big production out of it," Ludlow adds. "My main goal is not to be pure ethically; my main goal is to get the news. If it calls for having dinner with somebody and letting him pick up the tab, fine."

James Lowman, features editor of the Elmira, New York, *Star-Gazette*, who spent four years as a one-person news bureau in two small communities near Elmira, believes it is permissable to accept "lunches, Cokes, beers and so on from sources" in rural settings, where "a different set of ethics" is at work. "You have to remember that the person offering the treat has a set of ethics, too," Lowman said. "The moment you turn him down, you are questioning his own ethics. It hurts people for the reporter to turn the treat down. People are grossly offended by that in the small community."[2]

George E. Osgood, Jr., who covers Wellsboro, Pennsylvania, for the Elmira paper, has written that the "metropolitan dog-eat-dog . . . philosophy doesn't hold water in most rural communities." People in rural communities "know and trust each other, for the most part," Osgood said, "and neighborliness gets more than just lip service." He concedes that a reporter accepting a loaf of homemade bread from some public official's wife can be used by critics, "but there is likely to be a greater clamor...if such an offer is refused by a reporter too 'big-headed' to accept simple friendship and too set in his city ways to understand rural hospitality."[3]

Lowman and Osgood make sense when they argue that what might be seen as a freebie in an urban journalism setting is often a friendly gesture in a small town. But rural reporters share with their urban colleagues the risk of being pulled across that thin line between a friendly, neighborly gesture and an attempt to influence news policy through gifts of food and drink. You have to be able to get inside the heads of the givers and receivers to understand whether that line has been crossed. Some observers thought it had been crossed when President Reagan in his first year in office invited the some seventy reporters, TV producers, and photographers who covered him during his vacation on his Santa Barbara, California, ranch to come with their families to a little "company picnic." As the president and his wife, Nancy, circulated through the crowd, making small talk (everything they said, by prearrangement, was off the record) and kissing cheeks of the journalists' children, the members of the prestigious White House press corps sipped drinks and munched from buffet tables "creaking under piles of smoked salmon, tenderloin fillets wrapped in bacon, escargots baked in French dough, oysters on the half shell, a glorious assortment of cheeses, fresh fruit and a jelly-bean cake. Chefs stood ready to cook scampi au Pernod and fettucini Alfredo to order."[4] Such a party, when thrown by people you cover, strikes many journalists as at least a minor league freebie that ought to be avoided.

Merry Christmas! The gift givers can be a problem for journalists at any time of the year but Christmas really brings out their effusiveness. Here again, the Christmas presents to newsrooms and news people have decreased both in number and lavishness over the past two or three decades, but they still exist. Newspaper newsrooms of the 1950s often looked like the gift-wrapping sections of department stores as loot from all manner of givers would roll in. Some, like baskets of apples from a well-known Virginia senator, would be for everybody; others would be for specific writers or editors. Some of the gifts were sent to the journalist's home, or more often, to the bureaus and press rooms away from the main office. Tom Hritz of the *Pittsburgh Post-Gazette* tells how that worked at the press room of the City-County Building in Pittsburgh: "It would start with a trickle at the beginning of December. By Christmas week, the grungy little newsroom...was awash with the gratitude of the bench and bar: Scotch, bourbon, rum, rotgut — even champagne." The reporters would try to live by "The Rule" that you could accept it if you could eat or drink it on the premises, right then and there, Hritz wrote in his column.

But so much liquor would come in that, try as they might, they could not keep up with "The Rule." They would have to stuff gallons of gratitude and appreciation into shopping bags and take them home.[5]

Most public relations people have stopped sending gifts to newsrooms. Years of having them returned by the newspapers have discouraged the practice. Benjamin C. Bradlee, executive editor of the *Washington Post*, says that very few Christmas gifts are sent to the paper today and when they are, "they are turned away at the elevator and sent to Walter Reed Hospital and charity." (Interview, 5 June 1981.) At the smaller-community level, James A. Dunlap, editor of the Sharon, Pennsylvania, *Herald,* remembers how the "sports editor's desk would be piled high with liquor at Christmas time, but no more." Dunlap believes that his policy against accepting such freebies has stopped the flow of gifts that used to be common in his newsroom (Interview, 28 Oct. 1981).

Super Sports. The professional sports organizations that come out on top in their sport each year usually have rings or some other mementos made for the players. They also offer them to the sports reporters who cover that team, or they may give the reporters a less expensive gift. For example, when the Pittsburgh Steelers won the 1979 and 1980 Super Bowls, the players got rings cast especially for the occasion. "But when the Steelers came to the reporters and asked us if we wanted rings, we said no," Rick Starr, sports editor of the New Kensington, Pennsylvania, *Valley News Dispatch*, recalls (interview, 14 Nov. 1981). "But they came up with alternative gifts — cuff links one time and a watch or something the second time — all engraved, of course." Starr accepted these alternative gifts, but he says now that he wishes he had not and he will not accept any more such gifts, even if his fellow reporters do.

When the Philadelphia Phillies offered rings commemorating that baseball team's World Series victory in 1980 to the six reporters who covered them, most said they would like one, thank you. Craig Ammerman, executive editor of the now defunct Philadelphia *Bulletin*, blew the whistle on this gift giving in a column in which he claimed the *Bulletin* reporter was the only one to say no, although the *Philadelphia Inquirer* reporter had agreed to pay for his ring, worth about $2,000 (interview, 27 May 1981). After Ammerman's criticism of the acceptance of rings from the Phillies, Don Haskin, associate editor of the *Philadelphia Daily News*, said his paper's Phillies' reporter was not going to take a ring either. Then the Phillies' reporters for the Camden, New Jersey, *Courier-Post* and the Wilmington, Delaware, *News Journal* decided they did not want the rings after all, leaving only the writer from the *Philadelphia Journal*, who may have needed a free ring more than the others since that paper caved in a couple of months ahead of the *Bulletin*.

The public relations arms of the leagues and associations that run professional sports and put on the extravaganzas that decide the winners each year also try to take good care of the reporters. At the World Series, the Super Bowl, and other season-ending championship games, the leagues provide souvenir gifts, lots of free meals and drinks, elaborate press rooms, hospitality suites, and free video games, in addition to news releases and staged news conferences and interviews.

Ira Miller of the *San Francisco Chronicle* and Bill Lyon of the *Philadelphia Inquirer*, who have covered some Super Bowls and other championship finals, believe the gifts and freebies have decreased over the years. At the Super Bowl, for example, "all you get is coffee and a Danish" at the press room each morning, Lyon notes. "And they give you pens, brief cases and little plastic things." (Interview, 28 May 1981.) He says there's a free bar in the press room, but he doesn't drink. Miller agrees that the gifts are much less lavish than they used to be (interview, 2 Dec. 1980). He sees the juice and coffee he takes at the press room as a real service because the buses for the training camps of the two teams involved leave at 7 A.M. or so, before the hotel coffee shops are open. As for the free bar in the press room, Miller says "the writers don't seem to hang out there a lot."

But to Starr, whose paper near Pittsburgh has a circulation of about 43,000, covering the 1979 and 1980 Super Bowls was "a heady experience." (Interview, 14 Nov. 1981.) The National Football League gave each of the more than 1,500 reporters who covered the 1980 game a suit bag, a briefcase, and a note folder with a Super Bowl pen — "very classy," Starr comments. "They pick you up at your hotel in a bus, take you to a breakfast where you'll sit down and have a $7 to $8 breakfast. Then they'll put a coach up front who'll say a few newsworthy things. Then back on the bus to go to the other team's training site, where you have lunch and watch a workout. Then back to the hotel where the hospitality rooms are in full swing. One thing is planned for you after another. I mean, anybody could cover a Super Bowl. It's the easiest thing in the world to cover."

A tongue-in-cheek account of what it's like to cover a Super Bowl is provided by Fred Dryer, a former Los Angeles Ram player who with former teammate Lance Rentzel got himself accredited by *Sport* magazine to report the big game: "We acted just like regular beat-reporters. We ate and drank free all week, but we were unbelievable tippers. We slept in our suits. We blurted questions. We weren't interested in answers and we didn't wait for them."[6]

One reason the Super Bowl is "cleaner" than it used to be is that the APME Professional Standards Committee has monitored it. The committee decided in that same spirit to take a look at the 1980 Winter Olympics in Lake Placid, New York. It should have been called the "Freebie Olympics," concluded the APME report by Richard Benedetto of Gannett News Service. "Any enterprising journalist armed with shopping bags and a cast-iron stomach could have carted home scores of free gifts every day and drunk more free booze every night than any human could handle, with a gratis meal now and then thrown in for good measure," Benedetto wrote. The gifts he reported did not sound elaborate, but they were numerous. Cocktail parties and dinners for the reporters were held by Eastman Kodak, Xerox, Canon Camera, *Ski Magazine*, Finlandia Vodka, Rossignol Skis, the state of New York, K2 and Elan skis, the Austrian National Board of Trade, Adidas sports equipment, and Mr. and Mrs. Cornelius Vanderbilt Whitney.[7]

Convention Giveaways. The national organizations of journalists have been credited in this book so far with providing certain leadership in the development of ethical standards. But, unfortunately, they have also contributed to the notion that journalists are on the take, because of the way they used to run their national conventions.

The RTNDA was notorious in the news business at one time for filling its national conventions with freebies — cocktail parties, dinners, and entertainment sponsored and paid for by outside interests, such as automobile manufacturers. All that stopped about 1975, spurred by a CBS "60 Minutes" report on a salmon-bake party on a Puget Sound island that Chrysler threw for delegates to the 1973 RTNDA convention in Seattle. (That program, incidentally, embarrassed other journalists and some newspapers because it exposed freebies throughout U.S. journalism.) RTNDA has cleaned up its convention. Treasurer Lou Prato, news director of WDTN-TV, Dayton, Ohio, reports that the organization now charges an exhibition fee to "anybody there to do business with our delegates," including sponsors of hospitality rooms (interview, 9 Nov. 1981). Prato says some outside interests, such as the tobacco and railroad industries, still run hospitality suites during the conventions, but he claims the exhibition fees have "made us strictly honest."

The SPJ-SDX, perhaps the most idealistic of the national organizations of news people, had convention freebies in the old days. Old-timers in the society remember particularly the "Bloody Mary breakfasts" — booze, fruit juice, coffee, and Danish — sponsored every convention morning by the International Telephone and Telegraph Corporation. Steve Dornfeld, Washington correspondent for Knight-Ridder Newspapers and a national officer of SPJ-SDX, says the national board "adopted a purity policy in the early 1970s," decreeing that convention support would be accepted only from media groups (interview, 3 Apr. 1981).

The ASNE and the APME also allowed auto manufacturers and

other corporations to sponsor cocktail parties and buffets at one time. But they were eliminated sometime before 1970. The APME experienced some embarrassment, however, when the local organizers of its 1979 convention in Tulsa, Oklahoma, persuaded some big companies in the region to sponsor small dinner parties for all of the delegates and their spouses in various locations around Tulsa, including corporate dining rooms. "Tulsa Hospitality," they called it. Some of the editors had to "pay for their suppers" by listening to organized spiels from their sponsors, apparently hopeful of influencing national public opinion through the press. Embarrassed national officers made certain there was no "Phoenix Hospitality" night at the next convention.

Newspaper food editors keep the freebie tradition alive when they attend the annual Newspaper Food Editors Conference sponsored by the Newspaper Advertising Sales Association. The one hundred or so food editors who go to these conferences, which date back to World War II times, pay only a small registration fee because the meals and entertainment for the week are paid for by representatives of the food industry, who plan the conference program. Marion Burros described the 1980 conference for her *Washington Post* readers:

> Newspaper food editors met in Minneapolis last week. The annual conference is a round of business breakfasts, lunches and dinners, plus mid-morning and mid-afternoon snacks, cocktail parties and nightcap parties, an occasional meeting at which no refreshment is served. All of the events have been arranged to foster goodwill for the host food companies and often to impart information.

An example of one of the conference events was a press briefing and cocktail reception sponsored by Frito-Lay. Burros, who has since moved to the food section of the *New York Times*, wrote that the briefers maintained that Fritos are nutritious and have only 150 calories per serving, which would mean there would have to be sixteen servings in an eight ounce bag. "Food editors were not permitted to ask questions during the press briefing," Burros added.[8] Some food editors have stopped going to the Newspaper Food Editors Conferences and have organized an alternative group known as the Newspaper Food Editors and Writers Association, but the sponsored conferences have continued.

Freebies have also been part of the conventions and meetings of state organizations of journalists, publishers, and broadcasters, some of which used to give full credit in programs and other convention literature to outside sponsors of convention events. And although purity policies have eliminated virtually all outside-sponsored events from state journalistic meetings, some outside companies still run hospitality rooms in the hotels where the meetings are held.

Wherever large numbers of journalists congregate, you see companies and trade associations trying to get their attention and good will. The Association of American Railroads, for example, ran a free press lounge for the hundreds of reporters and media people who covered the 1980 Republican and Democratic national conventions in Detroit and New York City. Afterward, the association revealed that 24,722 media people entered its press lounges and consumed 37,200 half sandwiches, 114 kegs of beer, 159 gallons of coffee, 237 pounds of potato chips, and 268 pounds of pretzels.[9]

Free Tickets. Critics often question how the news media can be objective when their reporters are given free tickets to events they cover and review. It is true that the news media traditionally have accepted complimentary tickets for their reporters and photographers to cover sports events and to review plays, concerts, and movies. Whether getting in free has ever influenced the work of the reporter or reviewer is beyond the scope of this study, but it seems safe to say that it probably has not. Be that as it may, there is a definite trend for news organizations to pay to get their people admitted to events they are covering.

This trend is particularly visible in coverage of the arts. A survey by the AMPE Modern Living Committee in 1980 showed that about half of the 214 AP daily newspapers that responded were paying for tickets their critics used to review professional shows.[10]

Even in sports, where free rides are more cemented in tradition, newspapers are tentatively beginning to pay for tickets to events their reporters and photographers cover. Stephen D. Isaacs, CBS News producer, who was editor of the *Minneapolis Star* before it was merged into the *Tribune*, claims his paper paid for all tickets, including those for people covering games and cultural events (interview, 12 Nov. 1981). The one exception was Minnesota Vikings professional football games. Because it was very difficult to pay for the press box seat and sideline pass his reporter and photographer used to cover home games, Isaacs says the *Star* made an equivalent contribution to the Vikings Children's Fund. Another newspaper that pays for all its tickets is the Elmira, New York, *Star-Gazette*. The only exception, maintains executive editor Richard B. Tuttle, is for the photographer who goes into the event for a quick shot and leaves (interview, 14 Oct. 1981).

Despite the pay-your-own-way policies of papers like the *Star* and the *Star-Gazette*, most editors see nothing wrong in accepting free passes or tickets for people covering the event. But accepting free general admission tickets is quite another thing. That smacks too much of the old days when the circus advance man would drop off several free tickets in every newsroom where the circus was scheduled to appear. The advance man hoped, of course, that the free tickets would stimulate a little favorable publicity, and they often did. But the practice left a bad taste in some mouths and that is one of the reasons that acceptance of free general admission tickets by the news media is frowned on today.

When she was business editor of the *Trenton Times*, Perri Foster-Pegg wrote a column about being offered a ticket to hear Bruce Springsteen from a private box in the sports arena where he was drawing capacity crowds. Much as she wanted to go to the concert, she turned down the ticket because it was offered by the vice-president for public relations for the Prudential Insurance Company. She said Prudential wanted her to join some other reporters and a few Prudential officials in the plush, glass enclosed box. When she objected to the invitation, she said, the PR man suggested she come anyway and contribute the $12.50 ticket price to some charity. But that was not the point, Foster-Pegg wrote. He was not "asking me to meet Prudential officials in the company boardroom. He was asking me if I wanted to be a privileged guest at a sold out, highly coveted concert. It was a gift, and it didn't matter what it cost." Foster-Pegg says her colleagues on the staff were "split over whether I was being too righteous, or had responded appropriately."[11]

Sometimes a decision to start paying for all tickets can be costly. Michael J. Davies, president of the *Kansas City Star* and *Times*, recalls that someone once suggested that the Louisville papers, where he worked from 1968 until 1978, start paying for the seats they used to cover the Kentucky Derby (interview, 23 Oct. 1981). "We calculated it would cost us $50,000 to buy tickets for the seventy people we had covering it," Davies explains. "We decided we didn't want ethics that bad."

JUNKETS

Perhaps the most serious freebie ethically is the junket, a free trip paid for by a news source or some vested interest who picks up the tab for the journalist's transportation and often for food and lodging as well. There seems to be no question that junkets are on the decline among the bigger media, best able to pay to send their journalists where they need to go. The ASNE, which represents about 500 of the 1,730 dailies (and they tend to be the larger ones), finds fewer and fewer junkets each time it surveys its members. When it did so in 1979, responses from 274 editors showed that 81 percent refused free air fare or expenses from foreign governments, 80 percent refused free transportation to cover athletic events, 74 percent did not accept free travel from state government, 64 percent paid a pro rata share of the cost of traveling with a sports team, and 62 percent would not accept free transportation from a business or industry group, even to visit a project of specific interest to their communities. Comparing the 1979 results with those from earlier surveys in 1972, 1974, and 1977, the ASNE Ethics Committee concluded that "there has been a steady drop in the number of newspapers willing to accept free trips for any reason."[12]

The smaller newspapers and broadcast stations get fewer offers to take free trips and tend not to cover many stories outside of their circulation areas. But when junket opportunities do come along at their level, there seems to be less hesitancy about accepting them, ethics notwithstanding.

Two special areas of journalism — travel and entertainment — have been especially susceptible to free rides. Free trips have also been a problem for sports and political reporters.

Travel Writers. As Americans have been able to travel and vacation more, the news media, particularly newspapers and magazines, have tried to provide information to serve those needs. They have also hit a rich lode of advertising in doing so because the travel industry is large and active both here and abroad. Some parts of that industry — which includes private and government tourist agencies, airlines, cruise ships, and resorts — are willing to pay the expenses of travel writers to get publicity.

Robert W. Greene, assistant managing editor of *Newsday*, tells of the time he got called back from Rome because of a personal emergency (interview, 6 Oct. 1981). All he could get was a first class ticket on a Pan American Airways 747. "I found myself surrounded by free-lance travel writers," Greene recounts. "All of them were either riding for nothing or were on a discount." Greene says he gave their names to the *Newsday* travel editor when he got back, to assure that their contributions either would not be used or their stuff would be edited very carefully. "They were going to these places for nothing or almost nothing and then after a couple of weeks of wining and dining and having a good time, they'd come back and write puff stories." Greene put his finger on one of the principal problems in travel journalism: So much of it is done by free-lancers, out of the control to a degree of the editors who publish their material — and virtually all newspapers and magazines with travel sections do use free-lance stories.

Travel writers have a professional organization, the Society of American Travel Writers (SATW), but its code of ethics does not prohibit or even discourage accepting free transportation and accommodations. Like the outdoor writers' association, the travel writers' society accepts associate members from industry. It is another case of journalists being in bed with their news sources. In fact, the associate members in SATW are so numerous that when its code of ethics was recently revised by a special committee, "carefully selected to give equal representation" to active and associate members, industry representatives held half of the committee seats. The chairman of the committee was Glenn T. Lashley of the Automobile Association of America.[13]

"There's more freeloading, boondoggling, unprofessional, and unethical conduct in the travel field than in any other part of the industry," concludes John Bull, assistant to the managing editor of the *Philadelphia Inquirer,* who used to free-lance travel articles to other papers when he was on vacation (interview, 27 May 1981). He took some free trips to do his free-lance stories, and he reveals he invariably would find people in the group who were not legitimate reporters or writers. "When the New York public relations agents for the foreign tourist agencies can't fill the spots with genuine travel writers, they dig down and produce bodies," Bull contends.

Another insight into the travel junket business comes from David Shaw, media reporter-critic for the *Los Angeles Times* (interview, 25 Nov. 1980). He reports that a friend in the public relations department of SAS Airlines "is always after me to take free trips." Whenever they have an inaugural flight, Shaw says, "they fill it up with the press who ride free, round trip, to places like Stockholm and Copenhagen." Shaw does not take junkets, and neither do the people in the travel section of his newspaper. "We've been paying our own way in travel for years," says William F. Thomas, editor of the *Los Angeles Times* (interview, 2 Nov. 1981). "I don't know how you can make anybody think you're going to write an honest story about Bora-Bora when somebody spent $5,000 to fly you over there."

Eugene L. Roberts, Jr., executive editor of the *Philadelphia Inquirer,* discovered that one of his writers had taken a free $8,000 cruise with his wife only a few weeks after the paper had declared a formal policy of paying its own way and not accepting freebies (interviews 28 May and 15 Sept. 1981). The first thing the writer did when he got back from the cruise was to turn in a long article about it, complete with color photographs supplied by the steamship company. His resignation was requested and received.

Although papers the size of the *Los Angeles Times* and the *Philadelphia Inquirer* can eschew junkets and still cover travel news, smaller papers seem to have a harder time doing so. The *Sacramento Bee,* with a circulation of about half that of the *Inquirer* and a quarter that of the *Times,* had gradually weaned itself away from taking travel junkets. But travel section budget cuts in 1981, according to *Bee* ombudsman Art Nauman, have forced "the travel editor to swallow his pride and go back to the airlines and tourist agencies and say, 'Hey, I'd like to do a story about Bermuda, but I can't pay for it myself.'" (Interview, 2 Nov. 1981.)

As editor of the travel section of the *Chicago Tribune,* Alfred S.

Borcover no longer has to accept free trips to cover travel, but he remembers when he did, and he doesn't believe taking junkets is as bad as some journalists think (interview, 10 Sept. 1981). He explains that "even back in the days when we were taking freebies, Kermit Holt (then senior travel writer at the *Tribune*) and I reported things as we saw them. Our responsibility was still to our readers." Borcover, who served two terms as president of the SATW in 1973 and 1974, believes that junket taboos have resulted in many newspapers not covering travel at all or cutting way back on what they do cover. He maintains it is still possible to go on a junket and write fair and honest stories about it. "If somebody's going to be influenced by a Bloody Mary, heaven help us!" Borcover says. "Some newspapers have taken the whole ethics thing and driven it to ridiculous ends."

The *San Francisco Examiner* does not take travel junkets these days, but it did back in 1968 when Lynn Ludlow was sent out to the Philippines to report on the opening of the Manila Hilton Hotel. The junket also included three days in Hong Kong. Ludlow concedes that he did the obligatory piece on the Hilton, but he also did stories on poverty in the Philippines, dope smuggling in Hong Kong, and riot crowd controls in Hong Kong. In addition, on his own, he took a $168 flight to Vietnam, an area that had been rarely covered by his paper, and wrote a story about what it was like being a tourist in the middle of the Tet offensive. "So not all junkets are necessarily bad things," Ludlow concludes (interview, 29 Nov. 1980).

Covering the Entertainers. The American motion picture and television industry still likes the junket game, even though there are fewer players these days as more and more news organizations pay their own way. The three major TV networks and the top film studios, seeking advance publicity on new movies and TV shows, arrange special news media screenings, complete with interviews with stars, directors, producers, and others. To attract reporters, the networks and studios offer to pick up the transportation and on-site expenses of the journalists who attend the screenings. Many writers still accept such junkets, but the number of newspapers and magazines who reject them increases each year.

Back in the 1960s, the commercial TV networks started offering press tours of Hollywood studios to the thirty or so reporters covering television then. Not only would they pay full expenses, the networks would throw in side trips to Mexico, Hawaii, and San Francisco to interview "stars." About 1970, CBS, NBC, and ABC started coordinating their individual tours into the same periods of up to fourteen days every June and January, so that reporters could preview the new offerings of all three during one trip. More recently, PBS, the public TV network that is edging toward commercial status, joined in the coordinated tours. A survey in 1974 showed that about 70 percent of the journalists attending the Hollywood press tours had their transportation, hotel, and meals paid for by the networks, but a 1979 survey showed that the percentage had dropped to 30.[14]

While it is true that an increasing number of the some one hundred TV reporters who cover the preview tours pay their own transportation and hotel bills, almost all of the meals are provided by the networks. "And they are lavish," comments Sylvia Lawler, TV reporter-critic for the Allentown, Pennsylvania, *Morning Call*. She told her readers about one of the sponsored meals on the set of the "Little House on the Prairie" show:

> In the incongruous midst of the series' fictional pioneer town site of Walnut Grove, next to the Ingalls' parlor, dining room and the one-room schoolhouse and to the right of the town jail and Miss Nellie's Restaurant and Hotel, were two bars, a seven-piece band with singer and tables of mounded ice heaped with shrimp, West Coast Dungenness crab and planks of smoked salmon being sliced on the spot by waiters in black tie.
>
> Chasen's, the world-famous Beverly Hills restaurant, was caterer for the dinner of roast beef bordelaise, asparagus hollandaise, artichoke salad, and for dessert, Peach Melba. As a bonus, there was a side dish of Chasen's renowned chili, the chili Elizabeth Taylor used to have shipped to her wherever on the globe she happened to be filming.
>
> All served by waiters pouring Beaujolais wine at 18 round, red-clothed tables centered with bouquets of red roses and baby's breath.[15]

In addition to the lavish meals, the networks put on cocktail parties and run hospitality suites at which TV executives and personalities are usually available for interviews, Lawler notes. The hundred or so reporters who get invited to the press tours by the networks because they come from the larger TV markets organized themselves into the Television Critics Association in 1977 to provide a liaison with the powerful networks. Lawler believes that the association has also helped to "clean up" the tours, discouraging such practices as charging a fur coat to your hotel bill to be paid for by the networks, as some critic supposedly did in an earlier day.

Like TV reporters, the movie critics get frequent offers to junket to Hollywood or to wherever the film is being made. Some magazine and smaller newspaper critics take the junkets, but most of the larger newspapers seem to be paying expenses when their critics go. "The trend in the major newspaper markets is toward paying rather than accepting the studio's free junkets," observes Al Newman, vice-president of publicity and advertising for Metro Goldwyn Mayer studios in Los Angeles. Newman told the ASNE Ethics Committee that he cheered the "younger generation of hard-hitting journalists who are more honest in their reporting. . . . Naturally, the older practices of courting the press left a stigma, but the trend away from junkets — and a new breed of writer with a more honest approach — will better serve all concerned."[16]

Most movie producers today avoid the lavish press trips that some earlier producers arranged. They sometimes boomeranged when the journalists would write about how bad the junket was. And if the film was awful, most of the critics did not allow heavy wining and dining to keep them from panning it. So the typical press trip "is briskly businesslike," according to the *New York Times.* "It lasts two days, costs between $25,000 and $50,000, and consists of flying from 28 to 40 print and television journalists to Los Angeles for a screening, a relatively modest buffet dinner afterwards, and a day of interviews with the stars, director and producers." But there are exceptions: Univeral Studios recently flew fifty journalists to Athens for five all-expense-paid days of boat trips to Greek islands, interviews with the stars, and a preview look at "The Greek Tycoon," a movie that needed more than a junket to save it.[17]

Sports and Politics. Sports and political reporters frequently have to travel around the country to cover out-of-town sports events and national political campaigns. In the old days, it was common for such reporters to ride free on the trains and planes of the teams and candidates. But the free rides have virtually disappeared in political journalism, and they seem to be on their way out in sports reporting.

Virtually all the news media sending reporters to cover the president and national campaigns for the presidency pay the full cost of transportation. When the transportation is a chartered airplane, as it usually is, the news media pay a proportionate share of the full cost, which amounted to more than the price of a first class ticket for those reporters traveling with President Reagan. (Curt Matthews, Washington correspondent for the Baltimore *Sun* who sometimes travels with the White House press corps, says he is always "kind of shocked" when the president and the reporters land somewhere and he hears people standing at the fence saying, "It's outrageous that those reporters get to travel around with the president on my tax dollars" [interview, 3 June 1981].) Sometimes on state campaigns, reporters will accept a free ride with a public official or a candidate, but here too the policy of paying your own way seems to be taking over.

It is difficult to pay for the plane ride when the aircraft is military, as is sometimes the case when reporters cover military projects or need to get some place where the U.S. military is present but commercial airlines are not. News executives say it's "a pain in the neck" to get a bill from the military, but some, like Norman C. Miller, Washington bureau chief for the *Wall Street Journal*, persist and pay (interview, 29 Oct. 1981).

Sports reporters for the larger newspapers, magazines, and TV stations and networks usually pay their pro rata share when they travel on a plane chartered by the sports club they are covering. Many prefer to travel to out-of-town games on their own, however, giving up what advantage there is in being with the players and coaches to be able to travel on a schedule suited to the deadlines of the news organization they work for rather than those of the team. That deadline problem is what stimulated the *San Francisco Chronicle* to start paying the way for its reporters to cover out-of-town games. "We used to ride free on the charters," Ira Miller, sports reporter for the *Chronicle*, recalls (interview, 2 Dec. 1980). "But then in the mid 1970s we started flying back on commercial planes because we needed more time to write our stories." That led to the decision to pay full fare and let each reporter decide which method of travel would work best for that assignment. Miller said the *Chronicle* sports department spends about $80,000 a year for travel.

Many sports reporters for the smaller media still take free rides on team planes. They usually justify it by arguing that they would not otherwise be able to cover away games, since their publishers or managers won't pay to send them. But even small newspapers are gradually getting the idea that they tie the hands of their reporters when they put them in positions where they might feel obligated or beholden to certain sports organizations. The *Valley News Dispatch* in New Kensington, Pennsylvania, for example, pays its proportionate share when sports editor Rick Starr rides with the Pittsburgh Steelers to cover away games (interview, 14 Nov. 1981). That paper has about 43,000 subscribers. Most other small dailies in the Pittsburgh area do the same thing.

Junkets have been and are being offered to journalists other than those we have discussed so far in this section — travel and entertainment writers, and sports and political reporters. The top editors of daily newspapers also get invitations, particularly from foreign governments such as Israel and Taiwan, who apparently feel the way to influence the press is through the top. But the indications are that few editors are accepting such invitations today. Among the more than sixty newspaper editors interviewed for this book, for example, only three had ever gone on a real junket, and their junkets occurred at least ten years ago.

PERKS

As with congressmen and college professors, certain perquisites go with a journalist's job. Usually unspectacular, journalists' perks include such things as free or reserved parking, work space in pressrooms of government buildings, press cards from police and other governmental agencies to admit journalists to places the public cannot go, and (rarely) discounts at government stores.

Until recent years, the press galleries of the United States Congress, the pressroom at the White House, and the pressrooms in statehouses and city halls had one thing in common: the news media paid no rent for their use. That began to change in the 1970s, as the Watergate revelations sharpened sensitivities of both journalists and public officials about their relationships. Some of the larger news organizations are now paying for the space they use in government buildings. And in some state capitals, such as Sacramento, California, and Tallahassee, Florida, the news media have moved out of the statehouse and set up outside pressrooms of their own.

The movement to vacate or start paying rent for government pressrooms is still small, and it is more visible in the cities and state capitals than in Washington, D.C. Some news media have begun to make financial contributions to the U.S. Treasury for the facilities they use in the White House, Congress, and other government buildings, but the majority have not. Unlike some state governments, the federal government has declined to establish any sort of rent schedule. The *Wall Street Journal* makes a voluntary contribution of about $1,500 a year for government pressrooms in Washington, Norman C. Miller, Washington bureau chief, estimates (interview, 29 Oct. 1981). The appearance of not paying for space the press uses in government buildings bothers Miller. "We don't have an inalienable right to those facilities," he maintains.

Like Miller, news executives who are concerned about rent-free pressrooms provided by government contend that pressrooms are just another freebie from a news source. They also worry about government officials using the pressroom as a weapon, as Mayor Jane Byrne of Chicago appeared to do recently when she banned the *Chicago Tribune* from the City Hall pressroom in anger about something the *Tribune* had said about her. She thought better about it the next day and rescinded the ban, but many journalists shuddered at the thought that important work space could be removed at the flick of some politician's pique.

But Charles Seib, retired ombudsman for the *Washington Post*, does not believe "the public is short-changed" when the government provides working space for journalists covering it (interview, 9 Nov. 1981). He objects to free parking space for journalists, however.

Claude Sitton, editorial director of the Raleigh, North Carolina, *News & Observer* and *Times*, also objects to free parking space and telephones for reporters working in government buildings, but he sees a reason for government-provided work space (interview, 4 Nov. 1981).

Noting that his papers tried to pay rent for the pressroom in the statehouse but the state government said it could not come up with a rent schedule, Sitton believes the press serves "as a public surrogate" when it covers government. "The legislature, like other public bodies, has a responsibility to report on its proceedings, and we're acting as a transmission belt," he adds.

Seib and Sitton seem to be trying to distinguish between work space essential for journalists to do their job of reporting on government and perks that are merely special privileges, like free telephones and parking and discounts in government stores. That is a tightrope that a few news organizations like the *Wall Street Journal* have decided not to walk.

More Serious Perks. Another kind of perk that a few journalists have taken advantage of is that of using their positions for some sort of personal gain — accepting, for example, a discount price on a new car or a lower membership fee in a country club, offered to them because of the control they presumably have over publicity.

James Naughton, associate managing editor of the *Philadelphia Inquirer*, recalls that when he was a young reporter on the Cleveland *Plain Dealer* and in need of a new car, he asked around the office. "The auto editor told me to call General Motors PR in Detroit and get one at dealer cost," Naughton says. "You'd do the same thing when you needed new tires for your car. Nobody thought twice about it." Naughton believes today that he should not have done that (interview, 16 Sept. 1981).

Jack Landau, director of the Reporters Committee for Freedom of the Press, remembers that back in the late 1950s and early 1960s when he was working for the *Washington Post* "it was quite common for automobile company PR people to arrange factory-priced cars for journalists." (Interview, 24 Sept. 1981.) Landau started to arrange such a discount for himself, but he backed away from the deal after mentioning it to his editor, J. Russell Wiggins. "Wiggins said he could get GM to let him use a Buick for a whole year just on the hope that he might write a story saying he liked the car, but that would be bribery," Landau recalls. Then Wiggins told him: "Don't do it; it's unethical."

You do not hear much these days about such special deals on new cars for journalists, but as the report on outdoor writers in the opening of this chapter notes, the practice apparently still exists.

Another kind of perk, which some newspaper executives found out about when Gannett News Services (GNS) put the spotlight on it in 1979, is the sale of books sent to the papers for review. What many news executives apparently did not realize was that their book review editors were selling hundreds and thousands of books sent to them each year and pocketing the proceeds. The GNS story claimed that some editors were pocketing up to $1,000 a month selling books that did not belong to them to the Strand used book store in New York. This perk ended for some book review editors and at least two lost their jobs when the GNS exposé by Michael Cordts of the Rochester, New York, *Democrat & Chronicle* appeared. There were newspapers, however, that had already set up some system of disposing of the review books. The *New York Times,* for example, which probably receives more books for review than any other U.S. daily, sells most of the 37,000 books it gets each year, matches whatever proceeds result from that sale, and contributes the total to the New York Public Library. (A fuller account of Michael Cordt's investigation of the selling of review books appears in Chapter 6.)[18]

RESIST SEDUCTION, CODES SAY

The freebie problem is a comparatively new one in American journalism. At least, it was hardly mentioned in the early literature on journalism ethics in the 1920s. Today it is almost a fixture in the codes of ethics and standards of the news media and of journalistic organizations. This is not to say that would-be seducers of the press did not exist in the early years of this century. Obviously they did. But their efforts apparently were not perceived by press leaders as a serious threat to journalistic integrity. One theory as to why freebies came to be seen as a problem for journalism is that they grew out of public relations, which has developed in this country in this century, particularly since the 1920s. As government, business, and other segments of American society came to depend on the advice of professional propagandists and publicists, currying favor with the press soon came to be seen as a necessary or at least helpful step in communicating with the public at large. Currying favor has often translated into gifts, free tickets and trips, discounts, free drinks and dinners — the things newspeople call freebies.

If the history of freebies available to journalists could be graphed, the line representing the periods of greatest abundance would rise slowly through the 1930s and 1940s, reaching its highest point in the late 1950s and early 1960s, and would then drop slowly through the 1970s. The problem is a long way from being licked, most thoughtful journalists seem to feel, but freebies are not running wild as they did twenty years ago.

Bill Lyon, sports reporter and columnist for the *Philadelphia Inquirer,* sees fewer journalists willing to take freebies today than in the past "and fewer overt attempts to influence the media through gifts, junkets and the like." (Interview, 28 May 1981.) But he believes the freebies are still out there for the asking. "An unscrupulous journalist can damned near open his own pawn shop," Lyon adds.

One reason that freebies are decreasing as a problem in journalism is that news organizations, particularly the larger ones, are paying full expenses to send their reporters where the news is. Reporters do not need free tickets, meals, and rides to do their jobs. But some smaller newspapers and radio stations still count on some favors to get the news, particularly if it involves travel for their reporters.

Michael J. Davies, president of the *Kansas City Star* and *Times*, reminds metropolitan newspaper editors that it is easy for them to have high ethics, but it is tougher for the smaller papers (interview, 23 Oct. 1981). "The smaller paper editor has to say, 'If I don't take this freebie, then I don't cover the football game or I don't have a travel section,'" Davies holds. "The big guys should not be arrogant and look down their noses at the little guy who doesn't have many resources. Ethics are what you can afford."

Of the codes of ethics of national journalistic organizations, only that of the RTNDA says nothing about freebies. All the others give freebies a good tongue lashing.

"Newspapers should accept nothing of value from news sources or other outsiders," declares APME. "Gifts and free or reduced-rate travel, entertainment, products and lodging should not be accepted. The newspaper should pay its own expenses in connection with the reporting of the news. Special favors and special treatment for members of the press should be avoided."

The SPJ-SDX states that "gifts, favors, free travel, special treatment or privileges can compromise the integrity of journalists and their employers. Nothing of value should be accepted."

And the ASNE warns that journalists "should neither accept anything nor pursue any activity that might compromise or seem to compromise their integrity."

Two of the areas in journalism singled out because of their special problems with freebies — sports and travel — have some ethical guidelines on this matter from their professional organizations.

Five of the eleven Ethical Guidelines of the APSE deal with some aspect of freebies as follows:

I. TRAVEL, OTHER EXPENSES

The basic aim for members of this organization and their staffs is a pay-your-own-way standard. It is acceptable to travel on charter flights operated by teams and organizations, but the newspaper should insist on being billed. The newspaper should pay for meals, accommodations and other expenses of its sports staffers covering stories.

If newspapers allow writers to dine and drink at special, non-public places provided by teams or colleges, the papers should pay for food and drink consumed. . . .

IV. GIFTS AND GRATUITIES

Gifts of insignificant value — a calendar, pencil, key chain or such — may be accepted if it would be awkward to refuse or return them. All other gifts should be declined.

A gift that exceeds token value should be returned immediately with an explanation that it is against policy. If it is impractical to return it, the gift should be donated to a charity by your company....

VII. CREDENTIALS, TICKETS

As the result of untoward pressure by sports organizations, some newspapers advocate the payment of a reporter's admission to the event being covered. Where such overt pressures for favored treatment occur, the recommendation is that the newspapers adopt the firm policy of such payment. When there is a normal relationship, APSE considers acceptable standard press credentials and tickets, including parking, for those covering an event. However, sports editors should refuse to be placed in the demeaning position of requesting complimentary tickets for their relatives, friends or newspaper associates....

IX. USE OF MERCHANDISE OR PRODUCTS

APSE members and their staffs should not accept the free use or reduced rate purchase of merchandise or products for personal pleasure when such an offer involves the staffer's newspaper position. This includes the loan or cut-rate purchase of such things as automobiles, boats, appliances, clothing and sporting goods.

X. MISCELLANEOUS

Free or reduced memberships or fees in clubs or similar organizations should not be accepted.

As mentioned earlier in this chapter, the SATW adopted a revised Statement of Ethics and Code of Professional Responsibility by mail ballot in the fall of 1981. The society has both travel editors and writers and free-lance travel writers as members, and about half of its membership has associate status and comes from the travel industry. The sections of the revised code that have to do with freebies in general and junkets (the society prefers "familiarization trips") follow:

1. SATW recognizes the need for annual and ongoing scrutiny of its membership, eliminating those dilettantes who merely engage in travel journalism as a hobby, and at the same time demanding ever higher professional standards of admission to membership.

2. SATW will work cooperatively with publishers, editors and broadcast media toward achieving higher rates of pay for articles, photographs, films and other travel-related materials, while stressing the economic necessity for reimbursement of legitimate travel expenses so that all members may function in travel journalism

without even the appearance of compromising their integrity, so far as the public is concerned.

    3. SATW will maintain liaison with those segments of the travel industry which sponsor familiarization trips, while at the same time underscoring the complete independence of the travel journalist in reporting on the negative as well as the positive results of such trips, or to decide that the material justifies no report of any kind. In this connection, SATW emphasizes the advisability of sponsors providing advance documentation as to the variety of potential story material that might be developed by a familiarization trip, and stresses the negative impact on a journalist's productivity if too much time is devoted to unnecessary social events at the expense of free time to develop story materials. . . .

    5. The sole responsibility of the SATW member is to provide his/her readers, listeners or viewers with objective and independent reporting. SATW calls direct attention to the fact that some members represent publications which do not accept complimentary transportation, accommodations or other necessities or amenities of travel. Prospective hosts sponsoring familiarization trips at no charge to invited journalists are requested also to state in the invitation what the full rate or the press industry rate would be for such trips, giving those members who must pay all or part of the cost of any trip the option to do so. . . .

    7. Members shall not accept payment or courtesies for producing favorable materials about travel destinations against their own professional appraisal. . . .

    11. Members shall regard press trips as working opportunities and make every effort to obtain and report travel news accurately, without imposing excessive demands upon the hospitality of hosts. Any services required by a member, over and above those provided on a hosted trip, shall be paid for by the member. . . .

    13. Associate members shall neither accept nor pay money for acquiring new accounts, and shall not offer cash or any form of payment to editors and writers in return for editorial coverage.

The codes of individual news organizations are for the most part more specific in their freebie provisions, even spelling out the few minor gifts that staff members may accept.

Many of the approximately 150 journalists interviewed for this study said they believe the field is more ethical today than in the past. When asked why, most based their optimism on the decline in freebies. Perhaps because it is so visible, this area of journalism ethics is one that many journalists use as a measure of progress. Some of those interviewed seemed unwilling or unable to envision ethical problems beyond freebies and conflicts of interest; that is what ethics in journalism means to them.

But, as this book will reveal in the remainder of its chapters, the ethical problems of the news business go far beyond the relative simplicity of conflicts and freebies. It is entirely possible for a journalist to avoid freebies and conflicts of interest and still be a patsy for the power structure, or hurt people by unduly invading their privacy, or use methods in gathering news that throw suspicion on the news gathered, or act irresponsibly and without compassion in presenting news, or lie.

Reporters and Their Sources

"I'll quote you as an unimpeachable source, and you can quote me as highly reliable."

WHAT IF YOU LEARN, as editor of a metropolitan newspaper, that a promising new reporter in your Washington bureau had been romantically involved with a state official while covering politics for her previous newspaper two years ago? You also learn that she received a fur coat, a sports car, and other expensive gifts from this politician and that they shared an apartment. Do you ignore it? Do you reprimand her? Do you fire her? What right do you have to tell her who her friends can be and what gifts she can accept from them? Besides, this all happened before she came to work for you.

That is the sort of decision that faced the news executives of the *New York Times* a few years back when they learned that Laura Foreman, a 34-year-old reporter in their Washington bureau, had had an affair with a 54-year-old state senator and south Philadelphia political leader when she worked as a political reporter for the *Philadelphia Inquirer.* Her editors apparently learned of her relationship with Pennsylvania State Senator Henry "Buddy" Cianfrani when the Federal Bureau of Investigation questioned her as they were checking out Cianfrani on income tax evasion charges. At about the same time, the *Inquirer* itself broke a story reporting that the FBI was investigating Cianfrani and that he had been romantically linked with Foreman, who had left the *Inquirer* staff seven months earlier to join the *Times*'s Washington bureau. The *Inquirer* also reported that Foreman, while covering local politics for the paper, had accepted about $10,000 (the paper raised this estimate to $20,000 in later stories) in gifts, including a fur coat, from Cianfrani, who was legally separated from his wife at the time. The *Inquirer* story did not dwell on what was most bothersome to editors of the *Times* and the *Inquirer*: Cianfrani was both a news source for Foreman and a subject of many of her articles.

Inquirer executive editor Eugene L. Roberts, Jr., said his paper had not confirmed the close relationship between the reporter and the politician until she had been taken off the local political beat, and he did not learn about the expensive gifts until after she had left the *Inquirer*. The *Inquirer* did not take any action against Foreman; she left the paper for a better job in the Washington bureau of the *Times*.[1]

The *Times* editors took a harder line when they learned what Laura Foreman had done. They forced her resignation. Abraham M. Rosenthal, executive editor of the *Times,* reflects that the "penalty was severe but there was nothing else I could do." Foreman "violated a cardinal rule," Rosenthal says (interview, 7 Oct. 1981).* "She could not continue covering things in Washington, everybody in the Washington bureau agreed. And nobody wanted her here in the main office; her name was an embarrassment." It made no difference to Rosenthal that Foreman's violation occurred on another paper. "We don't tell our readers that our reporters start being ethical only when they come to the *Times,*" he explains.

Also involved in the decision to dismiss Foreman was David R. Jones, national editor of the *Times,* who has no reservations about the action the paper took (interview, 7 Oct. 1981). "If we had known about it when she was hired, we would not have hired her," Jones maintains. "Therefore, she was really hired, in a sense, under false pretenses, false credentials." He reports that the paper "took some flak" from women, who charged, in effect, that if Foreman were a man, she would not have been forced out. Jones denies that any double standard was applied in this case. "I'm not foolish enough to think that reporters, both male and female, do not occasionally shack up with news sources, but I'm not aware of it, and I have better things to do than to run a sex squad on my staff." Besides, he doubts that any other reporter has been involved with a source the way Foreman was. "If I were aware of any similar conflict of interest with any reporter on my staff, male or female, the result would

*See list of interviewees following Notes.

be the same," Jones contends. "A deep personal (particularly sexual) relationship with an important news source is a conflict of interest that merits dismissal."

Not only women raised the double standard question in the Foreman case. Richard Cohen, *Washington Post* columnist known for uncovering the corruption that led to Spiro T. Agnew's resignation as vice president, wrote that Foreman lost her job for breaking a rule made by men. The rule in her case was the "cardinal" one of not accepting "anything of value from anyone," Cohen said, but what "strikes you about the Foreman case is how it could not have happened to a man." Male reporters "have been having affairs with women they cover for as long as there have been reporters, women and spare time," Cohen observed. "It is somehow assumed that when a male reporter sleeps with a female source or with a woman connected with someone he is covering, he is using her — that along with her body, he gets, say, campaign secrets. In the Foreman case, we are assured she was not used by Cianfrani; that she could have been using him seems not to have occurred to many people. . . . The point is that for all Foreman may or may not have done, she is clearly being judged by standards that don't apply to men."[2]

Jay McMullen tells us about the way some male reporters have used female sources. In an *Esquire* article written by *Chicago Tribune* Washington correspondent Eleanor Randolph, McMullen is quoted as saying of his days covering city hall for the old *Chicago Daily News*: "I've screwed girls who worked at city hall for years. All those goddamn bluenoses who think you get stories from press conferences — hell, there was a day when I could roll over in the bed in the morning and scoop the *Tribune*. Anybody who wouldn't screw a dame for a story is disloyal to the paper." McMullen later married Jane Byrne, and he quit newspaper work when she became mayor of Chicago.[3]

Randolph, who was a friend of Foreman's, asked in her *Esquire* article: "What would have happened if Laura had been a man and Buddy had been a woman?" The answer is "a little muddy," she said:

> If a man took gifts valued up to $20,000 from a person he wrote about — love or no love — he would be in trouble. He would have a hard time convincing an editor that it was not a bribe, and in this area a man might have found himself in deeper difficulty than a woman.
>
> As for sleeping with the subject of stories, however, there is little doubt that until very recently a male reporter who took a female source or subject to bed had simply scored with more than a good story.[4]

After the *Times* dismissed Foreman and as the *Inquirer* became aware that most of the rumors staff members had heard about Laura and

Buddy were true, *Inquirer* editor Roberts assigned his Pulitzer Prize-winning investigative reporting team of Donald L. Barlett and James B. Steele to look into the entire mess. They produced a 17,000-word article examining the Foreman-Cianfrani affair in meticulous detail and reporting how various *Inquirer* editors were ignorant of or duped or looked the other way while the conflict of interest developed. Their blockbuster report revealed how, over a year and a half, a romance blossomed between the reporter and her political friend, and that he gave her more than $20,000 in gifts, including a sports car, a fur coat, jewelry, a TV set, stereo equipment, furniture, and a brass bed. Although he was living with two other women when Foreman came into his life, Cianfrani was soon concentrating his attentions on her, and they eventually moved into an apartment together. After Foreman had been covering local politics for about eight months, rumors reached some of her editors that she was having an affair with Cianfrani, but when Roberts asked her about it, she denied it. Roberts, true to his long-standing policy, trusted his reporter. But the rumors persisted and soon the affair was an open secret around town. Roberts and two subeditors questioned her again. She replied by complaining about rumors she said were being spread by reporters in the *Inquirer*'s city hall bureau who envied her accomplishments as the first woman ever assigned by the paper to cover local politics. The three editors read her complaint as another denial. By the time top editors accepted the rumored affair as a fact, Foreman had been reassigned to the national presidential campaign. They did nothing more about it because they reasoned that since she no longer covered local politics, her relationship with Cianfrani was her own business. Cianfrani continued to be one of her sources, however, because he helped lead Washington Senator Henry M. Jackson's campaign in Pennsylvania for the Democratic presidential nomination, and Cianfrani was a delegate to the Democratic National Convention, which Foreman covered. Shortly after the presidential campaign ended, Laura Foreman left the *Inquirer* for the *New York Times*.[5]

Foreman would not allow Barlett and Steele to interview her, and she made virtually no public statement in her defense at the time she resigned. But later she wrote an article for the *Washington Monthly* in which she argued that getting close to subjects was a good way to get stories. She talked mostly about former Mayor Frank Rizzo of Philadelphia in this piece but she also dealt with her Cianfrani problem:

> I think it's probably right that I was too close to one politician I covered — Buddy Cianfrani, the man I fell in love with. . . . As soon as was practicable I got myself transferred so that I wouldn't have to cover him anymore, and in the interim I mentioned him as little as possible and stuck as much as I could to what was commonly known. I

never slanted a story in his favor. If it was a bad situation, it was bad because we were in love, not because of the gifts Buddy bought me, which were the immediate cause of my downfall.

At another point in the article, in which she recounts several anecdotes about Rizzo that she learned about because of her closeness to him, Foreman wrote:

> Although my relationship with Buddy would never have started if I had been a standoffish, distance maintaining reporter, I wouldn't put it in the same category as my relationship with Rizzo. I think reporters should try to walk the narrow line of friendship with politicians they cover if it will help them write better stories. I don't think they should fall in love with them — that makes honest reporting well-nigh impossible.

Foreman does not say in this article that she ever told her editors she was having an affair with Cianfrani. But she concedes: "It was common knowledge around the *Inquirer* newsroom that Buddy and I were having an affair, and people may not have liked it, but there were no consequences for me professionally at that time. My editors continued to like my stories."[6]

While Laura Foreman was being let go by the *Times,* Cianfrani had his own troubles. He was arrested, tried, and sentenced to five years by a federal court for mail fraud, racketeering, and conspiracy. He pleaded guilty to accepting bribes to influence the admission of students to graduate schools and for arranging to place ghost workers on his state senate payroll. Shortly after serving twenty-seven months in the U.S. penitentiary at Allenwood, Pennsylvania, he and Laura Foreman were married.[7]

Looking back on the troublesome case, Gene Roberts is not sure he would do anything different (interviews, 28 May and 15 Sept. 1981). Foreman told him that "Buddy was just one other person she was dealing with." Checking out a complaint about the accuracy of a story is one thing, Roberts says, "but it's quite another matter to check out rumors about the romantic life of one of your reporters, staking out her apartment and all that. You have to have better ethics instruction for the staff before such things happen." He recalls that Foreman asked to be transferred from local politics, "but it was too late by the time she did." What Laura Foreman did "was a clear conflict of interest," Roberts says, that "grew with each passing month."

The Laura Foreman case is not the sort of thing that happens every day in the newsrooms of this land, but it underscores the ethical pitfalls in the delicate relationships between reporters and their sources. It is obvious to even casual observers that reporters rely heavily on human sources, people they interview and ask questions of. Documents and observation of an event, such as a game or a court trial, also provide reporters with material for their articles and broadcasts, but they get most of their information from other people.

FRIENDLIES AND UNFRIENDLIES

A friendship between a reporter and a news source does not have to go as far as the Foreman-Cianfrani relationship before it becomes troublesome, particularly for the reporter. Reporters who develop friendships with their news sources, seeing them socially as well as professionally, can easily fall into the trap of favoritism. Sometimes without being aware of it, reporters start taking care of their friends, looking out for them: When you need a good quote or a new angle on your story, call old pal Joe. When your old pal gets into the news, make him look good if you can. When you catch old Joe with his hand in the till . . .? Sources can also take care of their reporter friends, feeding them news or tips exclusively or at least ahead of their competitors, or filling them in on the sort of background information that makes their stories sound more authentic. A kind of a mutual back-scratching pact can easily develop.

It is understandable how such friendships occur. Reporters and their sources often have a lot in common. In most cases, reporters share and know much more than the average person about the source's chief area of interest. It is no wonder that politicians and political reporters, police and police reporters, coaches and sports reporters sometimes become friends. And in smaller journalistic settings, reporters and their sources are more apt to see and be with one another socially because the social network in smaller towns offers fewer opportunities for them to avoid one another. Friendships can easily spring from the church dinners, the evening softball, the Independence Day parade, and the daily contacts that make up the social life in small towns. Nevertheless, many reporters in both rural and metropolitan environments try hard to avoid deep friendships with their sources for fear of relationships that would or might interfere with the reporter's perspective and ability to treat news subjects fairly. But some take chances.

For example, when Roger Mudd of NBC News was working at CBS he was known around Washington as a friend of the Kennedy family, Jack W. Germond and Jules Witcover tell us in their book on the 1980 presidential campaign. Mudd and his wife were good friends of Ethel Kennedy, Robert's widow, but not particularly close to Senator Edward Kennedy. Although the Mudds often went to parties and casual evenings at Ethel Kennedy's home, where the senator was sometimes present, they had been in Senator Kennedy's home "perhaps three times on social occasions." Mudd only had the kind of social relationship with Senator

Kennedy "that many Washington reporters have with many members of Congress they have covered over the years," Germond and Witcover wrote.[8]

His friendship with some members of the Kennedy family caused Mudd to hesitate about taking on the assignment of doing an hour-long documentary for CBS News on Senator Ted Kennedy as a candidate for president. He did do the documentary, of course, and it became a major political event that some saw as contributing to the senator's lack of success in obtaining the Democratic nomination in 1980. Mudd's tough questioning, spurred perhaps by his not wanting to be seen as a "Kennedy insider," and the senator's often incoherent replies created a furor. The program also killed the Mudds' friendship with Ethel Kennedy and caused "a great freeze" to descend on Mudd from Senator Kennedy and his immediate family and staff.[9]

Another famous reporter-source friendship in the capital was that between David Stockman, President Reagan's budget director, and William Greider, then assistant managing editor for national news at the *Washington Post*. That friendship led to a series of eighteen sort of off-the-record but taped interviews that got Greider a big article in the *Atlantic Monthly* and almost got Stockman fired. The article related Stockman's personal doubts about his own budget estimates and about the Reagan administration's ability to balance the federal budget while cutting taxes. Stockman was quoted as saying that "we didn't think it all the way through" and "we didn't add up all the numbers" when the administration was trying to get Congress to pass its economic program in 1981. Stockman told a news conference that he understood the interviews by "an old friend of mine" were off the record, but that Greider understood them "to be off the record for use in the newspaper over the period in which our conversation occurred." Greider said his original understanding with Stockman was that he would not use any of the interviews immediately in the *Post* but would be free to write a longer, analytical article after the first phase of the budget battle was over.[10]

"My rule is I try not to become friends with my sources," says veteran Washington reporter Mike Feinsilber of the AP (interview, 23 Sept. 1981). "It's asking too much of human nature to separate the reporting function from your social function. This is hard because many of my sources are about my age and are fine people I'd like to have as friends."

Ray White, video production firm owner who edited the *Washington Journalism Review* until 1982, believes journalists "can easily be seduced by the desire to be liked, respected, part of the inner circle, close to power." (Interview, 1 June 1981). He feels the press can't do its job unless "it stays on the outside."

Concerned that the press has become "a power-groupy institution,"

Lyle Denniston, who covers the U.S. Supreme Court for the Baltimore *Sun*, maintains that Washington reporters "have dinner all the time with their sources." (Interview, 5 June 1981.) He asks: "How can you have sources to your house and have intimate personal relationships and be their adversary the next day if you have to be?" He claims the same thing happens in state capitals. "There's too much intimacy between reporters and sources," Denniston charges. "The press is a captive of government almost everywhere it has a relationship with it."

Ellen R. Findley of the *Sacramento Bee* worked in one of those state capitals as a reporter for the Baton Rouge, Louisiana, *Morning Advocate* (interview, 15 Feb. 1981). She recalls calling up an attorney "who was a very good friend" to ask him about the mayor's race. She was interviewing him for a story, but he thought they were talking as friends. When her story appeared, she says, "we both got a lot of flak — me from him, and him from the politicians he offended."

Women reporters often run into another kind of source problem. Findley says that many of the male news sources she dealt with in Louisiana practiced the charm of gentlemen of the Old South. This sometimes went beyond opening doors for a lady, inviting her to lunch, and helping her on with her wraps. "I got propositioned a whole hell of a lot," Findley says. She got out of it by "pretending to be dumb," rather than insulting the propositioner, she explains, "because 90 percent of the time he was a source I needed."

Elaine Tait, food and restaurant writer for the *Philadelphia Inquirer,* should get the most-gracious-squelch award for the way she rejected a news source who was making advances to her (interview, 12 Nov. 1981). She told him, "You know, I'm a married woman and I don't fool around — but boy, if I did, you'd be the first one." Tait reports she and the source got along fine from then on.

Broadcast journalists also may have a special source relationship problem, according to Brit Hume, Capitol Hill correspondent for ABC News, who has also worked for newspapers and the Jack Anderson column (interview, 4 Nov. 1981). He explains that in television reporting, because you often don't have as much time as you do in print, you "develop a handful of people who can help you ... and you come to depend on them. Then it becomes tough to take a shot at them." Broadcast journalists need access, he says — "that shot of Reagan walking toward the helicopter, even if what he's saying is pure word salad, is important in television. We have to be able to get to people, to be in the main scheme of things, to be known by the VIPs." Hume sees the risks in such a dependence on certain top sources. "You have to make sure you are not compromised by this need for access," he warns.

Hume recalls feeling uncomfortable while covering Vice President George Bush's campaign for the Republican presidential nomination in 1980 "because I found myself rooting for him." This is not too uncommon for TV reporters, Hume believes, because "in television journalism if your candidate is doing well, you're on the air, and if he's not, you're not." After Reagan moved ahead of him, Bush "gave a gracious speech praising Reagan," Hume relates. "So I wrote Bush a note telling him what a gracious speech it was and soon I got a nice reply. Now whenever I see Bush he is extremely kind to me," Hume says. "If I ever have to cover him, I'm going to have to watch it."

Some editors of larger newspapers rotate reporters on campaigns and beats, to minimize the "cozy" relationships that sometimes develop when reporters have to depend on the same sources again and again. But there are still reporters who have spent most of their professional lives covering one beat. They develop contacts from their long service covering the same area or subject, and that is often valuable. They also develop friendships, and that can get in the way. Editors acknowledge this problem when they, as they often do on the larger newspapers, assign reporters from outside a particular beat to move in on a special or negative story that the regular reporter could not do without losing some of his or her prize sources.

Socializing with news sources, even if they are not close friends, can present difficulties for reporters. What do you do, for example, when some VIP, cocktail in hand, starts talking about the merger deal his firm is making, or the secret committee report he just read? Some reporters say that anything they hear at a social gathering is fair game, but most figure it is fairer to call up the VIP or some other source the next day and try to get the "party talk" on the record in a more official way. Some avoid the problem by shunning such parties in the first place, or they socialize only with friends and have an agreement that reporting ends when the party begins.

Sources as Adversaries. A concept that has appeal for many journalists is that reporters are, or ought to be, adversaries of their sources, particularly political sources. An adversarial relationship between reporters and sources is necessary for the press to be a true watchdog of government and other important institutions of American life, this argument holds. We saw reporters as adversaries during the uncovering of the Watergate scandal that caused President Nixon to resign. The televised image of aggressive reporters like Clark Mollenhoff of the Cowles Newspapers and Dan Rather of CBS News pounding their tough questions at Nixon did not sit well with some viewers but many journalists cheered. They saw such aggressive reporting as necessary in fulfilling journalism's watchdog role, and appropriate because of the seriousness of the high level government shenanigans the reporters were trying to expose. So journalists talk a lot about hard balls and soft balls when they discuss interviews and news conferences, hard balls being the kind of tough questions Nixon got from many reporters in those Watergate days and soft balls being the easy ones that any savvy source can duck or knock out of the ball park.

But treating all sources as adversaries can be just as unfair to them and to the public as treating them all as buddies. Reporters who act as if most public officials are crooks or potential crooks are not only wrong in that assessment of all but a handful of public officials; they are apt to let their prejudices dictate both their questions and their news stories. And it is distressing when some reporters give the adversary treatment to even ordinary people caught up in and unsophisticated about the news, browbeating them with questions in a manner more appropriate in Hollywood fiction. As reporter Robert Scheer of the *Los Angeles Times* reminds us, "You have to be more careful when you're interviewing someone not used to being interviewed. You need to be fair to them." (Interview, 25 Nov. 1980.)

SECRET SOURCES

Journalists in the United States have come to believe that certain kinds of information cannot be obtained unless some sources are kept secret. Some sources will not talk for the record for various good reasons: They might lose their jobs, be physically harmed or even killed, or lose the trust of those from whom they are getting the information they are passing on to the journalists. Some of the major exposés of modern journalism would not have been possible without information that was obtained by reporters only because they agreed to protect the identity of some of their sources. Probably the most famous secret source in recent journalistic investigations was "Deep Throat," the name that Robert Woodward and Carl Bernstein gave to the anonymous insider who helped them break the Watergate cover-up for the *Washington Post*. But Deep Throat was only one of many secret sources Woodward and Bernstein used to develop their stories that contributed to the eventual resignation of President Nixon and the jailing of several White House aides.

Watergate is the kind of story journalists usually cite when they argue for their right to keep certain sources secret. Another is the exposé of organized crime, such as the series "Crime on the Waterfront" that the late Malcolm Johnson did for the *New York Sun* and that won him a 1948 Pulitzer Prize. His son, Haynes Johnson, reporter-columnist for the

Washington Post, contends that if his father "had used the names of some of his sources, they would have been killed. It's that simple." (Interview, 4 June 1981.) Source protection also was essential in the Watergate investigation, he believes. "People who told us things because they thought crimes were being committed that were literally destroying our democracy would have had their careers wrecked if they had been identified." (Malcolm and Haynes Johnson became the only father and son to have won Pulitzers for reporting when Haynes Johnson received one in 1966 for his coverage of civil rights clashes in Selma, Alabama.)

Because secret sources are important if not essential in exposing some society- or life-threatening conditions, journalists have sought laws to give them the right to protect their sources if called into court. They have also argued that the First Amendment guarantee of freedom to publish or broadcast is meaningless if it does not also guarantee them the right to gather information, even if it comes from secret sources. Although the latter argument has not gained widespread acceptance by judges, about half of the fifty states have passed so-called shield laws extending to journalists and their sources the protection that the common law has traditionally afforded to the privileged or secret communications between lawyers and clients, doctors and patients, clergy and flock, and husbands and wives. There has been talk of a federal shield law as well, but journalists are divided on that question, many arguing that it would be undesirable to set journalists up as a special privileged class. Others are concerned that "what Congress giveth it can taketh away," that such a law could be amended in the future in ways detrimental to journalism and press freedom.

Many reporters have gone to jail or paid fines since 1958 because they refused to reveal their sources to a court. Many of these punishments occurred in states that had shield laws but courts did not uphold them, usually for the reason that the journalist's "shield" had to yield to the Sixth Amendment rights of accused persons to a fair trial. The first reporter to go to jail to protect a source was Marie Torre, then a radio-TV columnist for the old *New York Herald Tribune.* It seemed like a trivial case at the time. She refused to identify the unnamed CBS executive she had quoted in her column to the effect that Judy Garland was being dropped from a forthcoming program because she was too fat. For this stand on principle, she spent ten days in jail for contempt of court.

Since the Torre incarceration in 1958, a parade of reporters and even a few editors have done time rather than give in to some court's insistence that they expose secret sources. Two of the best-known cases involved Myron Farber of the *New York Times,* who resided in a New Jersey jail for forty days because he refused to turn his notes over to the court in the murder trial that ended in the acquittal of Dr. Mario E.

Jascalevich, and William Farr of the *Los Angeles Times,* who spent forty-seven days in jail for refusing to reveal his sources for a story in the *Los Angeles Herald Examiner* that said the Charles Manson family had planned to kill a number of celebrities, including Elizabeth Taylor.[11] Although several other journalists besides Farber and Farr have been jailed for shorter periods of time, untold numbers of journalists have cooperated with courts to avoid being held in contempt. Since the stories of those who cooperate are not widely publicized, no one knows how many journalists have done so.

Supporters of the principle of confidentiality for journalists argue that a reporter is no better than his or her sources of information. If you cannot promise protection, many people will not talk. And if you give in when a judge orders you to reveal a secret source, other sources will clam up when you or other reporters go to them for information.

The legal argument for giving journalists the same privilege enjoyed by doctors, lawyers, clergy, and spouses but denied to most citizens is rejected by William A. Rusher, publisher of the conservative *National Review* and a lawyer. He believes the analogy that would equate the so-called reporter's privilege with the four types of communication treated as privileged at common law just will not hold up:

> All four common law privileges protect the communication, not the communicator. In all four, the identity of the communicator is known, but the substance of the communication may be withheld at the instance of the communicator in order to serve a greater public good — for example, to encourage clients to speak freely with their lawyers. In the case of a reporter and an anonymous source, the substance of the communication, far from being kept confidential, is blared around the world; what is kept secret is the identity of the communicator — the dubious theory being that anonymous revelations will serve the best interest of the American public.[12]

While agreeing that reporter's privilege is "an ethically justifiable doctrine in a small number of cases involving the very future of society," James W. Carey decries turning it into "the very essence of the journalistic relationship." Carey, dean of the College of Communications at the University of Illinois-Urbana, said he finds journalist Renata Adler's conclusion about journalistic privilege to be compelling: "There should be only rare and well defined exceptions to the rule that a journalist always reveals his sources; secrecy and journalism are contradictions in terms."[13]

Two editors with impressive credentials as reporters see material gained from confidential sources as useful for leads to on-the-record information, but not as a basis for news stories. Claude Sitton, editorial executive of the Raleigh, North Carolina, *News & Observer* and *Times,*

who distinguished himself covering civil rights and the South for the
New York Times, observes that "once you go beyond using confidential
sources for leads, you're on dangerous grounds." (Interview, 4 Nov. 1981.)
He believes that if a story based on information from secret sources gets
into the courts, the reporter is either held in contempt for not disclosing
the sources or "a judgment is awarded to the plaintiff on the grounds that
you don't have any defense because you refuse to come clean with the
court." At his newspapers, Sitton says, confidentiality is not given to any
source until he and the editor and reporter involved "have prayer
meetings," and sometimes not before he has conferred with his publisher
and their libel lawyer. Robert W. Greene, assistant managing editor of
Newsday, generally recognized as one of the top investigative reporters in
the country, argues that taking the easy route of building stories on
confidential sources instead of using them merely as leads can bring big
libel judgments that cause your paper to cease investigative reporting
(interview, 6 Oct. 1981). "If you can't reveal your sources when you're
hauled into a libel court," Greene explains, "it doesn't count as evidence
on either side."

Steve Dornfeld, Knight-Ridder Washington bureau reporter, knows
how a confidential source can lead to an important news story (interview,
3 Apr. 1981). He recalls that in his early days as a reporter on the
Minneapolis Tribune a judge he knew tipped him off the record that a
probate judge in another jurisdiction had appointed three political cronies
as appraisers of a huge estate for which they would be paid as much as
$10,000 apiece for doing not much more than signing their names. The
judge told him where to look and he ended up checking the records on
about 400 cases, which showed a pattern of appraisers appointed by
certain probate judges getting large fees based on percentages of the
estates for merely confirming the appraisals already made by trust
companies. In some cases, Dornfeld recalls, the appraisers signed their
appraisals on the same day they were appointed and walked away with
fees of $5,000 to $10,000, depending on the value of the estates. He got a
good story, and it was all on the record, but it would not have happened
without the confidential tip from the judge, whom Dornfeld says "had no
axe to grind."

However, reporters who grant confidentiality too easily can sometimes paint themselves into corners. This happened when a reporter in
the Madison bureau of the *Milwaukee Journal* was assigned to check out
a rumor that a Wisconsin state senator had financed a sex change
operation for a Madison man with whom he had had a homosexual
relationship. *Journal* managing editor Joseph W. Shoquist says the state
senator all but admitted the truth of the rumor to the reporter but the
reporter "made the terrible mistake of giving the senator confidentiality,

and that tied our hands for a month." (Interview, 19 Oct. 1981.) The story came out eventually, Shoquist relates, when the senator was picked up in a Milwaukee park by an undercover vice squad police officer.

The legal complications surrounding confidentiality and journalistic privilege are so interesting it is easy to lose sight of the ethical questions they raise: When, if ever, should a journalist agree to protect the identity of a source? How far should the pledge of confidentiality extend — just to publication or broadcast, or to court testimony as well? Is it ethical for a journalist to break a promise not to reveal a confidential source? Is a reporter violating a confidentiality pledge by disclosing such sources to his or her editor? How can we be sure that unscrupulous sources are not using confidentiality to avoid responsibility for passing on possibly damaging information? How can we be sure that reporters are not using "secret sources" to peddle their own opinions?

Editors Wary of Confidentiality. Editors of responsible news organizations have grown increasingly wary in recent years about the use of secret sources. Their concern seems to center on: (1) The possibility that the media are being used by sources who insist on secrecy, or by reporters who make up things and get them into stories by attributing them to so-called secret sources; (2) the possible loss of credibility when readers and viewers are not given specific sources of important information; and (3) the difficulties in defending against libel suits when judges refuse to consider proof of the accuracy of disputed stories if they are based on sources the media refuse to identify.

As with most things in this world, confidentiality in journalism has its degrees. Earlier in this chapter we discussed the top level of confidentiality — its use in a Watergate or organized crime sort of story that is of vital public interest and involves uncooperative and secretive people. Hardly anyone questions the use of secret sources by journalists trying to expose major cancers in the society. But secret sources are also used on less earthshaking stories, particularly those reporting on politics and government. Our newspapers are full of "administration officials said," "a White House source disclosed," "a source close to the governor said," "an authoritative source said," or simply "sources said." That is the way reporters fulfill the convention of attributing the information they have collected, without specifically naming their sources who, for one reason or another, have demanded secrecy (in the news business, such sources are called anonymous or "blind" sources).

Most journalists, even those who defend the use of secret sources on major and political stories, believe that too much reporting has been based on blind sources, particularly since Watergate. They see a mystique developing around the method as increasing numbers of reporters seem to think that their stories are more interesting and dramatic if they contain a secret source or two. There's also a suspicion among many editors that some reporters use anonymous sources because they are too lazy to pin down proper identification.

Norman E. Isaacs, retired newspaper editor and chairman of the National News Council until 1982, has been startled in recent years "by reporters calling up people and saying right away, 'If you don't want to be quoted, that's all right.' " (Interview, 7 Oct. 1981.) William J. Small, UPI president, says he wishes he had a dollar for every time a reporter has called him and said, " 'Look, why don't we do this off the record?' They're always shocked when I say I never talk off the record." (Interview, 5 Oct. 1981.) When she was managing editor of the Rochester, New York, *Democrat & Chronicle,* Nancy Woodhull remembers, one of her reporters turned in a story without any specific identification of its sources (interview, 16 Oct. 1981). Asked about this, the reporter said, "Well, gee, I didn't think they'd want their names used," says Woodhull, now managing editor for news of *USA Today.*

Greene of *Newsday* makes a more serious charge against the use of blind sources. "I've seen reporters who pass off their own ideas with anonymous sources," Greene declares. "I'm enormously suspicious of it." (Interview, 6 Oct. 1981.) And Richard Cunningham, veteran newsman who became associate director of the news council, opposes casual uses of confidential sources: "It annoys me to see some young reporter go off to the legislature or city council and start reporting 'observers said.' I know they haven't had time to develop good sources or a sense of what the consensus is among responsible observers." (Interview, 5 Oct. 1981.)

The loss of credibility when reporters are not able to name sources in their stories is the most bothersome aspect of confidentiality to some news executives. Attribution — telling the public where the information came from — is a cardinal principle of American journalism and one that obviously has to be bent when news comes from secret sources.

"Readers ought to know all you can tell them about where your information is coming from so that they can understand that information," says Donald Graham, publisher of the *Washington Post* (interview, 4 June 1981). "If you can't tell the reader exactly who said it, you ought to tell them as much as you can about what sort of person said it so that the readers can understand, if possible, what the source's motives were." Graham believes that reporters have a duty to get their information on the record, but he says that is not always possible in Washington. "If we ran no unattributed information, we would be taking a high moral stance, but we would be denying information to our readers."

Woodhull believes that when a source cannot be fully identified "we should say why. Was the person afraid of losing a job, afraid of taking sides? We should know the source's motive and share that with the reader as often as we can." (Interview, 16 Oct. 1981.)

What Graham and Woodhull advocate has been formal policy at the *Louisville Times* and *Courier-Journal* since 1976. The Louisville guidelines on anonymous sources say in part: "The reason for the source's anonymity should be explained in the story as fully as possible without revealing the source's identity. (If the reason isn't a good one, then the source shouldn't be quoted.)" Many other papers, including the *Kansas City Star* and *Times,* follow more or less the same rule.

Many journalists are worried about sources using them when they refuse to be identified with the information they pass along. Basing stories on unnamed sources "always involves manipulation," says Charles Seib, retired ombudsman of the *Washington Post* (interview, 9 Nov. 1981). "And the reader is almost always misinformed." Clark Mollenhoff, former investigative reporter who teaches at Washington and Lee University, has written that "any really experienced investigative reporter knows that many public officials who are quite reliable when speaking on the record will peddle a large amount of malicious misinformation when talking on a confidential basis. The investigative reporter must be constantly on guard against being used by clever informants who may make unjustified accusations against those whom the informants wish to damage."[14]

Secret sources have cost some newspapers when they were the basis of stories that brought on suits for libel. Some judges have demanded that the reporters of those stories disclose their sources, and when the reporters, as often happens, refuse to do so, the courts decline to listen to any proof that the story is true and accurate. Cognizant of this threat, the APME Freedom of Information Committee advised newspaper editors to take the following steps "in dealing with confidential sources":

> (1) In every investigative or sensitive story, make a serious effort at getting your sources on the record. Send the reporter back, and back again, even if it means warning the source that the newspaper might not use the story unless he is willing to go on record. Such a warning sometimes jolts a source into committing himself. After all, he usually wants to see the story in print or he wouldn't be talking with you in the first place.
>
> (2) If your source still refuses to go on the record, then ask if he would agree to being kept confidential EXCEPT in the event of a libel suit. You are only being fair to your source by explaining that a court could order you to name him.
>
> (3) If both these tacks fail, then it is time for a talk session with reporter, lawyer, and editors. Find out the trend of disclosure cases in your state. Weigh the measure of risk involved in doing the story

against the compelling nature of the story itself. Bottom line: Is the story worth the risk? Are you willing to accept the consequences?[15]

Blind Source Rules Tightened. Journalism suffered a severe black eye in 1981 when the *Washington Post* had to return a Pulitzer Prize for feature writing when the prize-winning article, the story of an eight-year-old heroin addict, turned out to be fabricated. The fabricator, a young reporter named Janet Cooke, was fired after confessing her hoax. The incident was a great embarrassment to the *Post* and the news business in general. It stimulated agonizing discussions about journalism ethics and credibility, and raised several questions about journalistic practices, including the widespread use of anonymous sources. (Other ethical questions evolving out of the Janet Cooke case are discussed in Chapters 7 and 10).

At the *Washington Post,* executive editor Ben Bradlee decreed that from then on at least one editor would have to know the identity of any anonymous source used (interview, 5 June 1981). "But you're kidding yourself if you think that's gonna stop another Janet Cooke," he warns. "It makes people feel better. If I feel I need to know a source, I'll ask, but there's no way to build an organization without trust. So I don't intend to spend a lot of time asking everybody the source of everything. But if I get in a shit sandwich again, I'm going to sure as hell know!" Bradlee also says the *Post* is "going to renew efforts that had probably lagged on maximizing attribution."

Some observers believe the stage was set for a Janet Cooke incident at the *Post* by Deep Throat, the anonymous source Robert Woodward used in his Watergate investigation with fellow reporter Carl Bernstein in the early 1970s. One well-publicized fact about Deep Throat, certainly known to those who work in the *Post* newsroom, is that his identity was never made known to *Post* editors at the time. Bradlee now admits he knows who Deep Throat is, but he would not say just when he found out.[16] He does say that in his lifetime, Woodward (who is now an assistant managing editor in charge of a special investigative reporting team at the *Post*) will be able to tell the world in the *Post* who Deep Throat was (interview, 5 June 1981).

After the Cooke affair, many newspapers did what Bradlee did — required that at least one editor had to know their "Deep Throats." Other papers that already had such rules reaffirmed them.

The policy at the *Kansas City Star* and *Times,* which predates the Cooke incident, is that anonymous sources are not used unless supervising editors know their identities and approve of their use. *Star* and *Times* president Michael J. Davies says that "essentially the reporter has to prove that he absolutely has to use that source, and then he must state in his story why the individual can't be identified." (Interview, 23 Oct. 1981.) Davies believes that most anonymous sources are "the result of lazy reporting" and that they should be used sparingly.

At the Rochester, New York, *Times-Union,* where the policy is to name sources unless there is some overriding reason not to, Anthony Casale, assistant managing editor before he moved to *USA Today,* says he insisted on knowing the identity of every blind source before a story was published (interview, 16 Oct. 1981). Sometimes he even interviewed the blind source himself after the reporter had already done so. "Reporters don't push hard enough to get sources on the record," Casale believes. Casale conferred with every one of the confidential sources for a series on police informers that his *Times-Union* staff produced; he got them to sign affidavits attesting to what they had told his reporters and agreeing to come forth if the paper was sued for libel. "We had to allow confidentiality on that series because people's lives were in danger," Casale says, but he took the opposite tack on another investigation, one of police brutality. "We felt that if we used unnamed sources, our findings would be dismissed," he explains. "Some sources would not go on record, but enough did" for the *Times-Union* to produce a series of articles detailing examples of police brutality suffered by thirteen victims who were fully identified.

Rituals of Confidentiality. Journalists have had to invent a variety of contracts with a confusion of labels to carry out their agreements of confidentiality with sources. They go by such names as "off the record," "without attribution," "for background only," and "on deep background."

Although often misunderstood and misinterpreted, "off the record" is the most common contract made between reporters and sources. It is supposed to mean that the information so embargoed cannot be published or broadcast, but frequently sources use it to mean they do not want to be identified with the information, which is what "without attribution" means to most journalists. And if that were not confusing enough, sources sometimes say that things are off the record when it is impossible for them to be so — such as a speaker at a public meeting of scores of people who asks that his very public remarks be "off the record." That speaker obviously does not know the meaning of the term. Off the record has become fashionable, says Robert Scheer, *Los Angeles Times* reporter (interview, 25 Nov. 1980). "Ask a guy on the street what time it is and he says, 'Off the record, it's 4:30.' "

That is why Scheer and most other reporters question sources when they ask for something to be off the record. Many times the source really means "Don't quote me" or "Don't use my name." And sometimes the source wants only part of what he or she is saying to be off the record.

Reporters who accept off-the-record information — some walk away if they are not able to get the source to cancel the embargo — usually honor it. But they generally find a way to get the information out. One way is to use it as a lead to ask questions of other sources who reply for the record. Another is to go back to the original source after circumstances have changed to see whether the information cannot now be put on the record.

Occasionally a journalist will violate an off-the-record pact, as did Claude Lewis, editor and publisher of the *National Leader*. The case involved Dom Manno, a twenty-three-year-old columnist for the student newspaper at the University of Pennsylvania, who shocked Philadelphia by writing that he hoped President Reagan would die from the shots he received in the 1981 assassination attempt. As associate editor of the late *Philadelphia Bulletin,* Lewis tried to reach Manno by telephoning the student newspaper but ended up talking "off the record" to another Penn student staff member who, in the course of the conversation, "expressed agreement with the proposition that 'President Reagan should be killed,'" Lewis wrote in his column. Lewis said he violated "this man's trust" because "I owe more allegiance to the president and the country than to people who hide behind the very freedoms we value, in order to express ideas that threaten us all."[17] Lewis said some months later he felt it would have been more unethical to have hidden from his readers what the Penn student told him than it was to break the off-the-record agreement (interview, 17 Sept. 1981).

"For background only" describes the arrangement when public officials or sources outside the government call in a group of reporters to brief them on some subject of public or at least news interest. The understanding in such briefing sessions can vary but it usually means that the briefer is not to be identified directly with the information. The State Department uses this device to provide background information to reporters assigned to cover that agency. It is commonly used to background reporters on impending federal and state budgets. Sometimes reporters set up the "for background only" sessions and invite public figures as high as the president to meet with a group of them and talk "without attribution."

"On deep background" came into the general language when Woodward used it to persuade Deep Throat to help him and Bernstein expose the Watergate scandal. Woodward "promised he would never identify him or his position to anyone. Further, he agreed never to quote the man, even as an anonymous source. Their discussions would be only to confirm information that had been obtained elsewhere and to add some perspective."[18]

One offshoot of the background briefing is the "leak," the word applied to information given to journalists that is not available to them through ordinary channels. That sort of thing happens when some person who is privy to private information decides, for one reason or another, to share that information with the world by feeding it to a single journalist or a small group of them. Sometimes the leaker is a government or political employee upset about what his agency or organization is doing. Some of Woodward and Bernstein's sources were disgruntled employees. Sometimes the leaker is a public official of some stature, who wants certain information out without having to have its release pinned on him or her.

These rituals have more meaning in the journalism of the nation's capital than anywhere else in the country. They come out of the relationships that have developed over the years between high-level politicians and high-level journalists. The skill of participants on both sides may account for their complicated arrangements, as with chess players who no longer play checkers because the game is too simple. When Henry Kissinger was secretary of state, he often slipped information to reporters who covered him that they were free to use as long as Kissinger was not specifically named as the source. There were often good diplomatic reasons for his desire not to be identified with certain information the public ought to have. But some in the business who knew this was going on wondered whether Kissinger's motives were always that pure, whether he did not sometimes use the journalists to help him with personal and political skirmishes in the Washington bureaucracy. Perhaps that was on Roger Mudd's mind when a later secretary of state, Alexander Haig, decided to talk to some reporters on a background basis and Mudd told listeners of the NBC Nightly News after a segment on Poland:

> Incidentally, a senior official who travels aboard Secretary of State Haig's airplane frequently said last night he will try to be more careful about his anti-Soviet statements because they might hurt Poland. The senior official wouldn't let his name be used, but he didn't say anything about hints. He has a brother who is a Jesuit priest; he once worked for Richard Nixon; he used to be a four-star general; and he recently said at the White House, "I am in control here."[19]

Washington Post editor Bradlee tried about 1970 to get the Washington press corps to boycott so-called backgrounders. Some of the big media went along, but not enough. As National News Council adviser Norman Isaacs recalls it, the boycott lasted only three or four weeks because "Bradlee was getting his brains beat out by the *New York Times,* which has always been the confidential source belt for Washington." (Interview, 7 Oct. 1981.) Bradlee believes the boycott would have worked if the *Times* had joined in — "we could have shut them down," he claims (interview, 5 June 1981). William J. Small supported the boycott as chief of the Washington bureau of CBS News then, but he says that "in the end we couldn't do it. All of our reporters felt handcuffed." (Interview, 5 Oct. 1981.) *New York Times* editor Abe Rosenthal agrees with Bradlee and Small that reporters and their news organizations "can be taken advantage of by backgrounders," but he believes reporters should still go to them (interview, 7 Oct. 1981). "They should have no obligation to write about the backgrounders if they turn out to be self-serving," Rosenthal adds. "I profited from many of them when I was a reporter, but I'm sure I was used many times."

Being used. That is what bothers journalists about arrangements that restrict their ability to tell the whole story — not just what was said, but who said it and why. As you can see from this discussion, however, journalists have entered into such arrangements, and some have even gone to jail rather than break their promises to keep certain sources secret.

WHAT THE CODES SAY

The codes of ethics of national journalism organizations do not have much to say about the kind of source relationship problem that Laura Foreman got involved in, although they undoubtedly assume that their conflict of interest prohibitions would include not sleeping with sources. Nor do many of the codes of individual media specifically discuss entanglements with news sources. Not surprisingly, one code that does deal with that problem is the one at Foreman's old paper, the *Philadelphia Inquirer,* which holds that "a staff member should not write about or photograph or make news judgments about any individual related to him or her by blood or marriage or with whom the staff member has a close personal or romantic relationship." The only national organization code that even touches on the Foreman-type problem is the APME code, which says under its Conflicts of Interest section: "The newspaper and its staff should make every effort to be free of obligations to news sources and special interests."

All of the national organization codes do deal, however, with the secret source issue, and all support the need for confidentiality with various qualifications. Here are the appropriate provisions:

From the APME: "News sources should be disclosed where ever possible. When it is necessary to protect the confidentiality of a source, the reason should be explained."

From the ASNE: "Pledges of confidentiality to news sources must be honored at all costs, and therefore should not be given lightly. Unless there is clear and pressing need to maintain confidences, sources of information should be identified."

From the RTNDA: "Broadcast journalists ... acknowledge the journalist's ethic of protection of confidential information and sources, and urge unswerving observation of it except in instances in which it would clearly and unmistakably defy the public interest."

From the SPJ-SDX: "Journalists acknowledge the newsman's ethic of protecting confidential sources of information."

Among codes and policies adopted by newspapers, news services, and broadcast stations and networks, the policy on anonymous sources of the *Louisville Times* and *Courier Journal* has been copied by many in the field. Issued on January 15, 1976, that policy reads:

> There has been increasing concern recently, both in and out of the building, about the use of anonymous sources in news stories.
>
> The concern revolves around these points:
>
> 1. The practice can be unfair to the reader. He doesn't know how much faith he should put in what an anonymous source is saying. One possible result of this is the erosion of our credibility.
>
> 2. It can be particularly unfair if the anonymous source is allowed to attack the credibility, character or motives of someone named in the story. The person being attacked — by name — has little or no defense from his unidentified attacker.
>
> 3. A news source sometimes will say something under the cloak of anonymity which he would not have the courage to say if he was being quoted by name. In most cases, he shouldn't be allowed to do this.
>
> 4. Occasionally, the use of anonymous sources can be a shortcut for the reporter, although not necessarily a desirable one.
>
> There is no denying that under some circumstances the use of anonymous sources is a legitimate journalistic tool. There are stories, particularly investigative ones, that would not be published if it were not for anonymous sources. However, we must exercise extreme caution.
>
> From now on, these guidelines should be followed when a reporter wishes to use an anonymous source in a story. They refer primarily to staff-written stories but should be applied whenever possible to wire stories as well.
>
> — The reason for the source's anonymity should be explained in the story as fully as possible without revealing the source's identity. (If the reason isn't a good one, then the source shouldn't be quoted.)
>
> — Information from an anonymous source should ordinarily be used only if at least one other source substantiates the information.
>
> — A supervising editor should be consulted every time an anonymous source is going to be quoted.
>
> — We should avoid letting anonymous sources attack someone's

character or credibility. If, in a rare instance, it is necessary to do so, we should not print the assertion without first giving the victim a chance to respond.

Because of Deep Throat and the Janet Cooke episode, it is interesting to note this attribution of sources section in the ethics and standards code executive editor Benjamin Bradlee has written for the *Washington Post:*

> This newspaper is pledged to disclose the source of all information unless disclosure would endanger the source's security. When we agree to protect a source's identity, that identity will not be made known to anyone outside *The Post.*
>
> Before any information is accepted without full attribution, reporters must make every reasonable effort to get it on the record. If that is not possible, reporters should consider seeking the information elsewhere. If that in turn is not possible, reporters should request an on-the-record reason for restricting the source's identity, and should include the reason in the story.
>
> In any case, some kind of identification is almost always possible — by department or by position, for example — and should be reported.[20]

The *Philadelphia Inquirer* shows concern about being used by secret sources in its news coverage policy:

> *The Inquirer* and its readers are best served when news sources are identified by name. Reporters should try very hard to present no information that they cannot attribute. On those occasions when an unnamed source is used, the news value should clearly warrant it, and every effort should be made to corroborate the source's statement through documents or other, attributed statements. Particular care should be taken to avoid permitting an anonymous source to use *The Inquirer* to attack an individual or organization.

The Operating Standards of NBC News see confidential sources as an important journalistic tool because "vital information, which serves the public's right to know, can be, and has been, obtained from sources who insist as a condition for furnishing the information, that their anonymity be protected." But NBC urges its reporters to try to find on-the-record sources for the same information to verify it if it is to be used. Unlike most of the other codes and policy statements dealing with confidentiality, the NBC Operating Standards dare to look into the jail cell:

> An employee who refuses to comply with outside requests to disclose the identity of a source may personally face legal proceedings, fines and jail sentences. In these circumstances, whether or not

to identify the source is a *personal* decision that must be made by the employee with no suggestions or directives by NBC News. However, if the employee refuses to identify the source (and this is a long-standing journalistic tradition and practice with which NBC News fully agrees), NBC News will support the employee fully in any resultant proceedings. This support will include journalistic guidance from NBC News management and legal guidance from the NBC Law Department. In addition, if the employee wishes to retain outside legal counsel, NBC News will pay the fees of such counsel after it and the employee have agreed on the need for, and the choice of, such counsel.

Lou Boccardi, executive editor and vice-president of the AP, worries about the loss of credibility with the public when nameless sources are used. In a policy memorandum to all of the domestic and foreign bureaus on 27 February 1981, Boccardi told AP staffers: "When someone asks not to be identified, ask them why and say so in the story. This is one very effective way to curb a practice that has grown up at the expense of OUR credibility, not that of the sources."

Isolating the problems evolving from the relationships between reporters and their sources as we have done in this chapter, we can see that secret sources seem to be the thorniest. Journalists appear to agree that there are times when granting secrecy to certain sources is the only way to get vital information, but there is less agreement on what level of threat to an individual or to society is required before secret sources can be justified, or whether there has to be any threat at all. There is a widespread belief in the news business that confidentiality is being given too readily, and that the public suspects information that is not pinned to specific sources. For credibility's sake, journalists need to work harder to get all information on the record.

The other reporter-source problems this chapter has examined are also important. The conflicts of interest that arise when reporters and news sources become too friendly are obvious evils. Reporters have to be wary of falling into cozy relationships with sources that inhibit their ability to be truthful in what they report from and about such sources. And treating sources as adversaries may be necessary in a Watergate-type situation in which sources try to lie to the public, but reporters have to be cautious about loosing their aggression on sources not deserving of that treatment. Aggressive reporting does not require the abandonment of civility.

Deception, Misrepresentation

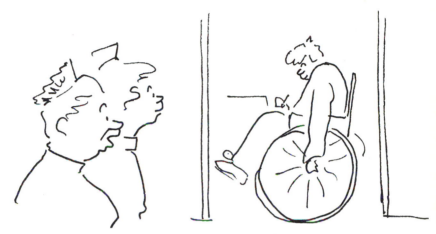

"Pretend you don't notice him — but make sure he knows how to spell your name right."

IMAGINE THAT YOU ARE EXECUTIVE EDITOR of this metropolitan daily newspaper. A veteran reporter on your staff has been doing an exhaustive study of the prison system in the United States. Now he wants to pass himself off as a criminal and spend a few days in some big state penitentiary to find out what it's like from the inside. This, of course, will mean that he will have to deceive some people because if the warden knows who he is, he will get special treatment, and if the other inmates know who he is, his life may not be worth a plugged nickel. But the reporter believes he can arrange to get himself incarcerated without the people at the prison knowing he is really a journalist.

Do you approve of your reporter posing as a criminal for a few days? Assuming that you can be satisfied that his security will be assured, do you tell him to go ahead with his plan to get himself falsely committed to a state prison? Does it bother you that he will not be able to identify himself as a reporter, that he will be carrying off a masquerade?

That is the kind of problem that confronted the editors of the *Washington Post* in 1971 when Ben H. Bagdikian wanted to get inside the

Huntingdon State Correctional Institution in Pennsylvania as a criminal, not as a visiting reporter. He had spent months investigating American prisons and jails, inspecting dozens of them and interviewing scores of prisoners, but he did not feel he could truly describe the psychological effect of being inside. Bagdikian did get himself committed as "Benjamin Barsamian," a prisoner awaiting grand jury action for murder, and he spent six days in the maximum security penitentiary in Central Pennsylvania. It was not easy getting in. He arranged it through the state attorney general and only the attorney general, his deputy, and the head of a confidential state police unit knew Bagdikian was a *Washington Post* reporter. No one at Huntingdon prison knew him as anyone but the prisoner two state policemen delivered in handcuffs as a "transfer" from a distant county jail. Bagdikian knew that the false identification was essential because if other inmates suspected that he was not a real prisoner, they would automatically assume he was a planted informer, "an occupation with high mortality rates." The warden and Bagdikian's fellow inmates did not learn his true identity until five weeks after his release when he described his experiences inside Huntingdon in the second of eight articles published in the *Post* under the label, "The Shame of the Prisons."[1]

Ironically, the executive editor of the *Post* at that time was Benjamin C. Bradlee, who seven years later would lead the successful fight on the Pulitzer advisory board to deny a 1979 Pulitzer Prize to the *Chicago Sun-Times* because that paper's entry had used deception. Bradlee and other prominent editors who sided with him thus turned what is known in the news business as undercover reporting into a major ethical issue.

Bagdikian says that back in 1971 Bradlee "did not disapprove of my passing myself off as a criminal. . . . The chief concern was security not the ethics of it." And Bagdikian, who teaches journalism ethics as professor of journalism at the University of California at Berkeley, still believes there was nothing unethical in his undercover reporting of life inside Huntingdon prison. "I believe that testing institutions that affect the public is one of the legitimate functions of journalism, so long as the test is of something important and it is done honestly," Bagdikian contends.

> The important thing in this case was not to alter the scene I was reporting, and then report this normal scene as accurately as I could. . . . If the warden knew I was a reporter, there isn't any question that he would have taken pains to place me in an untypical position for what he would conceive to be my own safety. If the prisoners had known I was not a real prisoner, either they would have acted abnormally with me or killed me as a suspected informer.

When Bagdikian ran into the warden at a conference on prisons some months after his article was published, the warden accused him "of unethical behavior, of coming into his prison under false pretenses." Bagdikian says he tried to explain, but the warden was too angry. "No warden or administrator likes to think he was spied upon for public use," Bagdikian adds. "In fact, I was pretty uncritical of Huntingdon because I had, from my past research, known that compared to most maximum security prisons it was one of the better ones, except for its size."[2]

Bradlee's opposition to undercover reporting seems to have its roots in the exposure by the news media of the Watergate scandal of the Nixon era, an exposure in which his newspaper played the leading role. "In a day in which we are spending thousands of man hours uncovering deception, we simply cannot deceive," Bradlee has said. "How can newspapers fight for honesty and integrity when they themselves are less than honest in getting a story? When cops pose as newspapermen, we get goddamn sore. Quite properly so. So how can we pose as something we're not?"[3] Although the Bradlee-authored standards and ethics section of the *Washington Post Deskbook on Style* makes no mention of undercover reporting and does not specifically prohibit using deception or misrepresentation to get a story, Bradlee insists that it is his paper's policy "not to deceive people." Asked to relate that policy to Bagdikian's masquerade and to a 1981 series in the *Post* by Neil Henry based on his posing as a vagrant, Bradlee explains that a "better statement of our policy" would be that "we do not lie about our profession, but we don't waste time telling everybody what our profession is."[4]

The *Chicago Sun-Times* entry that lost out in the special reporting category of the 1979 Pulitzer competition because of questions about its deceptive methods was regarded in the field as the ultimate in undercover reporting. In order to find out about reported shakedowns of small businesses by government inspectors in Chicago, the *Sun-Times* went into the tavern business. Reporters Pamela Zekman and Zay N. Smith posed as a couple from out of town and bought a tavern they decided to call the "Mirage." With help from Chicago's private, muckraking Better Government Association (BGA), Zekman and Smith operated the tavern in much the same way as the federal law enforcement agencies operate their so-called stings, providing opportunities for lawbreakers to break the law under surveillance. It worked. Scores of electrical and building inspectors were indicted for soliciting bribes to overlook deficiencies. The state set up a special tax auditing team, called the Mirage unit, to uncover tax fraud by accountants for restaurants, bars, and other cash businesses. The *Sun-Times* rocked Chicago with four weeks of exciting, dramatic articles by Zekman and Smith, illustrated with pictures taken by *Sun-Times* photographers from a concealed hideaway built above the ladies' and men's rooms. But the Pulitzer Prize went elsewhere — to reporters Gilbert A. Gaul and Elliot G. Jaspin of the *Pottsville* (Pennsylvania) *Republican* for a story about how a group linked to organized crime destroyed a coal operation. The Gaul-Jaspin effort did not involve any undercover reporting.[5]

Newspapers the size of the *Pottsville Republican* do not often do undercover reporting. The method is usually employed by reporters in larger cities, particularly those in competitive situations. The results of undercover reporting are often dramatic and exciting; they make good reading and viewing.

Undercover reporting — investigating something by having a reporter or reporters pass themselves off as insiders — is but one form of deception practiced by journalists, past and present. Reporters sometimes feel it is necessary to make their sources believe they are people other than reporters. Such misrepresentation can be as innocent as not identifying yourself and letting your source assume you are just another member of the public (as consumer reporters commonly do when they are doing price comparisons). Or it can be as devious as misrepresenting yourself to a source as a police officer, a coroner, or some other official whose questions are more apt to be answered than those of reporters.

An Honorable Tradition? Undercover reporting was not invented by the *Chicago Sun-Times*. It goes back at least to the 1890s when Nellie Bly (her real name was Elizabeth Cochrane) pretended to be insane in order to find out how patients were treated in the Blackwell's Island Insane Asylum. Her three articles for the old *New York World* were headlined "Ten Days in a Mad-house."[6]

And it is easy to find all sorts of undercover reporting going on in the 1930s, perhaps stimulated by the competition for dwindling depression dollars. Nellie Bly's inside report on a mental institution was repeated by the old *Chicago Times* in 1933 when it allowed one of its reporters to pose as mentally ill so that he could be voluntarily committed to the state mental hospital at Kankakee, Illinois, by another reporter posing as his brother. When the reporter was released by his "brother" a week later, he wrote about the dreadful conditions he had seen inside. His article was headlined "Seven Days in a Madhouse." Silas Bent, writing about this undercover report, said that it caused the *Times*'s circulation to go up considerably "but that was of minor importance in comparison with a drastic cleanup of the institution."[7] One of Nellie Bly's modern-day copiers is Doug Struck of the Baltimore *Sun*, who conned his way into the Crownsville (Maryland) Hospital Center, a mental institution. He wrote about the jaillike conditions he found during his six days as a patient there in a series of articles in the Annapolis *Evening Capital* headlined "Inside Crownsville."[8]

When the *Chicago Sun-Times* in 1980 exposed so-called accident swindlers — victims who fake injuries to collect insurance damages that they share with lawyers, doctors, and nurses who aid them — it may not have been aware that a precedent for that type of journalistic investigation had been set by Hearst's *San Francisco Examiner* in 1933. The *Examiner* reporter posed as an automobile accident victim to collect damages, just as *Sun-Times* reporters did in their investigation. The *Examiner* reporter's fake spinal cord injury enabled him to expose a racket that cost two doctors and two hospital orderlies their jobs and brought suspensions of two other physicians and eleven ambulance drivers and hospital stewards.[9]

When journalism historian Frank Luther Mott started collecting the best news stories and publishing them in a book each year, undercover reports were frequently included. The best news stories of 1934, for example, contained an exposé of the Drake estate swindlers that Arville Schaleben of the *Milwaukee Journal* did by pretending he was a prospective investor, and a description of what it is like being a transient and spending the night in a shelter for homeless men that William M. Pinkerton wrote for the *Omaha World-Herald.*[10]

If the Mott collections had continued, they undoubtedly would have reprinted some later-day examples of undercover reporting. A couple of investigations by *Newsday* should have made it. Back in 1953, a *Newsday* reporter, with the help of a judge, got himself sentenced to the Suffolk County jail on Long Island as a "burglar." He spent three months behind bars and when he came out he wrote a series detailing life in that particular jail, and reporting on the bribery, drug sales, and other illegal activity that went on there. And in the early 1970s, Robert W. Greene headed an investigative team at *Newsday* that produced a series on heroin imports that is still a model of team and undercover reporting. Greene tells of posing in France as a lawyer, even forging business cards and files, "to track down a high ranking official of the French secret service who had imported nearly ten tons of heroin into the United States." (Interview, 6 Oct. 1981.)* Greene says that what he did was the only and the most effective way to get his story, "and I'd do the same thing again tomorrow."

The Pulitzer Prize, despite what happened in 1979, has gone to undercover reporters. Edgar May of the *Buffalo Evening News* won a Pulitzer in 1961 for articles based on his taking a job as a social worker. Ten years later, the *Chicago Tribune* won a Pulitzer for a series by

---

*See list of interviewers following Notes.

William Jones reporting on collusion between police and private ambulance companies that he learned about by working as an ambulance driver.[11] The New York *Daily News* got a Pulitzer in 1974 for a series exposing doctors who were overcharging the Medicaid program that was done by a reporter and photographer posing as Medicaid patients with the knowledge and cooperation of New York Medicaid officials. Zekman, whose work on Mirage for the *Chicago Sun-Times* caused such a flap on the Pulitzer advisory board, shared in two Pulitzer Prizes for stories that were based on undercover reporting when she worked across Michigan Avenue on the *Chicago Tribune*. The first of these was in 1973 for a series on vote fraud that was done by reporters who posed as election judges, and the second was in 1976 for an exposé of abuses in two area hospitals, which were closed down as a result. She and other members of the investigative team at the *Tribune* learned about the abuses by working incognito at the two hospitals (interview, 8 Sept. 1981).

The Turn Around on Mirage. So why did the *Sun-Times* suddenly come up empty handed in Pulitzer competition for using methods that apparently had not handicapped entrants before 1979? The general answer seems to be that particularly since Watergate many of journalism's leaders have begun to question the use of deception and other "shady" methods to get news stories. They wonder aloud how journalists can point accusing fingers at the misbehavior of politicians and others in public life if journalism's own house is not in order. The more specific answer to the turnaround on the *Sun-Times* case is that there happened to be a number of those questioning editors among the fifteen on the 1979 Pulitzer advisory board, which makes the final selections after juries of journalists have narrowed the entries to the "best" in each of the various categories.

That predisposition against honoring undercover reporting continued to dominate the thinking of Pulitzer board members into the eighties. In 1982 the board again rejected the first choice of its jury in the public service category — a sixteen-part series by Merle Linda Wolin in the *Los Angeles Herald Examiner* that exposed sweatshop conditions and exploitation of illegal immigrants in the garment industry in Southern California. Wolin went undercover as a Brazilian immigrant and worked in several shops to observe conditions firsthand. Shunning the recommendation of its jury, the board, as it has often done in the past, shifted an entry from another category and awarded the Pulitzer Prize for public service to the *Detroit News* for articles on brutality aboard navy ships. The *News* had entered the articles in the local investigative and special reporting category. The chairman of the public service jury that recommended the *Herald Examiner* series, John M. Lemmon, managing editor of the Baltimore *Evening Sun*, praised his jury's first choice as an "excellent piece of reporting." Although he has reservations about undercover reporting, Lemmon said that he believes there was no other way to get the story Wolin went after.[12]

The Mirage story was also the first choice of the special local reporting jury in 1979, according to Joseph W. Shoquist, managing editor of the *Milwaukee Journal*, who headed that jury (interview, 19 Oct. 1981). He says he saw "nothing unethical" in what the *Sun-Times* did. "It wasn't even deception in a literal sense," Shoquist adds, "because they owned and operated the bar."

Zekman argues that "there was nothing we did in that project that I wouldn't do again. . . . We knew it might be controversial because it was advancing undercover reporting one step farther, in that instead of working in a business we were going to own a business. Working in a bar would not have told us what we sought. You had to own the bar to find out whether businessmen were being extorted by building inspectors." (Interview, 8 Sept. 1981.)

The editor of the *Sun-Times*, Ralph Otwell, believes the Mirage series was the most successful of the many undercover investigations that his paper has been doing for at least forty years (interview, 9 Sept. 1981). "It reached the most people in a way that they related to what we learned," Otwell says of Mirage, "and it documented something that had always been a truism in Chicago but yet had never been documented by anybody to the extent that we did it." Otwell, who sees irony in the opposition to the Mirage entry on the Pulitzer board because it came from "editors who had sanctioned undercover reporting before," claims that the public supports the technique. He points to a 1980 telephone poll in the Chicago area that the *Sun-Times* commissioned. The poll showed 60 percent of the 603 respondents approved of reporters not identifying themselves as reporters in doing their investigations, 35 percent disapproved, and 5 percent said they were not sure. The poll, which was taken February 16-19, 1980, under the supervision of Virginia Dodge Fielder, then editoral research manager of the *Sun-Times*, showed an even higher public approval of using hidden cameras — 62 percent approved, 30 percent disapproved, and 8 percent were not sure. Here is how the respondents said they felt about other investigative reporting techniques: using hidden microphones — 54 percent approve, 40 percent disapprove, 6 percent not sure; using unnamed sources — 55 percent approve, 38 percent disapprove, 7 percent not sure; paying people for information or interviews — 45 percent approve, 46 percent disapprove, 9 percent not sure.[13]

Otwell credits the private, not-for-profit BGA for stimulating many of the investigative and undercover projects in Chicago's news media.

One of BGA's methods is to work with journalists to expose wrongdoing in the city; two BGA investigators ran the Mirage bar with Zekman and Smith, and the organization was fully credited in the *Sun-Times* articles.

The snub on the Pulitzer did not discourage the *Sun-Times* from undercover projects. It has done at least four major ones since Mirage, in addition to other investigations that did not have to go undercover.

One of the *Sun-Times* undercover projects since Mirage required reporters to get jobs in legal abortion clinics in Chicago. Zekman says they were trying to "take the first look at the quality of medical care in those clinics since abortions had been legalized." (Interview, 8 Sept. 1981.) Working in the clinics was the only way to find that out, she believes, because "records are confidential and the women who go to the clinics won't talk." Other projects put *Sun-Times* reporters in the roles of accident victims in order to expose insurance fraud, of relatives of terminally ill people to show how the funeral industry takes advantage of people, and of dance teachers to report on the psychological techniques studios used to rip people off. Zekman, who left the *Sun-Times* in 1981 to set up an investigative unit at WBBM-TV, Chicago, claims that those articles resulted in the closing down of one private hospital and seven Fred Astaire dance studios.

One of the Pulitzer advisory board members in both 1979 and 1982, Eugene C. Patterson, views undercover reporting as "a fashionable trend I don't like to see encouraged." Patterson, editor of the *St. Petersburg Times* and president of the Times Publishing Company, said the Mirage series caused a debate on the Pulitzer board. "Some expressed concern that by honoring such reporting, encouragement to other journalists to do likewise would result," he said. "My personal feeling was that hard work and shoe leather could have unearthed the sources necessary to do the Mirage story, and most other such undercover stories. And I further feel that the press as a whole pays a price in credibility when a newspaper that editorially calls for government in the sunshine and candor in business shows itself disposed to shade the truth or mask its motives in its own method of operation, short of some extraordinary circumstance that would require a policy decision by the editor."[14]

After the Pulitzer Board declined to give an award to an undercover reporting effort again in 1982, Patterson explained that he had made his position clear on that issue in 1979, and the majority of the board continued to agree with him.[15]

A CONTROVERSIAL METHOD

Journalists interviewed for this book were almost equally divided on whether journalists should report undercover. But hardly anybody endorsed or condemned the method without some qualification. Those who favor it do not believe that it should be done casually on virtually every story that comes along. Those who disapprove of it believe there might be some special and rare circumstance in which the method might ethically be used.

Newsday's Greene is a strong advocate of undercover reporting, although he would not pose as a cop and he believes reporters still have to get all the documents and statements they can "because that's complete reporting." (Interview, 6 Oct. 1981.) But suppose "you get an indication that patients in a mental hospital are getting beaten senseless and are being robbed," Greene suggests. "You do not go to the public relations man for the mental institution and say 'Tell me the story.' And if you try interviewing the mental patients, you end up with thirty statements from people who have been adjudged mentally incompetent. The only way is to take the statements, because they are supportive, but also put somebody in there to observe what is going on."

Zekman makes much the same point. Undercover reporting to her is "a much more valid way to get at the truth of things than any other technique there is." (Interview, 8 Sept. 1981). She contends she is

> much more comfortable about doing a series about a nursing home abusing patients on the basis of my own reporters' observations than on the basis of charges made by the families of the patients — who are not there, who have no way of knowng whether mother fell out of bed or was pushed out, whether mother was attacked and cut or whether she fell or whether another patient cut her. The family can't possibly know. They may be willing to go on the record, but what kind of responsible operation is it to take such statements and go with them alone?

Zekman also draws the line at posing as a doctor, nurse, lawyer, or law enforcement officer because her lack of qualifications might hurt someone. The only undercover roles she has taken, she says, are those that she is as qualified to assume as the people doing that work, and roles in which she is not hurting somebody.

The executive editor of the *Philadelphia Inquirer*, Eugene L. Roberts, believes the *Sun-Times* "got a bum rap" from the 1979 Pulitzer board (interviews, 28 May and 15 Sept. 1981.) "I thought they did a good job of informing the people and taking the proper safeguards," Roberts contends. The *Inquirer* under his editorhsip has not gone in for undercover reporting — its specialty is the blockbuster investigative report in which three to sixty reporters almost literally exhaust some subject — but he believes it can be done in a reputable way.

Michael J. Davies has authorized undercover reporting on the newspapers he directs, the *Kansas City Star* and *Times*, but he has

misgivings about the method (interview, 23 Oct. 1981). "The problem
with journalism is that it's an inexact science at best," Davies observes.
"A couple of years ago we decided that the only way anyone was going to
find out whether the federal bureaucracy is as inefficient as everyone
says it is was to have a reporter work and live as a federal employee." The
papers hired a reporter from California, but instead of reporting to the
newsroom, she took a civil service examination and got a job in the
Kansas City regional office of the Health, Education, and Welfare
department. "We told her not to lie but also not to volunteer who she was
or what she was doing," Davies recalls. "She worked sub rosa for about
four months and then wrote a series of stories that resulted in one official
being indicted for running a sideline business out of his federal office. She
also described much waste and inefficiency, but told of some good people
working there."

Paul Janensch, executive editor of the *Louisville Times* and *Courier-
Journal*, does not regard the methods used on the Mirage project as "out
and out unethical." (Interview, 19 Oct. 1981.) What the *Sun-Times* did
was "passive subterfuge as opposed to active," he concludes. "They didn't
solicit bribes or other illegal acts." Another justification for the Mirage
series, adds Janensch, who was a police reporter in Chicago in the early
1960s, was that "it exposed a system that had never been exposed that
way before."

Joining Bradlee and Patterson in opposing underground reporting is
A. M. Rosenthal, executive editor of the *New York Times*. "Reporters
should not masquerade," he said. "We claim First Amendment rights and
privileges, and it's duplicitous for us to then pass ourselves off as
something other than reporters. Saying you'll get a better story or
perform a valuable public service doesn't change anything. It's still
wrong."[16]

Maintaining that "you should never misrepresent yourself," Haynes
Johnson, reporter-columnist for the *Washington Post*, believes there is "no
need for masquerades" in American journalism (interview, 4 June 1981).
"You don't have to go undercover to uncover things," he holds. When he
covered civil rights all through the South, Johnson recalls, he never felt
(as some reporters did) that he had to pass for somebody he wasn't. "I
dressed exactly the same as I always do for work, I told people I talked to
exactly who I was," he explains. "If you want to establish trust with
sources, you've got to be absolutely straight and not pretend you're
somebody else. Tell them why you're there, what you're there for, what
your purpose is, what you intend to do with it."

The trouble with undercover reporting, in the view of Brit Hume,
Capitol Hill correspondent for ABC News and former investigative
reporter for columnist Jack Anderson, is that "the public sees it as dirty

pool." (Interview, 4 Nov. 1981.) Using a method that the public perceives as "dishonest or slippery" gives any offended subject "a powerful weapon with which to attack you."

Another broadcast journalist, Bill Kurtis of CBS News, worries about what underground reporting leads to (interview, 8 Sept. 1981). "You're working in this office incognito and there are these confidential medical documents in a file," Kurtis hypothesizes. "Do you take them out of the building — which is larceny — to keep or copy, telling yourself it's not really stealing because what you are taking are 'ideas,' not physical property? . . . What's next? Breaking and entering? Burglary? Going into a psychiatrist's files at night? It's the direction that this is all leading to that journalists should be worried about."

David Shaw, media reporter-critic for the *Los Angeles Times*, is another who is bothered by undercover reporting. Conceding that there are times when there may be no other way to get a vital story, Shaw believes undercover reporting is sometimes used because "it's much easier to do it that way." (Interview, 25 Nov. 1980.) He cites as an example of what is troublesome about this method a report on conditions in a mental hospital done by another *Los Angeles Times* staffer, Lois Timnick. She used a phony name and posed as a psychology graduate student to work for two weeks in the hospital. While there she signed an oath not to divulge information or records about patients, Shaw relates, but in her article she wrote about what was in patients' confidential records, using pseudonyms for their real names.

William E. Deibler, managing editor of the *Pittsburgh Post-Gazette*, discourages undercover reporting on his paper (interview, 22 Oct. 1981). For example, when it was proposed to him that one of the paper's young interns should pose as a volunteer and work in a hospital being struck by county workers, he said he would permit it only if officials knew she was doing it as a reporter. "That didn't work," Deibler says, so the intern was not sent in. "We as journalists have to be very careful to observe the law, and not even suggest that we are a privileged class," Deibler believes. "After all, we'd get very upset if persons applying for jobs on our newspapers deceived us."

Another who is uncomfortable with undercover reporting is Phil Currie, vice-president/news staff development for Gannett Company, who admits he has used that method a couple of times when he was reporting. "A reporter gets trapped in one set of lies after another. . . . And sources can say, 'Gee, you lied to me,' " Currie explains (interview, 22 Oct. 1981).

Claude Sitton, editor of the Raleigh *News & Observer*, does not like undercover reporting or any kind of misrepresentation, but he "can see the necessity for it in rare circumstances." (Interview, 4 Nov. 1981.) He tells of sending a reporter into the fields of eastern North Carolina to take a job as a migrant worker "because we had tried every other means of getting that story and hadn't succeeded." The reporter got the job and worked with a crew for a week, but "he went back to the crew chief before doing his story and told the crew chief who he was and got his comments."

Reporter George Williams of the *Sacramento Bee* went undercover in the early 1970s and almost did not come back. As *Bee* ombudsman Art Nauman recalls, Williams got himself admitted to the state mental health system after considerable preparation, learning such things as how to act mentally ill and how to take pills but not swallow them (interview, 2 Nov. 1981). He used his own name but did not say he was a *Bee* reporter. After Williams had been in the receiving ward in Sacramento for three days waiting to be sent to the Napa Valley State Hospital, a new managing editor opposed to deception came aboard at the *Bee*. One of the new editor's first acts, Nauman recalls, was to cancel the assignment and chastise the city editor who had made it. "We had a hell of a time getting the reporter extricated," Nauman says. "Since then we haven't had any undercover projects at the *Bee*."

Some Representative Cases. Although the *Chicago Sun-Times* specifically and Chicago journalism in general are what come first to the mind when undercover reporting is discussed, other newspapers have also added to the literature on this controversial subject. Here are some representative cases:

THE NASHVILLE *Tennessean*. The *Tennessean* wanted to uncover the resurgence of the Ku Klux Klan in northern Alabama. Editor and publisher John Siegenthaler assigned veteran reporter Jerry Thompson to infiltrate that violent, racist organization. For sixteen months in 1979-80, Thompson pretended to be a retired, divorced, and racist Army sergeant taking up residence in Birmingham. It took him a while to be accepted by Klansmen he deliberately befriended, but they did take him in and for more than a year he was actually a member of the Knights of the Ku Klux Klan. The reporter played his role until December 1980 when he left Birmingham and the KKK, returned to Nashville and his wife and four children, and started writing articles that Seigenthaler said "identified the twisted nature, the violent character, the false appeal of Klan philosophy."

Conceding that the assignment was dangerous for his reporter, Seigenthaler believes that Thompson's findings justified the risk:

> He saw firsthand how Klan leaders exploit racial incidents in any community in this country to their own purposes. He measured a new dimension of the Klan movement: the effort to include wives and children within the circle of KKK activities. He discovered that there

are those who are not Klan members who give support and money to the KKK out of sympathy for its racism. Most of all, he established that any time robed Klan members gather, high on emotional rhetoric or on some more substantive intoxicant, carrying loaded weapons beneath their robes, they become potential carriers of violence. As he reported, they are dangerous to any community where they assemble.

Seigenthaler said there are some who do not share his view of Thompson as a journalistic hero who "performed a great public service." Klan members, of course, attacked the articles as distorted, sensationalized, and unfair, the editor said, and there are also people — "including some within the media — who may question the ethical considerations involved in Thompson's assignment. He did, after all, misrepresent his true identity." Seigenthaler indicated that journalistic ethics are not clear on that matter and added that in any event "no association of journalists has rules that impose effective restraints against those who abrogate rules of conduct."[17]

THE PROVIDENCE *Journal Bulletin*. This newspaper was a finalist for the 1982 Pulitzer Prize in public service and won the 1981 public service award of the APME for papers with circulations of 50,000 or more for investigative reports by Bruce D. Butterfield that exposed unhealthy and unsafe working conditions in the Rhode Island jewelry industry. As part of his massive investigation over eighteen months, Butterfield went undercover to work in four jewelry factories in Providence to get a feel for what it was like inside. He says he decided he had to do that because his interviews with workers convinced him that often the manner in which work is done and the materials that are used is what made the work dangerous (interview, 18 Nov. 1982). "I needed to see that," Butterfield explains. The reporter got his jobs through an employment agency that supplied temporary labor for the jewelry industry. He used his own last name and his real middle name, Dick, to avoid possible recognition of his by-line (seen frequently in his paper for the ten years he had worked there). He used his real address and social security number. No one questioned that he was anything but a guy looking for a day's work for cash. Butterfield went back to the three factories in which he observed questionable practices to interview their owners. "I wanted to tell them I had worked there and what I saw," the reporter says. "I wanted them to clarify why some things were done the way they were. They all claimed their plants were meeting whatever minimum standards exist for that industry."

This project was the first time Butterfield had ever reported undercover. He does not favor that method generally because he believes "it's important for journalists to announce themselves and for people being quoted by name to know they are dealing with a journalist." But undercover reporting is justifiable to obtain vital additional information that cannot be gotten any other way, he holds.

It is interesting to note that the judges in this APME competition — all newspaper editors and past presidents of the organization — apparently did not rule out the Providence entry because of its use of undercover reporting for at least part of its investigation. One of the runners-up, the *Los Angeles Herald Examiner*, used that method to an even greater extent.

THE *Los Angeles Herald Examiner.* Merle Linda Wolin, Latin affairs reporter for the *Los Angeles Herald Examiner,* transformed herself into Merlina De Novais, a poor illegal Brazilian, to work in several sewing factories and report on sweatshop conditions in the garment industry of Los Angeles. She played this role off and on for eight months in 1980 to produce a sixteen-part series that won at least two national awards besides being a finalist in the 1981 APME and the 1982 Pulitzer Prize public service competitions. She also used conventional interviews with people in the garment industry and public officials.

Wolin says she had to talk her editors into letting her go inside the sewing shops as an illegal alien because they were afraid for her safety and skeptical that a fair-skinned reporter from Cheyenne, Wyoming, could pull it off (interview, 16 Nov. 1981). She knew she could not pass as a Mexican or Central American, where most of the Spanish-speaking Latins in the garment industry come from, because she speaks Spanish with a blurred French accent, French being her first foreign language. So she decided to pass herself off as an illegal alien from Portuguese-speaking Brazil, because few Brazilians do that kind of work and the fact that Portuguese was supposedly her native tongue would explain her strange Spanish accent. With the help of a Mexican-born colleague, Wolin selected her clothing from a discount department store where many Los Angeles Latins bought their clothes. She figured that her sewing skills, learned at home and in a 4-H club in Cheyenne, would get her by. And they did. When she worked in the shops, she would work nine to ten hours a day and then sneak back to the newspaper to put her notes into the computer.

Wolin, who has since joined the news staff of the *Wall Street Journal*, believes undercover reporting should not be used for every story and can be abused, but it was the only way she could "find out what the lives of garment workers were like and how they endured." She believes undercover reporting is "controversial, not to the public, but only in the minds of certain newspaper editors who in a way are copping out from not going that extra step to really get the story."

THE *Milwaukee Journal.* The *Journal* used five reporters posing as patients to investigate Medicaid in the Milwaukee area in 1977. The reporters first were given medical examinations to assure that they were in good health. One was also given a Medicaid card that the *Journal* had obtained "from a high state official whom the paper took into its confidence," managing editor Joseph W. Shoquist relates (interview, 19 Oct. 1981). After Surgical Blue-Shield Care, which administered the Medicaid program, was informed by the *Journal* that the paper would pay all his bills, the reporter with the Medicaid card went to six doctors complaining of a sore throat. Five doctors prescribed medication, including chest and neck x-rays, antibiotics, lozenges, aspirin, blood sampling and throat culture, urinalysis, and cough depressants. The sixth doctor, at a Milwaukee clinic, told the *Journal* reporter: "Frankly, I don't see anything wrong with you. If there is soreness, I would only recommend that you go home and gargle with warm salt water. There is no need for medication." The doctor who made the biggest fuss about the first reporter's unsore sore throat was then visited by the other four reporters, one at a time. They all paid cash and at a counter in his office bought the drugs the physician prescribed — an antibiotic for each of them, plus cough syrup with codeine for two, and a cough depressant for a third.

Shoquist says the doctor who told all five of the well reporters they were ill was the only one the paper named and photographed in its stories. "He was running a pill factory," Shoquist explains. "He had fifty people lined up in the street waiting for his office to open at 8 A.M. He'd give them any drug they asked for." After the *Journal* broke its Medicaid story, the State Medical Examining Board investigated all five doctors and went to court to charge the one the *Journal* had identified, who then fled to Cyprus, according to Shoquist. "We did a public service by putting a major drug abuser out of business in Milwaukee," the editor claims.

The National News Council investigated the *Journal*'s stories after the State Medical Society of Wisconsin charged the paper with "unethical conduct." The council unanimously found the complaint unwarranted, hesitating only over the charge in the complaint about the "apparently fraudulent Medicaid card." The council noted on this point that the *Journal* recognized that the possession of the card "was a subterfuge" and "explained publicly that it would pay whatever costs were involved." The reporter did nothing that called for criminal prosecution, the council decision said, quoting an assistant attorney general for the state as saying that no Wisconsin law was broken because no criminal intent, "deceiving with intent to reap personal gain," could be proved. So the council decided the subterfuge was appropriate in this case.[18]

GANNETT NEWS SERVICE. Somebody at the Strand Book Store made a terrible mistake sending a letter to the book editor of the *Milwaukee*

Journal, inviting him to sell his review books and promising confidentiality. Book editor Robert W. Wells turned the letter over to *Journal* managing editor Shoquist, who was then president of the APME. Shocked by its implications, Shoquist asked Richard B. Tuttle as chairman of APME's Professional Standards Committee to look into the matter. Tuttle, from his position in Gannett's corporate headquarters in Rochester, New York, worked out an arrangement for Michael Cordts, then a reporter for Gannett's morning newspaper in Rochester, the *Democrat & Chronicle*, to investigate the nation's largest used book store, the Strand of New York City. Before Cordts got through and his stories were distributed around the country through the Gannett News Service in 1979, several newspapers were embarassed to learn that their book editors had been selling complimentary review copies to the Strand and pocketing as much as $1,000 a month. Most newspapers consider such selling by staff members to be an improper use of their positions for personal gain.

How could Cordts be so sure of his facts? He worked for two weeks at the Strand as a $2.85 an hour clerk, and discovered crates of books from various book editors, with their names on the return address labels. He usually had to mention those crates to the book editors he called before they would admit they had been selling books to Strand. For that reason, Cordts believes his undercover work was justified.

Cordts, who left the Rochester paper to join the *Chicago Sun-Times*, quoted Strand managers in his stories as saying that they had been "buying books from hundreds of newspaper reviewers." Yet Cordts was able to name only ten newspaper book editors who were doing it. Either the book store sources exaggerated or Cordts needed to stay undercover for longer than fourteen days. Incidentally, he donated the $280.84 he was paid by Strand to the Reporters Committee for Freedom of the Press.

Of the ten book editors named in Cordts's stories, two lost their jobs almost immediately. Larry Swindell of the *Philadelphia Inquirer*, who drafted the section of the *Inquirer's* ethics code that prohibited the selling of review books, resigned. Terry Anderson of the *Denver Post* was fired. One of the ten — Nancy Grape, who covers politics and does book reviews on the side for the Lewiston, Maine, *Journal* — came through the crisis of the investigation without a scratch. Cordts quotes her editor, A. Kent Foster, as saying, "If she was paid for reviewing I'd consider the books the property of the newspaper. But she isn't paid so what she does with the books is her own business."

Newspaper editors who are aware of the problem (Cordts said only one of the ten he snared was) see to it that review books for the most part are donated to libraries or charities.[19]

THE *Wall Street Journal*. Several times in the last two decades, the distinguished *Wall Street Journal* has sent reporters into the bowels of American business and industry to find out how things work from the inside. They have done this as workers, not as reporters. One famous *Journal* undercover reporting project was done back in 1967 by a student intern from the University of Michigan, Roger Rappaport. He worked for two weeks on an automobile assembly line in a Ford plant in Detroit, producing what *Journal* managing editor Laurence O'Donnell calls "a terrific story that told us all about blue collar blues" long before assembly line problems were generally known and talked about (interview, 22 Feb. 1982). O'Donnell, who was Rappaport's editor as Detroit bureau manager then, says Ford officials told him later that they found out who Rappaport was three days after he was hired, but they did nothing because they did not want to create an incident in the midst of negotiations with the United Auto Workers.

The most significant undercover reporting project by the *Journal* since then, in O'Donnell's opinion, was a controversial look at a Texas Instruments (TI) plant in Austin in 1978. Reporter Beth Nissen, who has since left the *Journal* for a reporting job with *Newsweek*, got a job as a $2.93 per hour solderer on an assembly line in the Austin plant to try to find out how TI had warded off unionization. At the time TI was the third largest nonunion company in the United States after International Business Machines and Eastman Kodak. Her article told of the very tight security system in the plant and of the heavy pitch against unions in the company's orientation program for new workers. It also reported pleasant working conditions, but only average pay and benefits, which caused a large turnover that was a natural deterrent to union organizing efforts. Nissen deliberately talked about unions with her fellow employees, which caused most of them to shun her. They called her "that union chick from Detroit," and said the company would find some reason to fire her if she didn't cool it. Nissen reported that she had planned to work a month at the plant, but she was fired after three weeks because she had falsified her application form by omitting the fact that she was a college graduate.[20]

O'Donnell reports that after Nissen was dismissed, she went back to TI officials to tell them that she was a reporter and to get their side of the story, but instead of talking to her, they went to New York to protest to *Journal* editors (interview, 22 Feb. 1982). They talked to Ed Cony, vice-president for news of Dow-Jones & Company, publisher of the *Journal* and other newspapers. Texas Instruments tried to get Cony to kill Nissen's story (interview, 20 Oct. 1981). "They threatened to sue us for trespassing and perhaps other things," Cony recalls. "I told them I could understand how they would get upset at the methods we used, but that they should not jump to the conclusion that we were out to do an unfair story on them." He urged them to talk to Nissen, which they eventually did. But O'Donnell says that the reporter did not get much from the response of TI officials that was useful in her story. "They were so upset about the way the story was done that they did not respond to the issues raised by the reporter," O'Donnell concludes, noting that Nissen's story reported in the fourth paragraph that the company "strenuously objected to the way in which the story was obtained."

The *Journal* got "lots of letters after the Nissen story expressing a deep sense of outrage that we had given ourselves the right to do something nobody else could do," O'Donnell adds. Among journalists also there was criticism because of the way Nissen openly engaged fellow employees in talk about unions, perhaps jeopardizing their jobs.

The *Journal* has done a few other less significant undercover reports since the TI piece, O'Donnell notes, but the paper has a feeling of caution about the use of that method. "The climate is just all wrong for this kind of reporting," the managing editor explains. "People resent the special privilege that the press assumes for itself, and they really don't like the break-and-enter mentality that a lot of reporters have." He observes that the *Journal* still considers using undercover reporting but with the realization that some serious problems have to be faced. "The biggest problem is entrapment," O'Donnell warns. "People don't know who you really are when they bare their souls to you, and then you smear them by invading their privacy." And "you have to bend over backwards" to give the employers or public officials involved a chance to comment. "A second problem is how honest are you going to be with the readers about how you got the story," O'Donnell suggests. "You've got to tell them how the hell you got in there, and if you lied and cheated, you've got to tell them that. So you'd better be prepared to suffer some loss of prestige."

If the story is significant and there is no other way to do it, the *Journal* might resort to undercover reporting, O'Donnell says, "but the managing editor has to be involved from day one... and you have to have confidence in the integrity of your reporter."

Cony is equally cautious. "Deception is an uncomfortable technique to use," he believes. "Maybe sometimes the results are sufficiently in the public interest that you can make peace with your conscience, but as soon as you do, you are aware that throughout history a lot of people thought ends justified the means, and some terrible things happened as a result."

MISREPRESENTATION

Undercover reporting always involves some degree of misrepresentation by journalists to their sources. Even when journalists merely pose as members of the public, their motives are still to get a story, which sets them apart from other members of the public and results in their misrepresenting who they really are to the people they deal with while undercover. But as with most things, there are degrees of misrepresentation. And misrepresentation occurs in some conventional as well as undercover reporting.

The telephone changed news reporting in many ways, speeding up the process but also enlarging opportunities for inaccuracy and making it easier for reporters to misrepresent themselves to sources on the other end of the line. I recall with embarrassment showing my first journalism class a film on reporting that I had not screened, and watching with horror as the reporter picked up the phone in the pressroom to call someone involved in a crime and said, "Hello, this is O'Neill down at police headquarters." Thus was born a healthy caution about the use of audiovisual aids in teaching.

Ethical journalists do not try to make people believe they are cops. That stuff supposedly went out with Harry Romanoff, the legendary reporter for the old *Chicago American* who was called the "Heifetz of the newsroom" for the way he played the telephone. Legend has it that he would pose as a police officer, a coroner, or even a governor to get a story.[21] He once got the mother of mass murderer Richard Speck to talk to him by telling her he was Speck's attorney.[22] But although Romanoff has been dead since 1970, his methods live on. Craig Ammerman, who was New York City bureau chief for the AP when Elvis Presley collapsed, recalls that there was a thirty- to forty-minute period after the singer had been taken from his Memphis mansion in an ambulance when no one was able to get any information from police (interview, 27 May 1981). "A guy on my staff with a New York City voice called Memphis police and said he was Sergeant Kelly of the New York Police Department and was curious about what was going on. And they told him," Ammerman says. "We didn't use very much of what they told us, but we used it to confirm that Presley was dead and that he probably died of a drug overdose."

A variation of the Romanoff method is related by Les Whitten, novelist who was senior reporter on the Jack Anderson column for twelve years (interview, 2 Sept. 1981). Whitten tells of a colleague he heard telephoning from Robert Kennedy's political headquarters to someone in that organization and saying, "I'm calling from Bobbie Kennedy's headquarters here in Washington. What the hell's going on with such and such?" Whitten concedes that "the guy got a peach of a story but I thought what he did was very unethical."

Executive editor Roberts of the *Philadelphia Inquirer* believes reporters "have an obligation to get the news out . . . and not passively accept handouts and police rules in emergencies." (Interviews, 28 May and 15 Sept. 1981.) This can sometimes mean doing things to get across police cordons, "short of falsifying credentials or breaking into an office," Roberts adds. He remembers once when he was covering a murder case as a reporter for the Raleigh *News & Observer* that he picked up a stethoscope from a desk in a hospital and walked nonchalantly into the emergency room where police were questioning a suspect. No one stopped him as he went into the interrogation room and heard the suspect confess to police. "I didn't lie to anyone," Roberts says. "We're not obligated to wear a neon sign."

Roberts and other reporters who covered the tense South during the civil rights movement in the late 1950s and the 1960s often did not object to being mistaken for federal agents. It was safer that way. This meant dressing more stylishly than many reporters like to — coat, tie, and a hat — and it didn't hurt to stuff your notebook inside your coat in such a way that it might be taken for a shoulder harness for a gun. Claude Sitton, now editor of the Raleigh *News & Observer* but who, like Roberts, covered civil rights for the *New York Times,* remembers how he and a reporter for *Time* magazine were having a cup of coffee in a little Mississippi town when a fight broke out in the restaurant between some red necks and a group of freedom riders. They sat there in their Brooks Brothers suits, London Fog raincoats, and hats, and witnessed the whole thing. The next day, Sitton says, the local paper reported that the riot had been witnessed by two FBI agents (interview, 4 Nov. 1981).

There were times, though, when civil rights movement reporters did not want to look like federal agents. Roberts felt that reporters had a right to report what was going on in high schools that were being desegregated, even though local authorities would not let them in. So he would stash his "FBI clothes" in a bush somewhere, slip on a sweater and "blend in with the students." (Interviews, 28 May and 15 Sept. 1981.) Editor Tuttle of the Elmira, New York, *Star-Gazette* did the same thing when police blocked reporters from entering the University of Mississippi campus in the turmoil after James Meredith became that school's first black student (interview, 14 Oct. 1981). Tuttle, who was reporting for the *Miami Herald* then, says "that kind of posing does not bother me." And Sitton recalls that there were times when the only safe thing for a reporter to do was to "take off your shirt, roll it up and stomp on it, put it back on inside out, and go down and sit on the bank and chew grass."

In a more recent life-threatening news situation, Bill Kurtis of CBS News tells of moving through a market in Tehran with a camera crew the day after America's abortive mission to rescue the Iranian hostages (interview, 8 Sept. 1981). Kurtis says his guide and interpreter — after hearing whispers of, "They're Americans. Let's kill them." — suggested that Kurtis pretend to be French. "You bet!" Kurtis told him.

Misrepresentation may have saved Kurtis's life in Tehran, but another time it cost him a story. He went to Bangkok for WBBM-TV, Chicago, in 1981 to get a story about the illegal smuggling of animals into the United States. He reports that the woman who set up the deal for him told authorities that he was from an advertising agency. When he got there, he was not allowed to film. "I couldn't complain as a journalist would," Kurtis explains. "If I had been straight with this guy I would have been able to tell him that he was going to be indicted in Chicago as a co-conspirator — 'and if you're clean you'll let us in, and if you don't we'll go back and say you wouldn't let us in, and that will look bad for you.' But I was unable to do that. So I lost the story I came to get."

David R. Jones, national editor of the *New York Times*, recalls that when he was Pittsburgh bureau chief for the *Wall Street Journal* he slipped a reporter into a union meeting unrecognized. Jones himself could not get in; he had to wait outside because he was known to officials of the United Steel Workers union. "My reporter wore a sports coat that day and just walked into the meeting," Jones relates. "If he had been asked, he would have identified himself as a reporter and probably been thrown out of the meeting, but he wasn't asked." Jones believes that it is unethical for a reporter to pose as someone else, "but you don't have to announce yourself. A reporter should be able to go anywhere an ordinary citizen can go and not wear a press card in his hat." (Interview, 7 Oct. 1981.)

Claude Lewis, editor and publisher of the *National Leader*, would not misrepresent himself over the telephone, but he recalls slipping on a white coat a couple of times to get a story (interview, 17 Sept. 1981). Once he did that to pass as a physician in order to get into a hospital room to interview a patient for the Philadelphia *Bulletin*. He found that the man, who was being held for shooting himself and about eight people in Cherry Hill, New Jersey — killing some and injuring others — was being held in the same recovery room with many of his victims. Another time, working for *Newsweek* in the sixties, he and other reporters were trying to find out what was going on in a New York hotel room in which the owner of a major league baseball franchise was negotiating with some people to sell the team. When the people in the room sent down for some food and a waiter rolled up with a food tray, Lewis talked him into letting him don his jacket and take the food into the room where he got some idea of what was happening. "I just stood around and listened for a while," Lewis recalls. "I was a natural part of the scene — you know, a black guy with a tray."

About thirty police officers were discharged or suspended after Alex Dobish, reporter for the *Milwaukee Journal*, got an interview with a woman who claimed she had been taken out of her jail cell to a police stag party where she was forced to perform sexual acts on the stage with several policemen. Dobish got the interview by putting on a good suit, picking up his briefcase, and striding confidently into the hospital where the woman was being held. He did not say who he was, but hospital officials must have assumed he was a lawyer because they let him go to the woman's room. Dobish's managing editor, Joe Shoquist, says he both "reprimanded and complimented" the reporter (interview, 19 Oct. 1981).

A good illustration of how opinion divides among journalists on misrepresentation, whether it be active or passive, is provided by Gene Roberts and his counterpart at the *New York Times*, executive editor Abe Rosenthal. Both of them had reporters recently who donned coveralls to get close to airplanes involved in news stories. Rosenthal chastised a new reporter who tried to pass as an airline mechanic to get near the plane in which the wife of defecting Soviet ballet star Alexander Godunov was being detained.[23] When an enterprising *Inquirer* reporter put on a similar costume and succeeded in getting into a hijacked plane being held at the Philadelphia airport, Roberts not only approved; he gave the reporter a bonus (interviews, 28 May and 15 Sept. 1981).

Some Lesser Deceptions. Some types of misrepresentation and deception are acceptable even on papers with ironclad "no masquerading" rules such as the *New York Times*. Restaurant reviewers, consumer reporters, and travel writers find it more honest to be a little dishonest sometimes.

Restaurant critics who want to avoid any special treatment they might receive if the restaurant knows it is being reviewed usually hide their identities. If they make reservations, they do so in some other name. David Shaw, media reporter-critic for the *Los Angeles Times,* observes that to avoid being recognized some critics wear funny hats or wigs, eyeglasses one time but not another, go with different people each time, or deliberately show up ten minutes late so that the rest of the party is already seated (interview, 25 Nov. 1980).

Elaine Tait, restaurant critic for the *Philadelphia Inquirer*, tries hard to keep from being known, but "more important than all that cloak and dagger stuff is knowing what you're doing — being informed, honest, and sober." She never drinks wine with her meals when she is reviewing "because I need to be as sharp as I can." (Interview, 12 Nov. 1981.) Although most newspapers and magazines never run photographs of their restaurant reviewers, the *Philadelphia Inquirer* and the *Detroit News* run promotion ads with pictures of their reviewers. Tait says she "sort of objects" to her picture being used but she doubts that many people would recognize her because newspaper pictures are "so one dimensional." She says that if she senses she is known in some restaurant, she orders prepared food (such as the soup of the day) and other things that cannot be whipped up at the last minute.

Reporters trying to find out how consumers are treated by various kinds of retail businesses almost invariably do their checking as ordinary customers and not as reporters. Most, however, identify themselves as reporters to get comments from owners and managers after they have done their research. This not only helps balance their stories; it ameliorates any feeling among the retailers who have been checked that they have somehow been taken advantage of.

Responsible travel writers — there are plenty of the other kind as we learned in Chapters 3 and 4 — often find it best to travel as ordinary citizens. Alfred S. Borcover, editor of the travel section of the *Chicago Tribune* and a former two-term president of the SATW, has sent writer Kermit Holt on a number of tours incognito. In 1981, for example, Holt signed up for one of those whirlwind budget trips to Europe — nine or ten countries in twelve or fourteen days. His report showed both goods and bads, Borcover says, and the tour company wrote to them later saying that it was trying to correct the problems Holt had noted (interview, 10 Sept. 1981). A year or so earlier, Holt signed up for one of the first tours of China, not as a travel writer but as just another tourist. "Craig Clairbourne may have taken a gourmet tour of China," Borcover notes, "but our man, who traveled the way most Americans will have to travel to China, found the food was not so hot."

WHAT THE CODES DON'T SAY

The codes of ethics and standards of national journalism organizations do not specifically deal with undercover reporting, deception, and misrepresentation, but some of the policy statements of individual news organizations do. The Operating Standards of NBC News, for example, state that "misrepresentations by NBC News personnel (of their identity or of any other material fact), even though intended solely to expedite an investigation, are generally *not* necessary and should be avoided." It goes on to say that in those "isolated and infrequent situations" in which concealing your identity seems necessary, an appropriate executive should be consulted.

Similarly, ABC News cautions its reporters not to "disguise their identity or pose as someone with another occupation without the prior approval of ABC News management." An example of a permissible disguising of identity, ABC News states, is the story that has become almost a cliché of local TV news — a reporter taking an automobile in good repair to various repair shops to see who's naughty and who's nice.

Two recent books on investigative reporting address the problems of reporters misrepresenting themselves or deceiving people. In their chapter on the "Ethics of Investigative Reporting," David Anderson and Peter Benjaminson, investigative reporters for the *Detroit Free Press*, suggest that posing as someone else is frequently necessary even if it is dishonest. They write:

> The reporter is often left in the classic ethical dilemma: He's damned if he does and damned if he doesn't. By lying to the double-dealing official, the reporter will shock many people's ethical sensibilities. But if the story doesn't appear, that corrupt official will continue to enrich himself at public expense.
>
> Most reporters use deceptive methods to gather information — on the theory that in a democracy the public's right to information outweighs a public official's right to expect complete candor from journalists. Deceptive methods are justified, however, only when greater harm will be done the public if the information remains concealed than the harm done individuals by its publication. A reporter should never resort to questionable methods if the information can be obtained in any other way.
>
> In those cases which are difficult to judge, most reporters tend to err on the side of dishonesty to obtain the information. The underlying assumption is that society has more to gain from an accurate, thorough reportage of events than it has to lose from the discomfort of the corrupt. Most professional journalists would prefer not to find themselves in a position of withholding important information from their readers simply to avoid worrying about their own personal ethics. Their overriding goal is to inform the public.[24]

Clark R. Mollenhoff is more specific in his guidelines. The veteran investigative reporter turned journalism professor sets down seven basic rules for investigative reporters that assure ethical conduct. His rule five says in part: "Ask straightforward questions that go to the heart of the problem, and do it in a serious manner. Don't use tricks or pretense to get people off guard. Don't use a false name or identity, and particularly do not impersonate a law enforcement official."[25]

As has been shown, many journalists do not agree with Mollenhoff's clear advice to avoid deception and misrepresentation. This probably accounts for the lack of attention paid to reporting by subterfuge in the national and in most individual media codes. Many journalists see this as a nonissue. They argue that undercover reporting has an honorable tradition and should not be sacrificed to Watergate-spawned concerns about the methods reporters use to get their stories. But the issue has been raised — and by some of the big guns of American journalism. Journalists need to come to grips with it.

CHAPTER SEVEN

Anything to Get a Story

"You know what you can do with your New Journalism. What I want are straight, dull news stories — and keep 'em short!"

LET'S SAY YOU ARE A WIRE EDITOR on a daily newspaper in California. From one of the wire services you get a news story that begins like this:

> LOS ANGELES — The $100,000 Lamborghini Countach shoots up the on-ramp at 65 mph in first gear, 80 mph in second.
>
> Once in the fast lane, the speedometer inches toward 200 mph. Signs along the deserted freeway flip past in a blur and gentle curves become hairpin turns. Make a mistake at that speed and both car and driver would likely disintegrate in flight.
>
> This is a "banzai run" with an outlaw racer, a man pursuing an illegal, dangerous and expensive hobby that goes beyond the speed limit and even beyond the reach of the law. For these racers, speed is a kind of intoxicant.
>
> "Military jets take off at 200 mph," the driver of the Countach says with a terse laugh. "If this car had wings..."
>
> He eyes the Ferrari Boxer and Vector Twinturbo V2 behind him in electronic rearview mirrors. The exotic cars in this high-speed caravan are barely visible out the Lamborghini's tiny back window: "It's the Italian philosophy of driving," he said of his sports car. "You don't have time to look back."

Indeed, looming suddenly ahead is a dreaded black and white cruiser of the California Highway Patrol. The distance eaten up in a second, the sports cars rocket past in a flash. As seen in the mirrors, the patrol car seems to be hurtling backwards as if shot from a cannon. Are its red lights turned on?

"Doesn't matter — might as well try to catch a Russian spy satellite," sneers the driver, who asks not to be identified. Nevertheless, some banzai runners take no chances — they've installed switches in their cars to flip off their tail lights and make their vehicles more difficult to follow.

By the time the patrol radios for help, the banzai runners will be hiding safely in some small town miles up the coast, slinking down back streets, maybe parking in a dark alley until things cool down.[1]

The rest of the story tells of police surprise that this new "sport" is as organized as it is and describes the banzai drivers as former race car drivers or the "newly rich," such as rock stars, actors, and Middle Eastern princes. Would you publish this story, assuming you had space? Would you question the story? Does it bother you that the writer of the story, who presumably was on the banzai run described, has protected (by not identifying) the drivers who obviously were breaking laws?

When this story was sent out by the AP to its member papers in California and Nevada, many published it. Three weeks later, they had to publish what the AP calls a "corrective." The story was partly phony and partly plagiarized. The reporter who wrote it, Gloria Ohland, had not been on the banzai run she described, or on any run. What she portrayed as if she had been a witness or participant was fabricated. She also had lifted parts of the piece from an article that had appeared nine months earlier in *New West* magazine. In addition, she attributed statements to a California Highway Patrol officer who denied that he had ever talked to her, and who said that the patrol had not had a problem with banzai runners.

When AP executive editor and vice-president Louis D. Boccardi confronted Ohland, she eventually admitted in the course of several telephone conversations that her story was a misrepresentation. The 29-year-old reporter decided then and there that she had no future with the AP and she resigned. She had been with the AP in its Los Angeles bureau for two and a quarter years. Before that, Boccardi reports, she had worked briefly in Minnesota as a part-time reporter for the AP. She graduated from St. Olaf College in Minnesota with a degree in English and did graduate work in mass communications at the University of Minnesota in 1977-78, but did not receive a degree.

Boccardi, who wrote the corrective himself, calls the episode "a

serious lapse in our standards." (Interview, 8 Oct. 1981.*) Ohland did not
fabricate the phenomenon of banzai racing, Boccardi concedes. "But she
misrepresented the circumstances under which the story was gathered,
she took some material from a magazine without credit, and she
inaccurately attributed some quotations."

An editor in the Los Angeles bureau, Steve Loeper, was officially
reprimanded for not inserting in Ohland's story the fact that it was a
"composite," her impression of what a banzai run would be like based on
taking brief rides and talking to banzai sports car drivers. He found out it
was a composite when he passed along to Ohland questions about the
story that editors in AP headquarters in New York raised when they
were considering the story for national transmission. But Loeper said he
decided against changing the story because it "was a representative
portrayal of a typical banzai run."[2] Boccardi is pleased that his New York
editors raised the right questions, but he says what happened in the
banzai run story is "easy for a reporter to do and hard for an editor to spot.
We are so vulnerable to the integrity of our reporters."

The AP found out about the misleading and plagiarized story from
David Shaw, media reporter-critic for the *Los Angeles Times*. Shaw was
asked by his editors to look into Ohland's story after another *Times*
reporter, Paul Dean, found that her story did not jibe with what he was
turning up in his research for an article on the Lamborghini Countach.
Shaw talked to Ohland, who told him that her description of the banzai
run was a composite. "I just couldn't think of any other way to write the
story," Shaw quoted Ohland as saying. Asked why she did not say in her
story that she was writing a composite, Ohland told Shaw, "I didn't feel it
was necessary." After reading to her similar passages in her story and in
a *New West* article by David Barry, Shaw said Ohland told him she had
read Barry's article and had gotten her sources from it, but she did not lift
phrases from it for her story. However, she said she might have
unconsciously taken some material from the *New West* article. Shaw in
his report showed that several phrases and sentences that appeared in
Barry's article as the author's own observations came out in Ohland's
story as statements made by other people. Shaw also said that much of
Ohland's story was similar to Barry's "in structure, tone and actual
wording."[3]

Besides being an embarrassment, the Ohland story is one of several
that have caused questions to be raised about the reporting and writing
methods that some journalists use: fabricating news stories, plagiarizing,
making up quotations, embellishing the facts so much that a false picture

---

*See list of interviewees following Notes.

is presented, breaking laws to get a story, ambushing sources, eavesdropping, using hidden cameras, and buying information. These are not methods that are often used, but that they are used at all is disturbing to those seeking a more ethical journalism.

FAKERY

Unfortunately, one of the surviving traditions of American journalism is the manufacturng of news. Hoaxes, they used to be called. Perhaps the most celebrated journalistic hoax was the lengthy account, complete with drawings, of the manlike creatures with wings discovered to be living on the moon. This discovery of the "man-bats" and other lunar life was supposedly made by a Sir John Herschel, employing a giant new telescope. This nineteenth century version of pure baloney published in the *New York Sun* in 1835 helped that paper achieve the largest circulation of any daily in the world.[4]

The hoax did not die with the turn of the century. In the late 1950s when the *San Francisco Examiner* and the *Chronicle* were battling toe to toe for the largest circulation in town, the *Chronicle* started publishing a series of articles by outdoor writer Bud Boyd that put it ahead of its chief competitor. Boyd's articles, called "The Last Man on Earth," told how he and his family were surviving in the wilderness, living off the earth, like modern-day Robinson Crusoes. Lynn Ludlow, veteran reporter for the *Examiner,* recalls that his paper countered Boyd's circulation-winning series by sending its top investigative reporter to check out Boyd's claims. The *Examiner* reporter finally tracked down the Boyd family campsite, where he reportedly found canned food, tools, and other amenities of civilized life. When the *Examiner* published its exposé, the *Chronicle* sued, Ludlow reports, but the suit was dropped when the two papers entered into a joint operating agreement five or six years later.

Several years ago the *Boston Globe* startled readers with a page one report that said the state had released piranha into the streams and rivers of Massachusetts and they were eating up all the trout. That is why fishermen were having such poor luck that particular season. The story went on to say that the state had had this vat of the voracious piranha left over from an experiment and simply dumped them into the streams to get rid of them. Great story. Only there was not a bit of truth to it. Sal Micciche, former *Boston Globe* ombudsman, explained that the piranha story was buried in a field and stream column written by the paper's outdoor writer. The copy editor in sports who processed the column thought the writer had missed the lead. "The story went up the ladder of editors, and all felt it was a terrific story," Micciche said. "In fact, it was so good it didn't belong on the sports pages. It was news. Big news.

Page one news." When someone finally got around to asking the outdoor writer about the item, it had already been published and the uproar had begun. The writer explained that "he was being tongue-in-cheek with respect to the complaints of the trout not biting," Micciche said. The mood was so gloomy around the *Globe* that day that no one laughed when a copy editor suggested that the correction be headlined, "Yes, we have no piranha today."[5]

The piranha story is more in the nature of an April Fool's joke compared to the fakery of some modern journalists, like Gloria Ohland. The new art of journalistic fakery skillfully weaves fact and fiction into a concoction that is difficult for editors and news consumers to spot.

Janet Cooke and Jimmy's World. The *Washington Post,* a newspaper that has been a leader in setting higher ethical and professional standards for journalism, sent back a 1981 Pulitzer Prize for feature writing because the reporter admitted she had counterfeited the article that won it. Man-bats from the moon again!

The story that embarrassed the *Post* was a dramatic account of an eight-year-old heroin addict. The writer, Janet Cooke, gave him the name, "Jimmy," and her page one article was headlined, "Jimmy's World: 8-Year-Old Heroin Addict Lives for a Fix." Illustrated by a moving drawing of what *Post* artist Michael Gnatek, Jr., imagined Jimmy would look like as he was getting a fix, Cooke's article began:

> Jimmy is 8 years old and a third-generation heroin addict, a precocious little boy with sandy hair, velvety brown eyes and needle marks freckling the baby-smooth skin of his thin brown arms.

The article went on to paint a dreary and hopeless picture of "Jimmy's world" in Southeast Washington where he lived with his mother, an ex-prostitute, and her lover, Ron, a pusher who got Jimmy hooked on heroin. Jimmy wanted to be a dope dealer like Ron, the article said, and "he doesn't usually go to school, preferring instead to hang with older boys between the ages of 11 and 16 who spend their day getting high on herb or PCP and doing a little dealing to collect spare change." At the end of the article, Cooke described Jimmy being "fired up" with an injection of heroin:

> Ron comes back into the living room, syringe in hand, and calls the little boy over to his chair: "Let me see your arm."
> He grabs Jimmy's left arm just above the elbow, his massive hand tightly encircling the child's small limb. The needle slides into the boy's soft skin like a straw pushed into the center of a freshly baked cake. Liquid ebbs out of the syringe, replaced by bright red blood. The blood is then reinjected into the child.

Jimmy has closed his eyes during the whole procedure, but now opens them, looking quickly around the room. He climbs into a rocking chair and sits, his head dipping and snapping upright again, in what addicts call "the nod."

"Pretty soon, man," Ron says, "you got to learn how to do this for yourself."[6]

The story of Jimmy saddened, outraged, angered, and upset many Washingtonians, including Mayor Marion Barry, who ordered a search for the child. Police Chief Burtell Jefferson threatened to have Cooke and *Post* editors subpoenaed if they did not reveal who Jimmy was. *Post* lawyers replied that the paper had a right under the First Amendment to protect its sources. As Robert U. Woodward, then assistant managing editor-metro, put it, "We went into our Watergate mode: Protect the source and back the reporter."[7]

Cooke had told her editors that the dope pusher in her article, Ron, had threatened to kill her if she told anyone who he was. No editor pressed her to identify Jimmy or his family. Instead they stood by her and succeeded in scaring off Washington officials. But three weeks after the story appeared, veteran managing editor Howard Simons was still worried about Jimmy. He ordered city editor Milton Coleman — who had shepherded Cooke's story from the moment she said she had heard of an eight-year-old heroin addict until it got into print — to find Jimmy. "Take Janet with you," Simons said. Coleman told Cooke what Simons wanted them to do, but before they got around to it, Cooke informed Coleman that there was no need to go. She said she had revisited the house and found that the family had moved to Baltimore. So that was that. Exit Jimmy.

Two months later, Coleman was pushing his supervising editors to nominate "Jimmy's World" for a Pulitzer. The *Post* entered the Cooke article in the competition for general local reporting. It ended up winning the Pulitzer Prize for feature writing after the Pulitzer advisory board moved it from the general local reporting category where it was about to place second. The jury of editors that had screened the local reporting entries had recommended that the prize in that category go to the Longview, Washington, *Daily News* for that small paper's coverage of the eruption of nearby Mount Saint Helens; it found Cooke's article "gripping and powerful," but put it second to the Longview entry. So the Pulitzer board, as it has done in the past, moved the *Post* entry and awarded it the Pulitzer for feature writing even though that jury of editors had not even seen the Cooke article. The only vocal dissent on the board came from Eugene C. Patterson, editor and publisher of the *St. Petersburg Times*, who said he considered the story "an aberration" that should never have been published.

Cooke, who had been on the *Post* news staff a little more than eight months when her "Jimmy's World" made page one, had herself a Pulitzer at the age of 26. But the imagination that had gotten her the prize also brought her down. She had exaggerated her background and credentials when she applied at the *Post,* and on her biographical material she provided when the paper put her in for the Pulitzer. She claimed when she applied to the *Post* that she had two years on the Toledo *Blade* and was a Phi Beta Kappa graduate of Vassar College; she also said she could speak or read French and Spanish and had won an award from the Ohio Newspaper Women's Association. The biographical form she filled out for the Pulitzer entry claimed that in addition to graduating from Vassar, she had a master's degree from the University of Toledo and had studied at the Sorbonne; she added Portuguese and Italian to the foreign languages she claimed to know and reported six awards from the Ohio association. When the Toledo *Blade* started to do a "local gal makes good" story, it found that the biography transmitted by the AP from the Pulitzer form did not jibe with *Blade* records. Informed of the discrepancies, AP checked with Cooke, who said the biography she had submitted was essentially correct. *Post* editors were then brought into the act and Cooke's house of lies began to tumble. By early the next morning, the young reporter had confessed to her editors that "Jimmy's World" was a fabrication. She said she never encountered or interviewed an eight-year-old heroin addict. He was a "composite" of young addicts social workers had told her about. Most of her biography was also fiction: she had gone to Vassar but only for her freshman year, and then she returned to her home town and got a bachelor's degree in English from the University of Toledo; she had won one award from the Ohio Newspaper Women's Association; she studied French in high school and college but was not fluent in it. Cooke resigned, and the *Post* returned her Pulitzer with apologies.[8]

Why did she do it? At the time her fakery was discovered, Cooke refused to be interviewed, but about nine months later, she allowed Phil Donahue to interview her on NBC's "Today" show for the usual $400 to $500 actor's pay plus expenses. She said to Donahue that after spending about two months looking for the eight-year-old heroin addict her sources told her was out there, her "whole mindset was in the *Washington Post* mentality: He must be there and it's being covered up; I must find him." She decided to make up an eight-year-old addict, she said, because "the last thing I could do was to go to my editor and say, 'I can't do it.'" Cooke said she does not "excuse what happened: It was wrong; I shouldn't have done it. . . . I simply wanted . . . not to fail." Asked why she lied on her job application, she said she believed she would not have been hired otherwise and she felt "a need to be perfect."[9]

A *Post* staffer who knew Cooke, reporter-photographer Linda Wheeler, recalls conversations they often had when both would be working late in the newsroom. "She was attractive, but also friendly and nice," Wheeler relates. "I talked to her a lot about the Jimmy story, a story that went way beyond anything I could do. I was very impressed by that story, and I believed it." (Interview, 24 Sept. 1981.) When Cooke's Pulitzer Prize was announced, Wheeler remembers congratulating her and asking whatever happened to Jimmy. "She looked me straight in the eye and said, 'You know, I was back there a couple of weeks ago and the women who were dealing out in front of the building told me that the mother and kid were still gone and that Ron was looking for me and they told me not to go in.' " Wheeler believes Cooke "lived her lies" and was not conscious of them.

"The ultimate tragedy of the Janet Cooke episode was that it was so predictable," in the view of Lyle Denniston, U.S. Supreme Court reporter for the Baltimore *Sun*. "The power groupie, the fame-driven person runs through this profession now in great numbers. I don't think people respect truth very much: they respect theater and they respect excitement, but truth isn't a driving proposition anymore." (Interview, 5 June 1981.)

The Case of Michael Daly. While journalism was still reeling from the embarrassment of Janet Cooke, a young columnist for the New York *Daily News* resigned after the London *Daily Mail* attacked him for writing "a pack of lies." The columnist, 29-year-old Michael Daly, was called back from Ireland by his editors when he could not satisfy their questions about a column he wrote which began:

> BELFAST — Peering over the hood of an armored car, gunner Christopher Spell of the British Army watched a child not yet in his teens fling a gasoline bomb against the front of the Northern Bank of Falls Road. . . . A soldier to Spell's right raised his SLR rifle and fired two shots. A 15-year-old named Johnny McCarten fell. . . . "If I'm lucky, the little Fenian will die," the soldier said.[10]

The column went on to tell in eyewitness detail how the British Army patrol had fired real bullets, instead of the nonlethal rubber or plastic ones. It focused on the soldier, Christopher Spell, reporting that he had watched a comrade shot, and how he saw similarities between himself and the working-class Catholics in Northern Ireland. The *Daily Mail* maintained that although a British trooper had shot a Catholic boy that day, there was no soldier in the British Army named "Christopher Spell." No member of that troop could have seen a comrade shot, the *Mail* claimed, and Daly also erred in reporting the date that the troop had arrived in Ireland and the route it took that day. Daly admitted using a pseudonym for the soldier and recreating scenes that he had not witnessed. One of his supervisors, James Weighart, executive editor of the *News,* said he is not convinced that Daly had ever been with that troop.[11]

One of Daly's admirers, Craig Ammerman, executive editor of the Philadelphia *Bulletin* when it went out of business early in 1982, saw Daly as "the godson of Jimmy Breslin," another *Daily News* columnist. Daly, according to Ammerman, merely imitated Breslin when he "used composites or enlargements." (Interview, 27 May 1981.)

Michael J. O'Neill, former editor of the New York *Daily News,* says it was Daly who suggested he resign (interview, 8 Oct. 1981). "I didn't say a word to him," O'Neill adds. O'Neill admits, however, that he had challenged two previous stories Daly wrote out of Washington. "So when the Irish story blew up," O'Neill reports, "I resolved to act because of public perceptions of the credibility of the paper." Accepting Daly's resignation obviously saddened O'Neill, who says that "in time, I would love to get Michael back."

Daly had been with the *News* three years when he resigned and took up free-lance writing, later joining the staff of *New York* magazine. He is a 1974 graduate of Yale, and attended Phillips Academy at Andover, Massachusetts. Before joining the *News,* he had worked as a writer for the *Village Voice* and the Courier-Life newspapers, a chain of weeklies in Brooklyn.

The Cooke, Daly, and Ohland fakeries differ in one important way from some of the famous hoaxes of the old days. The man-bats hoax, for example, was a project of the entire newspaper, not a counterfeit that a writer conned his or her editors into legitimatizing through publication. Maybe that is a measure of progress.

The New Journalism. Unfairly perhaps, what has come to be known as the New Journalism took a lot of the rap for the explosive fictions crafted by Janet Cooke, Michael Daly, and Gloria Ohland. New Journalism is the label that has been put on the technique of writing fact articles as if they were short stories or novels, using the devices and modes of fiction writing to make the articles more dramatic and interesting. Practiced by skillful writers and reporters like Tom Wolfe and Gay Talese, New Journalism has produced some lively articles and books that have also been fairly truthful. Younger writers have imitated the style of Wolfe, Talese, and other New Journalists — and this frequently has brought them applause and promotions from newspaper and magazine editors eager to publish more interesting styles of writing. But a few have practiced their New Journalism without the careful research and reporting — saturation, Wolfe calls it — needed for truthful portrayals. A fabricated piece of journalism is even more harmful when it is so beautifully written that readers are bedeviled into believing it.

Free-lance writer Teresa Carpenter, who got the 1981 Pulitzer Prize for feature writing that had originally been awarded to Janet Cooke, was chastised by the National News Council for one of the three articles in *Village Voice* that won her the prize. The council investigated her story about Dennis Sweeney, the young man who was sentenced to a psychiatric center for murdering Representative Allard K. Lowenstein in 1980, and concluded that it was "marred by the over-use of unattributed sources, by a writing style so colored and imaginative as to blur precise meanings, and by such reckless and speculative construction as to result in profound unfairness to the victim of a demented killer.[12] The council was particularly disturbed by this paragraph in Carpenter's article:

> After the shooting, in fact, there were rumors that Lowenstein and Sweeney had fallen out as the result of a lover's quarrel. Everyone simply assumed that Lowenstein had approached Sweeney. (Now, from his cell at Rikers Island, Sweeney denies that they ever had a relationship. Once while he and Lowenstein were traveling through Mississippi together, they checked into a motel. According to Sweeney, Lowenstein made a pass and Sweeney rebuffed it. Sweeney is not angry with Lowenstein, he claims. Nor does he feel any shame. It's just that Lowenstein wasn't always above board.)[13]

Would you assume after reading that paragraph that the writer had interviewed or talked to Sweeney at Rikers Island? The council and many other critics of the article believe most readers would make that assumption. In fact, Carpenter did not talk to Sweeney. Although Carpenter and the *Village Voice,* a New York weekly tabloid, did not cooperate with the council in its investigation, she told the *New York Times* that the statements attributed to Sweeney came from third parties. She noted that none of the statements were in quotation marks. "The reader has to trust me when he or she is reading the piece," Carpenter told the *Times.* "I do not feel compelled to attribute each and every piece of information to its source. I don't mean to sound arrogant, but I do mean to sound confident."[14]

The *Wall Street Journal* also interviewed Carpenter and reported that she had never even met Sweeney. The *Journal* plucked the following passage from her article as representative of the "liberties taken in the name of the so-called New Journalism":

> Sweeney was utterly alone.... Lowenstein, he was sure, had willed the murder of San Francisco Mayor George Moscone in 1978, as well as the 1979 DC-10 crash in Chicago.... The plan he devised contained a simple and chilling logic. He would confront Lowenstein

and demand assurances that in the future he would leave Sweeney, his family, and others alone. If he got those assurances, Sweeney intended to drive home to Oregon. . . . If not, he would have to destroy his tormentor.[15]

Asked how she could write about what Sweeney was thinking without talking to him, Carpenter told the *Journal* she did not mean to imply that she had talked to Sweeney. "It's very cumbersome to say, 'According to sources close to Sweeney,' " she commented. She said the passage above about Sweeney's thoughts was derived from interviews with Sweeney's attorney and another man who talked to Sweeney after the killing and requested anonymity. "I knew in my gut that this is what Sweeney was thinking," Carpenter said. "It's incumbent upon me to make judgments. Otherwise I'm shunting off responsibility and being terribly cautious, and being a clumsy writer in the process." Carpenter said Sweeney wrote to the *Voice* disputing a few points in her story but not its main thrust or the passage quoted above.[16]

Haynes Johnson, reporter-columnist for the *Washington Post,* is turned off by much of what passes for New Journalism. "When Tom Wolfe and the people who call themselves the New Journalists use composite characters and tell us what people are thinking because they've talked to so many of them, well, they're just playing God," Johnson says (interview, 4 June 1981). "I find that pretentious." He believes there is a need for more polished writing in journalism. "But you don't make up quotes and composite characters and label it as journalism," Johnson says. "It's something else, and should be labeled as something else."

Another tradition in journalism that has contributed to some fakery is the embellishment that once powerful rewrite men added to the bald facts gathered by reporters, some of whom were called legmen. Rewrite men and legmen have all but disappeared in newsrooms today (if they existed, obviously they would have to be called rewrite and legpersons), but the tradition of embellishing stories lives on. "Good editors have to watch for trimmings that writers have added and cut the crap out," says Claude Sitton, editorial director of the Raleigh *Times* and *News & Observer* (interview, 4 Nov. 1981). "You have to watch your good writers particularly. They don't like rough edges and they'll knock them off everytime." Donald Haskin, associate editor of the *Philadelphia Daily News,* is cheered that newspapers have done away with old-time rewrite men who could hype quotes and embellish stories, but he sighs: "Those crusty old bastards would never dream of doing what Janet Cooke did." (Interview, 27 May 1981).

Plagiarism. One of the ethical sins that Ohland committed in the "banzai run" story that forced her resignation from the AP was that she plagiarized parts of it. She apparently lifted sections of an article from *New West* magazine and passed them off as her own words. That's serious enough when a college student does it, but it can be career smashing for a professional writer.

Yet anyone who has been in journalism very long knows that a mild form of plagiarism goes on all the time. News organizations and reporters save clips of news stories and articles they may need again, sometimes informally in pockets, drawers, and briefcases, and sometimes formally in news department libraries, traditionally called morgues. When these clips are pulled out for help in doing a story, words, phrases, and whole passages frequently are lifted and repeated. This is no big deal when the stuff being lifted is from your own publication, but it is more serious when the words and ideas are picked up from other writers and publications without credit, as is sometimes the case.

The more serious kind of plagiarism, however, is the kind that the *Washington Post* had to deal with a few years ago. Benjamin C. Bradlee, executive editor, recalls that a new young reporter — "a brilliant Radcliffe graduate" — wrote a story about singles apartments in the area (interview, 5 June 1981). "The next day someone called us and pointed out that six paragraphs of her story were taken verbatim from Salinger's *Catcher in the Rye*," Bradlee says. "I was stunned. We had to fire the girl." The editor says that the young woman underwent psychiatric care for about six months and then got back into the news business with one of the Detroit papers, but then committed suicide.

When Steve Lovelady first joined the *Philadelphia Inquirer* as an associate editor after reporting for the *Wall Street Journal,* he started searching through *Inquirer* clips to determine who the good and not so good writers were (interview, 16 Sept. 1981). *Inquirer* executive editor Eugene Roberts remembers how impressed Lovelady was with one very well written article he found, but something about it seemed familiar to him. The next day he remembered. No wonder it seemed familiar. It was his article — one he had done for the *Journal* — that an *Inquirer* reporter had plagiarized. Roberts says the reporter was let off with a warning, but had to be dismissed about a year later when *Fortune* magazine informed him that one of its articles had been picked up verbatim by the same writer (interviews, 28 May and 15 Sept. 1981).

Hoaxes on the Press. In this era of media events and staged "news," it is no wonder that some people might try to put one over on the press. Most of these hoaxes get caught before they become full-blown news stories, but not all of them.

Take the cockroach pill story, for example. It told how a group of people in New York was hooked on pills that gave them the same qualities that make the cockroach impervious to man's assaults. The story was transmitted throughout the land by the UPI and was used in about 175 daily newspapers, including the *Chicago Tribune,* the Louisville *Courier-Journal,* the *Philadelphia Inquirer,* the *Washington Star,* the *Pittsburgh Press,* and the *Dallas Times Herald.* The story was phony, the invention of Joseph Skaggs, a teacher of journalism at New York's School of Visual Arts with a fondness for Franz Kafka.

To make a point to his class about the gullibility of the press, Skaggs came up with the idea of a mad scientist who had developed a marvelous cure for mankind, cockroach juice. Drawing on Czech author Kafka's *The Metamorphosis,* Skaggs decided to call himself Dr. Josef Gregor and his research institute Metamorphosis (in the story by that name, Gregor Samsa is a character who awakens one morning to discover that he has become a giant insect resembling a cockroach). Skaggs and his students ran off dozens of press releases, prepared presentations by "patients" who could claim various cures from taking Dr. Gregor's roach pills, and invited all the major news media in New York to a news conference. Five reporters showed up, including one from UPI.[17]

UPI's major competitor, the AP, did not buy the cockroach pill story, but it got very much involved in the street violinist hoax about the same time. What happened was that an advertisement appeared in the *Village Voice* offering $1,000 to find a street violinist. The ad explained that this millionaire Florida investment banker had heard a young woman playing the violin on the streets of New York and wanted her to appear in a concert he was arranging in Carnegie Hall, but he did not get her name because he had to rush off to catch a plane. The New York *Daily News* did a big story on the ad and the search, and then another when the street musician was found through a friend. The AP picked up the story at this point, after Jerry Schwartz of the New York bureau had checked it out by calling the Florida millionaire. "He sounded legitimate," Schwartz recalls, "and he had run such concerts before in South Florida," concerts that gave undiscovered musicians a chance to perform (interview, 13 Nov. 1981). Schwartz also checked Carnegie Hall and found that the guy indeed had rented it for a concert and was selling tickets at the reasonable price of three to five dollars, which would just about pay for the rent for the hall.

Five days after the AP transmitted Schwartz's story across the country, a newspaper in Ft. Lauderdale, Florida, carried a report that the ad and search for the street musician was a hoax. Schwartz got back on the story and found the Florida banker in a New York hotel. "The man admitted he had lied, but claimed he had done it to promote the concert," the AP reporter explains. "He said he had been told that that was the only way he could get any publicity for it." The banker had indeed discovered a young woman violinist playing on a New York street and had enrolled her in the Manhattan School of Music with the understanding that she would agree to go along with the hoax. A friend of the musician also agreed to help by "finding" the missing street violinist and telling the *Daily News* about it. Schwartz wrote a 450-word corrective story.

The two hoaxes that duped the UPI and the AP were innocent in nature compared to the fakery of a young free-lance writer who sold a fabricated and plagiarized article to the *New York Times Magazine.* The *Times* apologized on the front page when it discovered that twenty-four-year-old Christopher Jones had made up his account of a trip with Khmer Rouge guerrillas to Cambodia that had appeared in its Sunday magazine on 20 December 1981. Jones admitted he had invented the article from his imagination and recollections of two 1980 visits to western Cambodia, according to the *Times.* In fact, he lifted material from an article he wrote about one of those visits that had been published in the Asian edition of *Time* magazine. He also confessed to plagiarizing a passage from André Malraux's *The Royal Way,* a novel set in Cambodia.[18]

It was the plagiarizing that did him in. About two weeks after the Jones article appeared in the *Times Magazine,* Alexander Cockburn wrote in the *Village Voice* that the ending of the article was evidently stolen from a Malraux passage depicting a blind Cambodian minstrel. The *Times* sent off a letter to Jones demanding an explanation and cancelling an assignment he had been given for another *Times Magazine* article, but he never replied. Then when the *Washington Post* quoted a Khmer Rouge official in Bangkok as saying that Jones had not visited the guerrilla enclaves in 1981, *Times* executive editor Abraham M. Rosenthal put three staffers on Jones's trail. They found him in Calpe, Spain. Jones eventually confessed to Rosenthal's bulldogs that he had intended to return to Cambodia in 1981 — he showed them a letter from Khmer Rouge officials authorizing his return visit — but he did not have enough money to pay for the trip. So instead, he holed up for a month in a seafront apartment owned by his parents and a hilltop villa he shared with a fifty-two-year-old German woman, and wrote his fictitious account. When his manuscript was finished, he and the woman drove to Locarno, Switzerland, to mail it to New York, apparently to give the impression that he had flown from Thailand to Switzerland to rest after the rigors of his jungle adventure. Jones also sent in a forged expense account, including a fake bill from a Bangkok hotel.

Rosenthal said that the *Times* had checked on Jones and "was informed by a publication for which he had worked in Asia that he was a reliable journalist." His manuscript was also checked, but apparently not thoroughly enough. Rosenthal said the major mistake was not showing the Jones article to one of the *Times*'s specialists on Cambodia. "We do not feel that the fact the writer was a liar and hoaxer removes our responsibility," Rosenthal added. "I regret this whole sad episode and the lapse in our procedures that made it possible."

Quote Tampering and Such. Quotation marks are supposed to say to the reader, "What's inside here are the exact words of whoever is being quoted. Verbatim." And most of the time what we read in the press inside quotations marks is a reasonably accurate facsimile of what the source said. Careful writers do not use direct quotation unless they are sure they are presenting the exact or nearly exact words of the speaker; if they are not sure, they use indirect quotation, paraphrasing what the speaker said as accurately as possible and not enclosing any words in quotation marks.

But there is also a convention in journalism of "cleaning up" quotations that are ungrammatical or that contain obscene or offensive language. And there is another convention, not so often employed or talked about, of tampering with quotes to make them more exciting and interesting, or making up quotes. Sharp editors who have been around a while recognize and destroy some versions of the exaggerated or made-up quote: Anything said by an unnamed taxi driver is suspect ("As one veteran cab driver put it, 'When you got a mayor who won't tip, you got a city in trouble.' "). Reporters who yearn to summarize or moralize in the manner of essayists or editorial writers have been known to slip their judgments into their news stories through the mouths of such unnamed observers. These brief betrayals of truth that get into print probably do not do much damage to humankind, but they are dishonest and can cause a loss of trust in truthful reporting.

Sometimes the quote tampering gets more serious. Wayne Thompson, associate editor and veteran reporter and editorial writer for the Portland *Oregonian,* was suspended without pay for eight weeks when he fabricated some quotations from an interview with Washington Governor Dixy Lee Ray. The nightmare that occurs to all reporters who use tape recorders became reality for Thompson when his recorder malfunctioned without his knowing it during an hour-long interview with the governor. He could make out parts of the tape when he got back to his office, but feedback from Governor Ray's tape recorder hummed out many of the governor's words on Thompson's tape. Because his paper had already promoted the upcoming interview with Ray to its readers and because he could make out about fifteen quotes clearly, Thompson decided to try to reconstruct other quotes from his notes and the imperfect sound of his tape. That was a mistake. The governor complained, sending the paper a transcript of the interview from her own taping of it to show that twenty statements attributed to her were inaccurate or fabricated. The *Oregonian* ran a lengthy retraction and punished Thompson, who at the time had had twenty-six years of experience in the news business.[19]

Advice columns have been standards in American newspapers for a long time, and almost every daily in the country today carries "Ann Landers" or her sister, "Dear Abby." Many papers in recent years have gone in for action line or hot line columns that try to respond to questions from readers seeking help or advice with almost any problem you could imagine. In most such features, the persons seeking advice are allowed anonymity. That opens the door for various kinds of fabrication, from the silly letters Ann Landers gets from Yale undergraduates pretending to be "Panting Patty from Paducah" or "Swinging Sally from Syracuse," to the more serious manufacturing of letters by staff members of the newspapers publishing the advice columns. Rich Stim, a San Francisco rock musician, confessed in a *Columbia Journalism Review* article that by the time he reached his fifth and last year as editor of the hot line column for the Bloomington, Indiana, *Herald-Telephone* he was creating more than half of the questions he got. As with car thieves who start by shoplifting pencils, Stim started small. He made up two questions once — by turning two facts from the *World Almanac* into readers' queries — in order to leave work early to practice with the rock band he had joined. Nobody said a word. So he was soon making up one or two questions for each of his columns. Stim's editor unconsciously encouraged the practice when he selected the questions for the "best of the Hot Line" column at the end of that year and chose a majority from those Stim had dreamed up.[20]

More recently the *Philadelphia Daily News* started a new advice column by psychologist David Stein called "Ask David." The column started out on its first day answering questions from "Frustrated Mom, East Falls," "Perplexed, S. Phila.," and "Mark, Mt. Airy." As the column warmed to its task, letters appeared from "Irritated Hubby, Ardmore" complaining that his wife's "best friend is a lying creep," and from "Carol, Bala Cynwyd" who was concerned that her husband was too liberal because he told their young daughter details about their lovemaking ("Your husband's no liberal, he's a pervert," David replied). But when David printed a letter from "Worried, Kensington," asking advice because after twenty-two years of marriage her husband "all of a sudden wants to tie me down to the bed during sex," that was too much for Clark DeLeon, who writes "The Scene" column for the *Philadelphia Inquirer.* DeLeon snooped around and reported that all those heavy letters David had received had been written by *Daily News* staff members. *Daily News* editors said the in-house efforts would end as soon as enough legitimate letters started rolling in. "Sign us, 'Cynical, South Philly,'" DeLeon concluded.[21]

The journalistic fakery we have examined in this chapter is not an everyday occurrence, but it does happen often enough to be disturbing both to practitioners and consumers of U.S. journalism.

DUBIOUS METHODS

Journalists get criticized for some of the methods they use to get the news. Nobody disputes such conventional reporting methods as observing and recording a public event, interviewing people in their work places or homes, or doing library research. But when journalists lie or break laws or use sleazy tactics to get a story, observers wonder whether the ends justify such means, whether their methods do not color or distort the news they produce.

Robert Scheer, who as editor of *Ramparts Magazine* helped develop so-called guerrilla or counterjournalism, has said that "some of the most important stories of recent years have involved theft, burglary, seduction and conning people." Scheer, who has become more conventional as he has progressed from *Ramparts* to the *Los Angeles Times,* makes it clear that he does not believe in using such extreme methods unless you're dealing with a story vital to the public interest. Scheer is not happy with the thought that he'll probably be most remembered for his 1977 comment that when dealing with politicians who are trying to hide things from the public, "the journalist's job is to get the story by breaking into their offices, by bribing, by seducing people, by lying, by anything else to break through that palace guard." During an interview by Ken Auletta shortly after that remark to the A. J. Liebling convention organized by now defunct *More* magazine, Scheer tried to emphasize that he does not support the use of dubious means to get most news stories. He said he does not want to be thought of as a guy whose "main contribution to journalism is to advocate going through the second story. I mean, if I had to make a choice ... between a young journalist going to the library or breaking into an office, I'd pick the library."[22] Interviewed more than three years after his oft-quoted comment to the *More* convention, Scheer says flatly that he regrets he said it (interview, 25 Nov. 1980). "I don't believe it's a mark of character or intelligence to stick with things that are dumb," he explains.

James C. Thomson, Jr., curator of the Nieman Foundation at Harvard, has noted that the ends of journalism "are so patently lofty, yet the means often so tawdry." Thomson concludes from his discussions with nearly a hundred of the country's finest young journalists who have studied at Harvard as Nieman Fellows that in their minds "the clean and beautiful ends" of journalism "can justify virtually any means." Yet the same journalists who believe that anything goes in the pursuit of truth express uncertainty and self-doubt about how far they would or should go or whether they would or should break a law. He also finds "a shrinking from 'playing God'; and a deep-seated cynicism about the purity of the journalist's own craft . . . while seeking out that pure commodity, 'truth.'"[23]

Most Americans tell Gallup Poll researchers that they approve of investigative reporting but not of four principal methods used by investigative reporters. Part of the explanation for this seeming contradiction may be the way Gallup worded its question when it asked 1,508 adults in more than 300 locations:

> As you probably know, the news media — TV, newspapers and magazines — often do "investigative reporting" — uncovering and reporting on corruption and fraud in business, government agencies, and other organizations. In general, do you approve or disapprove of investigative reporting by the news media?

The response showed 79 percent approving, 18 percent disapproving, and 3 percent with no opinion. But how can anybody be opposed to uncovering corruption and fraud?

The question Gallup researchers asked about investigative techniques is probably a better reading of how Americans feel about some of the methods so-called investigative journalists use to get certain kinds of stories. The same adults were asked:

> Now, I am going to read to you a list of techniques the media sometimes use when they are doing investigative reporting. Please tell me whether you approve or disapprove of each technique. . . . Using hidden cameras and microphones? . . . Having reporters not identify themselves as reporters? . . . Running stories that quote an unnamed source rather than giving the person's name? . . . Paying informers for their information or testimony? [Ellipses theirs]

The highest percentage of approval was given to the use of unnamed sources (covered in this book in Chapter 5), a technique 42 percent said they approved of, but 53 percent said they disapproved and 5 percent had no opinion. Using hidden cameras and mikes (to be discussed later in this chapter) was approved of by 38 percent, while 58 percent said they disapproved, and 4 percent had no opinion. Paying informers (also to be discussed later in this chapter) was approved of by 36 percent, but 56 percent said they disapproved and 8 percent had no opinion. The lowest percentage of approval was given to reporter misidentification (covered in Chapter 6), a technique only 32 percent said they approved of, while 65 percent said they disapproved and 3 percent expressed no opinion.[24]

Eavesdropping. Nice people don't eavesdrop, but journalists do. Or as William F. Thomas, editor and executive vice-president of the *Los Angeles*

Times, puts it, "Nice people don't eavesdrop unless they have to." (Interview, 2 Nov. 1981.) Most (but certainly not all) journalists do not regard listening in on other people's conversations with the naked ear as a high-level ethical sin. But eavesdropping with electronic devices or telephone wire tapping is fairly generally condemned as a reporting method.

During the early part of the crisis after the Three Mile Island nuclear power plant breakdown, two *Philadelphia Inquirer* reporters pretended to be a couple of bickering lovers so they could stay in a hotel corridor to eavesdrop on a meeting of public relations executives for the utility. Each time a hotel official or some guest would come by, the two reporters, Julia Cass and Jonathan Neumann, would strike up a lovers' quarrel — which ranks right up there with picking your nose as a surefire way to get other people to look away. Many times reporters use what they hear from eavesdropping only as a lead, but Neumann and Cass did a story on what they heard through the hotel room door. Neumann explained that they had tried for days to talk to the officials inside but were always told that the head of public relations for the utility was too busy discussing the "nuclear question." But the conversation inside "was about the press question," Neumann said. "About how to get us off their tail. They had lied to us."[25]

The *Inquirer* told its readers how Neumann and Cass got their story and got no real public criticism of the method they used, reports executive editor Roberts. "We have to have high standards," Roberts believes, "but we can't get so finicky about ethics that we use them as excuses for not doing our jobs. . . . There's no ethics in being docile and the pawn of whoever wants to prevent you from getting the story." (Interviews, 28 May and 15 Sept. 1981.)

Robert Giles, executive editor of the Rochester, New York, *Times-Union* and *Democrat & Chronicle,* opposes electronic eavesdropping, but old-fashioned eavesdropping does not bother him as much (interview, 15 Oct. 1981). He tells of using that technique twice in his reporting days on the *Akron Beacon Journal.* Once he listened at the door after being thrown out of a meeting of the area labor council. Labor officials were furious at him when his story was published. Another time he listened through a basement window of a hospital as police talked to the mother of a kidnapped infant whose body had just been found. Other reporters were "milling about" inside the hospital getting nothing. Giles says he got no flak on the second story. Even though he had those two experiences with the method, he still believes it should be used rarely and "with great caution."

When public officials go behind closed doors, few reporters hesitate to listen in if they can. Jack Severson, of the *Philadelphia Inquirer* has done that and he has listened in as lawyers and clients conferred in witness rooms at court houses, but he says he has never gotten anything more than leads to information that might be usable (interview, 18 Sept. 1981). "I've never based a story merely on what I heard through the door," Severson says, "and I've never eavesdropped except in public buildings."

"If a public agency goes behind closed doors to deal with public matters," declares Raleigh editor Sitton, "our reporters may stand at the door and try to hear what's going on, and I must say I've never reprimanded any of them for doing so. If the public's business is being dealt with, the public has a right to know." (Interview, 4 Nov. 1981.)

Getting caught while eavesdropping is embarrassing and not in keeping with the image most journalists like to project. Journalists do not ordinarily like to be thought of as practitioners of what Charles Puffenbarger, assistant financial editor of the *Washington Post,* calls "Peeping Tom journalism." (Interview, 23 Sept. 1981.) But, of course, they do get caught.

Jack Landau, director of the Reporters Committee for Freedom of the Press, got caught when he was covering negotiations between the port of New York and the longshoremen's union when he was working for the AP (interview, 24 Sept. 1981). Landau climbed on a chair and put a water glass to an opaque glass panel to hear what was being said in the closed meeting. After he had listened about ten minutes, one of the longshoremen left the meeting to go to the men's room and spotted him on the chair with his ear to the water glass. "All of a sudden I looked down from my chair to see a delegation of burly men rushing at me and screaming, 'The goddam press! We're breaking off negotiations!' " Landau, who had to call in a story that negotiations had broken off because an AP reporter was caught eavesdropping, feared that he was going to be fired, but his editor never said a word to him.

Two reporters for the high-minded Louisville newspapers embarrassed their news bosses when they got caught eavesdropping on a police meeting in 1974. The reporters — Howard Fineman of the *Courier-Journal* and Jerry Hicks of the *Louisville Times* — were arrested as Fineman was lying on the floor while Hicks had his ear to the door of a room in which the local Fraternal Order of Police was holding a closed meeting. The reporters had a tape recorder with them, but they said they had not used it. Charges against both reporters were eventually dropped. What was going on that was important enough for them to take the risk they did? The police wanted to discuss the action of their chief in bugging their squad cars to check on possible police misbehavior.[26]

Michael J. Davies, who was managing editor of the *Louisville Times* when the two reporters were caught, says "the resultant publicity was awful." (Interview, 23 Oct. 1981.) The publisher, Barry Bingham, Jr., "issued a statement saying that this was a terrible thing to do, but every once in a while we have to do it," Davies recalls, "which didn't sit well with anyone outside the papers." Davies, who is now president of the *Kansas City Star* and *Times,* opposes eavesdropping. "We should conduct ourselves the way other people do," he concludes.

An editor who is personally offended by journalistic eavesdropping, James Wall of *Christian Century* magazine, suggests a test for deciding when it and other dubious methods should be used. "You have to ask," he says: "Are you seeking the truth? Are you hurting anyone? Does the public need to know?" (Interview, 9 Sept. 1981.)

Hidden Cameras. A photographic form of eavesdropping is to take pictures of people without their knowing it. The *Chicago Sun-Times* did that in its famous Mirage investigation of bribery and shakedowns by government inspectors. Hiding in a compartment above the toilet rooms of the Mirage Tavern the paper bought for that project, photographers took pictures of police officers and inspectors as they accepted bribes from the reporters posing as owners of the tavern. The principal reporter on that assignment, Pamela Zekman, claims the paper was very careful not to publish any photo that showed ordinary patrons of the bar who were not known to the *Sun-Times* people on the project (interview, 8 Sept. 1981). "We were concerned about hurting someone who had done nothing wrong, such as someone involved in an affair." Although she would not support using a hidden news camera in a private home, Zekman considers it to be an acceptable technique in a public place, like the Mirage. "Sometimes it's crucial to have the credibility and authenticity that photographs can give you," says Ralph Otwell, editor and executive vice-president of the *Chicago Sun-Times* (interview, 9 Sept. 1981).

Although she does not believe the *Washington Post* would allow secret cameras, reporter-photographer Wheeler concedes that her editors permit the use of long lenses that allow photographers to be so far away from their subjects that the subjects do not always know their pictures are being taken (interview, 24 Sept. 1981). Wheeler used a long lens to photograph a District of Columbia police decoy pretending to be asleep on a doorstep with a portable radio at his feet. From a rooftop across the street, Wheeler photographed a thief stealing the radio and striding confidently down the street into a police ambush, where he was arrested. "If people are in a public place," she says, "they're fair game for photographers."

Another example of the unseen camera occurred recently in Milwaukee, where *Journal* reporters and photographers observed and photographed city garbage collectors "at work." *Journal* managing editor Joseph W. Shoquist explains that the collectors had only enough work to occupy about four to five hours a day. So they would fill out the rest of the day sitting in taverns, playing pool, washing their cars, and the like (interview, 19 Oct. 1981). The photographs helped the *Journal* illustrate the problem in a way that would not have been possible if the collectors had known they were being photographed.

Television news has also discovered the hidden camera technique. KPNX-TV in Phoenix used that method to expose insurance salesmen who made fraudulent claims in order to sell policies to old people. Reporter David Page and photographer Bill Timmer worked with the state insurance commissioner and the Grey Panthers to check out information Page got from a dissatisfied insurance salesman. The Grey Panthers put the news team in touch with Winnie Lockwood, who allowed them to build a closet in her home from which they could secretly photograph her living room through a one-way glass. They took videotape pictures of several insurance agents assuring Lockwood that the policies they were selling provided coverage beyond Medicare that they did not actually provide. Then Page interviewed the agents in their offices, where they told him just the opposite of what they had told the elderly woman. After the stories Page and Timmer developed were broadcast, the license of one insurance salesman was revoked, several were suspended, and one insurance company had to make refunds totaling $400,000 to policyholders who bought their policies because of false sales pitches.[27]

Another ethical problem for photographers is the posed or reenacted shot. Not all posed or reenacted shots offend reality, of course, and about the worst you can say about most of them is that they are dull. And there has been a tolerance for staged news photographs, even when they do tamper with reality. One of the most famous photographs to come out of World War II, Joe Rosenthal's "Raising of the flag on Iwo Jima," was staged. He asked the Marines to raise the flag a second time, using a larger flag that would show up better in the photograph.[28]

But some reenactments are beginning to trouble journalists. Don Black, features editor of the *Statesman-Journal* in Salem, Oregon, tells of a photographer at another paper who was sent out to get a shot of young people smoking in the lounge of the local vocational-technical school (interview, 10 Nov. 1981). The photographer got to school at the wrong time — the lounge was empty. "So he rustled up a couple of kids, gave them some cigarettes and set up the picture he was sent to get," Black recalls. "The paper got into a big hassle, because one of the kids did not smoke and came from a family that felt strongly against smoking."

The *St. Petersburg Times* and *Evening Independent* dismissed a veteran photographer who set up a stunt picture and was photographed doing so by a photographer from the rival *Tampa Tribune*. Attempting to liven up routine picture coverage of a football game between Eckerd

College and Florida Southern, the St. Pete photographer, Norman Zeisloft, asked a barefoot student in the stands to print "Yea, Eckerd" on the soles of his feet. The student agreed, his girl friend did the art work, Zeisloft got his picture, and so did the *Tampa Tribune.* "It was a hard call," said *Times* executive editor Robert Haiman, but "one of the cardinal sins of a journalist is to tell a lie." "It was just a whimsical little picture," said Zeisloft.[29]

Checkbook Journalism. While not a common practice in American journalism, paying for information or exclusive rights to an interview still occurs. It is a method of reporting generally condemned in the United States, but more widely practiced in Great Britain, where even some public officials ask to be paid for granting interviews. The argument against it in this country, in addition to its costliness, is that it tempts informers to lie for cash, to merchandise facts.

The kind of checkbook journalism that has gotten the most attention when it has happened in this country is the payment of large sums of money by big media for exclusive rights to some VIP's story: the $100,000 that CBS paid in 1975 to H. R. Haldeman, Nixon's top White House aide, for two televised interviews; the presumably large but undisclosed sums that *Life* magazine paid in the mid 1960s for the exclusive right to the personal stories of the U.S. astronauts, thus covering up blunders in the space program that were not revealed until Tom Wolfe dug back into that material for his 1979 book, *The Right Stuff.*[30] Movie companies and book publishers occasionally pay for exclusive rights to someone's story, but those media are not in the news business and most observers see less harm in their trying to tie down interesting stories that are only peripherally in the public interest.

But most of the paying for information in U.S. journalism occurs at a much lower level than Haldeman and the astronauts, and the money that is passed comes in smaller denominations. When black activist Eldridge Cleaver was in exile, he demanded $2,000 from Claude Lewis for an interview for the Philadelphia *Bulletin.* Lewis talked him down to $200. He says he got a fine interview for his money, but he "felt shaky about it because there is a danger that people will tell you anything for money." (Interview, 17 Sept. 1981.) When Robert W. Greene, assistant managing editor of *Newsday*, was doing his now-famous investigation of heroin imports to this country, he had to bribe Turkish police for leads (interview, 6 Oct. 1981). "Nothing is done in Turkey unless you pay bribes." Even though he did it, Greene feels checkbook journalism is a bad practice.

The AP surprised everybody in the news business when it paid a coal miner for his exclusive first-person account of the 122 hours he spent entrapped in a Pennsylvania mine that collapsed in 1977. The AP declined to say at the time what it paid the anything-but-wealthy miner. But James Donna, a deputy director of the newsphoto agency Gamma-Liaison who was the AP editor on the coal mine story by Lee Linder of the Philadelphia bureau, believes the payment was small — something like $2,000 (interview, 8 Oct. 1981).

William F. Thomas, editor of the *Los Angeles Times*, remembers being "lambasted in all the righteous organs across the land" for printing a confession in the Manson trial that he obtained by paying some official of the court (interview, 2 Nov. 1981). "It was clearly a document I was not supposed to have," Thomas concedes. "I paid quite a bit for it, but you never have to pay as much as people think." Thomas contends he did it because "everybody in the entire community was on edge, wondering whether there were more of those people around and what in hell made them do what they did." But the press could not find out what actually happened and what the Manson gang's motives were because "court officials were trying to protect the court record in order to get a clean conviction." The document Thomas got was a transcript of a taped interrogation of one of the women in the Manson group. "She unburdened herself, and, oh, God, what a story!" Thomas adds. "It was important to everybody."

Chet Fuller, *Atlanta Journal* reporter, opposes buying information for a story, but he recalls paying a male prostitute $40 to talk to him. He said the prostitute, who told him he could have made $120 for the time he gave him, provided valuable background for an article on male prostitution. Fuller claims he "would not have been able to penetrate that world otherwise," and he does not regret paying (interview, May 1981).

A dissent from the prevailing feeling against checkbook journalism comes from Jack Landau, director of the Reporters Committee for Freedom of the Press (interview, 24 Sept. 1981). Landau argues that newspapers buy information all the time when they pay to publish memoirs from important people, such as Dwight Eisenhower and Henry Kissinger, and when they pay for syndicated columns. Newspapers are also willing to pay for photos of some news event they did not cover, but they would not pay for some eyewitness account of the event, Landau notes, adding: "Checkbook journalism may be a bad practice economically, but I can't see the legal distinction between purchasing the kind of information publications do from one category of person but not another."

But Landau was virtually the only one of the approximately 150 journalists interviewed for this study who had even a slightly kind word to say for checkbook journalism.

The Ambush Interview. Is it fair for a reporter to surprise a news source with tough and sometimes embarrassing questions? That depends, most journalists would reply.

It depends first on who the news source is. If it is a public official who is evading the news media, or someone involved in illegal or questionable practices, then it is all right to use what is coming to be known as the ambush interview — surprising the source by catching him on the street or somewhere away from his or her home or office, or surprising the source by unexpected questions. But many journalists object to ambush interviews of any sort if they are on film or videotape. In other words, it is permissible for a pencil reporter working for print media to ambush a source, but it is not usually acceptable for a television reporter and photographer to do so. Why the distinction?

Fred Friendly, former president of CBS News and a professor at Columbia University, has called ambush interviewing "the dirtiest trick department of broadcast journalism." He believes that when viewers see a TV reporter chasing a source down the street, the impression they get is of "the honest reporter asking the honest question, and the crooked interviewee being unavailable." The truth could be "exactly the opposite," Friendly said, noting that saying no to a television camera is everyone's First Amendment right.[31]

Friendly made that comment on a documentary that Bill Kurtis of CBS News did when he was chief anchor at WBBM-TV, Chicago. Kurtis agrees with Friendly's view of the ambush interview if the interviewee is a private person. He maintains that the technique is acceptable if the person being asked questions is a politician used to talking to reporters. His objection to such an interview for private persons is that "you run the risk of not being fair, of making an innocent person look guilty." One alternative method he has used is for the TV reporter to approach the source on the street, with the camera well back, to ask if the source will respond. If the source agrees, then the camera moves in; if the source declines to talk, then you still have film to use to report that the source has declined to comment.

"60 Minutes," CBS News's highly rated investigative reporting program, has not gone in for the kind of ambush interview that shows the interviewee being chased down the street by a reporter and photographer, but it has used the technique. However, Don Hewitt, producer of the show, has come to believe that ambush interviewing "has been abused." In a 1981 program in which "60 Minutes" examined itself with a panel of journalists and media observers, Hewitt agreed with Ellen Goodman, *Boston Globe* columnist, when she said it is impossible for a source to say "no comment" to a TV reporter with the camera on, the way he might with a print reporter. "He always looks bad," Goodman claimed. "The camera is an inherently unfair weapon." Hewitt commented that the ambush interview is, "in effect, asking a man to testify against himself. You shouldn't do that."[32]

Brit Hume of ABC News agrees that some ambush interviews are questionable, but he points out "there are circumstances when you have no real alternative." (Interview, 4 Nov. 1981.) When he was working for ABC's "Close Up" series, he followed a Department of Agriculture official to Rome and had to put the same question to him fourteen times before he would answer it. "It's fairer to your source if you can notify him in advance that you're going to interview him," Hume concedes, "but if you're dealing with some miscreant, it's legitimate to catch him somewhere and put the question to him. Calling people to account is part of what we do."

William J. Small, UPI president and former head of NBC News, objects to using the ambush interview just for dramatic effect, but he feels that it is important to allow the "accused" to have his or her say (interview, 5 Oct. 1981). In Small's view, when "NBC Magazine" showed reporter Jack Perkins running down the street after a portly photographer he had just accused of photographing young girls in the nude, it was the photographer, not Perkins's, who turned that into an ambush situation. NBC got no negative reaction from Perkins's losing foot race, according to Small.

Print reporters do not get their pictures in the paper chasing news sources, but they, too, use confrontational tactics on occasion. And quite often, they get interviews with reluctant sources by telling them they want to discuss some unfrightening subject and then once into the interview switching to questions the sources have been trying to duck — getting an interview with a developer, for example, by telling him you want to do a piece on how his housing developments have contributed to the economy of the area and then pulling some "time bomb" questions out of your pocket about some shady deal he was involved in back in Memphis. *Phildelphia Inquirer* editor Severson admits he has used that technique and he sees nothing wrong with it as long as there is no TV camera recording it (interview, 18 Sept. 1981). "We're not dealing with retardees," he argues. "They can duck the questions."

Sources, like the developer in the preceding example, frequently have reasons for not wanting to talk to reporters. When they have secretaries in their offices to protect them, the reporter's task is all the more difficult. One journalist who is said to have developed a sure-fire way of getting reluctant sources to the telephone is investigative reporter Seymour Hersh, formerly of the *New York Times*. Developing legend has it that after Hersh has been turned away about seventeen times, he says to the reluctant source's secretary: "You tell him if he doesn't call me back in five minutes, we're going to go with the sodomy story."

Taking and Breaking. Most journalists like to think they would not break a law to get a story, but as a matter of fact, they do it often. Usually, though, the laws they break are not serious ones: exceeding speed limits to get to a fire, parking illegally to be near the scene of a story, trespassing on private property after a fire or some other tragic event, things of that sort. But sometimes journalists have gone beyond minor infractions when the stakes have been high.

Les Whitten, novelist who was the senior investigator on the Jack Anderson column for twelve years, admits that he once committed a felony by taking some papers out of a U.S. senator's files, copying them, and returning them the next day. He had help from a person he would not name who opened the Senate office door for him and gave him the letter of the alphabet he should seek in the files. "It was a hell of a story that helped prevent a multi-million-dollar insurance fraud, and I couldn't resist it," Whitten admits, "And I'd probably do it again." (Interview, 2 Sept. 1981.) Whitten believes that government documents belong to the people and reporters should not be afraid to "liberate" them in certain serious situations.

A Rochester, New York, *Times-Union* reporter lost his job for stealing evidence, according to his managing editor, Larry Beaupre, and his executive editor, Robert Giles (interviews, 15 Oct. 1981). The reporter, who had gone to a house where police had rounded up a group of suspects, found two envelopes on the floor, evidence apparently dropped or overlooked by the police. The reporter picked them up and brought them back to his office, where he used material in the envelopes in his story. When the city editor asked him about the unattributed information in the story, the reporter confessed. "He said he'd seen it done that way in the movies," Beaupre recalls. This same reporter had earlier offended his editors when he turned his notes over to a defense attorney in a case he was covering. After the second incident, "his lawyer advised him to take a resignation," Giles adds.

Most journalists draw the line at breaking and entering or stealing, but they would not turn their backs on stolen material that came their way. One of the arguments the U.S. government made when it tried to stop publication of the Pentagon Papers by the *New York Times* and the *Washington Post* was that the papers were stolen property. But the journalists on the *Times*, *Post*, and other newspapers got those papers not by stealing them but by accepting them from Daniel Ellsberg, who had been a government consultant. Editor Bradlee of the *Post* observes, "I still don't know whether Ellsberg stole them or had a right to have them." (Interview, 5 June 1981.) Ellsberg, an antiwar activist, wanted the papers published because they revealed how the U.S. government had gotten steadily enmeshed in the Vietnam war. He made copies available to a few members of Congress, hoping in vain to get them out to the public that way, before he started slipping copies to newspaper journalists he knew.

Once they got hold of the copies, editors of the *New York Times* and the other papers Ellsberg made them available to had to decide whether to defy the convention of not publishing government secrets and whether to publish materials that had probably been stolen. An important related question was: How can we not pass these documents on to the public now that we have them? What right do we as journalists have to suppress material so obviously in the public interest? As you know, the *Times*, the *Post*, and other newspapers decided to publish. That was in 1971. None of the dire predictions of the Nixon administration about what was going to happen to the country if the papers were published has yet materialized.

Would a stolen secret government report as important as the Pentagon Papers be published by most newspapers today? Chances are it would. William E. Deibler, managing editor of the *Pittsburgh Post-Gazette*, seems to speak for many when he says, "If I had a document that showed that Lee Harvey Oswald worked for the CIA, no matter how it got in my hands, it would be printed." (Interview, 22 Oct. 1981.)

WHAT THE CODES SAY

What was most shocking to many journalists about the fabrications of Janet Cooke, Gloria Ohland, and Michael Daly was that they violated a principle that is so basic to journalism that you don't have to talk about it and you don't even have to write it down. Everyone who gets into journalism is supposed to understand that lies and fakery are simply not allowed. Fiction has no place in journalism.

Because the principle of not lying, not making things up, is so well understood, the codes of ethics of national news organizations do not deal with it in any very specific way. There is no provision in any of them that says simply: "Journalists don't lie!" Perhaps there should be, in view of the recent resurgence of fakery in journalism.

To most journalists, the accuracy standard means getting your facts right and presenting them honestly. And it also means being truthful. So we find in all the national codes some proviso against inaccuracies.

Among the codes of individual news organizations, there appears to be the same assumption — that truth telling is so basic to the business that spelling it out would be like instructing your staff to breathe in and out. But some specifically mention plagiarism. The *Washington Post*, for example, states that "attribution of material from other newspapers and media must be total. Plagiarism is one of journalism's unforgivable sins."[33]

The other concern of this chapter — the dubious methods journalists sometimes use to get news — is not dealt with at all in the national codes. The national journalistic organizations apparently do not view the use of such methods to be widespread enough to merit attention. This was indicated when, in one of the interviews for this book, Casey Bukro of the *Chicago Tribune*, principal author of the SPJ-SDX code, turned aside a question about checkbook journalism because he said it so rarely occurs in American journalism (interview, 10 Sept. 1981). However, some of the codes of individual newspapers and broadcast networks do contain advice about methods of gathering news.

The *Philadelphia Daily News* advises that "in gathering the news, staff members should avoid conduct that could reasonably be considered unethical or illegal."

The NBC News code deals with eavesdropping, hidden cameras, and paying interviewees. It warns that the

> unauthorized use of an electronic, mechanical or other device to intercept (and, in some situations, to record) the contents of a telephone, wire or private oral communication is a crime under federal law and under the laws of some states. As a consequence, no such interception or recording should be attempted until the facts have been reviewed by the Law Department or an appropriate Vice-President of NBC News.

Regarding hidden cameras, the NBC News code states that they may be used "to record occurrences in public places, such as streets and parks," but "the use of hidden cameras in buildings or locations which are not public but which the public is invited to enter, such as stores, restaurants and common areas of apartment houses or office buildings, should be undertaken only after consultation with the Law Department and an appropriate NBC News executive." NBC reminds staff members that they also need to consult with superiors if they plan to use hidden cameras in private places.

NBC News opposes paying persons for interviews "for initial use in hard news or hard news oriented broadcasts." It adds, however, that management might approve payment for interviews "in very special circumstances," such as "the broadcast of memoirs of public figures."

The law-breaking problem is addressed by CBS News in a provision in its code that states CBS News "personnel will not knowingly engage in criminal activity in the gathering or reporting of news, nor will they encourage or induce any person to commit a crime." The provision goes on to discuss exceptions, such as technically violating the law to buy liquor in a dry state or handguns for "reports on how easy it is to acquire these articles." But, the CBS News code adds, there are "acts which cannot be countenanced, no matter how important the subject under investigation, the most obvious example of which would be injury to another person. Between these extremes lie many hard questions."

The CBS News provision on electronic eavesdropping and hidden cameras expresses great concern about what federal and state laws do and do not allow and prohibits its newspeople from using these methods in any case where they may be illegal. It concedes that hidden cameras can be used in public and semipublic places (defined in the same way as the NBC code provision above), but not in a private place unless the subject has given permission to do so.

While prohibiting payment to a news source for a story or news release, ABC News policy recognizes these possible exceptions:

> (1) An author, reporter, commentator, teacher, entertainer or other professional or expert, who appears in his professional or vocational capacity....
>
> (2) A public figure for participation in a broadcast which is in the nature of an electronic version of the person's memoirs.
>
> (3) A consultant, who may or may not appear on broadcasts, who is employed to provide information and expertise that we cannot duplicate by our own efforts....
>
> (4) Persons who own rights to an already completed work (book or movie), or work in progress, that we plan to use.
>
> (5) In foreign countries, persons such as British members of Parliament who customarily receive small honoraria for giving broadcast interviews.

In his "Seven Basic Rules" for investigative reporters, Clark R. Mollenhoff addresses some of the concerns of this chapter. "Don't exaggerate or distort the facts or the law," he states in rule four. "There is enough wrong in our society that you don't have to fabricate or exaggerate anything.... efforts to sensationalize will discredit your investigation in the long run." Mollenhoff's sixth rule warns:

> Do not violate the law unless you are prepared to take the consequences. Any time you violate the law to obtain information you develop a vulnerability that can destroy your credibility as well as the story you are pursuing. Such behavior gives errant public officials an opportunity to get the spotlight off their corruption and misman-agement and to focus instead on excesses of the press. If you give the problem sufficient study, there is usually a legal way to obtain information, although it may require more patience than a burglary. Learn how to use the Freedom of Information Act. Know government records. Know information policies and procedures — information is your business.[34]

Sometimes the folklore of the newsroom can provide guidance for journalists fortunate to work for organizations that have had wise and thoughtful leaders, such as the late John Dougherty, who was managing editor of the Rochester, New York, *Times-Union* and *Democrat &*

Chronicle. Anthony M. Casale, who was assistant managing editor of the *Times-Union* before joining *USA Today*, says he still lives by Dougherty's words: "We don't lie, we don't steal, we don't misrepresent ourselves." (Interview, 16 Oct. 1981.)

The fakery and dubious methods discussed in this chapter fortunately are not often employed in the practice of journalism in this country. But it does not take much of such unethical behavior to pollute the entire enterprise and erode public confidence in the news process.

C H A P T E R   E I G H T

That's Shocking!

PICTURE YOURSELF AS THE MANAGING EDITOR of an afternoon newspaper in a medium-sized city. One of the stories brought to you for decision is a report about a forty-nine-year-old woman who doused herself in gasoline and then set fire to herself on a quiet suburban street this morning. Horrified residents of the area smothered the flames with blankets; fire fighters and an ambulance crew treated her there on the street and then took her to a hospital, where she is near death. Your city editor did not know of this unusual incident in time to send out a staff photographer, but one of the residents who helped smother the flames took some photographs and has loaned you his roll of exposed film, from which your photo department has printed up two photographs for possible publication.

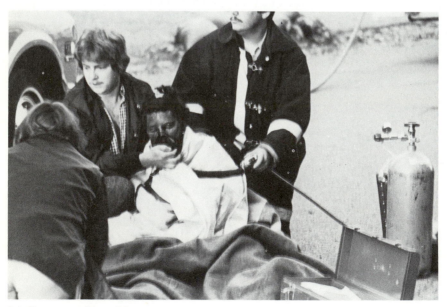

8.1. Rescue workers giving oxygen.

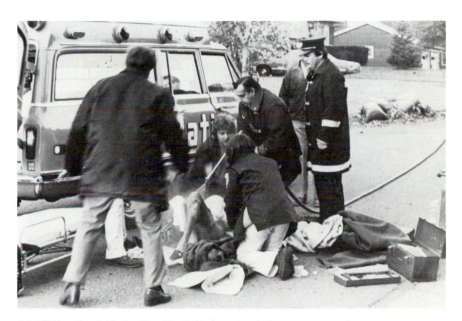

8.2. Victim of suicide by fire. *Fire fighters and ambulance crew members fight to save the life of a woman who tried to take her own life by setting fire to herself. Should these pictures have been published?*

What do you tell your news staff to do with this story and pictures? Would you be inclined to publish the story and both pictures, or the story and perhaps only one picture, or the story alone, or a picture alone, or nothing at all? If you are squeamish about running either the pictures or story on this incident, what is it that makes you so? Shouldn't people in your town know that one of their neighbors has acted in this highly unusual way?

This is the sort of decision that faced the editors of the Rochester, New York, *Times-Union* when a woman attempted suicide by fire in a surburban community about a mile from her own home, where she had left a suicide note. There was no question in the *Times-Union* newsroom that day that a story on this strange incident had to be published, but the photographs were a different matter. "We thought about it for a long time before deciding to run one picture on the back of the local news section," contends Nancy Woodhull, then managing editor of the *Times-Union*, now managing editor for news of Gannett's new national daily, *USA Today* (interview, 16 Oct. 1981).* The picture that was used (Fig. 8.2) was probably worth page one, Woodhull says, but "you have to be considerate of readers . . . who welcome you into their homes every day and expect you to handle things in a certain way."

The woman who set fire to herself died later that day, after all editions of the *Times-Union* had gone to press. It turned out that she had been under psychiatric care — no surprise, of course — and that she had quit her job as a junior high school teacher only two months earlier. She left a husband, mother, and five children.[1]

The *Times-Union* got a lot of criticism for using the picture, and none of the letters of protest it printed noted that the picture was on the back page of the local section and not in what editors would regard as a more prominent position. The letters, many of which came from friends of the dead woman, concentrated their protests on the picture, which the letter writers saw as tasteless and as compounding the anguish of the surviving family.

Woodhull, who consulted executive editor Robert Giles, among others, before deciding to run the controversial photograph, believes the critics overlooked the fact that the woman did what she did in a public not private place — "in the middle of the street." Besides, she explains, "the world needs to know this is what happens to a person if pushed to the brink. . . . This is what we're talking about when we talk about mental health facilities and mental health care."

The photograph probably would not be run in the *Times-Union* today. Larry Beaupre, who succeeded Woodhull as managing editor, believes that he would not have used it because a story without any photographs would have been sufficient (interview, 15 Oct. 1981). The picture's "value" did not "offset its grisly impact," Beaupre adds. He would have the support of his former assistant managing editor, Anthony Casale, who went along with the decision to publish the photo at the time but says he would not run the picture today (interview, 16 Oct. 1981).

What this case study tells us, among other things, is that pictures usually have more impact on people than written words. Their capacity to shock exceeds that of language. People are shocked by both visuals and

---

*See list of interviewees following Notes.

words, of course, and editors and television news directors and producers tiptoe when they have to decide whether and how to present news material that might be shocking.

Another word that is used to describe what this discussion is all about is "taste" — the sense of what may be done or said without giving offense or committing an impropriety. All journalists seem to believe that they have to be aware of taste in the material presented to the public, but some do not see taste as an ethical problem. This chapter will try to show that extreme violations of taste — shocking words and visuals — are ethical issues in that they force the journalist to make what is basically a moral decision: If the news is shocking, how much, if any, should be screened from the public?

DISTURBING PHOTOS

Ralph Otwell, editor of the *Chicago Sun-Times,* recalls the photographs U.S. newspapers ran during the Vietnam War of Buddhist monks burning themselves to death. Those self-immolation pictures were shocking, he admits, "but they were important in telling the story of that war and people's reaction to that war." (Interview, 9 Sept. 1981.) Otwell does not believe, however, that all such photos should be published automatically. "If an emotionally unstable woman goes down to the civic center plaza and sets herself on fire," he explains, "we would not use that picture."

Otwell's paper and most others in this country published many photographs from the Vietnam War that startled readers. Remember the little Vietnamese girl running naked and screaming down the street after her village was bombed? Or the close-up photo of the Viet Cong prisoner as he was executed with a shot to his head from a pistol being held two inches from his ear by a South Vietnamese officer? Or those TV pictures of South Vietnamese soldiers cutting the ears off the dead Viet Cong soldiers? (Younger readers may need to be told that the South Vietnamese were on our side.)

It should not be surprising that news pictures from a war would be disturbing. War is disturbing. But news photography depicts a lot of violence and tragedy in peacetime as well. A study by photojournalist Lil Junas showed that 56 percent of the winners in the top two news photography competitions in the United States were pictures of violence and tragedy. The Pulitzer Prizes have been particularly partial to such pictures. Junas found that twenty-six of the forty Pulitzer awards for news photography between its beginning in 1942 and through 1981 went to pictures showing violence and tragedy. She discovered that thirty-two of the sixty-three "pictures of the year" recognized by the National Press

Photographers Association and the University of Missouri School of Journalism between 1944 and 1982 were photographs of violence or tragedy. In addition to the fifty-eight winning photos that depicted violence or tragedy, Junas said eighteen winners "were related to or results of tragic and violent situations — like refugees fleeing a war area and rescues from fires and accidents."[2]

When he was ombudsman for the *Washington Post*, Charles B. Seib wondered in writing about the differences in the way readers and news editors looked at photos. When the *Post*, along with most other daily newspapers in the land, prominently displayed photographs of a woman and a little girl falling from the collapsed fifth floor fire escape of a burning Boston tenement, many readers complained. Seib reported he got about seventy such calls the day the photos ran, more than he had ever received as ombudsman. He said many of the callers were more hurt than angry, expressing sorrow that the *Post* had "sunk to pandering to the most morbid instincts." But when he checked about the *Post* newsroom, he found no second thoughts about running the dramatic fall photos, only some discussion of how such photos should be displayed. "It is not too far-fetched to suggest that the Boston pictures and the reactions to them shed some light on the strained relations between the press and the public," Seib wrote. "Our professional 'little shells' can diminish our awareness of the human and humane feelings of the reader in matters far beyond picture selection."[3]

The Boston fire photos won a 1976 Pulitzer Prize for Stanley Forman of the *Boston Herald American*. The woman he photographed in her fall from the fire escape balcony was baby-sitting the little girl. The woman was killed. The little girl survived because she landed on the body of her baby-sitter. Forman said he thought he was photographing a dramatic rescue as he stood on the back of a ladder fire truck clicking off shots of a fire fighter on the ladder reaching for the woman and child. Just as the fire fighter's hand touched the arm of the woman, the metal balcony of the fire escape started falling. Forman was not certain what was happening but he kept his motor-driven camera aimed at the scene. He said he started following the girl down and then he realized what was going on. He completely turned around because he did not want to see her hit the ground.[4]

Tom Kelly, director of photography for the Pottstown, Pennsylvania, *Mercury*, won a 1979 Pulitzer Prize for some shocking photos of another tragedy. Alerted by the police radio in his car, Kelly was the first journalist to arrive at a home near Pottstown where a young man had barricaded himself after killing his pregnant wife, stabbing his six-year-old daughter in the eye, and seriously injuring his 71-year-old grandmother. The grandmother, lying stabbed on the lawn, was the first to be rescued by the police. They then talked the berserk young father into releasing his daughter. Kelly says he could not stop the tears from his eyes as he photographed the little girl, blood covered from head to toe and pleading with the police not to hurt her daddy. Then police went in after the man, and as they brought him out he broke free about four feet from Kelly. The photographer believes he must have reacted automatically because he does not remember taking the picture that his paper used to lead off the fifteen photos it published the next day (Fig. 8.3).

8.3. Berserk young murderer. *Blood-stained murderer breaks loose from police. Is this too shocking for your family newspaper?*
(Photo by Tom Kelly, the *Mercury,* Pottstown, Pa.)

The photographs Kelly took that afternoon, which were distributed by the AP and used all over the country, were "shocking and very emotional," he admits (interview, 8 Jan. 1982). But he does not believe the press should "hide what's going on. It's life. It happened." He said all of the pictures the *Mercury* used to tell this tragic story "may have been shocking or horrifying, but none was distasteful."

Kelly's editor, Robert J. Urban, says "we knew we'd be criticized for using" the photographs, and they were (interview, 26 May 1981). Urban remembers that most of the criticism was to the effect that the paper had given undue emphasis to a horrible crime. "We saw it as a life-and-death drama that we were obligated to show to our readers," the editor explains.

Another case that gave editors a decision as to whether news photos justified the shock occurred when the U.S. government sent a mission to Iran in 1980 to rescue the hostages and then had to abort it when a cargo plane and a helicopter in the mission collided and exploded in the desert. Both major wire services transmitted some stark photographs of the charred bodies of U.S. servicemen killed in that collision. Most newspapers ran them, but they got a lot of protests from their readers. Ombudsman George Beveridge, in defending the use of those "ghastly" pictures by his newspaper, the now defunct *Washington Star*, wrote that "newspapers were obliged to print them because they gave readers a dimension of understanding of the situation and the people involved that written words could not possibly convey." The *Boston Globe* received more than 200 calls and letters protesting the use of a picture of a charred body. *Globe* ombudsman S. S. Micciche held that this was a case where the event was so historic that it outweighed all other considerations. "We would have been derelict in our obligation to print the truth and reality if we had banned the use of that picture," Micciche said. But editors of the small daily in Gulfport-Biloxi, Mississippi, the *Sun*, told their readers that they tore up the AP photos of the charred bodies because it would have been "the poorest kind of taste to display those ghastly pictures." The *Sun* said the "decision was based on common decency and simple good taste."[5]

Some readers and viewers aim their "poor taste" criticisms at visuals that show presidents and other VIPs in unsightly or embarrassing lights. News photographers in an earlier day were unusually respectful of presidents, as were reporters. Franklin D. Roosevelt, for example, was not often shown in a way that gave readers any clear idea of how difficult it was for him to get around in the braces he had to wear because of infantile paralysis. Years later President Ford might have yearned for that kind of "protection" as he was photographed slipping on stairs, bumping his head, and doing other things that gave him a reputation for clumsiness. And Governor George Wallace, after the assassination attempt that crippled him, was frequently photographed in his wheel chair or as he was being carried onto an airplane or being helped to a podium.

The FDR treatment was also lacking when President Carter fell while jogging in Georgia, three days after he turned the White House over to President Reagan. Photographer Charles Kelly of the AP was there shooting a jogging picture when Carter tripped over a curb and fell forward to the pavement, slowing his fall with his hands. A single photo and a four-picture sequence were sent out by AP to all of its clients, most of whom used at least some of the pictures the next day. Reader reaction was strong, many accusing the AP and newspapers that put the pictures on page one of kicking the man while he was down. Louis D. Boccardi, executive editor and vice-president of the AP, claims that he understands the reaction the pictures brought from some people, but the photos "were perfectly valid" because it happened in public to "one of the most public persons in the world." Boccardi notes that the AP never heard from Carter personally about the fall photos (interview, 8 Oct. 1981.) Edwin Guthman, editor of the *Philadelphia Inquirer*, which heard from several angry readers after displaying two pictures of the Carter fall on page one, apologized for running the photos in such a prominent position and for the facetious caption, but denied that his paper was trying to rub salt in Carter's wounds. Guthman said he was glad to see in the public reaction "a sense of fairness and humane concern for Carter, a genuine outpouring of sympathy and decency." He added that the paper had learned from the criticism.[6]

Guthman's comments should not be read to mean that news photographers and editors are thinking of retreating to the softer attitude that dictated their depiction of crippled President Roosevelt. Rightly or wrongly and with some exceptions, journalists today keep a fairly consistent heat on presidents, senators, governors, and other top public officials, and if those officials slip or stumble in public they are apt to land on page one.

Another kind of taste problem for editors and television news directors occurs when news includes photographs of nudity. Elizabeth Ray comes to mind. She was the woman who claimed to be the mistress of Ohio Congressman Wayne Hays while she was being paid $14,000 a year to be a secretary on his congressional staff who never had to come to the office. Shortly before she broke the news of her illegal employment by Congressman Hays, Ray had posed for *Playboy* magazine, which provided the AP with a bare-breasted photograph of her. The APME did a survey and found that only 24 of the 138 editors who responded had used the partially nude picture, and 20 of them said they cropped it to avoid showing the woman's breasts. APME Photo Committee chairman Joseph M. Ungaro concluded that "editors don't think the public is ready for nudity in the newspapers."[7]

A student newspaper published at a large university can take greater risks with shocking photos than, say, a newspaper in a small to medium-sized community that tries to appeal to families. Editors presume that the audiences for a college student newspaper and a community newspaper are different. But the *Daily Collegian*, student newspaper at the Pennsylvania State University, still had to defend itself against critics after it published a picture of a young woman winning a wet-T-shirt contest by stripping the shirt (Fig. 8.4). Letter writers and other protesters said the picture was in poor taste and was insulting to women. To which *Collegian* columnist Kathleen Pavelko replied that the wet-T-shirt contest, which had attracted hundreds of people to a local bar, "was like the streaking incidents of 1974; not in its nudity, but as a student phenomenon and a possible trend on American college campuses. The contest was a slice of student life." Pavelko said the editor consulted with many staff members before deciding to run the photo. The photo "did not pander to anyone's prurient interest," she wrote. "In fact ... it was a strong argument for the women's point of view; the reaction of the men on the left was caught beautifully — tongues out, eyes bulging. I could think of no better way to illustrate the ugly reaction of the crowd that night."[8]

Another kind of nudity problem for editors comes up in pictures of human birth. Don Black sold an interesting set of photographs to *People*

8.4. Wet T-shirt. *Young college males recognize a winner in wet T-shirt contest. It was published. Should it have been?*
(Photo by Randy J. Woodbury, *Daily Collegian*, University Park, Pa.)

magazine after his own newspaper, the Binghamton, New York, *Evening Press*, would not use them. The pictures told a story of an obstetrician in that area who taught fathers how to deliver their own babies, with the OB standing by. Black's photos showed a father delivering his own 9½-pound son and a look of joy on the mother's face seldom seen anywhere. That was in the mid 1970s. Black, who is now features editor of the Salem, Oregon, *Statesman-Journal*, believes that public acceptance of such material is much greater now and thinks his paper would publish those photographs today (interview, 10 Nov. 1981).

While he does not feel newspapers should publish shocking pictures for shock's sake alone, Black sees a danger in journalists being "too timid." He contends that "failing to run an important news picture for fear of reader response is indulging in a form of censorship." But many editors are still timid about publishing shocking pictures, worrying about whether the shock will not get in the way of the message the picture is supposed to communicate. This caution is more noticeable, for understandable reasons, in the smaller newspapers.

OFFENSIVE LANGUAGE

One of the things young reporters quickly learn is that the people they cover sometimes use language their editors will not let them publish. Some solve this problem by cleaning up such language as they write their stories. Others try to keep it in when it is part of the news, arguing that when a source says "horse shit," it is dishonest and misleading to change it to "horse manure."

One such reporter is David Shaw, media critic for the *Los Angeles Times*, who feels strongly that there are no words that should not be used in the newspaper. But he runs into arguments with his editors all the time, he admits, even though the *Times* is more liberal on language than most newspapers. "I remember once having to trade a 'shit' and an 'asshole' for a 'ratshit,' " Shaw says (interview, 25 Nov. 1980).

Shaw may or may not be typical but many younger writers see their newspapers as being too conservative about the kind of language they will print. Executive editor Boccardi of the AP has felt some pressure from younger AP staffers (interview, 8 Oct. 1981). Boccardi concedes that standards on offensive words have loosened up in society and the media, but he does not favor "a wholesale letting down of barriers." He wonders whether the younger reporters pressing for more liberal use of language in news stories "will feel that way when they have eight-year-olds reading newspapers."

Boccardi's views are shared by most newspaper editors in this country who see their audiences in terms of families and who worry about what children should or should not read. And the size and location of the newspaper usually make a difference, editors of smaller newspapers tending to block obscenities and other kinds of shocking language that might be permitted in a metropolitan newspaper. Radio and television journalists are even more cautious about allowing offensive language on the air.

Obscenities. The Federal Communications Commission (FCC), which regulates broadcasting in the United States, has a 1978 Supreme Court ruling to back up its right to reprimand broadcasters who use any of seven words the FCC has said are obscene, indecent, or profane. The court decided that the FCC had a right to chastise WBAI, a Pacifica Foundation station in New York City, for broadcasting a monologue by comedian George Carlin, in which he used all seven of the FCC's filthy words — shit, fuck, cocksucker, motherfucker, piss, cunt, and tit. Although this decision sent a shiver through American broadcasting, news departments have continued to air occasional obscenities, banking on the traditional reluctance of the FCC to mess with news and the First Amendment. Many TV stations in 1980, for example, used portions of transcripts from the ABSCAM tapes of conversations between congressmen and undercover FBI agents that were sprinkled with vulgar and obscene words.[9]

Commenting on the Supreme Court's decision in the Pacifica case, Russell Baker wrote in his *New York Times* column that what the court found offensive about the seven words, which refer to bodily wastes or sex, "was not the subject matter they dealt with, but the use of Anglo-Saxon vocabulary to discuss it." Impishly, he continued:

> All seven words have long-winded Latinate synonyms which are commonly used without producing a blush outside the most sheltered backwaters of society. Anyone who undertook court action against a broadcaster for saying "micturition" or "defecation" into a microphone would doubtless be dismissed as a crank or a fool.
>
> But let the same subject be broached in one-syllable Anglo-Saxon words and the Supreme Court assembles to ponder the implications for the future of the Republic. Very few persons, one suspects, would be much offended if, on tuning in their home tubes, they were to hear someone refer to "sexual intercourse," "practitioner of fellatio," "female reproductive canal," "incestuous male issue" or "female mammary glands.". . .
>
> Something about the Anglo-Saxon tongue has the power to make us see red. Or, in the case of the seven unspeakable words, blue. This may go back as far as the Norman invasion of England when the conquerors from France tried to destroy Saxon culture and, in the process, succeeded in stigmatizing the Saxons as crude barbarians.[10]

Publishing one of those Anglo-Saxon words on page one of the Dayton, Ohio, *Journal Herald* in 1975 cost Charles Alexander his job as editor. The word with all that power was used by a U.S. Treasury agent explaining to authorities how it happened that he shot and killed another law enforcement man in a furious quarrel. "Goddamn it, you are fucking with my family," the treasury agent shouted. "You are fucking with my future.... I'll kill you first." Five days after that quotation was published and almost a hundred readers complained, the angry owners of the *Journal Herald* forced Alexander to resign.[11]

Writing later about his decision to print the quotation, Alexander said the news story in which it appeared told how the minor argument escalated to "a state of rage that resulted in a struggle for life between two armed law enforcement agents." He said the story "vividly detailed the erosion of all the restraints that characterized civilized beings, finally culminating in the ultimate obscenity — homicide. But homicide is a socially acceptable obscenity in print. Vulgar language, to some, is not." Alexander argued that journalists have to start telling "the whole truth" if they want to be believed, even though that may require indelicacy. "The reality of truth will have to supplant the illusion of propriety," he declared.[12]

The flap in Dayton reminded John McCormally, then editor and publisher of the Burlington, Iowa, *Hawk Eye*, of the time his paper "used that ultimate 12-letter obscenity (in a story attempting to show what caused nice policemen to lose their cool and hit protesting college students on the head)." This upset a woman reader who called his home one evening when he was not there, McCormally revealed in a letter to *Editor & Publisher* magazine, "but my 11-year-old daughter, as she'd been trained to do, asked: 'May I give him a message?' 'Yes,' replied the woman, 'tell him if he doesn't quit printing that filth, I'm gonna quit taking his fucking paper!' "[13]

Newspaper editors and broadcasters dug into their dictionaries of synonyms and thesauruses to report a racist "joke" that caused President Ford to fire the guy who told it, Earl L. Butz, who had been secretary of agriculture for five years. The "joke" not only made use of vulgar barnyard language, which Butz often lapsed into despite his high cabinet position; it slurred blacks. But most Americans never found out exactly what it was he said that so upset his boss, because only a handful of newspapers and magazines and no broadcast stations carried his remarks verbatim. Those who did not ignore the "joke" altogether resorted to euphemisms.

The news media first learned of the Butz "joke" in a report on the 1976 Republican National Convention in *Rolling Stone* written by John Dean, former White House counsel to President Nixon. Dean said that on the plane coming home from the convention he got into a discussion with Pat Boone and Sonny Bono. They were joined shortly by a man Dean did not name in his article but identified as "a distinguished member of Ford's cabinet." Dean asked the unnamed cabinet secretary why convention delegates had given such a cool reception to a speech by their vice presidential nominee, Senator Robert Dole:

> "Oh, hell, John, everybody was worn out by then. You know," he said with a mischievous smile, leaning over the seat in front of Pat and me, "it's like the dog who screwed a skunk for a while, until it finally shouted, 'I've had enough!' "
> Pat gulped, then grinned and I laughed. To change the subject Pat posed a question: "John and I were just discussing the appeal of the Republican party. It seems to me that the party of Abraham Lincoln could and should attract more black people. Why can't that be done?" This was a fair question for the secretary, who is also a very capable politician.
> "I'll tell you why you can't attract coloreds," the secretary proclaimed as his mischievous smile returned. "Because coloreds only want three things. You know what they want?" he asked Pat.
> Pat shook his head no; so did I.
> "I'll tell you what coloreds want. It's three things: first, a tight pussy; second, loose shoes; and third, a warm place to shit. That's all!"
> Pat gulped twice.[14]

It took some simple sleuthing by the staff of *New Times* magazine to find out who Dean's foul-mouthed storyteller was. The now-defunct magazine reported that it simply checked the traveling schedules of Ford's cabinet members, all eleven of whom had attended the convention, and found that Butz was the only one who flew from Kansas City to Los Angeles on August 20, the day after the convention ended. Dean would not "confirm or deny" that Butz was the storyteller, and Butz refused to comment, but *New Times* got Pat Boone to confirm that it was Butz who told the "joke." "I took it as a joke," Boone was quoted as saying, "but I didn't think it was funny. I felt it was inappropriate language for anyone. He knew he was talking to a reporter, and he may have thought what he said was unprintable. It occurred to me right then that it might be printed. I cringed for him."[15]

The major wire services picked up the story, of course, and editors had to decide how much if any of Butz's remarks would be used. The AP, as it sometimes does, put out two versions of its story, "one you could publish in the church bulletin," AP's Boccardi says. The version that hardly any paper used quoted Butz verbatim. The other version said: "Butz, in his comments, referred to blacks as 'coloreds' and discussed in derogatory terms what he said were their sexual, dress and bathroom preferences." AP's competitor, the UPI, handled the offensive comments with the paraphrasing, "good sex, easy shoes and a warm place to go to the bathroom."[16]

The *New York Times*, which has a reputation as the most bluenosed of major U.S. dailies, reported that Butz had referred to blacks as "colored" and said they wanted only three things that he "listed, in order, in obscene, derogatory and scatological terms." After Butz resigned, the *Times* loosened a bit and used the euphemisms "satisfying sex, loose shoes and a warm place for bodily functions — wishes that were listed by Mr. Butz in obscene and scatological terms." The San Francisco *Examiner & Chronicle* employed the old crossword puzzle trick: ". . . first, a tight p----, second, loose shoes, and third, a warm place to s---."[17]

Some newspapers told their readers that Butz's comments were too raw to publish but adult readers could see them at the office or write in for copies. More than a hundred persons visited the Erie, Pennsylvania, *Morning News* to read the "joke" for themselves. About three hundred fifty showed up at the *Lubbock* (Texas) *Avalanche-Journal*, including a farmer and his wife who drove seventy miles to copy the "joke" to show their neighbors.[18] The somewhat larger San Diego *Evening Tribune* got three thousand letters in a week from readers responding to the paper's invitation to write in if they wanted a copy of what Butz really said.[19]

Charles B. Seib pointed out in his *Washington Post* ombudsman's column what can happen when newspapers blue-pencil controversial remarks by public officials. Seib said that Republicans, including then vice presidential candidate Robert Dole, were putting out the story that Butz's language was no worse than what Jimmy Carter had been quoted as saying in *Playboy* magazine. That was the famous interview in which Carter, who was then running as the Democratic candidate for president, used such words as "screw" and "shack up" and admitted that he had "looked on a lot of women with lust." Seib held that since Butz's exact words were not as widely publicized as those of Carter, the public had no basis on which to make a comparison. "And somehow, I think Carter comes out the loser, even though Butz is the man who lost his job," Seib wrote. "Again I am not arguing that the words Butz used should have been published. Nor am I arguing that Carter's words should not have been published. I do say, though, that the press finds itself in a strange position on the dirty language front."[20] (Seib's paper told its readers what Carter had said but waffled on Butz's more extreme language, reporting that he had said "coloreds" wanted "good sex, loose shoes and a warm place to dispose of bodily wastes.")

That racist revelation to John Dean was not the first time that Butz put his foot in his mouth publicly. During the height of Watergate, he called Senator Sam Ervin "senile." And after Pope Paul VI had criticized birth control as a means of combating world food shortages, Butz quipped to the press — in a mock Italian accent — "He no playa da game, he no maka da rules." Butz got back in the news more recently when he paid a $10,000 fine and served 30 days of a five-year sentence for income tax evasion. He was to be on probation for the balance of the sentence.

Loose-Mouthed Heroes. Many Americans were surprised and shocked when they read court transcripts of tape recordings President Nixon had made in his White House office during the Watergate scandal. His language was salty, to say the least, employing three of the FCC's seven verboten words as well as some of the milder swear words. Americans saw or heard these because most news executives decided that the revelations on the tapes were too important to doctor. Oh, some used the crossword puzzle technique (f---ing, and the like) but Americans got the idea: Nixon, in private, at least, used a rich vocabulary.

It made a difference to editors that the language they might otherwise paraphrase, disguise, or delete came from the top guy in the government. "If the president of the United States says 'fuck,' I'm going to quote him," observes Benjamin Bradlee, executive editor of the *Washington Post*. Abraham Rosenthal, executive editor of the *New York Times*, put it this way: "We'll take 'shit' from the president of the United States, but from nobody else."[21]

VIPs below the presidential level are not always quoted verbatim when they utter an obscenity or profanity. It depends on the story, the circumstances, and the judgment of the editors involved. When people who figure in the news use obscene or vulgar language, most editors and news directors follow the same general rule: keep the language in if it is essential or germane to the news story; otherwise, delete it. There is obvious disagreement among news executives, however, on what is germane and then on whether the dirty words need to be disguised somehow. So it becomes quite a game.

Many newspapers editors, for example, agreed that when Democratic presidential candidate George McGovern climbed over a fence and told a heckler to "kiss my ass," that had to be reported. David Broder, *Washington Post* reporter-columnist who was covering McGovern then and reported exactly what the candidate said, believes that "any public statement by a president or presidential candidates ought to be quoted as accurately as possible." (Interview, May 1981.) But James Naughton, who was there for the *New York Times*, could not get that quote in his paper (interview, 16 Sept. 1981). *Times* editors were not persuaded by Naughton's argument that the comment "exhibited an awful lot about the state of mind of that candidate at that point in his candidacy which was important for the reader to know."

Another presidential candidate, George Wallace, gave Broder "more of a problem with his language," not because of obscenities, but because of grammatical slips (interview, May 1981). He tried to quote Wallace literally when he'd say "ain't" and "he don't," but that made it seem that he and other reporters were putting a "Dogpatch label on him." So the standard of literal quotation for presidential candidates becomes arbitrary, Broder adds, "because none of us speaks absolutely correct grammatical English in everyday life."

The *New York Times*, which obviously does not believe in Broder's literal quotation standard except perhaps for presidents, decided to change Senator Barry Goldwater's words when he said that "every good Christian should kick Falwell in the ass." The senator was responding to conservative religious leader Jerry Falwell's statement that Christian groups should be mobilized against Justice Sandra O'Connor's appointment to the United States Supreme Court. The *Times* quoted Goldwater as saying that Falwell should be kicked "in the posterior." This caused an interesting little problem for the *San Diego Union*, which used the "posterior" quote in its story from the New York Times News Service, to which it subscribes. At least one reader complained that he had heard what Goldwater actually said on television and wanted to know why the paper felt it had to clean up Goldwater's language.[22] Good question. Other wire services and newspapers quoted Goldwater verbatim or did not put quotations marks around the word "posterior" as if that is what the senator said.

The AP paraphrased a verbal outburst by former Attorney General Richard Kleindienst when he was on trial for perjury in Phoenix. AP's Boccardi reported that as a Senate investigator left the witness stand after testimony and walked past the defense table, the AP reporter heard Kleindienst say to the witness, "You goddamn whore." The reporter checked outside the courts with the witness, who confirmed the "whore" remark and said Kleindienst also had called him a "lying son of a bitch." Shortly thereafter, Kleindienst offered apologies all around, saying he had just lost his temper. The AP decided that the exact words were not essential "to convey the fact that Kleindienst had the outburst," Boccardi wrote in an internal newsletter, *Prose & Cons*. The story that went out over the AP wire said, "In a bitter outburst marked by obscenities, Kleindienst called Gray a 'whore' and a liar as Gray walked past the defense table after testifying."[23]

Barry Commoner, in an obvious attempt to get some attention for his minor party campaign for the presidency in 1980, used "bullshit" in a radio ad. That became a news story that gave editors another chance to play their game. The *New York Times* called it a "barnyard expletive" and then referred to it as "Bull———!" The *Philadelphia Inquirer* said

Commoner used an "epithet" and then spelled it out as "b——s——." The *Los Angeles Times* and the *Washington Post* used the word.[24]

Since most newspapers will not print the word "bullshit," the AP usually communicates it without actually spelling it out, Lou Boccardi explained. It came up in a story out of Fort Riley, Kansas, about an army major who had been relieved of command and transferred because he chanted an obscenity while passing in review before a general who commands the base. The story never told what the word was. Boccardi said the AP's Kansas City bureau was advised to find out. It did. The story was rewritten to explain that the major had used a "barnyard epithet" and on second reference "bull----" was used. The story also carried a "flag" at the top, as AP usually does, warning editors that the story contained offensive language.[25]

The late Mayor James Daly of Chicago gave Chicago journalists a somewhat different problem in reporting his expressions. James Hoge, editor in chief of the *Chicago Sun-Times*, recalls that Daly, who used a "colorful brand of fractured English," would often get upset when he was quoted and would claim that he had been misinterpreted (interview, May 1981). "Don't quote what I said, quote what I mean," he would insist. Hoge believes Daly had a good point and his paper tried to "quote what he meant" as often as it could, "except in an occasional feature story on his malapropisms."

Sports reporters and editors could use a phrase similar to "barnyard epithet" — something like "sandlot epithet" or "playing field profanity" or "locker room expletive" — to report on the foul language of many professional athletes. Instead they duck and bob.

"You can't quote most pro athletes verbatim because of obscenity," contends Bill Lyon, sports reporter and columnist for the *Philadelphia Inquirer* (interview, 28 May 1981). "You have to launder their words." Lyon believes that in his experience, at least, baseball players have the "filthiest mouths," with hockey players second, and football players third; "basketball players may have the cleanest mouths," he suggests. In addition to heavy profanity and obscenity, many athletes "butcher the English language," Lyon notes, and sports writers have to ask, "How far should we go for the sake of complete accuracy if it makes an athlete appear to be illiterate?"

George Langford, sports editor of the *Chicago Tribune*, says his section eliminates obscene and profane quotes from athletes "except in rare instances where the language they used is germane to the story." He claims they clean up the language for the readers, not to make the athletes look good (interview, 8 Sept. 1981).

Rick Starr, sports editor of the *Valley News Dispatch* in New

Kensington, Pennsylvania, usually edits out offensive language but he sometimes substitutes the word "bleep'" and occasionally he uses an offensive word (interview, 14 Nov. 1981). One of the times he used a verbatim quote was when Pittsburgh Steeler lineman Joe Greene reacted to new rules that caused a flag to be thrown against Steeler linebacker Jack Lambert for hitting an opposing quarterback. "We play faggot football now," Greene reportedly said. Starr explains that he warned his managing editor that the quote was going to be in his column, and the editor let it stay.

The "bleep" technique to which Starr referred is one sports editors often use, although it is not usually seen in other parts of the paper. The *Miami Herald* gave us an example of that device when it reported Clemson football coach Danny Ford's reaction to the news that the NCAA was investigating his program for alleged recruiting violations. "I don't bleeping have to talk about the bleep," the *Herald* quoted Ford as saying. And for readers who did not understand whatingodsname Ford was saying, the *Herald* story elaborated: "I don't give a bleep what nobody thinks."[26]

Stories edited with such skill and a sense of propriety must be what Drake Mabry, managing editor of the *Des Moines Register* and *Tribune*, had in mind when he told the APME: "It takes a dirty mind to edit a clean newspaper."

Slurs on People. Some news stories that contain no obscene language can still offend some group in the community or society. What would you do, for example, with a news story during a presidential campaign quoting one of the candidates as telling this joke to a group of supporters on his bus:

> How do you tell who the Polish one is at a cockfight?
>   He's the one with a duck.
> How do you tell who the Italian is at the cockfight?
>   He bets on the duck.
> And how do you know the Mafia was there?
>   The duck wins.

That, in case you did not recognize it, is an ethnic joke, possibly offensive to people of Polish or Italian descent. It was told by President Reagan as he campaigned through New Hampshire.[27] Robert Scheer, who studied and interviewed candidate Reagan in depth for the *Los Angeles Times*, would report that particular ethnic joke only in the positive sense: "I tell ethnic jokes. You hear them everywhere. We expect these guys to be human and open, and the minute they show some of that, we slam them.

That's a double standard." Besides, Scheer adds, "it's absurd to suggest that Reagan doesn't like Italians or Poles; there is nothing in his history to suggest that." (Interview, 25 Nov. 1980.)

Scheer was involved in two other flaps about VIPs using words that shocked some people. He was one of the editors of *New Times* when it tracked down Earl Butz as the teller of the racist story that cost him his job as secretary of agriculture. He also did the *Playboy* interview with Jimmy Carter that upset many people. Writing about the Carter interview afterward in *New Times*, Scheer said he had no premonition that Carter's utterance of "screw" and "shack up" would cause a furor. "I just didn't know that they were still dirty words," he said. To illustrate how that part of the interview made Carter come alive, Scheer said his 76-year-old mother told him she found it "reassuring" that "Carter is not an uptight Baptist." Scheer's piece ended with a plea to "reward Carter's honesty with our votes. There must be more of us who 'shack up,' 'screw,' and love it, than those who are still frightened by the words."[28]

Although ethnic sensibilities are more often rubbed wrong by entertainment or drama in movies or on television, it still happens occasionally in news. Philadelphia news media took a beating from Greek-Americans for reporting the murders of two men the Pennsylvania Crime Commission had identified as members of the "Greek mob." The protests to politicians and law enforcement officials as well as to news executives was led by Peter J. Liacouras, then dean of the Temple University School of Law. Most of the news executives stopped using the term in their follow-up stories, but the *Philadelphia Inquirer* continued to refer to the "Greek mob." Its managing editor, Gene Foreman, insisted that the *Inquirer* tries "very hard to keep bias, including ethnic bias, out of our news reporting. Unfortunately, the problem in this case is that the crime organization involved in the news calls itself by an ethnic name and is known by that name by the people who deal with it, including line police officers.... It is wrong for anybody to infer that by reporting the organization's name we express our approval of it."[29]

The word "faggot" that Joe Greene used to describe what some rule changes had done to professional football has been a troublesome one for news executives. The first time I saw that word in a news story was in an article by a young sports writer on a university student newspaper. He used it to describe a college wrestler, thinking that it meant someone small and fast like a "leprechaun." (That topped an earlier experience with a high school friend who wrote in the school paper about "row upon row of little yellow concubines," thinking he was describing cottages or small houses.)

The *Los Angeles Times*, the *New York Times*, and other newspapers decided they had to use "fag" and "faggot' in order to report a story about a judge whose language upset the gay community in the Los Angeles area. In sentencing a Mexican who had crossed the border illegally, U.S. District Judge A. Andrew Hauk reportedly said: "I don't know what's happening. We let all these Iranian ignoramuses in, but not this young man who wants to support his child. And he isn't even a fag, like all these faggots from Cuba we're letting in." Homosexuals, led by two fellow judges and a deputy city attorney, protested that the language the judge used demonstrated that he was personally prejudiced against the homosexual minority. Their protests in this case were aimed at the judge and not the newspapers that printed what he said.[30]

Feminists have demanded that journalists and other public communicators avoid language that stereotypes and insults women or ignores the changing role of women. Newspaper style books have undergone a flurry of changes in recent years as editors tried to meet at least some of these demands. Some, like "chairperson" for "chairman," were resisted stoutly, but news executives found more reasonable, for example, the insistence that fire fighter and mail carrier be substituted for fireman and mailman to reflect the entrance of women into those callings. Careful writers now try to avoid language that suggests men are always wage earners and women are always homemakers.

SLIPPERY STANDARDS

Journalists have a very difficult tight rope to walk between prudishness and sensationalism in their selection of words and pictures. Public mores do not stand still: what was shocking to Americans born early in this century does not shock their grandchildren. And what does it mean when seventy people, or three hundred, call in to protest some picture or some language in an article? Do such protesters represent larger numbers, perhaps a majority, or are they merely the self-appointed censors who make up a small minority of the audience for any news medium?

You would think that the one code of ethics that would deal with the problem of shocking photographs would be that of the National Press Photographers Association. But theirs is a disappointing statement, written in vague and general language that reads more like a pledge for entering some monastic order. Just a sample:

> Our standards of business dealings, ambitions and relations shall have in them a note of sympathy for our common humanity and shall always require us to take into consideration our highest duties as members of society. In every situation in our business life, in every responsibility that comes before us, our chief thought shall be to fulfill that responsibility and discharge that duty so that when each

of us is finished we shall have endeavored to lift the level of human ideals and achievement higher than we found it.

Nor are the codes of other national journalistic organizations of much help in deciding what to do about shocking words and pictures. The Code of the Ethics of the SPJ-SDX declares, "the media should not pander to morbid curiosity about details of vice and crime." The ASNE Statement of Principles advises that journalists should "observe the common standards of decency." The RTNDA code directs that newscasts exclude "sensationalism or misleading emphasis in any form." The only mention of this problem in the APME code is in its definition of a "good newspaper" as being, among other things, "decent."

The wire service that all APME members use does not have a code of ethics as such, but executive editor Boccardi issues periodic advisories to his worldwide staff that amount to the same thing. In a statement on obscenity, Boccardi reminded AP staffers:

> We do not use obscenities on the wire unless there is a compelling need. Where there is a way around them, and there *almost* always is, take it. Similarly, we do not want the wire peppered with the "hells" and "damns" that sprinkle the speech of many people. Leave them out. Good writers and reporters don't need cusswords to make their work graphic and effective.

Some of the codes or operating standards of larger newspapers and television networks deal with shocking language in considerable detail. For example, the *Philadelphia Inquirer* code maintains that "our policy on the use of profanity, obscenity and blasphemy is based on the premise that the *Inquirer* should appeal to the widest possible audience . . . and offer a G-rated product every day." The *Inquirer* requires that its staffers must ask, "Is any important journalistic purpose served by the use of the questionable language?" Then it offers its editors these guidelines:

> A. The use of any questionable language is almost exclusively limited to quoted material. It should be rare indeed that our own writers use it.
> B. Generally, when a news subject utters profanity, obscenity or blasphemy in an interview with one or two reporters, we will not use it. The decision becomes more difficult when the number of listeners is larger and the personage of the speaker more important. When President Carter said in public of a potential campaign opponent, "I'll whip his ass," that was deemed to be a situation in which the verbatim quotation was justified.
> C. Sometimes language that is not in itself profane, obscene or blasphemous might be objectionable on the ground of taste. On the other hand, we should not hesitate to write in clinical terms of

matters pertaining to the human anatomy, sex and excretory functions when relevant to the news.

D. In most cases, when language is deleted from a quotation, an ellipsis will be inserted to indicate that something is missing. Occasionally — and on approval of a ranking editor — it is permissible to *suggest* the word or phrase used without actually publishing it. This is done by using the first letter of the word, followed by an em dash: "The mayor told the reporter, 'If you print that story, I am going to kick your a——.' " The use of *bleep* and *bleeping* as substitutes for profanity is restricted to the sports pages.

E. Most decisions concerning the use of questionable language should be resolved by departmental editors and copy chiefs. These line editors may determine when circumstances warrant the use of expletives such as *hell* and *damn*. Line editors may also authorize the use of such terms as *goddamn, son of a bitch* and *bastard* when the speaker is a reasonably important person, the audience is a fairly substantial one, or the quotation is in a long, serious piece in a section of the paper such as Review and Opinion or Today magazine.

    1. When the circumstances are not clear-cut, or if stronger language or a question of taste is involved, the executive editor or managing editor must be consulted. In the absence of both of these editors, the assistant managing editor in charge must be consulted.

    2. Hard-core obscenities such as *shit, fuck, piss, cocksucker* and their variations may be used *only* on the express approval of the executive editor or the managing editor.

The *Washington Post* also gives detailed advice on shocking material in its *Deskbook on Style*. Benjamin C. Bradlee, executive editor, wrote a sort of introductory statement on taste that declares: "We shall avoid prurience. We shall avoid profanities and obscenities unless their use is so essential to a story of significance that its meaning is lost without them." One of several guidelines under Profanities and Obscenities further on in the deskbook says the "use of nude pictures can be justified only if they provide significant information or understanding that would otherwise be lacking in the story."[31]

Both the *Inquirer* and the *Post* seek through their written codes to advise their news staffs how to avoid sexist language. That section in the *Post* code is especially instructive. For example, it lists several gender-free terms that may be substituted for words and terms that offend many women, such as: business executive or manager for businessman; photographer for cameraman; member of Congress, representative, or legislator for congressman; council member for councilman; supervisor for foreman; reporter or journalist for newsman; flight attendant for steward or stewardess; humanity, humans, or the human race for man or mankind; adulthood for manhood; synthetic or manufactured for man-made; worker or work force for workingman.[32]

The *Chicago Sun-Times* in its Professional Standards urges its news people "to communicate with their readers in the way that readers communicate with each other" even though that may mean using "language (including profanity) which in the past may have been considered taboo." The *Sun-Times* then tells its staffers they have to judge the appropriateness of the language to the story. "If the language is not appropriate or obviously intended to shock, rather than inform, it should be deleted, whatever its nature or no matter how innocuous it might be. If the language is appropriate to its particular context, it should be allowed to stand."

In its Operating Standards, NBC News directs that "audio or visual material which is considered coarse or offensive by a substantial portion of the audience must be avoided to the fullest feasible extent." It adds that management may make an exception if the news is significant, if the offensive material is relevant, and if the material is not so offensive that it outweighs the need of the public to know and understand. "And, in no event, may any such material be used for its shock effect or as the basis for humor."

The Production Standards of CBS News are similar. They offer the Nixon Watergate tapes as an example of news in which offensive language had to be used. "It was decided that the anticipated objectionable language would be broadcast because of the historical and journalistic importance of reporting the [congressional impeachment] proceedings as they actually took place," the CBS code states.

The ABC News policy states that "morbid, sensational or alarming details should not be included in broadcasts unless they are essential to the factual report. Obscene, profane or indecent material must also be avoided." ABC requires that problems involving objectionable material "must be resolved in light of contemporary standards of taste, the state of the law and the requirements of newsworthiness."

As journalists wrestle with the genuine problem of how much offensive material should be passed on to the public, the question has to be asked: If journalists routinely hold back or disguise certain words and pictures, is the public getting — and should it get — the most accurate reflection of real life that journalists can provide? Frankly, most news executives seem to view their audiences as less able than they are to handle shocking words and pictures. "Our readers aren't ready for that," they claim. No sane observer wants all of U.S. journalism to suddenly start imitating the sensationalism of the *New York Post* or the *National Enquirer*, but perhaps it is time for news executives to ask how well they serve us if they treat us all as eight-year-olds.

CHAPTER NINE

Privacy

"I don't know — using the names of these raped Sabine women might stigmatize them for life."

SUPPOSE YOU ARE THE MANAGING EDITOR of a metropolitan daily newspaper and you have to decide how far to go in identifying eight men who have died in a fire at a homosexual film club. Most of the men are married. None is well known in your city: one is an aide to a congressman, one is an army major, one is a former pastor; the other five hold ordinary jobs. Six other men were injured seriously enough to require hospitalization, but authorities have withheld their names and other identification. Because flames blocked the front door of the club, the only unlocked exit, firemen had to smash through a locked rear door to reach the dead and injured men, who had been watching all male, X-rated films on the second floor.

Would you identify the dead men fully — name, age, address, job, and survivors? Would you tell your readers that the death scene was a homosexual club? Would you press authorities to name the injured men?

The editors of the *Washington Post* and the late *Washington Star* had to decide how far they would go in identifying eight victims of just such a fire. Basically, the *Star* decided to identify them fully and the *Post* did not.

Both revealed the nature of the film club, the Cinema Follies. Neither paper published the names of the injured.

The ombudsmen for the two competing papers discussed their different approaches to this story in columns about a week after the tragedy. Charles B. Seib of the *Post* said his paper's "main motivation in not using the names was compassion for the wives and children of the men."[1] George Beveridge of the *Star* wrote that "the identity of the victims in a local tragedy as substantial as this one was so vital an element of the story that the printing of the names never arose" as an issue in the minds of *Star* editors who handled the story.[2]

Seib saw something "disquieting" in the *Post*'s decision because, "in effect, *Post* editors said that homosexuality is so shameful that extraordinary steps had to be taken to protect the families of the victims. We will report the tragedy fully, they said, and tell you what we know about the men who died. But we won't tell you who they were." Seib questioned whether the *Post* approach did not underscore "the stigma of homosexuality" just at the time that "efforts are being made to bring it out and address it as a social fact?"[3]

Beveridge used stronger language to question the *Post*'s decision:

> Post editors say two factors figured in their decision: First, a doubt that the fire victims' presence at the gay-oriented establishment conclusively proved anything about their actual sexual preferences; and second, a concern about the identifications' impact on the families of the fire victims, some of whom may have been "secret" homosexuals.
>
> The first of the Post's factors, to my mind, lands with a thud. For while I haven't the slightest idea who at the Cinema Follies that evening was or wasn't a homosexual, the question strikes me as being entirely beside the point.
>
> The purpose of those stories, in The Post and The Star alike, wasn't to disclose or suggest the sexual preferences of anyone. The stories were written solely because eight human beings who happened to be in a certain place at a certain time, tragically died in a fire. That was news. I won't argue that the sexual orientation of the Cinema Follies added no element of additional reader interest to the story. But the point is that eight deaths in a fire at the Kennedy Center, or an uptown X-rated movie, for that matter, would be no less a story. The victims would be no less or no more important to the story in those instances than they were in the Cinema Follies fire. And I can't, for the life of me, imagine a like tragedy in any other location in which the victims should not be identified as a matter of legitimate reader interest.[4]

Seib agreed that the *Post* should have fully identified all of the fire victims. "By all the measures we normally use, the names were news, and the business of a newspaper is to print the news," he wrote. "Any other course results inevitably in confusion and precedents that cause trouble later."[5]

Beveridge also expressed concern about precedent. While "it is hard to imagine that anyone fails to share the Post's compassion for the families of the fire victims," the *Star* ombudsman wrote, the *Post's* failure to identify the victims of the disaster amounted "to a sort of double standard of press responsibility that is much easier started than stopped."[6]

In his post-mortem on the *Post's* decision not to fully identify the victims in the homosexual film club fire, Seib said he suspects that if a poll could be taken, "the public would favor the course the *Post* took" because the "public generally feels, I think, that the press is much too insensitive to the harm and pain it can cause innocent people."[7]

The question of whether a journalist should or should not reveal or suggest the sexual proclivity of a person who figures in the news is a privacy question. Although invading the privacy of news subjects is usually thought of as a legal matter — the kind you discuss with your lawyer — it is really more of an ethical question: How much of any person's private or personal life should journalists publicize and under what circumstances? The developing law on privacy — based mostly on court decisions in privacy and libel suits — is better at telling journalists what they cannot do than what they should do.

PRIVACY LAW AND ETHICS

You will not find a right to privacy mentioned in the United States Constitution. But since the early part of this century, the courts in this country have increasingly accepted the legal concept that citizens have a right to be let alone. Various opinion polls indicate widespread public support for this idea. One poll by Louis Harris Associates showed that three out of four people questioned urged a guarantee of privacy, equating the right of privacy with the "unalienable rights" of the Declaration of Independence — "life, liberty and the pursuit of happiness."[8]

News organizations often have to defend themselves against suits alleging both libel and invasion of privacy because those two legal theories overlap. For example, litigants may claim that they were libeled (defamed or suffered injury to their reputations) by the publicizing of private facts about them. But defenses against libel and privacy differ. In libel suits, the oldest major defense is truth. Another is qualified privilege, protecting the news media from libel convictions for truthfully reporting government proceedings and records. A third major defense against libel is fair comment and criticism, designed to protect the news media's right to comment on the public performances of people who voluntarily put themselves in the limelight — politicians, entertainers, athletes, and the like. The best defense against a privacy suit, on the other hand, is newsworthiness. If the defendant news organization can show that the offensive item was news and it was accurate, it usually wins suits brought for publicizing private facts.[9]

So the decision about whether and when journalists should invade someone's privacy is largely an ethical rather than a legal one. If the private facts publicized are legitimate news — and courts have been liberal in defining that — chances are slim that a privacy suit will be successful.

When journalists are faced with a decision about publicizing private facts, they have traditionally granted less privacy to public officials and figures than to ordinary or private persons. The "prominence" of people who get into the news has long been a criterion of newsworthiness: What happens to a Senator Kennedy or an Elizabeth Taylor is seen by journalists as being more interesting to the public than what happens to John and Jane Doe.

Privacy for VIPs. How much does the public need to know about the private lives of public officials and personalities? Not an easy question, in this day and age. Many Americans, remembering Wilbur Mills and Richard Nixon, seem to want journalists to at least monitor enough of the private lives of politicians to be able to tell us what kinds of people they are. And most editors today act as if they sense a growing appetite in the public for news and gossip about people, particularly big-time entertainers and artists, but also big-time politicians. Gossip journalism has found a home even in such respectable newspapers as the *Washington Post*, and it is a major part of the content of most of the schlock journals people buy by the millions at supermarket checkout counters.

Public office holders have traditionally been scrutinized rather diligently by the press, which believes a major reason for its constitutionally guaranteed freedom is so it can serve as a watchdog of government. This vigilance, however, had been mostly a nine-to-five thing. Journalists had taken the view that public officials should be able to lead private lives, just like the rest of us. This tolerance even extended to looking the other way when the bad personal habits of some office holders surfaced while they were on duty. It was common in an earlier day for journalists not to report drunkenness, philandering, and senility on the part of some members of Congress and other office holders. Former Congressman Wilbur Mills, chairman of the House Ways and Means Committee, "was a prime example," observes David R. Jones, national editor of the *New York Times* (interview, 7 Oct. 1981).* "The guy was falling down drunk, but the

---

*See list of interviewees following Notes.

press in general portrayed him as one of the great legislative leaders in American politics. Now, he himself says that his drinking affected his job."

The tapes of private conversations in President Nixon's White House office and the many books that have been written about him since he resigned the presidency in 1974 were shocking to many people because they revealed a rather foul-mouthed man who had trouble holding his booze and distinguishing right from wrong. That is not at all the picture that the news media in general had projected of him prior to Watergate. Admittedly, reporters covering Nixon were seldom able to get close enough to him to observe habits that might rub off on his public performance, but part of the reason we learned about some of Nixon's unflattering personal qualities only after he left office is that most reporters were reluctant to invade his privacy. When you're covering the president, you do not go snooping around inquiring about his bedroom or bar habits.

But, for better or worse, the press seems to be paying more attention these days to the private lives of public officials and reporting them to the public when they affect the jobs the officials are responsible for. Michael J. Davies, president of the *Kansas City Star* and *Times,* believes that public officials, like everyone else, are entitled to privacy from the press "until their private lives affect their public duties." (Interview, 23 Oct. 1981.) When he was an editor in Louisville, he reported a private matter involving the mayor of that city. Davies recalls that Louisville firemen went on strike and no one could find the mayor — who had told everyone he was going to Atlanta to some conference. "The paper tracked him down in New Orleans, where he was having an affair with his secretary," the editor reveals. "We printed that."

Robert W. Greene, assistant managing editor of *Newsday,* believes the press has to invade the privacy of public officials to determine whether they are violating their public trust (interview, 6 Oct. 1981). "And when celebrities try to make themselves household words because that puts bucks in their pockets, they must open themselves up to scrutiny by the press," Greene contends. "This doesn't mean that we should be muckraking around in this stuff all the time, but the point is that, in principle, when people offer themselves on the public market-place, they should be prepared for a rather withering examination."

Although he believes the news media no longer protect the drunkards and letchers who get to Congress and high public office, Brit Hume, Capitol Hill correspondent for ABC News, objects to the way journalism has treated some relatives of public persons (interview, 4 Nov. 1981). "We ought not make relatives public persons by extension," he suggests. "I have thought for years that we ought to leave certain members of the Kennedy family alone — particularly Jacqueline Onassis, who has sought to be a private person. We ought to leave her the hell alone. And sons and daughters who don't try to take advantage of their special positions, we ought to leave them alone, too." Hume holds that the "governing standard" in invading the privacy of public persons and officials *and* their relatives ought to be whether or not some issue of public policy has been raised.

Hume regrets the story he did back in the early 1970s when he was working for columnist Jack Anderson about Randy Agnew, Vice President Spiro Agnew's son. Hume tracked down young Agnew in Baltimore and confirmed that he had broken up with his wife and moved in with a male hairdresser. Anderson assigned Hume to get the story and he used it in the column because the vice-president often pontificated about child rearing. Hume says he is "more ashamed of that story than anything I've done in journalism. I'm sorry about it to this day."

Hume strikes a sore spot in his criticism of publicity given by the media to relatives of the mighty. Editors who have given big play to stories involving such relatives argue that they are justified because the stories tell us something about the public persons or officials.

A VIP relative story that raised some eyebrows was the report of the arrest in 1975 of the forty-one-year-old daughter of then Senate Republican Leader Hugh Scott. Marian Concannon was one of twenty persons arrested early one morning in drug raids near Philadelphia. Concannon, divorced mother of eight children who was supporting herself by driving a circulation truck for a Doylestown, Pennyslvania, newspaper, was charged with selling $100 worth of hashish to a state undercover agent. Most of the stories identified Concannon in some detail but did not name any of the other persons arrested in that day's sweep. The *Philadelphia Inquirer* ran a 500-word page-one story on the Concannon arrest, illustrating it with two pictures — one of her modest home and one of Concannon with a sweater over her head being led to arraignment. *Inquirer* editors may have felt that this final paragraph of the story justified the play they gave it: "Her father has been a strong supporter of presidential moves to tighten drug controls, and in 1971 supported President Richard M. Nixon's opposition to the legalization of marijuana."[10]

Steve Lovelady, associate executive editor of the *Inquirer,* was not on the paper when the Concannon arrest story was run, but he sees it as a legitimate news story (interview, 16 Sept. 1981). He puts it in the same class as a more recent story in the *Inquirer* reporting that the man who was about to marry then Mayor Frank Rizzo's daughter was a convicted bookmaker. "Our phones rang off the hook," Lovelady claims. ' "For chrissake,' they said, 'can't you even leave his daughter alone?' " Lovelady argues that if the daughter of the top editor of the *Inquirer* got arrested or was about to marry a bookmaker, that also would be news and would be reported.

Another case that evoked public criticism was the widely used story of Mary Tyler Moore's only son dying from a self-inflicted gunshot wound. The son, twenty-four-year-old Richard Carlton Meeker, Jr., was a mailroom employee at CBS Television in Los Angeles at the time. Many of the stories about his death noted that the actress had suffered another tragedy two years earlier when her twenty-one-year-old sister died of a drug overdose and said that in her latest movie, "Ordinary People," she played the mother of a son with suicidal tendencies.

Charles B. Seib, retired ombudsman for the *Washington Post,* is critical of allowing the law to set the ethical standards for privacy (interview, 9 Nov. 1981). He contends that journalists have been handicapped in their thinking about privacy by the stiffer tests that courts require in libel suits brought by public officials or persons. "When we ask ourselves, 'How public is this person whose privacy we're about to invade?' " Seib continues, "what we mean is, 'How far can we go?' " Seib believes that "compassion has to come up occasionally" when journalists try to decide whether and how far to invade someone's privacy.

Privacy of Ordinary People. When ordinary people get caught up in the news somehow, journalists — for that moment at least — tend to treat them like public figures. It does not seem to matter whether the private persons thrust themselves into the news (such as demonstrators for a cause) or fall into the news through no action of their own (such as victims of a public accident). Many journalists worry, however, about hurting people who fall into the news and are not seeking publicity. "I don't want to hurt people unnecessarily," observes Claude Sitton, editorial director of the Raleigh *News & Observer* and *Times,* "but sometimes that may be necessary. I regret it and we don't do it lightly." (Interview, 4 Nov. 1981.)

A recent incident in Cocoa, Florida, provides us with a good example of the sort of problem created for editors when a private person gets involuntarily involved in a newsworthy event. Anne M. Saul, managing editor of Cocoa *Today* before she became a news editor for *USA Today,* explains that the Cocoa paper had to decide how much coverage to give to a story about a woman who was abducted by her estranged husband and held captive by him for about two and a half hours while police surrounded their former home (interview, 21 Oct. 1981). The woman was grabbed by her ex-husband, who had a gun, as she left her job at an electronic plant. He pushed her into his car and drove her to their former residence, where he threatened her and made her take off all of her clothes. Sheriff's deputies, called by a coworker of the kidnapped woman, surrounded the house, keeping the press and spectators behind a roped off area. Suddenly there were shots inside. The deputies rushed the house and brought out the woman, who had only a small hand towel in front of her. It turned out that the shots had been fired by the husband as he killed himself. The problem for *Today* editors was not whether to publish a story of this unusual event — there was no question about that — but whether to use a photograph of a plainclothesman rushing the woman out of the house with only a hand towel to hide her nudity. The decision was to use the photograph on page one.

The woman later sued the paper for invasion of privacy, and she won a damage award from a Florida jury of $10,000, much below the more than $7 million she sought. The woman's attorney appealed the judgment, but the Fifth District Court of Appeals decided against the woman, ruling that since what the newspaper reported was newsworthy and true, no invasion of privacy had occurred. Her attorney then appealed to the Florida Supreme Court, which had not acted on the matter as this is written.

9.1. Kidnap victim. *This photo of a woman being escorted by a police officer from the home where her estranged husband had been holding her hostage raised an ethical question for editors of the local newspaper. They published the photo on page one. (Face masked here, but not in original photograph.)*

In his arguments to the jury, the woman's attorney contended that the paper should have cropped the photo above the woman's waist. In response, the executive editor when *Today* published the photo, Charles Overby, testified that he decided against cutting out the lower portion of the picture because that would have eliminated the motion of the woman and the officer running during a "dramatic rescue attempt." Overby said that if the picture had shown her private parts, "we never would have considered" running it.[11]

Pittsburgh editors faced an unusual privacy decision when a local television station planned to run a made-for-TV movie about a teenage prostitute entitled "The Two Lives of Carole Lentner." A local man went into federal court in Pittsburgh seeking an injunction to stop KDKA-TV from running the movie because its principal character had the same name as his thirteen-year-old daughter. The judge refused to accept the man's suit, but the TV station withdrew the film anyway. Although he disagreed with KDKA's decision "because this was clearly a First Amendment issue," William E. Deibler, managing editor of the *Pittsburgh Post-Gazette,* says his paper covered the court proceedings and KDKA's withdrawal announcement "for the record," but did not interview the father and daughter or try to get a picture of her (interview, 22 Oct. 1981). "That would have been overstepping the bounds," Deibler feels.

SOME SPECIAL PRIVACY PROBLEMS

Some kinds of news and news subjects cause special problems for journalists who have to decide about publicizing private facts. News stories involving homosexuals, rapes and other sex crimes, juveniles in trouble with the law, and suicides are almost always troublesome, but they are merely the most obvious areas of privacy that journalists have learned to be cautious about.

Even something as routine as reporting someone's age in a news story can upset people who see their age as a private matter. Smaller and medium-sized newspapers seem to get the heaviest criticism for this practice. "We don't always use ages, particularly of older women," notes James A. Dunlap, editor of the Sharon, Pennsylvania, *Herald* (interview, 28 Oct. 1981).

Addresses, another standard way of identifying people in news stories, also seem to some citizens to be a private matter, particularly those whose homes have been burglarized or who have suffered some criminal act that is apt to be repeated. Newspapers, large and small, have taken to reporting general addresses (such as 5400 block of Elm Street) when homes have been hit with routine burglaries.

News of mentally retarded people who get in trouble raises a red flag in most newsrooms. Sometimes the problem can be solved simply by not identifying the retarded person as such; some editors have chosen to ignore minor stories about retarded people in trouble if no community interest is involved. But one young editor who apparently had difficulty spotting red flags got run out of Marceline, Missouri, in the late 1970s when residents strenuously objected to his treatment of a local retarded man. Randy Miller, who took over the editorship of the weekly *Marceline Press* when he was fresh out of the University of Missouri journalism school, published a page one story and a full page of photos about a thirty-two-year-old retarded man who had to be subdued by police after he showed up at work with a twenty-gauge shotgun, hit his plant manager, and threatened his foreman. Angry readers protested by phone calls and letters, one accusing Miller of "capitalizing on the infirmities of this young man." Another letter signed by four people said that Miller's article and photos of the retarded man might be acceptable in large cities, "but in a town the size of ours, where everyone is a neighbor to everyone else in the community, such pictures and articles can only cause resentment and dislike." Then Miller reopened the wounds by reprinting one of the photos of the man in his year-end review of memorable local news events. Shortly after that, people in Marceline heard that the retarded man had committed suicide in Colorado. Whether he or his family had seen the year-end photo was not known, but Miller left Marceline on the advice of the police chief, who said he had heard rumors of threats to the young editor's life.[12]

Homosexuals, Transsexuals. As we saw in the case study that opened this chapter, the sexual orientation of people who have fallen into the news can become a thorny issue for reporters and editors. Public acceptance of homosexuals and the gay life-style undoubtedly has increased in this country over the past two decades, but sensitive journalists know that hanging a homosexual label on someone can still hurt. The ethical problem for editors is deciding whether the homosexual identification is relevant to the news being reported. It obviously would be in a story about an admittedly homosexual junior high school teacher fired because of his homosexuality. It just as obviously would not be relevant in a story about a local businessman who is homosexual being awarded a prize for beautification of his business site. But in between those rather easy calls lie many news situations in which the decision for editors is far from simple.

Perhaps the best known recent case and one that ended up in the courts is the story of the ex-marine who knocked aside the gun hand of Sara Jane Moore as she aimed a 38-caliber revolver at President Gerald

Ford. Moore's shot was deflected, missing the president as he left a San Francisco hotel to get into his limousine. Almost immediately Secret Service agents and police wrestled Moore to the ground and arrested her. And the hefty marine veteran, thirty-three-year-old Oliver W. Sipple, became an instant hero.[13]

Three days later newspaper and broadcast editors in California and around the country had to decide whether to reveal to their publics that hero Sipple was probably homosexual. Would you? Members of the ASNE were asked at their next convention whether they would publish an exclusive story that a citizen who knocked away a gun aimed at the president was a homosexual. Only 126 editors said they would; 383 said they would not publish such a story. But when they were asked whether they would publish such a story if some other news medium used it first, the replies were almost exactly opposite: 344 said yes, 91 said no.[14]

The second question put to ASNE members was most like the actual situation in the Sipple case. There was no suggestion that Sipple was gay in any of the news reports published and broadcast in the two days after he apparently saved the president's life. But then Herb Caen, in his widely read *San Francicso Chronicle* column that other news people call a newspaper within a newspaper, reported that two San Francisco gay leaders were "proud" of Sipple's heroism and remarked, "Maybe this will help break the stereotype." Caen identified one of the leaders as "gay politico" Harvey Milk, who had gotten help from Sipple in his later-to-be-successful campaign for city supervisor. Picking up on the Caen item, *Los Angeles Times* reporter Daryl Lembke located Sipple and filed a story noting that although Sipple "declined to characterize his sexual prefer-ences," he admitted that he was a member of the "court" of Mike Caringi, who had been elected "emperor of San Francisco" by the gay community. Lemke's story was carried on the *Washington Post-Los Angeles Times* news wire and picked up by both major wire services.[15]

One of the newspapers that ran Lembke's story was the *News* in Detroit, where Sipple's mother and father lived. The *News* published a follow-up story the next day reporting on how relatives and others who knew Sipple when he was growing up in Detroit reacted to the revelation that he "was a prominent figure in San Francisco's gay community." The story reported that his mother, Mrs. Ethyl Sipple, "said her motherly pride is tarnished by the stories about her hero son," and quoted her as saying, "We were very proud of Oliver, but now I won't be able to walk down the street without somebody saying something." The story also said that Sipple was a high school dropout, and that he was honorably discharged from the marines and placed on 100 percent disability because of mental adjustment problems from Vietnam combat, during which he was wounded twice.[16]

About this time, Sipple and his attorney, John E. Wahl, called a press conference in San Francisco to denounce news stories about him. Sipple read a statement that said his "sexual orientation has nothing at all to do with saving the president's life." That same day, the *San Francisco Examiner* reported that "gay activists," noting that Ford had personally thanked the police officers who helped subdue Moore but had not done the same for Sipple, "wondered whether Sipple was being shunned by the White House because of his identification with San Francisco gay politics." The White House denied this and quickly released copies of a letter from the president to Sipple dated the same day, in which Ford expressed his "heartfelt appreciation" for Sipple's quick action that "helped to avert danger to me and others in the crowd."[17]

Sipple sued columnist Herb Caen, the *San Francisco Chronicle,* the *Los Angeles Times*, and five out-of-state newspapers for invading his privacy. The suit claimed that the publicity about Sipple's homosexuality brought him "great mental anguish, embarrassment and humiliation" and caused his family to abandon him after learning about his sexual proclivity for the first time through the news stories. Lawyers for the *Los Angeles Times* argued that Sipple, by becoming involved in an event of worldwide importance, had wittingly or unwittingly injected himself into the "vortex of publicity," thus relinquishing "a part of his right of privacy to the extent that the public has a legitimate interest in his activities." To counter Sipple's argument that his homosexuality was not newsworthy, the *Times* maintained that reporting his sexual orientation gave the gay community the favorable publicity it had demanded, because Sipple's action was heroic and helped break the stereotype of homosexuals as effeminate and helpless. The *Times* also said the story was "hot" because it raised the issue of whether President Ford discriminated against gays. Another argument by the defendants was that Sipple's homosexuality was already known by many people, through his participation in well-publicized activities in many cities other than San Francisco.[18]

The California trial court threw out the suit against the five out-of-state papers because it said it did not have proper jurisdiction. The non-California newspapers he sued were the *Denver Post*, the *Chicago Sun-Times*, the *Des Moines Register*, the *Indianapolis Star*, and the *San Antonio Express*. Observers wondered why Sipple and his lawyer had not also sued the *Detroit News*, the paper he alleges revealed his sexual orientation to his family, or two other San Francisco newspapers that gave thorough coverage to his homosexual connections — the *Examiner* and the *Sentinel*. The *Examiner* is owned by the Hearst chain and is published afternoons under a joint operating agreement with the morning *Chronicle*. The *Sentinel* is a gay-oriented newspaper.[19]

Although the San Francisco County Superior Court dismissed

Sipple's case on a summary judgment without comment in 1980, Sipple's lawyer filed a motion for a new trial, arguing that a jury, not a trial judge alone, should decide whether "reasonable people" were offended by revelation of Sipple's homosexuality. At this writing, that appeal is pending.[20]

Another California newspaper, the Oakland *Tribune*, lost the first round in its legal battle for the right to report that a college student body president had had a sex-change operation. The newspaper appealed a jury verdict that would award $775,000 to Toni Ann Diaz, who went by the name of Antonio Diaz before her secret sex-change surgery. After the operation, Diaz became the first woman elected student body president in the history of the College of Alameda. Then she was selected to be the student member of the Peralta Community College Board of Trustees, which governs Alameda and other community colleges in Peralta. Diaz sued the *Tribune* for invasion of privacy after the paper published a column stating that Diaz was "no lady, but is in fact a man whose real name is Antonio." The columnist also remarked that her physical education classmates should reconsider their showering arrangements. The jury agreed with Diaz that her sex change was her business alone and not newsworthy.[21]

The Rochester, New York, *Democrat & Chronicle* took a different tack from the Oakland paper when it decided not to report the transsexuality of a local woman who got into the news. When a surrogate mother in California refused to give up the baby, the donor father and his wife, who lived in Rochester, sued. Reporter Nancy Monaghan, now a national editor of *USA Today*, found out that the reason the couple had gone to a surrogate mother was that the wife was a transsexual (interview, 16 Oct. 1981). Monaghan says her editors decided at that time that the transsexuality of the wife, who was a dispatcher at the local police department, was not relevant to the story. When the suit came up for hearing, Monaghan was sent to Los Angeles to cover it. But the hearing never came off, Monaghan reports, because the lawyer for the couple advised them to drop their suit. He did so after conferring with the judge, whose reaction to the news that the wife in the suit was a transsexual caused the lawyer to feel his clients might be better off filing another suit later. Although the woman's transsexuality was never mentioned in open court, a reporter for the *Los Angeles Times* found out about it and was going to report it the next day. Monaghan says she pleaded with her editors to let her explain as well, but they insisted that unless she could attribute it to the judge, she not mention it in her story. The judge had earlier told Monaghan off the record that the transsexuality of the Rochester woman was revealed to him in his private discussions with lawyers in the case. Monaghan went back to the judge the next day and persuaded him to go on the record, and she was finally able to report what she had known all along.

Monaghan's managing editor then, Nancy Woodhull, is not so sure now that the paper made the right decision in not reporting the woman's transsexuality in initial stories (interview, 16 Oct. 1981). "After it all came out, the couple appeared on the Phil Donahue show," she notes.

Woodhull and other editors who have to decide when homosexuality or transsexuality are relevant to the news do not have an easy task. Publicly identifying homosexuals and transsexuals as such may not be as harmful to them as it once was, but, as we have seen, suits for privacy invasion are still a risk. The ethical argument for not identifying homosexuals unless it is extremely relevant to the story is that the identification can stigmatize the person — cause him or her to lose a job or an apartment, or to be alienated from relatives and friends. But Seib holds to his view that the *Washington Post* carried that reasoning too far in not fully identifying the eight men who died in the homosexual film club fire reported at the opening of this chapter (interview, 9 Nov. 1981). "We were saying that some things are so stigmatizing that we declared those eight men to be non-persons," Seib observes. "It was demeaning to the men who died."

Rape and Sex Crimes. Another troublesome area of news is that having to do with rape and sex crimes. The convention in U.S. journalism has been to withhold the identification of rape victims unless the victims are well-known persons or unless the victims are also murdered. The reason for such self-censorship is that rape is seen by many as a crime that often stigmatizes its victims so that they become double victims, so to speak. But this convention of protecting the woman who alleges rape is being challenged by some journalists. And the U.S. Supreme Court, in a 1975 case involving a Georgia TV station's broadcast of a young rape victim's name, held that the media cannot be sued for violations of privacy when the victim's name comes from court records.[22]

One of the leaders in the movement away from the general policy of automatically withholding the names of rape victims is Claude Sitton, editorial director of the Raleigh newspapers, who was chairman of the ASNE Ethics Committee in 1980-81. It has been the policy for many years at his newspaper to identify both the victim and the alleged rapist at the time he is arrested and charged, Sitton reports (interview, 4 Nov. 1981). Until the arrest, the rape victim is not identified. "But once the charge is made, we do not feel we have a right to decide between the guilt or innocence of the man charged," Sitton explains. "We do not print her name again generally until the case is in court and she is on the stand. ... If the guy pleads guilty, we don't print her name again. But so long as the matter is an open question before the courts, we print the victim's name."

Sitton can recall three or four cases in recent years in which the alleged rapist was found to be innocent or the charge dropped, "but they suffered damage to their reputations anyway." Another case he feels supports his policy was one in which a black teenage boy was arrested after a white teenage girl charged that he raped her at the state fairgrounds. "We published the names of both and the circumstances," Sitton recalls, and as a result other boys came forward and told police they had had sexual relations with the girl that day and she "had invited it all." Sitton believes the publicity helped calm community emotions in this case, which twenty-five years ago "would have led to a lynching." Sitton admits the "policy causes us a lot of pain, but we don't feel we have a right to play God and say who is guilty and who is innocent."

The *Durham* (North Carolina) *Morning Herald* and the *Northern Virginia Sun* in Arlington have similar policies. The *Herald* in a recent eighteen-part series of editorials defending its policy said: "No one seems concerned that the newspapers, along with the police and courts, could be exploited as a weapon against a man by a woman seeking to ruin him." The *Herald* also argued:

> In any other criminal case, the concern for the rights of the defendant seems paramount; great suspicion is directed at the motives and integrity of the prosecution witnesses, the police, the entire judicial system . . . until it comes to the rape charge. Then . . . suddenly they have faith in the judicial system. Suddenly they don't seem to have ever heard of the idea that a defendant might possibly be innocent — the victim either of honest mistake or malice.[23]

Another who questions the conventional policy is *Newsday*'s Greene, who feels that "in modern society it is not as shameful to be a victim of rape as it used to be." (Interview, 6 Oct. 1981.) Greene contends that withholding the name is a "holdover from the age when women had to be protected." He can imagine cases in which a man goes on trial for rape and because of newspaper policies the public has no idea who the raped woman is. "Yet somebody may have been with that complainant that night thirty or forty miles away and would have come forward to police if he had known the name of the woman who complained."

The Rochester, New York, newspapers follow the conventional approach of not identifying most rape victims, but they had a dissenter when Nancy Monaghan was a metro editor of the *Democrat & Chronicle* (interview, 16 Oct. 1981). "Rape is not the only crime that has psychological implications for the victim," Monaghan reasons. She does not see how a paper can protect a rape victim and then turn deaf ears to a seventy-year-old woman who pleads with you not to report her burglary because she fears the burglar will come back again if you do.

Larry Beaupre, managing editor of the other Gannett paper in Rochester, the *Times-Union*, believes Monaghan's minority view may be the policy on most newspapers in twenty years (interview, 15 Oct. 1981). "But readers are not yet ready for us to change."

Paul Janensch, executive editor of the *Louisville Times* and *Courier-Journal*, recognizes the agitation within journalism for a change in the policy of withholding the names of most rape victims (interview, 19 Oct. 1981). "Maybe the policies will all change in ten or twenty years," he says, "but today, rightly or wrongly, the crime of rape carries such a stigma for the victim, particularly in our community."

But even when news organizations hew to the predominant policy of protecting rape victims in most cases, it does not always work out the way it's supposed to. The 6,300-circulation Winfield, Kansas, *Courier* did not identify two women who testified in court about how they were raped. But the two women were so upset about the *Courier*'s detailed story that they complained to the National News Council, maintaining that practically everybody in that small community of 12,400 knew they were the two women who testified. The women and most of the writers of the twenty-three letters to the editor the paper published the next three days complained that the story was sensationalized and it would deter future rape victims from testifying. (In this case, after the two women testified at his preliminary hearing, the accused rapist pleaded guilty and was sentenced to more than a hundred years in prison.)[24]

The news council staff found that the rape hearing story was written by a reporter three months out of college and was turned in just at deadline. The publisher, Dave Seaton, who was filling in for his vacationing managing editor, explains that the story struck him as "rough," but two thoughts pushed him toward publishing it (interview, 5 Mar. 1982). One was his feeling that the paper had often been criticized for being too cautious and protective of the community. The other was a concern that the citizens of Winfield needed "to know how severe rape cases are. I felt the town was very reluctant to face the danger. . . . Both these rapes occurred because of the long habit of keeping doors unlocked. I had not expected so vivid and detailed a story, but since the names were not used it seemed to me then to be justified. I cannot accept the charge of sensationalism. That implies deliberate motivation. Our purpose was totally different. We were trying to alert the community."

Seaton told news council investigators if he had it to do over again he would show the story to other senior staff members and hold it for another day to get an account that would convey the seriousness of the situation, but with more delicacy. "We learn by experience," he said.

The news council rejected the charge that the reporting on this story was sensationalized but noted a *Courier* editorial indicating that future coverage would be handled more cautiously. The council also recommended that leading organizations of journalists make a major study of community attitudes toward sex crimes and the attendant problems of reporting such crimes.[25]

The story of another rape victim who indicts the news media for the way they covered her tragedy even though they never used her name is told to us by her friend, Susan Seliger, in the *Washington Journalism Review*. Seliger wrote that her friend was brutally raped and beaten by a man in Baltimore. For the next six hours, the victim was with police, "dredging up the details, poring over mug shots. The model citizen." She was beginning to feel better by the next day, but the news reports then brought the whole experience back to her. The *News American* reported her street and the hundred block of her apartment; WBAL radio, using a UPI story, revealed that she was a director at such and such a television station, which clearly identified her for many people since she was the only female director at that station. Because of the address in the newspaper report, she never returned to her apartment except to move. When she went back to work at her TV station, she found she was treated differently. One coworker said to her, "Gee, you don't look very beaten up." Seliger says her friend feels that the way the media covered her rape stank. "My right to privacy was already stripped from me by that one individual," the rape victim said. "Now it's been totally invaded. And I wasn't the one who did anything wrong."[26]

Most American newsrooms are also very cautious about reporting sex crimes other than rape. Many ignore the routine arrests of prostitutes and their clients, even though police departments frequently pressure the news media to report the names of men accused of using prostitutes on the theory that publicity would be a deterrent. The media do report on prostitution when it becomes a major problem in their communities or when some better known person is arrested, such as the priest who was picked up in a raid on a bordello in Rochester, New York, recently. Unfortunately for him, a local television station videotaped the raid, and the story was used in all Rochester media. He was transferred, according to Anthony Casale, assistant managing editor of the Rochester *Times-Union* before moving to *USA Today* (interview, 16 Oct. 1981).

Juvenile Offenders. A sixteen-year-old boy leaves a homemade bomb in his locker, causing the evacuation of 2,800 students from his school. A nine-year-old surrenders to the FBI to face a bank-robbing charge. A fourteen-year-old is arrested for shooting and killing a classmate in the corridor of their junior high school. Should any of these juveniles be fully identified in news stories?

These are all actual cases. Only the nine-year-old was not fully identified, but his picture was on TV and in the newspapers in New York City, where he lived. The other juvenile offenders were fully identified in news accounts of their crimes.

By and large, journalists have gone along with the predominant view in the justice system of this country since World War II that people under eighteen should be treated differently than adults when they get in trouble with the law. And this has often meant downplaying the news about juveniles and identifying them usually in only a general way, such as "a fifteen-year-old high school student." But this protective attitude is being challenged by many journalists concerned about the increased incidence of juveniles committing major crimes, such as murder, rape, mugging, and armed robbery. A respected newspaper like the *Philadelphia Inquirer*, for example, publishes full identification of juveniles at the time of arrest and trial whenever it can.

Reporters are not always able to get complete information from police and courts on juvenile cases. Often officials are bound by law not to release names and other information to the media, and juvenile proceedings are conducted in secret rather than in open court. But when the charge against the juvenile is a very serious one, such as murder, most state court systems treat the juvenile like an adult with open records and proceedings. And there are times when news people defy the system and give full publicity to a case, even though officials clam up and do not or cannot cooperate. This happens when the news organizations decide that some public interest demands fuller publicity than the law encourages, and reporters then seek out their own sources of information.

The Elmira, New York, *Star-Gazette*, which ordinarily protects juveniles accused of lesser crimes, decided to vary from that policy when the son of a high official at the Corning Glass Works and two other juveniles were arrested for what they saw as a prank — stealing a bottle of laughing gas. "Half of Corning knew about the prank," comments executive editor Richard B. Tuttle (interview, 14 Oct. 1981). For that reason, plus the fear of being accused of covering it up because of the prominent position of the father of one of the boys, the *Star-Gazette* identified all three boys, even though the Corning *Leader*, the newspaper published in that town, ran a story without the names.

Another kind of high school prank in the Philadelphia area created a special ethical headache for editors because the boy who did it was the son of one of the editors. What happened was that a smoking homemade bomb was found in a student locker, causing officials to evacuate 2,800 students from a Cherry Hill, New Jersey, high school. After a Philadelphia police bomb squad removed the bomb and said it had the destructive force of a hand grenade, a sixteen-year-old sophomore was arrested and charged as a juvenile with causing or risking widespread injury or damage and criminal intent. Police under New Jersey law were bound not to release his name, but reporters found out that he was David Bellune, son of Jerry Bellune, editor of the editorial page of the now defunct Philadelphia *Bulletin.*

The *Bulletin* had never been a newspaper that exploited people in the news, particularly juveniles, and that was especially true in its final years under executive editor Craig Ammerman. "If the Cherry Hill bomb had been left there by just another John Doe without any record of offense, we wouldn't have used the name," Ammerman explains, "but we had to do it because it was Jerry Bellune's kid." (Interview, 27 May 1981.) After the *Bulletin* printed David Bellune's name, Ammerman explained in his Sunday column that his newspaper and its key officials were public figures who had to be treated like other public figures. "If, for instance, the publisher were arrested for drunken driving (which he hasn't been), or was a principal in a divorce suit (which he once was), we would publish a story," the editor wrote. "We do the same thing if the mayor or governor or some other public figure is involved." Ammerman concluded, however, that the way the press treats the offspring of public figures "is not fair to the children." He said David Bellune "didn't get to pick his parents" and "did not ask for notoriety."[27]

"I was in a difficult spot," Jerry Bellune says (interview, 3 Nov. 1981). "Craig Ammerman called me at home to say that they knew it was David, that they had it from at least two sources, but he'd prefer that I confirm it before the *Bulletin* published David's name." Bellune declined to confirm it on the record. Then he got a call from *Bulletin* publisher, N. S. "Buddy" Hayden, who had been reached in Chicago by Ammerman. Bellune recalls Hayden saying that "our First Amendment concerns have to override. We've got to publish the name and I want you to confirm it." Bellune talked it over with his wife and they decided to release a statement confirming that it was David who was arrested, but that they did not believe he was guilty.

The *Bulletin* was the first to publish David's name, but the Camden *Courier-Post* and the *Philadelphia Inquirer* soon used it also. The *Philadelphia Daily News,* which has a very small circulation in South Jersey, ran the story without naming David. The fourth Philadelphia daily in business then, the *Journal,* which folded shortly before the *Bulletin,* did not report the story at all. James Naughton, associate managing editor of the *Inquirer,* believes his paper would have used the name even if Bellune had not released it and even if the *Inquirer* had been the only paper in the area to do so (interview, 16 Sept. 1981).

David Bellune was put on probation for a year. It turned out that the Philadelphia police bomb squad had been wrong about the bomb he made. It was only a smoke bomb and badly designed at that, his father points out. "If it had gone off right, everyone would have known it was a smoke bomb." David Bellune told juvenile court that he made the device and ignited it because "it was getting near the end of the year; things started getting monotonous and I thought I'd break up the monotony."[28]

The whole incident "has enormously affected our lives," Jerry Bellune says. He sees himself as a public figure and he believes "it was unfortunate that my son got penalized for that, because it was not his fault. But intelligent people accept that as part of the bitter that comes with the sweet of notoriety. You don't have to like it, but it's part of the price you pay for being who you are."

Bellune claims that what happened to David has changed his views about publicity for juvenile offenders. "I have been sensitized by that experience," Bellune adds.

> I am a hell of a lot more circumspect about what I publish. My feeling about the public's right and need to know has not been changed, but now I weigh that against factors such as: Does this child have a chance to be rehabilitated, and by publishing his name am I going to impair that chance? Does the community really need to know the child's name? I think I may have considered those questions before, but not with the understanding I have now.

Lyle Denniston, U.S. Supreme Court reporter for the Baltimore *Sun,* believes the press ought to go easy on the children of public figures (interview, 5 June 1981). "When David Kennedy gets arrested in a drug bust in New York, if it's news for other reasons, OK, print it. But if it's only news because he's David Kennedy, let the kid alone, for God's sake," Denniston urges. "It's hard enough to grow up being a kid in this society."

David Bellune, of course, was the first of the three juvenile offenders mentioned in the opening discussion of youths in trouble with the law. The second, the nine-year-old, had stolen $118 by pointing what appeared to be a pistol at a New York City bank teller. His lawyer alerted court reporters that the child was going to turn himself in, and about thirty reporters and photographers showed up to cover it. In their stories and captions, they identified him only as "Robert."[29] The third, the fourteen-year-old boy, was arrested for killing a schoolmate. Both Charleston, West Virginia, dailies decided to name him in their stories, in defiance of a state law that prohibited newspapers but not other news media from publishing the name of a juvenile charged with crime, unless a judge approved. The *Charleston Daily Mail* and *Charleston Gazette* fought the case to the U.S. Supreme Court, which in 1979 declared the West Virginia law unconstitutional because it infringed on freedom of the press and discriminated against newspapers.[30] All three of these cases were, in one way or other, unusual. The prevailing practice in American journalism is to protect the ordinary juvenile accused of crime unless the crime is very serious or very public.

Suicides, Deaths. Most people in this land seem to think it is important that they and their friends and relatives be allowed to die with dignity. No problem for journalism in most cases. Most news stories or obituaries reporting the deaths of people are about as inoffensive as anything that gets printed or broadcast. But every once in a while editors have to decide how much of the circumstances of death are relevant in reporting the death to the public.

Suicides present difficulties. Some newspapers are beginning to not label suicides as such in routine death reports. One editor who is questioning the need to report it in all cases is James A. Dunlap, editor of the Sharon, Pennsylvania, *Herald* (interview, 28 Oct. 1981). "If someone jumps off a bridge or a public official takes his own life, then we have to report it," Dunlap agrees, "but a newspaper has to be compassionate and be aware of the grief it can cause families." Two recent suicides in that community caused Dunlap to question the need to report suicides in all cases: both involved men in their eighties who took their own lives in the privacy of their homes. Most papers, however, report most suicides because they believe important causes of death are facts that readers should know. Some report suicides in news stories but not in the obituaries, which are usually what people clip to store in their family Bibles.

Editorial director Sitton of the Raleigh newspapers tells of a difficult exchange of correspondence with a Methodist minister in nearby Goldsboro, North Carolina, who was angered by the way the Raleigh papers reported a suicide (interview, 4 Nov. 1981). The head of a water and sewer system in the town had been charged with carnal knowledge of three teenage girls, Sitton says. When three deputy sheriffs went to his office to serve the arrest warrants, the man excused himself, went into the bathroom, and shot himself. The minister objected that reporting what the man had been charged with caused great grief to his family. Sitton wrote the minister that "the charges were a factor in the suicide, that the arrest warrants were a matter of public record, that everybody in Goldsboro knew what was going on because it is such a small city, and that it would hurt the paper's credibility to conceal those charges." Sitton claims he "gets more and more mail on subjects of this kind today. People are very sensitive to anything that smacks of an invasion of privacy."

INVADING PRIVACY TO GET THE NEWS

In the process of gathering news, journalists often invade privacy by what the law of privacy calls intrusion. They do this sometimes merely by asking questions of people caught up in the news — not just public figures more accustomed to answering reporters' queries, but ordinary people as well.

"We are by nature invaders of privacy," concedes James Naughton, associate managing editor of the *Philadelphia Inquirer* (interview, 16 Sept. 1981). Public officials are "fair game" for aggressive reporting, Naughton believes, but ordinary people "often are unsophisticated" and have to be protected. "The press is sometimes too zealous," he adds.

News of tragedies often pushes journalists to invade the privacy of grieving survivors. "Some smart people ask dumb questions when they have to intrude on grief," observes Brian Healy of CBS News, Washington, alluding to broadcast journalists who jam microphones into the faces of people after a tragedy (interview, 25 Sept. 1981). Print reporters often intrude in much the same way. A Chicago reporter who had imposed on a grieving family to write a story about a child who had choked to death on a Christmas tree ornament was ordered by his editor to call back to ask the family what color the ornament was.[31]

Too many reporters take advantage of people who are unsophisticated about the media, Healy believes. After more than a dozen years in television journalism, he contends that if he personally got involved in something criminal or embarrassing, "I'd tell the members of my family to keep their mouths shut."

During the many years that this country has been involved in wars, reporters have had to interview surviving family members whenever some American serviceman was reported killed. Usually they also had to ask the family to loan them a photograph of their dead son, brother, or husband. The same intrusion occurs when people are killed in domestic accidents and crimes. Reporters who have had to face this unpleasant task express amazement at how often people are kind to them and willing, almost eager, to talk. I recall being assigned to interview parents and borrow a photograph of an eighteen-year-old woman who had been murdered by her nineteen-year-old sweetheart, who then killed himself. The young woman's father, sitting alone on the back porch steps, talked freely about his daughter and loaned me what must have been the family's prize photograph of the daughter, posed in a full-length gown.

Sometimes reporters and photographers enter private property after a fire, or a crime, or some other human tragedy — unless police stop them, which does not always happen. Jerry Thompson, reporter for the Nashville *Tennessean,* once beat the police to the scene of a celebrated Nashville murder case. He went into the house just before police arrived and was inside when he heard a police sergeant order the house sealed so that no journalists would be allowed in. Thompson quickly found a picture of the dead woman in an upstairs room and threw it out the window. Fortunately for him, the picture landed safely on some shrubbery and Thompson was able to retrieve it. He was proud that his paper was the only medium to have a photo of the dead woman for three days.[32]

Covering families of the fifty-two American hostages in Iran brought on many privacy invasions by journalists. Ramon Coronado, reporter for the *Fort Collins Coloradoan,* described the mob of journalists who covered the family of Marine Sergeant Billy Gallegos of Pueblo, Colorado, as the family awaited the call, which did finally come, that their son and the other hostages were coming home. "The media camped in the sloped front yard, an area no bigger than two spaces in a parking lot," Coronado wrote. "Electrical cords, telephones, television sets, radios, tape recorders, microphones, cigarette butts, coffee cups and paper from fast-food restaurants blanketed the ground. In the back, the alley was filled with television news trucks manned with technicians." About three dozen of the reporters and photographers were allowed inside the small home, but some had to stay outside. As those inside jostled for better positions, one journalist knocked a ceramic plate off a wall, Coronado reported. Photographers stood on furniture, breaking one table. A reporter from Colorado Springs was caught looking in the family's mail. "There is no question that the press should have been at the Gallegos home," Coronado concluded. "A story like the release of the hostages and how their families have been affected is of concern to us all. But perhaps the press lost sight of the fact that the Gallegoses were not just a story but are people. People with feelings and the need for privacy."[33]

It needs to be said here that many journalists conducted themselves properly in covering the hostage story, and many became close friends of the hostage families, whom they covered off and on for the fourteen months of their ordeal.

Robert Giles, executive editor of the Rochester, New York, *Times-Union* and *Democrat & Chronicle,* once wrote out some ground rules for reporters who have to cover disasters and human tragedies — what he calls "news that nobody likes." With the preface that the one quality he likes to find in a reporter is compassion, Giles suggests these ground rules:

> Say you are sorry, and mean it.
> Show a sense of feeling without abandoning the story.
> Do not ask dumb questions.
> Do not break and enter in search of pictures or a comment.
> Establish a trust with family and friends.
> Make sure they understand that what has happened is news.
> Try not to be part of the story.
> Be prepared to listen. Survivors . . . need to ventilate many kinds of feelings: anger, sorrow, disbelief. Some do this by talking.
> Avoid the temptation to run with the pack.[34]

WHERE ARE THE GUIDELINES?

Guidelines on privacy, such as those suggested by Robert Giles in the preceding section, are few and far between in American journalism. A beginning journalist turning to the written codes and standards would find very little help in deciding how far to go in gathering and writing news involving private matters. Perhaps this paucity can be explained by the heavy reliance that many journalists place on the law to guide them in matters of privacy. But the law of privacy in this country provides an inadequate set of rules that are often difficult to apply to particular news situations.

This is not to say that journalists are unconcerned about privacy. Newsrooms are full of unwritten rules in this area — not publicizing the names of most rape victims or juvenile offenders, for example. But there are many other privacy questions that newsroom folklore usually does not acknowledge, let alone address, except in the most general way.

Paul A. Poorman, editor of the *Akron Beacon Journal,* sees privacy as the foremost ethical issue for journalism in the future (interview, 8 Apr. 1981). "It's a complex problem because privacy is increasingly a legal concept," Poorman explains.

> But there are some strong moral issues raised by privacy: Why do we run all those pictures of grieving relatives? Why do we delve so deeply into the private lives of public officials? There are often good reasons for doing these things, but we tend to get carried away. And unless the newspaper industry becomes aware of privacy as a simple question of fairness and as a moral issue as well as a legal issue, others will write those laws for us.

Poorman believes it is very evident in this changing society "what our readers want, even though they may be ambivalent. Our readers want to read everything they can about Rita Jenrette, but they don't think it's fair when we print the names of rape victims. They are able to make those distinctions, and we'd better be able to make those distinctions."

The codes of ethics of national organizations of journalists either ignore or say little about what Poorman sees as the field's "foremost ethical issue." The APME code states that the newspaper "should respect the individual's right to privacy." The RTNDA urges that "broadcast journalists shall at all times display humane respect for the dignity, privacy and the well-being of persons with whom the news deals." The SPJ-SDX calls on journalists to "show respect for the dignity, privacy, rights and well-being of people encountered in the course of gathering and presenting the news" and calls on the news media to "guard against invading a person's right to privacy."

Some newspaper codes contain guidelines on the special problem areas dealt with in this chapter on privacy. The *Chicago Sun-Times,* for one, states that it will not (except in unusual instances):

(1) Use the name of a rape victim.

(2) Use the name of a child whose parents may be involved in scandalous conduct or scandalous litigation.

(3) Use the name of a juvenile involved in a misdemeanor. When juveniles are involved in felonious crimes — shootings, stabbings, armed robbery, etc. — that are given prominent display, the disclosure of their names should be considered an integral part of the story. While it is our desire to protect juveniles, it is also our duty to our readers to inform them fully about the identity of criminals, young or old, in major stories.

(4) Involve innocent members (adult or minor) of a person's family, merely because that person figures in a crime story or in an episode of a scandalous nature.

(5) Resurrect a person's past unless it is germane to an important current story.

(6) Engage in any form of race or religious labeling, except where such identification is necessary to accurate understanding of the story.

This section of the *Philadelphia Inquirer* code deals with some privacy questions:

C. The name of a rape victim is not published unless there are extraordinary circumstances, as determined by the managing editor or the executive editor or, in their absence, the assistant managing editor in charge.

D. The name of a person under 18 accused of a crime is published unless there are extraordinary circumstances, as determined by the managing editor or the executive editor or, in their absence, the assistant managing editor in charge. If the person's identify is withheld by the police, this fact should be stated.

E. When we report that a person has been accused of a crime, we incur an obligation to follow the case to trial and report the disposition.

F. We do not use specific addresses of victims of crimes, witnesses or persons accused of crimes, for such persons often are harassed. Such addresses are obscured by referring to a nearby intersection, as in *Broad Street near Callowhill Street,* or, if that cannot be determined, by using a block number, as in *the 200 block of Doone Road,* or, especially for short suburban streets, by deleting the house number, as in *Emery Lane, Phoenixville.*

The problem of broadcast journalists who jam microphones in the faces of accident victims or their relatives is faced in the codes of CBS and

NBC News. The CBS code directs that such interviews should normally be avoided "except when they are essential to the story" and then they should be conducted with restraint and only after the interviewee has given permission. The NBC code explains that because "there must be complete sensitivity to the emotional state and physical condition of people who have been involved in tragic or traumatic situations," no interviews will be conducted with such people unless it is "clearly relevant and essential to the story."

It is obvious that most Americans highly value their privacy. It is also obvious that journalists have not given enough thought to how they might best deal with the conflicting pulls of privacy and of public curiosity. Journalists probably never will be able to eliminate their intrusions into private matters because some are necessary to serve the public good, but they must strive to bring them under control. Too often there is no forethought about whether the public interest to be served justifies invading someone's privacy. More discussion and agreement on sensitive and compassionate as well as practical standards is needed in this chaotic area of journalism ethics.

CHAPTER TEN

Journalists, Citizens, or Human Beings?

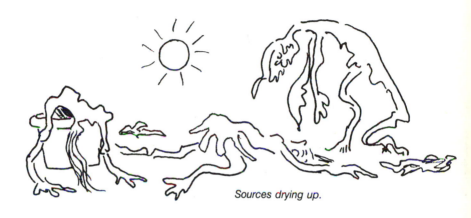

Sources drying up.

IMAGINE THAT YOU ARE A PHOTOGRAPHER for a daily newspaper. As you are driving over a bridge on your way to work early one morning, you spot a man and a woman struggling near the railing. You stop your car and get out, instinctively slinging your camera over your shoulder. Now the man is on the outside of the bridge railing and the woman is on the inside, desperately trying to stop the man from jumping into the swirling river nearly one hundred feet below.

What do you do? Take the picture or try to save the man? Maybe you can do both? But is there time to do both? What do you know about jumpers anyway? Why doesn't somebody else stop?

These were the kinds of questions that went whirling through the mind of William T. Murphy, Jr., that morning. This happened to him as he was driving from his home in Vancouver, Washington, to his job at the *Oregon Journal*, the now defunct afternoon daily in Portland. His route took him across the Columbia River. Halfway across the bridge, Murphy saw the struggling couple and stopped his car and got out (interview, 27 Mar. 1982).* "At first they didn't notice me," the photographer said later.

---

*See list of interviewees following Notes.

"The man was in his mid-40s, I'd guess, a husky guy. His wife was trying to hold onto his arm. She was screaming and pleading with him." Murphy took one picture (Fig. 10.1) and then another one just as some kid on a bicycle pedaled by, passing within two feet of the woman as she struggled to keep her husband from jumping (Fig. 10.2). Other cars crossing the bridge slowed when they reached that point but none stopped at first.

10.1. A suicide leap. *This is the scene that photojournalist William T. Murphy, Jr., found when he stopped his car on a bridge connecting Washington state and Oregon.*

10.2. "That's not the right thing to do, pal," *photographer Murphy says he shouted at the man struggling to free himself from his wife's weakening grip. The unidentified bicyclist did not stop.*

Murphy tried to remember how suicide prevention experts had dealt with jumpers back in Boston where he had worked for the old *Herald-Traveler*. "One thing was for certain," Murphy confided. "I didn't want to try to rush the guy because I thought he'd jump for sure. I got within ten feet when he noticed me. I started talking. 'That's not the right thing to do, pal,' I said. 'Come over here and we'll talk about it.' " The jumper stared at Murphy but said nothing. A van on the bridge stopped and a young woman looked out. Murphy screamed at her to get the state police "at the end of the bridge." Then he remembered something else from Boston: if you insult someone about to jump, he might come back and try to take a poke at you. "Hey, you coward, that's a coward's way out," Murphy yelled. "Come on back here, you coward." It didn't work, Murphy added. The guy "leaned out and was gone." The photographer took a picture of the man falling away from the bridge (Fig. 10.3). He took a total of five pictures. About then, Murphy noticed that the young woman from the van had gotten out and was standing fifty feet away watching the man jump to his death.

10.3. The man jumped *to his death in the swirling Columbia River nearly one hundred feet below. The photographer then noticed that the young woman he had asked to go for the police was still there on the bridge, watching the suicide.*

After his pictures were published in the *Oregon Journal* and in other newspapers across the country that subscribed to the UPI photo service, angry letters and phone calls started coming in. "Don't the ethics of journalism insist that preservation of human life comes first, news second?" asked a woman in Philadelphia. "He let a man die for the sake of a good photograph," a New Yorker wrote.

Murphy was in agony. He had taken his pictures, but he had also tried to help the man. "Why didn't someone else stop?" he asked. "I don't know what I could have done differently. I am a photographer and I did what I have been trained to do. I did all I could."[1]

The uncertainty Bill Murphy felt is not unique to journalism. Any one of us is apt to get caught between the obligations of our jobs and our obligations as citizens and human beings. But it seems to happen more often to journalists because so many of the normal duties of citizenship — such as testifying in court — often conflict with the job of being a journalist. And in some journalists' minds, even humanistic instincts can get in the way of doing their jobs.

DISPASSION/COMPASSION

One of the definitions of objective reporting — which most journalists still try to practice despite widespread doubts in the field about its achievability — is that the reporter is a spectator and not a participant in what he or she covers. The discipline of objective reporting, it is said, requires a dispassionate approach to the gathering and presentation of facts. Reporters are not supposed to get involved in their stories; they are not supposed to become part of the story; they are supposed to be neutral observers.

If that conventional wisdom of contemporary journalism is taken literally, then Bill Murphy was foolish to agonize about whether he did the right thing. Of course he did the right thing. He did what he gets paid for doing — taking news pictures. So why did it haunt him for months afterward and why did so many readers rail at him for doing his job? The answer, it would appear, is that both Murphy and his critics believe journalists are human beings even when they are doing the work of journalism, and Bill Murphy the human being was supposed to do something to help another human being in trouble. In this way of thinking, Bill Murphy was no neutral observer on the bridge that morning. He was a human being who makes his living taking news pictures and he was ten feet away from a fellow human being intent on jumping to his death.

It is unfair to suggest that if Murphy had dropped his camera and concentrated on trying to help restrain the suicidal man that he would have succeeded. He apparently felt that if he rushed to the woman's aid, the man would have pulled away from her that much sooner.

(On two occasions after the bridge jump incident, Murphy used his first-aid training to help automobile accident victims [interview, 27 Mar. 1982]. He recalls pulling an older man out of his wrecked car and turning off the engine after a two-car collision near Sandy, Oregon. He bandaged another victim of that crash, using a first-aid kit he carries in his car, and then wrapped her in his coat because she seemed to be going into shock. He took no pictures until the ambulance crew arrived. Another time, because he was in a rented car when he came upon an accident, Murphy had to flag down a passing car to get bandages to wrap around an injured man's head. Murphy remembers with some bitterness that after the second accident, the *Journal*'s chief photographer chewed him out for trying to help because that would expose the paper to a law suit.)

The point in telling Bill Murphy's story is not to imply that he should have done anything different or that anyone else would have been able to handle the bridge suicide any better. His experience illustrates the frustrating dilemma that journalists face when they have to decide whether to help people or go for the story or picture. Or to put it another way, when they have to decide whether to substitute compassion for dispassion.

Room for Compassion? American newspapers and other news media are well known for their charitable campaigns: Beating the drums for contributions to United Way, to help the needy at Christmas time, to send city kids off to the country for "fresh air" vacations, or to rebuild the fire-damaged home of a local family. One of the awards in the Gannett chain's annual competition for the newspapers and broadcast stations it owns is the Good Neighbor Award, which recently went to the San Bernardino, California, *Sun* for mobilizing the community to help victims of a major forest fire. Second place went to Cocoa, Florida, *Today* for collecting funds for Christmas toys after the Salvation Army's toy locker was burglarized in November.

Although such charitable campaigns represent a sort of institutional compassion, they cannot be read as signs of a growing compassion in the practice of journalism. Journalists are not so sure they can afford to be compassionate in all new situations. "It might be compassionate to suppress a story reporting the arrest of the publisher for drunken driving," says Louis D. Boccardi, executive editor and vice-president of the AP, "but that might be disastrous for the credibility of the newspaper." (Interview, 8 Oct. 1981.) Boccardi recalls that when he was a young reporter covering the courts, he was asked many times not to put certain things in the paper. "Compassion might dictate that you not report certain things, but there are other considerations" for journalists, Boccardi believes. Although he's not ready to embrace "compassion" as a prerequisite for work in journalism, Boccardi agrees that journalists should "have a regard for human life."

Diane Benison, managing editor of the Worcester, Massachusetts, *Evening Gazette*, also has trouble seeing a place for compassion in news work (interview, 19 Oct. 1981). "One of the curses of this business," she argues, "is that you're expected to have your pores open, to be able to feel, to be able to empathize with people, and yet to eviscerate yourself to do your job, just as if you were a machine."

Other journalists more readily accept a place for compassion in journalism. Anthony Casale of *USA Today* tells a story of a police reporter for the Rochester, New York, *Times-Union* who exchanged himself for a woman hostage being held captive by a robber barricaded in a house (interview, 16 Oct. 1981). The criminal had threatened to kill the woman if he was not allowed to talk to a reporter. After the exchange, the reporter escaped and the robber killed himself. But because "he became part of the story," the reporter was reprimanded by his editor, who put out a memorandum that the next reporter who did anything like that would be fired. Casale is not sure what he would do if that same thing happened to him. "You can't be more objective than you're able to," he reasons. "If it's a matter of saving a life or something that can't be replaced, there's an obligation beyond your professional one."

Two other photojournalists interviewed for this book said they had taken first-aid training because sometimes they get to accident scenes ahead of everyone else. One is Linda Wheeler, reporter-photographer for the *Washington Post*, who claims she always gets her picture, but she also tries to help people if they need it (interview, 24 Sept. 1981). "The picture is in the paper only one day," she adds, "and I have to live with myself every day." Wheeler says that when she covers news of accidents, fires, and other tragedies, "I try to turn things around. I try to put myself in the victims' shoes and try to be very gentle."

Bob Gay, a photographer who worked for three different dailies in West Virginia, took paramedic training and instruction in law enforcement and fire fighting, "just in case." (Interview, 16 Nov. 1981.) He explains that at the time he was "working in a remote area" and felt he ought to be "completely prepared." Besides, "if you know what a paramedic has to do to keep someone alive, then you won't get in his way. And if you know what a 357 Magnum will do, you'll have a hell of a lot more respect for an officer when he has to draw one." Gay has never "done anything as dramatic as saving someone's life," but a couple of times at bad accidents he has helped paramedics extricate victims from cars. He has held intravenous bags and helped load people into ambulances. When he did that, of course, he had to put his camera aside. "A human life is a hell of a lot more important than a picture," Gay declares. "Some people can stand there and say, 'It's just not my job,' but I can't."

Michael J. Davies, president of the *Kansas City Star* and *Times,* who believes journalists "have to have as much compassion as possible," maintains that his papers "could have done a sob story every day" after the balcony collapsed and killed 113 people in the Hyatt-Regency Hotel there (interview, 23 Oct. 1981). Instead, they concentrated on why the accident happened and downplayed the "blood and guts" so as not to make things any worse than they were for the surviving families. "We deliberately did not run any gory photos," Davies claims. And when they felt they had to run a picture of bodies in the morgue, "we burned out the faces of recognizable people."

Seattle Times editors had to decide whether to publish a photograph of a dead boy that was apt to be the first notification to his surviving family that he had been killed. That sort of problem does not arise with most shots of accident or disaster victims because authorities almost invariably notify next of kin before news and photos can be published. But the dead boy in this photograph was unidentified. It was the famous photo of the body of a young boy in the back of a pickup truck after the 1980 eruption of Mount Saint Helens. Most editors thought that picture, taken from a helicopter by photojournalist George Wedding of the San Jose *Mercury-News,* was one of the best and most telling news photos to come out of that volcanic eruption in Washington state. But Seattle editors knew there was a good chance that the dead boy's family lived in their circulation area.

The *Seattle Times* ran Wedding's photo, distributed by the AP. "I think we had to run the picture," day picture editor James Heckman explained.

> It made me uncomfortable, especially wrestling with the inevitable conclusion that family members might well identify the victim. But we are chronicling an incredible event and ... publishing history. The photograph in question likely will be the picture — or one of the pictures — used in the years ahead when the awesome fury of the eruption is detailed.[2]

The dead boy's maternal grandfather was the first of the family to see the photo of his eleven-year-old grandson, Andy. The grandfather had picked up a paper at his motel where he was staying during a visit to his daughter's home in a semirural area southeast of Seattle. What the photo did not show were the bodies of Andy's father and his nine-year-old brother, Mike. All three had been asphyxiated by volcanic ash that carpeted their campsite, four and one-half miles west of the mountain.[3]

Editors of another western newspaper, the Spokane, Washington, *Spokesman-Review*, got criticized for a lack of compassion when they gave up a quarter of their front page to a picture of a local lawyer. The picture showed a woman struggling against two police officers trying to arrest her after she drove her car off a bridge into the Spokane River. She was charged with negligent driving and driving under the influence of intoxicants. The woman in the picture was a public defender whose client, a convicted rapist, had been sentenced earlier that day to life plus three terms. It was not her best day.

After the photo of the lawyer appeared on page one next to the story of her client's sentencing (her picture, that story, and a picture of the convicted rapist took up more than half the page), the *Spokesman-Review* got a flurry of protesting phone calls and letters. Managing editor Don Gormley defended the use of the photograph, which he called "a splendid news picture" that told the story "better than words could possibly do." A second justification for running it was that it was "clearly news," the editor argued in an editorial. "A driver zipping off a bridge into the Spokane River is not a common occurrence. When the driver then struggles with police, that makes it a little better story. When the driver turns out to be a public defender in a widely publicized and important trial, the story gets more compelling." The photo was neither in bad taste nor unfair, Gormley contended. It was "made in a public place of a public incident." Gormley then asked readers to tell him whether they would have printed the photo, by filling out and sending in a ballot. Of the 1,776 ballots returned, 1,231 favored using the photograph and 545 opposed it.[4]

About two-thirds of the ballots were accompanied by notes and letters. "The sobering part of the exercise," Gormley wrote, "was reading a couple of hundred letters telling us rather bluntly that we are insensitive, brutish boors, lacking in compassion, eager to destroy somebody's career and reputation. . . . It doesn't really take the edge off to know that more than twice as many letters applauded the use of the picture. When a couple of hundred people take time to write and tell you what a creep you are, you feel wounded."

Columnist Bob Greene seemed to be arguing for compassionate interviewing in a recent column in *Esquire* magazine. Since almost none of the people he interviews ever asks not to be named, Greene says he suggests it if the topic they discussed is sensitive or potentially embarrassing. The interviewee is often surprised when he suggests not printing his or her name, Greene adds, because one of the tricks he uses is "to make an interview subject feel so comfortable and so warm that he cannot conceive of being betrayed by this nice fellow who is asking the questions and making the notes." Greene continues:

As often as not, though, the person I'm with has never been interviewed before. He is wary at first; it takes a while to make him understand that this is not a surgical procedure. There are tricks to that, too; I will stumble around in my conversation. I will make my questions sound exceedingly dumb; if he is having a few too many drinks, I will drink right along with him. I may or may not be a likable person in real life, but I can be a likable person in an interview situation; it's just another trick I have learned.

So at the end of our talk, . . . chances are he would willingly give the okay to use his name. What he doesn't know is that the sight of his words and his world in cold print, in front of hundreds of thousands of strangers, is going to jar him. . . .

I decided a long time ago in situations like those, I had the obligation to help protect a person even if he didn't know enough to protect himself.[5]

Mike Feinsilber, Washington reporter for the AP, shares Bob Greene's concern (interview, 23 Sept. 1981). "Sometimes I'll tell some innocent person I'm interviewing, 'Don't tell me anything you don't want in the newspaper,'" Feinsilber explains. "I don't like to take advantage of someone's inexperience in dealing with reporters." Feinsilber also often "gives news sources a chance to collect their thoughts." When he has to get a reaction comment from someone, he usually calls the person, explains the situation, and then offers to call back in ten minutes or so for a comment. "I find I get better information and better quotes that way, and people appreciate it," Feinsilber adds.

"Compassion is basic to good ethics and good journalism," in the view of Joseph W. Shoquist, managing editor of the *Milwaukee Journal* (interview, 19 Oct. 1981). He feels it is important for journalists to have "a regard for people as human beings, not be so hard-nosed about everything, and understand where people are coming from and why they do the things they do."

On Saving Janet's Jimmy. Jimmy lived for almost seven months. He was created on the front page of the *Washington Post* by Janet Cooke— "Jimmy" was what she called the eight-year-old heroin addict she wrote about — and he died almost seven months later when she confessed she had made him up, then turned in her Pulitzer, and left the news business. (An account of this fakery and its aftermath appears in Chapter 7.) The most compelling of the many ethical issues raised by the fabrication, in the minds of some observers, is the issue of whether the *Post* should not have tried to help poor Jimmy instead of turning him into a front page tearjerker.

The two ethical issues that received the most attention right after the fakery was disclosed had to do with the deception itself and the use of anonymous sources (pseudonyms for fictitious people, as it turned out in this case). But to Charles B. Seib, retired ombudsman for the *Post,* the more serious question was: "Why were the *Post* editors so willing to let Jimmy die?" Seib notes that the massive postmortem *Post* ombudsman William L. Green, Jr., did on the matter after the *Post* returned the 1981 Pulitzer Prize the story had won made no mention of any concern for Jimmy. Green's report had lots to say about "the editors' enthusiasm over the story," Seib wrote in *Presstime.* "There was deep concern for Cooke's safety" after she claimed that Jimmy's dope-dealing guardian had threatened her life. "But not a thought for Jimmy."[6]

Seib said a *Post* editor told him privately, before Cooke admitted the story was phony, that if he had it to do over again, he would handle the story differently. "Before publishing the story, he would put pressure on Jimmy's mother to get the child into treatment," Seib said the editor told him. "The *Post* could have footed the bill, he said. There would have been no need to bring in the authorities." If the *Post* editor had done that, "if he had allowed a humanitarian instinct to rise briefly above his enthusiasm for a smashing story," Seib wrote, "there is a good possibility that he would have uncovered the deception and the story would have died aborning."

Seib is not alone in his feeling that the *Post* should have tried to help Jimmy, assuming that he did exist. Thomas J. Bray, associate editor of the editorial page of the *Wall Street Journal,* asked, "Why didn't the *Post* scrap the story and insist that the reporter report this pathetic case to the authorities? Was the story in this instance really more important than 'Jimmy'?"[7] John Troan, editor of the *Pittsburgh Press,* wondered why somebody at the *Post* had not said, "Hey, let's get this kid out of his horrible predicament, get him the help he needs — and then run the story. That way we might not only win a prize but — even more important — save a life."[8] John Bull, assistant to the managing editor of the *Philadelphia Inquirer,* believes that "the real problem with the Janet Cooke story was the *Post's* insensitivity to the life of the child. When everybody said please tell us who he is, we want to save his life, the *Post* arrogantly went into its bunker of confidential sources and First Amendment, and ... the poor kid ... could have died for all anybody at the *Post* cared." (Interview, 27 May 1981.)

Bill Green, now back at Duke University after serving a year as *Post* ombudsman, claimed the "*Post* was under seige for four or five days after 'Jimmy's World' was published. It was under seige not because the story was challenged, but because the community was convulsed with feeling about the boy himself. 'Let's save the boy! How dare you play God!' they shouted at us." (Interview, 3 June 1981.) Green said he tried to explain in a column why the *Post* felt it could not name the boy, why Janet Cooke's promise of anonymity had to be kept.

Benjamin C. Bradlee, executive editor of the *Post,* acknowledges the legitimacy of the question Seib and others have raised, but he says "we talked ourselves into the position that we were focusing on a social problem and we would do the community more good by focusing on it than by going to the cops with a story we thought would put our reporter in physical jeopardy." (Interview, 5 June 1981.) Bradlee admits he is uncomfortable with case-by-case ethics on when journalists should report crimes they learn about to the police.

In its overall investigation of the *Post*'s counterfeit, the National News Council looked into the question of whether authorities should or should not have been told who "Jimmy" was. The council report quoted Robert Woodward, then assistant managing editor in charge of the metro staff, as saying that the *Post* had been wrong in deciding to go with the Jimmy story instead of telling authorities about him. The *Post* was in a "morally untenable position," having witnessed a crime and saying "to hell with" the eight-year-old victim, Woodward told council investigators. The council commented on this issue in its report:

> Neither the complaint nor the ombudsman's report addressed what the Council believes to be a pivotal issue in this case: the human concern that a journalist as citizen ought to have for an 8-year-old child whose life is being criminally endangered. The Council's investigation shows that there was no adequate discussion among *Post* editors of a question that admittedly presents an uncomfortable dilemma for news organizations — whether to fulfill their obligations as citizens and report the crime to the police or to stand on the principle that it is the journalist's obligation to publish the story to call attention to a social problem. The Council regrets that even after the story was published, the *Post*'s editors failed to try to help the mortally endangered child they believed to exist.[9]

Journalists seem to have learned many lessons from the "Jimmy's World" case. It might be hoped that one of them is the lesson of compassion — that it is all right to act like a human being even in a business that worships independence, noninvolvement, and dispassion.

COOPERATING WITH GOVERNMENT

American journalists are no longer "on the team." That expression came from a remark that Admiral Harry D. Felt reportedly made when he met Malcolm Browne, one of the early AP correspondents covering the Vietnam War: "So you're Browne," Felt said. "Why don't you get on the team?"[10] The admiral was expressing his anger at Browne and other correspondents who were beginning to defy the official line in their reporting of that war in the early 1960s. American war correspondents had not acted that way in World Wars I and II and in Korea. Their patriotism came out in the positive, morale-boosting stories they filed.

The spirit of cooperation between the press and government that prevailed during America's wars in the first half of this century seemed to carry on for a while after World War II. During that war and for the period after it known as the "Cold War," some U.S. journalists worked or cooperated with the young and still small Central Intelligence Agency (CIA). It was only natural that our spy agency would turn to journalists, many of whom had contacts in and special knowledge of other countries. But the love affair between the CIA and some journalists did not last long because of something that was happening between the press and government in this country.

As the U.S. government grew in size and complexity during and after World War II, it became obvious to government leaders that effective communication with the citizens was required. American business had already discovered this essentiality some years earlier and had turned for help to a new breed of specialist — the public relations expert. Government soon followed suit, adding scores, then hundreds, and finally thousands of such specialists to the public payroll. Today, in both government and the private sector, no major enterprise is without public relations counsel.

With the help of its public relations specialists, government began to find better ways to assemble and package information so it was more apt to be used by the press. It also found other ways of communicating with the public, so that it did not have to depend entirely on independent, nongovernment channels of communication. And somewhere along the line, government discovered that certain kinds of information were better than other kinds, that you did not have to tell the people everything. Image making and manipulating information to certain ends became instruments of government strategy. Even the lie was not out of the question, as the press and the country learned in 1960 when the government said it was not using the U-2 plane to spy on the Soviet Union, and then the Soviets produced the captured pilot of a downed U-2 who said that was just what he was doing. And in 1962 Arthur Sylvester, spokesman for the Pentagon under Presidents Kennedy and Johnson, admitted that the lie had been added to the government's public relations arsenal when he told a meeting of journalists: "I think the inherent right of the government to lie — to lie to save itself when faced with nuclear disaster — is basic, basic."[11]

Well, this was something new. It was one thing for the press to cooperate with government, as it did in World War II, to keep news from the public. But having the government manage the news, even to the extent of lying, to keep information from the press was more than most journalists were willing to take. So in Vietnam, reporters began to ask tougher questions and to go out on their own without military escort to find out what was happening. One reporter, Harrison Salisbury of the *New York Times,* even went to Hanoi, the enemy's capital, to file reports that cast doubts on Pentagon claims that we were not bombing civilian targets in North Vietnam, only military targets. Salisbury's stories in 1966 and the increasingly critical coverage by all reporters and photographers covering Vietnam undoubtedly contributed to the snowballing public disenchantment with that war, which eventually forced the government to disengage us from the conflict without victory.

The more aggressive and less cooperative attitude of the press toward government also was expressed in the publication by the *New York Times* and other periodicals of the secret Pentagon Papers and by the coverage of the Nixon administration, which brought about the resignation first of Vice President Spiro Agnew and then of Nixon himself in 1974. Some leaders of journalism believe the press may have overdone its aggression in the period right after Watergate, and the watchdog's growl has tempered a bit of late, but the press is certainly not back on the government's team.

Working with Police. Most journalists do not become war or even foreign correspondents, but virtually all of them have covered police. Police news is an important and standard part of the content of newspapers and broadcast news programs. Covering crime news, though, raises some sticky ethical questions having to do with how much cooperation, if any, should exist between journalists and police or law enforcement officials.

Most journalists seem to believe that at the working level a little cooperation between reporters and police is usually not harmful, but they draw the line at becoming just another arm of law enforcement. There seems to be considerable disagreement, however, about how much cooperation is acceptable.

William F. Thomas, editor and executive vice-president of the *Los Angeles Times,* warns that "you never cooperate with law enforcement in a way that jeopardizes your independence." (Interview, 2 Nov. 1981.) For example, his paper refused to cooperate with police who wanted staff testimony and photographs of college student riots back in the sixties and early seventies. "Helping police that way would have hurt our effectiveness as journalists." But Thomas believes that if a journalist is walking down a street and sees a crime, there is no reason why he or she should not testify. As a city editor for many years, Thomas concedes that he often cooperated with law enforcement by trading information. "You do this very quietly and it helps you both."

The way Robert W. Greene, assistant managing editor of *Newsday,* sees it (interview, 6 Oct. 1981):

> All the cops are required to give a police reporter are the basic skeleton details on the blotter report. But they give him more, plenty of background. They volunteer that information. Now there comes a time when the reporter and the police are each working on the same thing, both convinced that the other is working toward the same good end, and so you prime the pump by exchanging information.

Greene, a longtime officer of Investigative Reporters and Editors, says that "a vast majority of reporters I know cooperate with government agencies — senate committees, local police, district attorneys — given certain circumstances." Greene believes journalists do not have a right to withdraw from society. "To say that we will not cooperate when we have seen a crime committed, that because we're reporters we don't have to testify, is to say that we're not citizens, that we're privileged people," he adds.

A considerable degree of press-government cooperation was evident when the *Chicago Sun Times* bought and operated the Mirage Tavern to expose shakedowns by city inspectors (detailed in Chapter 6). Editor Ralph Otwell, who believes that journalists witnessing a crime in progress have a duty to report it, points out that the reporters who posed as operators of the tavern made daily reports to the Illinois Department of Law Enforcement (interview, 9 Sept. 1981). Their memos "summarized their encounters with various inspectors in cases where the inspectors were soliciting bribes." The principal reporter on that undercover reporting project, Pamela Zekman, who later moved to WBBM-TV, Chicago, says the agency "understood that they were not to make arrests while our investigation was still going on, because if you arrest the first inspector in a chain of inspectors, that's the end of the project." (Interview, 8 Sept. 1981). The department started making arrests when the investigation was finished but before the *Sun-Times* published its report. Otwell emphasizes that the paper would not have collaborated with law enforcement "if there had not been an actual crime being or about to be committed" because "we don't want to be perceived of as an arm of law enforcement."

Press-police cooperation occurs perhaps more often in areas less urban than Chicago. When Richard P. Cunningham, associate director of the National News Council, was one of two reporters on the *Durango* (Colorado) *Herald,* he worked with a police officer to trap a bootlegger (interview, 5 Oct. 1981). While the police officer observed, Cunningham picked up a prostitute who worked for the bootlegger and asked her to get him some dope. She took him to the bootlegger's house, where he gave her a marked ten dollar bill. She came back empty-handed twice, but finally returned with a bottle of liquor. At this point, Cunningham signaled and the police officer came in with his "big dog" and arrested the bootlegger. With the help of Cunningham's testimony, the bootlegger was convicted of selling without a license. Cunningham, who was twenty-six at the time, remembers that the bootlegger used to "perch like a vulture on the edge of a reservation, victimizing Indians." It would not have been possible for such a small paper to do that story the conventional way, interviewing Indians and officials, Cunningham believes. "This was a quick and dirty way to do it and it worked."

When she was a reporter for the Baton Rouge, Louisiana, *Morning Advocate,* Ellen R. Findley of the *Sacramento Bee* often traded information with a United States attorney there (interview, 15 Feb. 1981). "I don't view it as an ethical violation to give him a piece of information I have run across," she said. "He's not an enemy." For his part, the legal official kept her informed about his cases, which enabled her to write fuller, more accurate stories and often allowed her paper to get a jump on a story. Findley also cooperated with state narcotics officers, who once let her go with them on a big raid, with the understanding that some of what she learned she "would not print right away." She got a lot of information that eventually she was able to print.

Tom Kelly, director of photography for the Pottstown, Pennsylvania, *Mercury,* also does not believe in being an arm of law enforcement, but he does not hesitate to supply prints of automobile accidents he has photographed to state and local police when they need them (interview, 8 Jan. 1982). And he admits he occasionally takes special shots for police who request them for their records. "It's no real big deal," Kelly adds. "We have to have good relations with police. They tip us on stuff and cooperate with us, too."

James A. Dunlap, editor of the Sharon, Pennsylvania, *Herald,* favors cooperating with police if it serves the purpose of better law enforcement (interview, 28 Oct. 1981). "My feeling is that we're for law enforcement," Dunlap comments. "If we have a picture that will help them catch a criminal, let them have it. I want criminals arrested as much as anybody else. I would cooperate. They don't have to subpoena me."

While he believes the press should avoid being "partners with law enforcement or government," Michael J. O'Neill, former editor of the New York *Daily News,* agrees with Dunlap on photo requests from police (interview, 8 Oct. 1918). Many newspapers and television stations oppose giving police prints or video tapes of any pictures unless they have been published or broadcast, but O'Neill believes that "if we have a photo that will help the cops solve a murder case and we accidentally didn't run it, there's no crime in giving it to them. We are citizens, too."

William J. Small, veteran TV news executive who now heads UPI, would not turn over to police tapes and films that had not been used on the air, but there are times, he concedes, when you try to find ways to cooperate (interview 5, Oct. 1981). When he was president of NBC News, Small recalls that "the FBI asked for our outtakes to see if John W. Hinckley, Jr., [charged at that time with trying to assassinate President Reagan] had been at any Carter or Reagan rallies. We culled through our tape files and put the pertinent ones on the air."

Claude Sitton, editorial director of the Raleigh *News & Observer* and *Times,* does not take a hard line on cooperating with police (interview, 4 Nov. 1981). "I don't go out and spy for the cops, and we don't take what cops tell us as gospel," Sitton declares, "but we've gotten some very good stories from law enforcement people." Sitton recalls that when he was covering a "highly volatile racial situation" in St. Augustine, Florida, for the *New York Times* in the sixties, he spotted a man he knew to be psychotic, "a bomber and a very dangerous individual." Sitton says he went to an FBI man and told him what he'd seen, "and I would do it again today."

Although he wouldn't let himself be recruited by the CIA as some foreign correspondents did in the old days, CBS News producer Brian Healy concedes that he did work with a "guy I knew to be a spook," when covering Iran (interview 25, Sept. 1981). Healy, who worked out of London for CBS for several years, believes that in Iran there was a lot of "very informal trading of information" between journalists and government people. Healy adds that if the government wanted to ask him about some place he had been, "I would not refuse."

Leslie H. Whitten, novelist who was senior investigator on the Jack Anderson column for twelve years, believes "cooperating with law enforcement and government agencies is quite proper as long as it is not done at the expense of your integrity. We're all citizens." (Interview, 2 Sept. 1981.) He remembers that when assassination threats against Senator Edward Kennedy and others would be phoned to Anderson's office, "we'd go immediately to the Secret Service." Another time, when prisoners told them that they were being shot at by their prison guards, they went to the FBI. "But when we're asked for our sources, outtakes, or notes, we've got to resist unless there's some overwhelming reason to cooperate," Whitten adds.

When Lives Are at Stake. Most editors in recent years have been willing to cooperate with police when asked to hold up publicity that might put a life or lives in danger. In cases of kidnappings, for example, the news media are often asked to delay their stories so that the kidnappers will assume that police or the FBI have not been called into the case. Authorities believe that if publicity is delayed, they have a better chance of securing the safe release of the kidnapped person or persons.

The famous Patty Hearst kidnapping in 1974 brought just such a request from authorities to news media in the San Fransisco Bay area. All of them held off their stories for twelve and one-half hours, except the Oakland *Tribune,* where publisher William F. Knowland insisted on printing the story. He told his editors that this was no ordinary kidnapping, that too many people had heard the gunfire when Hearst was abducted, and that there was no way of keeping such big news quiet. Afterward journalists joined police in condemning the *Tribune* for being the only news medium in that area to print the story during the blackout.[12]

When the APME Professional Standards Committee asked 328 editors if they agreed with San Francisco area media acceding to delay publicity, 260 said they agreed, 40 disagreed, and 28 were not sure. The AP was one of the news organizations that held up its Patty Hearst kidnapping story at the request of police and the FBI, which brought a protest from one of its prominent members, Robert Haiman, executive editor of the *St. Petersburg Times.* Haiman argued that the press should have "learned a lesson from the *New York Times*'s unfortunate decision to suppress news of the Bay of Pigs at the request of President Kennedy" in the early sixties. "The Kennedy appeal was made to the integrity of the *Times* with a heavy foot on the pedal of responsibility, ethics and concern for the lives of the 'brave invaders,' " Haiman added. "The *Times* weighed that and agreed not to publish. Afterward, both the *Times* and the White House wished they had done otherwise." This brought a reply from AP executive editor Boccardi, who defended what the AP did in the Hearst case as "the ethical, responsible thing to do. To have rushed out in a life be damned headline splurge would have been in my view, nothing short of irresponsibility on our part."[13]

More recently, in the Detroit area, the AP joined two newspapers and two radio stations in holding up a kidnapping story until a sixteen-year-old hostage could be freed. The five news organizations found out one morning that the night before three armed young men had kidnapped the wife and three sons of General Motors executive William Schulenberg. The kidnappers locked their victims into the trunk of the family Cadillac, after shooting holes in the lid for air. Two of the kidnappers drove off with the victims; one stayed behind with Schulenberg to explain that he was to get ransom money. Overnight Schulenberg was able to raise $54,000 and the kidnappers released his wife and two sons, ages twelve and fourteen, but said they would hold the sixteen-year-old son until the ransom was in their hands. About this time, reporters began to find out what was happening, but police urged them to hold off for fear that any news stories would tip the kidnappers that police were in on the deal. All five held their stories until midday when the sixteen-year-old was freed. The three kidnappers were tracked down and arrested, and all the money was recovered.[14]

Boccardi, who authorized the Detroit bureau to hold up its story on the Schulenberg kidnapping, did the same in 1981 when an armed man in South Carolina had holed himself up in a house surrounded by police. A psychiatrist told police that the man, who was suffering acute depression, might kill himself or some police officers if he heard a news report about himself on the radio. Boccardi says he does not "think we lose very much by delaying a bit in a life-threatening situation." (Interview 8, Oct. 1981.)

The U.S. government got cooperation from the news media when it asked that news be withheld in the case of six Americans who were outside the U.S. Embassy when the Iranian militants took it over. The six hid out in Tehran under the protection of the Canadian Embassy until the Canadians could sneak them out of Iran. The *New York Times*, NBC, CBS, *Time*, and *Newsweek*, among others, found out that the Canadians were sheltering the six Americans but did not put out any stories for fear that the lives of those in hiding would be in danger. Officials as high as Secretary of State Cyrus R. Vance pleaded with the news media that found out about the story not to publish or broadcast it. Seymour Topping, managing editor of the *New York Times*, who got a call from Vance on the matter, said it was not difficult to cooperate in this situation because it would not have served "the public interest in any way for us to print the story" and it would have endangered American lives.[15]

Although two journalists in recent years have served as mediators in prison riots — Tom Wicker of the *New York Times* at Attica prison in New York state and Chuck Stone of the *Philadelphia Daily News* at the state prison in Graterford, Pennsylvania — many journalists disapprove of that practice. The National News Council surveyed forty-five newspaper editors and broadcast directors on that question and found that only nine had no reservations about journalists serving as peacemakers in prison riots, the holding of hostages, or similar situations. Twenty-seven opposed such participation, and nine had varying degrees of reluctance on the subject.[16]

The Taboo of Testifying. Many journalists are wary of witness stands in court and grand jury rooms. They fear that giving testimony encourages the impression that they are in bed with cops and courts, which would scare off some news sources and cause the public to question the evenhandedness of their reporting on the justice system. Another objection is that some prosecutors and defense attorneys subpoena reporters to testify about matters that police and defense investigators should be digging up.

Journalists can resist subpoenas — and many do — but their success in invoking the reporter's privilege not to testify usually hinges on whether they are being asked to talk about what they learned more or less confidentially in the course of news gathering. If they saw a crime committed while walking their dog, they have no special First Amendment right not to testify. But Jack Landau, director of the Reporters Committee for Freedom of the Press, tells of a time he advised two reporters to testify even though the murder they witnessed happened while they were on the job (interview, 24 Sept. 1981). They were doing an undercover reporting project in 1980, posing as derelicts in order to investigate flop houses in their Texas city. In one flop house they saw a man shot and killed by another man. The reporters called Landau because they wanted to plead First Amendment immunity and not testify as to what they saw. "I told them the whole point of reporter's privilege is that everybody knows you are a reporter, and sources come to you as a reporter, and trust you as a reporter," Landau explains. "You did everything you could to not let them know you were a reporter. So how can you turn around and claim the First Amendment is going to be undermined, when you did everything you could to hide your First Amendment connection?"

The *Washington Post*, which has a long-standing practice of resisting subpoenas directed to its reporters, observes in its deskbook that "testimony by reporters in court cases concerning their news-gathering activities will discourage many persons from talking freely to reporters, because they will be afraid that what they say may end up in litigation." This is true whether the reporter is asked to reveal confidential or nonconfidential information, the *Post* states. "The mere fact that a reporter appears on the witness stand to testify concerning his or her news gathering has a chilling effect on many potential sources of information." The *Post* notes that the First Amendment protection of news gathering has been recognized in a number of cases in which subpoenas have been struck down. "In particular," the deskbook adds, "there has been a tendency by the courts to recognize the First Amendment right of the reporter not to testify in cases where the information sought by the subpoena can be obtained by an alternative means."[17]

A Los Angeles TV reporter was criticized by other journalists when he voluntarily testified in a murder trial. Reporter David Lopez of KNXT,

Los Angeles, claimed that William G. Bonin during the course of an interview in the Los Angeles County Jail confessed that he had killed twenty-one young men and boys in 1979 and 1980. But the confession was off the record; Lopez agreed to go off the record with the understanding that Bonin would not tell anybody else "anything we talked about." This was in January 1981 while Bonin was awaiting trial on charges of committing twelve murders. Lopez claimed that Bonin broke his word to him not too long after the "confession" by telling a reporter for the *Orange County Register* some of the things he had told him. Lopez tried to get his station to let him report the "confession" now that Bonin had talked to another reporter, but his bosses told him they felt such a story would jeopardize Bonin's right to a fair trial. In late June, five months after he got his off-the-record interview, Lopez contended that Bonin broke his word again by negotiating for a movie deal. This time the station let Lopez go on the air.[18]

After his story aired, Lopez was called twice to testify. He resisted, claiming the newsman's privilege of confidentiality under the California shield law, which a judge upheld both times. But once the judge had upheld the shield law in his case, Lopez felt he had fulfilled his responsibility as a reporter. "I have two kids and I come from a family of eight," he confided. "If my kid was killed and someone could have done something and didn't come forward, I could never forgive him." Lopez volunteered to testify as a prosecution witness and told the court in great detail what Bonin had said to him eleven months earlier. When Lopez stepped down from the witness chair, he said to reporters: "I'm a citizen first. I feel as though a hundred-pound weight has been taken off me." (Bonin was later convicted of the first degree murder of ten victims and sentenced to death.)

Two reporters who went to jail for resisting court orders to testify, Myron Farber of the *New York Times* and William Farr of the *Los Angeles Times*, criticized Lopez. "I would have testified if I were the only witness to see someone kill someone else, but this is not the case" with Lopez, argued Farber, who spent forty days in jail in 1978 for refusing to give a New Jersey court his notes on a story about a doctor standing trial for murder. Farber concluded that Lopez had "injected himself in the case" on behalf of the prosecution. The state ought to try Bonin "on the quality of the evidence it gathered ... and not on what Lopez, in a purely journalistic attempt, accomplished on his own," Farber added. Farr, who spent forty-seven days in jail for refusing to disclose the source of a story he wrote about the Charles Manson murder trial in 1970, disagreed with Lopez's claim that he was a citizen first and a reporter second. "Bonin talked to him because he was a reporter, not a plain citizen," Farr contended. Farr also criticized Lopez for breaking his pledge of confidentiality to Bonin, maintaining that when reporters break their promises to sources, other sources dry up.

Lopez should not have taken the confession off the record in the first place, in the view of Eugene Patterson, editor and president of the *St. Petersburg Times*. But once he did, he was duty-bound to tell authorities, Patterson said. "I don't think journalists can get themselves in the position of using the First Amendment to shield someone for murder."[19]

Washington Post reporter Thomas Zito was not walking his dog when he saw a cop shoot a man on the street. He was on assignment in New York, riding in a cab, when he saw a guy arguing with a cop on the sidewalk. The guy threw a punch. The cop retaliated, first with his night stick and then with his gun, seriously wounding his assailant with two shots. In his page one story in the *Post* telling about his witnessing the shooting, Zito said he had notified the district attorney that he had seen the whole thing "and would cooperate." Zito was in New York to interview Bob Leuci, a former policeman whose life story has been made into the film, "Prince of the City."[20]

Chicago investigative reporter Pamela Zekman has never resisted a subpoena to testify, although she has not been subpoenaed often (interview, 8 Sept. 1981). Zekman says she objects to prosecutors trying to base their cases on her testimony. "We don't want to do their work for them, but if they need us in some small way, I feel we have to help," Zekman says. "We aren't above the obligations of a normal citizen. If you witness a crime, you have an obligation to testify."

Newsday's Greene has testified before numerous congressional and legislative committees and as a witness at more than sixty criminal trials. "Yet I have never encountered a source who avoided me because I did so," maintains Greene, regarded as one of journalism's top investigative reporters. Although he would not disclose a confidential source, he claims he has always been willing to turn over his notes when asked. Greene explains that he has testified because "I believe my craft calls upon me to be a reporter of facts, not a keeper of them."[21]

Greene sees no reason for reporters to refuse to testify about information they have gotten on the record from a source but did not, for space reasons, publish (interview, 6 Oct. 1981). And even if reporters agree to protect the identity of a source, they have no reason not to testify about the information, Greene believes. "It is not easy for the public to understand why we are withholding information we have not made any contract with our sources to withhold," Greene contends. "We are more and more appearing to the public as some sort of privileged class. The public despises privileged classes."

Pre-Trial Publicity. The press and the bar have been "dating" heavily in recent years, getting together in numerous conferences to discuss standards, ethics, and procedures in their frequently conflicting callings. The basic issue in these discussions and confrontations is whether media coverage of crime and the legal process does or does not get in the way of justice. At the extremes of the argument are the journalists who want absolute freedom to cover crime the way they see it even if that stirs up the populace, and the lawyers who seek a pure justice through a process that is conducted in a vacuum immune from the stones and shouts from the street. The numerous press-bar discussions seem at least to have given both journalists and lawyers a better understanding of their differing approaches to news versus evidence, charges versus convictions, justice versus advocacy, and a free press versus a fair trial.

Ethical issues are raised by the way the news media cover crime: Should reporters play cop and investigate crimes on their own? Should the media report confessions or prior police records of accused persons when those matters may not always be used as evidence in a trial? Should reporters interview and report statements of people who are apt to be witnesses in the trial? Should the media so emphasize certain very interesting cases that community opinion is aroused against a defendant, making it more difficult to draft an impartial jury?

There is a community and public interest in reporting crime, of course. Journalists have an obligation to watch the criminal justice system — from arrests to sentencing — in the same way they are supposed to watch the other branches of government. The public is well served when diligent news reporting assures against secret arrests and trials, both contrary to an open and civilized society.

But what still bothers many people is the way some segments of the news media hysterically report certain crimes, way out of proportion to their news value and often pandering to the basest instincts. The "Son of Sam" case comes to mind, but it is an unfair example because the journalistic sins it illustrates were committed primarily by the *New York Post* and to a somewhat lesser degree by the New York *Daily News*.[22] Neither tabloid is typical of American journalism.

But the *Minneapolis Tribune* is. Yet it was sharply criticized by two University of Minnesota journalism faculty members for following the standards of "William Randolph Hearst, the patron saint of Yellow Journalism" in its sensationalized coverage of a 1977 double murder in Duluth. The faculty members, Arnold H. Ismach and Everette E. Dennis, were also critical of the St. Paul and Duluth newspapers and the *Minneapolis Star* but claimed the *Tribune* came closest to old Hearst standards in its "peep-show" reporting of the murder of Elizabeth Congdon, an eighty-three-year-old heiress, and her night nurse. The murdered heiress was a prominent person, but only in Duluth, and "her death had little import for the public," Ismach and Dennis wrote.

"Tribune stories told about the reclusive life of Miss Congdon, cast suspicions on the background of her regular nurse and repeatedly offered clues and details about the case," they added. The paper's "exhaustive coverage" continued after the husband of Miss Congdon's adopted daughter, Roger Caldwell, was charged with murder. The defendant and his wife were depicted "as unsavory characters," Ismach and Dennis said, and such detailed accounts of the evidence against Caldwell were published that the press "has, in effect, portrayed him as guilty" before the trial.[23]

Replying to Ismach and Dennis, Charles W. Bailey, then editor of the *Tribune*, said his paper's coverage was based in large part on official and public court records. He added that the "basic yardstick used by the *Tribune*'s editors in judging what we should or should not print was whether we believed it would have" an adverse effect on the defendant's ability to get a fair trial. "We may have been wrong, of course," Bailey conceded.[24]

Because of pretrial publicity, judges moved the separate trials of Roger and Marjorie Caldwell out of Duluth. After his trial in Brainard, Minnesota, Roger Caldwell was convicted of two counts of first-degree murder and sentenced to two consecutive life terms in prison. Marjorie Caldwell was acquitted on charges of being an accomplice, after a trial in Hastings, Minnesota. Joseph Kimball, who reported the case from its beginning for the *Minneapolis Tribune*, admits that the case "received an inordinate amount of coverage" by Minnesota news media, "but it was a tailor-made newspaper case." (Interview, 26 Mar. 1982.)

Reporting by the *Chicago Sun-Times* and its since-folded sister paper, the *Daily News*, contributed to community hysteria that helped wrongly convict a Chicago man of Nazi war crimes, in the view of Flora Johnson of *Student Lawyer* magazine. It all started when the Israeli government leaked to a *Chicago Daily News* correspondent a list of eighty-nine Nazi war crimes suspects. The name of Frank Walus was one of more than ten Chicago residents on the list. The *Daily News* then began a series of "exclusive reports revealing war crimes allegations against more than 10 Chicago-area residents." The revelation about Frank Walus, who was called "Fritz Wulecki" in the story "to avoid any possibility of prejudicing the ongoing federal investigation," was headlined: "Nazi Jew Killer Living on SW Side." The story quoted two eyewitnesses describing in gruesome detail the atrocities "Wulecki" committed. It also quoted an Israeli Ministry of Justice attorney as saying the case against "Wulecki" was "airtight" and "one of the best" of the cases about to be filed against alleged Nazis. "Eighteen days later, when charges were brought against Frank Walus, everyone recognized him as 'Wulecki'," Johnson wrote.[25]

When Walus came to trial, the Chicago newspapers, particularly the

Sun-Times, "which had picked up the cudgel against Walus" after the *Daily News* folded, prominently featured the testimony of witnesses against Walus. Eleven Jewish survivors of the Nazi occupation of Poland testified that some thirty-five years earlier they had seen Walus beat people, murder women and children, and send people to concentration camps. But when Walus finally got to tell his side of the story, the *Sun-Times* buried it. Walus testified that at the time the witnesses said he was doing all those things, he was actually a teenager working on German farms; he said he was among the 2.5 million Poles the Germans rounded up and sent back to Germany to work as virtual slaves. Feelings were high: Walus was convicted, stripped of his naturalized U.S. citizenship, and ordered deported to Poland. But two years later a court of appeals said it would be "an intolerable injustice" not to retry Walus and that a new trial "almost certainly" would clear him. Nine months after that, the government decided it didn't have enough evidence to justify a retrial and dropped the charges against Walus. It had been a terrible mistake in identification. The Israelis, the U.S. prosecutors, and the press had gotten the wrong man.

These two cases from Minneapolis and Chicago, while not as damaging to the image of press responsibility as the coverage of the "Son of Sam" murders in New York, indicate that journalists still do not earn straight A's for their reporting of crime news. The press in this country has obviously progressed a long way from the Yellow Journalism of an earlier day, but the line between responsible reporting of pretrial criminal investigations and sensationalism still gets crossed.

STANDARDS HARD TO COME BY

The matter of when and if journalists should show compassion toward the people and the news they deal with is virtually ignored in all of the codes or operating standards examined for this study. That is not surprising. Compassion, in addition to being a word that many macho journalists do not even like to hear, does not easily translate into a standard or a guideline. ("Be compassionate in the following circumstances. . . . don't be compassionate in the following circumstances. . . .") Also it is hard to legislate a human emotion like compassion, which comes easier to some people than it does to others.

The *Washington Post* touches on the matter of journalists not getting involved in what they are reporting — the dispassion side of the dispassion/compassion issue — in its deskbook guideline on the reporter's role: "Although it has become increasingly difficult for this newspaper and for the press generally to do so since Watergate, reporters should make every effort to remain in the audience, to stay off the stage, to report history, not to make history."[26]

At the same time that there is a lack of written guidelines and standards suggesting that compassion might be acceptable on occasion, there is great concern among journalists about the image of the news business. Various fears about how the press is perceived are often expressed — that the press is arrogant and aloof from people, that journalists try to set themselves up as a privileged class, that journalists do not really care about anyone or anything as they get their stories and move on. Such images may be undeserved, but many journalists believe they already exist in the minds of the public or could be put there quickly by the continuation of certain bad practices in the business.

Although compassion cannot be turned on and off like a faucet, encouraging more of it in news work and presentation might improve the public's perception of the entire enterprise. It also might improve the perception of news work by journalists themselves, many of whom seem to get cynical at an early age. The folklore of the news business is mostly hardnosed, Humphrey Bogart-like. Any feelings of sympathy or tenderness are better expressed off duty.

Perhaps it is time in news work to start honoring compassion more and cynicism less.

The codes of ethics, particularly in broadcast journalism, have more to say about the free press versus fair trial issue. The absence of specific advice on that issue in the codes of most newspapers and national newspaper organizations may be explained by a fear of free press versus fair trial guidelines. Many editors have refused to agree to such guidelines when they have been pushed by state bar associations because courts in some cases have applied those guidelines as standards the press is supposed to adhere to, not as voluntary procedures.

The code of the RTNDA states that "in reporting matters that are or may be litigated, the journalist should avoid practices which would tend to interfere with the right of an individual to a fair trial."

The NBC, CBS, and ABC news standards on the free press versus fair trial matter are more detailed. NBC notes that "under our judicial system, verdicts must be based on evidence heard in the courtroom. As a consequence, if we report information which would not be legally admissable or available in the courtroom, it may have a prejudicial impact on the judicial proceedings." NBC then offers these general guidelines:

> When we report news about crimes and criminal proceedings, detailed references to such matters as (1) the existence or content of confessions or (2) prior criminal records or (3) the identity or potential testimony of witnesses have the potential to interfere with the processes of justice....
>
> There are some situations, however, where such information not only may, but should, be reported. If, for example, we are investigat-

ing or exposing wrongful behavior by government officials, or a wrongful deprivation of civil rights, or a wrongful imprisonment or any other miscarriage of justice, we must seek out and report every available and relevant fact.

CBS News, after warning in language similar to that in the NBC code about the ways that pretrial publicity can cause miscarriages of justice, explains the kinds of situations in which such publicity might be appropriate:

> We still must fulfill the vital watchdog role of the press, particularly in the administration of justice. Consequently, where there are public policy reasons to do so, we *can* pursue every lead and report it — so long as it relates directly to a story or exposé about the administration or miscarriage of justice and improper action or inaction of officials. Watergate was, of course, a paramount example of this. The Wetumpkta story is a more obscure and less dramatic example: There, a young black was hauled out of his car by the county sheriff and dragged into jail, and then was found dead in jail — and there was no indictment and no charge against the county officials. After a reasonable time had elapsed and it became apparent that there would be no official pursuit of the case, we reported eyewitness and other evidence that the sheriffs had brutally beaten the black. Here was a case where, indeed, the evidence went to the guilt or innocence of the sheriffs. But it was apparent that nobody was doing anything and hence there seemed clearly to be a miscarriage of justice. In such cases no holds, except careful and responsible reporting, are barred and we go full-speed ahead. So, too, if a seemingly innocent person appears to us to be in the process of being railroaded to jail, we can and ought to report any evidence that we can find.
>
> One other point — where a crime has been committed and there is no warrant or arrest or indictment for any particular person, we certainly can interview eyewitnesses (staying away, as is normally the case, from explicit fingering and identification of the alleged criminal by name) and carry the pictures and description of the suspected fugitive released by the police. Further, where the police themselves or government officials violate the American Bar Association guidelines and publicly announce, in newsworthy circumstances, particular evidence pointing to the guilt of a person including confessions or prior police records, it is not incumbent on us to censor them if our news judgment otherwise indicates that some or all of their statements are worthwhile carrying. An extreme example of the latter is the instance where the Dallas Chief of Police waved a rifle in front of everybody and said that this was the rifle that Oswald had used and that he was clearly guilty. So, also, is the Nixon reference to Manson's guilt before Manson's conviction. These are

things that we could not, and should not, suppress. Mr. Nixon and the police official may have been totally wrong, but we cannot put ourselves in the position of playing God and pretending, in these particular circumstances of significant public interest and importance, that the events didn't happen.

ABC News urges that its news people "be sensitive to the accused's right to a fair trial and the potential prejudicial effect of prior publicity." The ABC News guideline on crime reporting also says:

> We should give careful thought on a case-by-case basis before reporting confessions or other detailed "evidence" which directly links a particular individual to a crime. Even if the information comes from the police or prosecutor, it is untested in court and may not be admissible at trial (for example, if a confession is ruled to be not voluntary). On the other hand, if the police hold a news conference to discuss particular evidence, their actions and opinions may be newsworthy and under most circumstances we should feel free to report them.
>
> The dictates of fairness are of particular relevance where individuals are accused of crimes. While "alleged" is a useful word connoting something unproved, we should also seek out the accused for comment and consider other opinions that run counter to the allegations.
>
> While we wish to proceed with caution in this area, we are not limited to reporting only what the police or prosecutors have done or are about to do. There will be instances where the very point of our story is the failure to prosecute or undue delays in an official investigation, or evidence of miscarriage of justice. In such cases, we may determine that the fullest reporting of facts is justified and necessary.

The *Washington Post* deskbook deals with crime and court coverage. "We should take care to report crime news with caution and accuracy, to bear in mind the rights of the accused and to leave the deciding of guilt or innocence to the courts," the *Post* declares. "Be especially careful about these points:"

> 1. Guilt of accused or arrested persons must not be conveyed or implied in the stories or headlines....
>
> 2. Statements to police officers, reporters or prosecutors are not confessions. The term *confession* should not be used either in headlines or text unless we are dealing with an acknowledgment of guilt given by a defendant in a courtroom. Accused persons *state*, *relate*, *report*, *explain* or otherwise elaborate upon a criminal situation in remarks to police. We prefer to avoid the use of even such words as *admit* or *acknowledge*.

3. Reports of trials should accurately reflect the proceedings. Reporters and editors should give the prosecution and the defense fair coverage. . . .

6. Persons charged with a violation of the law should be given the opportunity to reply to such charges, if possible.

7. Do not routinely report arrest records of suspects in crime stories. . . . A record (and it should include disposition) may be used only after clearance with a departmental editor. Particular effort should be made to avoid prejudicing a trial by publishing the record of a suspect immediately before trial.

8. We avoid publishing pictures that might prejudice the trial of defendants. . . .

10. As a general rule, we name persons charged with crimes. However, in "trend" or "survey" stories, where one or a few cases are selected as examples, the departmental editor should carefully weigh whether to use those names — particularly if they would not have otherwise seen print. . . .[27]

ABC News is one of the few news organizations that tries in its code to guide its journalists on questions of when and if they should cooperate with government. After stating that it "disapproves of most forms of cooperation with government agencies . . . because it can compromise, or have the appearance of compromising, the First Amendment freedom and independence of the press," ABC News says cooperation might be all right in situations involving threats to human life or national security and in cases where a crime has been, or is about to be, committed. "In such situations, the responsibilities of good citizenship and good journalism must be reconciled," ABC adds, warning, however, that all "invocations of national security" cannot be recognized because "history reveals too many instances where claims of national security have been used wrongly to cover up information that should have been reported." Another kind of cooperation seen as possibly acceptable to ABC News is accompanying police on a narcotics raid or in undercover or "sting" operations. The only specific example in the ABC code of a time when journalists should not cooperate with government is in this prohibition: "A reporter must never use his or her identity as a journalist to ask questions or perform any investigative function on behalf of the police or any other government agency."

Existing codes, however, lack much advice on the more general underlying questions posed by this chapter: Aren't journalists also citizens and human beings? Shouldn't they live up to the obligations of citizenship and humanity that apply to all of us?

If, as Robert Greene suggests, journalists are seen as a privileged class when they decline to testify or cooperate with government investigations, perhaps it is time for journalists to start explaining their reasons for not doing what other citizens are expected to do. The process of justifying their uncooperative behavior to the rest of us might force journalists to more thoughtfully separate the legitimate refusals from the less legitimate ones. There are certainly occasions when journalists, in order to serve the greater good of truthful reporting, have to say no to courts, government investigators, and other human beings in need, but a knee-jerk no every time cooperation is asked makes journalists appear to be the despised privileged class that Greene warns about.

Incompetence, Irresponsibility

Reporters pursue hot story.

ASSUME YOU ARE A DOCTOR practicing general medicine in a medium-sized city. You enter the doctor's lounge of the hospital just after checking on your patients and are greeted by a fellow general practitioner who says, "Now we know how you can afford that new house!" Then he shows you an article in that morning's local newspaper reporting on fees charged by various medical specialists in the area. Your name is listed at the top of a column of general practitioners for charging $35 for an initial office visit. Your actual fee schedule is $15 for the first office visit, and $12 for each subsequent visit, with slight additional charges for longer revisits.

Does this mistake upset you? Or are you inclined to shrug it off? If you are upset, what do you intend to do about it? Will it do any good to complain to the paper?

When this happened to Dr. Gary A. Hogge, he was angry. He called one of his patients who was an editor of the newspaper, the Louisville *Courier-Journal*. Hogge contends that the editor promised to look into it and get back to him that day, but he did not. When Hogge had not heard from his editor-patient after a week, the doctor called the paper and asked to speak to the reporter whose by-line was on the erroneous article, Robert L. Peirce. Because the reporter was not in just then, Hogge unloaded his complaint on city editor Bill Cox and demanded a retraction. Again he was told that the editor would check into the matter and call him back. But another week passed without a call from the paper. His anger escalating, Hogge called city editor Cox again and was told flatly that no retraction was going to be printed because the article was based on Medicare statistics. Hogge said that after an exchange of some unpleasantries, Cox suggested he talk to reporter Peirce, which Hogge did. The doctor told the reporter that he should have checked the Medicare figures with the doctors — at least those at the top of the price range — because such statistics are "notoriously unreliable." Hogge said Peirce's response "floored me." The reporter "told me (1) he didn't have time to check his figures and (2) even if he had checked with me, he wouldn't have changed anything in the article. It was by now apparent that the *Courier-Journal* was tired of fooling with this insignificant country doc who had the effrontery to challenge its omniscience," Hogge said.[1]

When he asked Peirce whether he had any recourse other than legal action, the doctor said he was surprised when the reporter gave him the name of the National News Council. Nowhere in the *Medical Economics* article he wrote about this experience does Hogge report any cognizance on his part or that of the *Courier-Journal* people he talked to of that newspaper's ombudsman, whose job it is to deal with complaints like his. This despite the regular publication by the Louisville newspapers of the name and address of both their news ombudsman and the news council.

The *Courier-Journal's* news ombudsman then, Frank Hartley, did get involved when Hogge complained to the news council. Hartley investigated the complaint for the newspaper and in his response to the news council supported the article and the two staffers who had dealt with the physician. Hartley found that (1) the paper had hired an outside computer firm to double-check its own study of the Medicare printouts; (2) Peirce had interviewed at random 60 of the 400 physicians listed; and (3) when Peirce found out that charges for an initial visit can vary because of billing inconsistencies, he inserted that explanation at the top of the list of doctors and their charges, directly above Hogge's name.

News council investigators found that Hogge did not deal directly with Medicare and instead asked his patients to file for whatever reimbursement they were due. The council suggested that since Hogge's "billing form was less than ideal," some of his patients might have submitted blanket fees instead of itemized ones, which would have skewed his Medicare "profile." The council report said, however:

The *Courier-Journal* listing was accurate insofar as the Medicare computer records listed Dr. Hogge's charges. What seemed essential was a direct check with Dr. Hogge and all others listed in the top rank of fees recorded, the most sensitive area in the lists. It is clear such a recheck with Dr. Hogge would have brought instant protest and a deeper check. However, the newspaper opted for random checking. Moreover, the newspaper's statement seeking to clarify differentials was not fully informative. *The Courier-Journal's* motivation was sound and the paper did publish a patient's letter supporting Dr. Hogge's view. Nevertheless, Dr. Hogge was done an inadvertent injustice and the complaint is found warranted.[2]

The *Courier-Journal* reported the council's finding on its front page and executive editor Paul Janensch apologized to the doctor in his column ten days later. Janensch said he accepted the council's decision "without a quibble" and explained that the error "was a collective one and shouldn't be ascribed to a single individual." Hogge said he "was surprised to get anything near this much redress of injustice. It shows that if you're right — and willing — you *can* fight 'bad press' — and even win."[3]

Hogge might not have fared so well — nor been so gratified by the result — if he practiced in a city whose newspapers cared less about providing channels for complaints and machinery for public accountability. The Louisville *Courier-Journal* and the *Louisville Times* were the first newspapers in the country to set up an ombudsman to deal with readers' complaints and have been longtime supporters of the news council. Yet Hogge's complaint sort of fell through the cracks. Janensch admits that it was not well handled "or it wouldn't have gone as far as it did." (Interview, 19 Oct. 1981.)*

News people make mistakes. ("Doctors bury their mistakes," some editor once said. "We print ours.") But news people are also better at making errors than they are at correcting them. Although newspapers and the broadcast media are making much greater efforts these days to admit and correct their mistakes, many errors still go unnoticed or are deliberately swept under the rug. If an error such as the one in the preceding case study can go uncorrected for five months in a newspaper with the reputation for high standards and ethics that the *Courier-Journal* enjoys, then journalism is a long way from being able to claim that it fully and promptly corrects all its mistakes.

Errors are often caused by incompetence or irresponsibility, or both. Whether journalism has more incompetent and irresponsible people than other orders in American life is impossible to determine, but it certainly has its share. This chapter examines some of the incompetence and irresponsibility that has damaged the news business.

---

*See list of interviewees following Notes.

WHY SO MANY ERRORS?

Pollster George Gallup, Jr., found in 1980 that when people were asked what their own experience has been with newspaper reports of things that they knew about personally, about one in three (34 percent) said the paper had gotten the facts wrong. The 47 percent who said newspaper reports they knew about personally were accurate was much lower than the 70 percent who replied that way in a 1958 poll. Gallup also found that people "who feel the press has been inaccurate in treating news items relating to their own lives are more likely to favor stricter curbs on the press than are those who feel the facts were dealt with accurately."[4]

There are all sorts of explanations for inaccuracies in news reports. Some are caused by carelessness — some reporter or editor not taking that extra step to check a fact or a quote. Some mistakes come out of ignorance — the journalists processing the news report lack the knowledge needed to recognize errors or to prevent themselves from making them. Deadline pressures can cause mistakes. News sources sometimes give out "bum" information and reporters and editors are not sharp enough to challenge or check it. Some subjects journalists have to deal with are so complex and fuzzy that errors can easily occur in the process of simplifying these subjects for mass audiences.

Carelessness. Carelessness or thoughtlessness causes many errors in the processing of news. Even respected newspapers like the *New York Times* and *Washington Post* are not immune.

The *New York Times* once published a column by Tom Wicker that had been written (and published) seven months earlier. Associate editor Charlotte Curtis explained that someone pushed the wrong button on the *Times*'s computer, calling up the old column instead of the fresh one that was supposed to appear that day. No one at the *Times* apparently caught the error because the outdated column ran in all three editions. But dozens of readers noticed that the column discussed President Reagan's tax cut proposals — long since enacted into law. Curtis noted that such an error could not have happened in the precomputer days when used type was automatically destroyed. The next day the *Times* ran the correct Wicker column, dealing with Reagan budget cuts, with an explanation that a "regrettable editing lapse" caused the error.[5]

Mechanical problems also took the rap when the *Washington Post* failed to run a crucial story in a series of reports from St. Louis on a five-day trial involving Senator Thomas Eagleton. His niece and her attorney were being tried on charges of extortion. The *Post* omitted the story on the day that Eagleton's niece and her attorney admitted that the allegation of homosexuality with which they had threatened the senator was totally false. This was another computer error, compounded by the fact that the *Post* was at the time changing over to a new printing system. But it was also a human error by a makeup editor who should have noticed that the story was "dummied," scheduled to appear on a particular page, according to William L. Green, Jr., *Post* ombudsman at the time. Green later wrote in his column that the omission deprived readers in the city where Eagleton spends most of his professional life "of the words of his accusers that would have documented the Senator's denials. It should not have happened."[6]

The *Post* got egg on its face again when it dug into the background of John W. Hinckley, Jr., the young man accused of trying to assassinate President Reagan in 1981. In its 10,000-word report put together by eight reporters was a 31-word passage, right after a description of Hinckley's purchase of handguns during the eighteen months he was a student at Texas Tech University in Lubbock. The passage read: "A penchant for guns hardly strikes anyone as ominous in free-wheeling Lubbock, where some university students carry guns to class and the pistol-packing frontier tradition runs deep and long."[7]

The good people of Lubbock took exception to that picture. Their complaints spurred ombudsman Green to discover that one of the reporters on the *Post* article, Chip Brown, had based the offensive passage on material he lifted — without independent verification— from a similar article about Hinckley in the *Philadelphia Inquirer* three days earlier.

Donald C. Drake, who wrote the *Inquirer* story that the *Post* reporter used as his source, believes that although his story did say that guns were common in Lubbock, "it didn't give the sense that Lubbock was a wild town, but quite the opposite." Drake calls attention to this section in the *Inquirer* story:

> An official in the Lubbock office of the Federal Bureau of Alcohol, Tobacco and Firearms confirmed yesterday that records showed that Hinckley had purchased at least six handguns over 18 months from various Lubbock pawnshops.
> "Should that have raised a warning signal somewhere?"
> "Naw," the official said. "We have people that buy a hundred or two hundred a year around here."
> Rolf Gordhamer, who directs psychological testing and counseling at Texas Tech, said it was quite common for students to carry weapons at the college.[8]

Drake sees not only a difference in tone between this segment of the *Inquirer* story and that in the *Post*, but "a small but important difference in the actual information reported." Carrying "weapons at the college," as the *Inquirer* said, is substantially different from the *Post* statement that "students carry guns to class," Drake points out. "The thought of a student carrying a pistol in a classroom is much more disturbing to me, as a reader in a northeastern city, than the image of them carrying a gun outside on campus for target shooting or some other sporting activity," Drake adds. The *Inquirer* further quotes Gordhamer as observing:

> "Seriously, this is frontierland. People do have guns. Their grandparents were pioneers. There are a lot of small towns and isolation, and change comes very slowly. People shoot rattlesnakes and coyotes and," he paused to laugh, "trespassers."
>
> "Still," Gordhamer said, "the campus is placid, the calmest, quietest place I've ever seen. Basically, the kids obey authority. They don't protest or march up and down the streets here. They take life pretty easy. They just kind of enjoy it. People out here believe in mother, apple pie and The American Flag."

"As you can see," Drake explains, "the *Inquirer*'s picture of Lubbock is much more complex than the one suggested in the segment of the *Post*'s story....I think this is a particularly interesting example of how the basic facts in two stories might be the same — Lubbock is a town where guns are common and pioneer independence predominates — but one story, the *Post*'s, leaves the impression that Lubbock is the set for a John Wayne movie and the other, the *Inquirer*'s, suggests something more like Thornton Wilder's 'Our Town.' "

The *Post* corrected the passage about Lubbock twenty-five days after it ran. The correction said that the article "presented an inaccurate depiction of Texas Tech University and the city in which the university is located, Lubbock. Texas Tech students do not carry guns to class, as the article stated, and the city itself is a quiet town with orderly and law-abiding citizens. There is no 'pistol-packing' tradition in Lubbock, as the article incorrectly implied." The *Post* also carried four letters from Lubbock, all disagreeing with the implications in the *Post* reference to the city and the university.[9]

The Hinckley story also caused an embarrassing error by the AP. The AP's Chicago bureau paid $3,000 to a free-lance photographer for a photograph of "Hinckley" and two other members of the National Socialist Party of America dressed in their neo-Nazi uniforms. The shot was supposedly made at a party demonstration in St. Louis in 1978. But when reporters for the Oklahoma City *Daily Oklahoman* showed the photo to two neo-Nazis they interviewed, the party members said the picture was not of Hinckley. Hinckley's family in Evergreen, Colorado, also said the picture was not of their son. It turned out the uniformed young man in the picture resembled Hinckley but he was really James Gaither Whittom of Shreveport, Louisiana, a former member of the Nazi group. The AP killed the picture two days after it was distributed and had run in many newspapers, and instructed clients to destroy file copies.[10]

Diane Benison, managing editor of the Worcester, Massachusetts, *Evening Gazette*, believes many errors in news reports are caused by "a lack of thought." (Interview, 19 Oct. 1981.) She tells of one of her reporters, "not an insensitive guy," who wrote in his story about a woman who had been raped that "the woman was not injured." When she questioned him about it, he was not able to see immediately what she objected to. So she asked him to imagine that his wife had been raped and how would he feel if the news story about it said she had not been injured. He got the point.

Ignorance. H. L. Mencken took the same dim view of the business that fed him as he did all other orders of American life, with the possible exception of Gibson drinkers. "There are managing editors in the United States, and scores of them," Mencken wrote in the twenties,

> who have never heard of Kant or Johannes Müller and never read the Constitution of the United States; there are city editors who do not know what a symphony is, or a streptococcus, or the Statute of Frauds; there are reporters by the thousand who could not pass the entrance examination for Harvard or Tuskegee, or even Yale. It is this vast and militant ignorance, this widespread and fathomless prejudice against intelligence, that makes American journalism so pathetically feeble and vulgar, and so generally disreputable.[11]

Ignorance in the newsrooms was also a target in the best of the early books on journalism ethics, Nelson Crawford's *The Ethics of Journalism.* "Not corruption," Crawford wrote,

> but ignorance, inertia, and fear — the same type of ignorance, the same type of inertia, and the same type of fear that permeate American life — are the fundamental causes for the failure of American newspapers in giving the public the facts which the public has a right to demand. Persons who come to this country from Europe, familiar wih the better newspapers there, are astonished at the ignorance displayed by American reporters and copy-readers about the simplest matters.[12]

Unfortunately the ignorance Mencken and Crawford saw in the U.S. journalism of the twenties is still a problem. Errors in news reports, some serious, occur every day because some journalist doesn't have the knowledge or intelligence to get the facts straight. Perhaps it is asking too much of journalists that they have at least above-average knowledge of the many subjects they deal with every working day. But citizens depend on the information they get from the news media to guide them in the decisions they must make at the polling place, the market place, and in their lives in general. Bum information leads to bum decisions.

An example of the kind of problem journalists face in keeping their knowledge current in order not to mislead people is presented by changes in chemical and biological warfare. The National News Council investigated this problem when a reader, Robert Gulack, complained about a headline in the New York *Daily News* that said, "Haig charges: Soviets Use Germ War." The head was on a report of a speech by then U.S. Secretary of State Alexander Haig in which he implied that Communist forces had used toxins derived from living organisms in Laos, Kampuchea, and Afghanistan. Gulack complained that "germ war" was a more frightening term than what Haig was talking about, which was chemical warfare using poisons sometimes referred to as "yellow rain." After getting no satisfaction from a telephone conversation with the managing editor of the *News*, Gulack wrote a letter to the editor, but the paper never published it. His letter said in part: " 'Germ war' is something quite different and far more scary than the use of poisons, because germs reproduce themselves in an uncontrollable manner. It is important for your readers to realize that Haig did *not* charge the Soviets with using plague as a weapon of war."[13]

Editors of the *News* defended their use of "germ war" as an "acceptable vernacular phrase" and especially "valid in page-one headlines because of space limitations." John H. Metcalfe, assistant to the editor of the *Daily News*, told the news council that he thought Gulack was "straining at a semantic gnat." He argued that "germ" is not a scientific word, and "germ war" does not connote "plague" to the average reader. "The distinction between a living microorganism and a poison produced in nature by living organisms is not likely to be readily made by the reading public — or considered all that significant," Metcalfe claimed.

But the news council decided it was "significant" and said it was "unfortunate that the *News* did not publish" a correction or Gulack's letter, which did make the distinction between chemical and biological warfare that the *News* failed to make.

News council investigators also examined thirteen other newspapers around the country and found only two that used "germ" warfare in their headlines on the Haig speech of 13 September 1981. One was the *News-Sun* in Waukegan, Illinois, which changed to "chemical warfare" the next day. The other was the *Los Angeles Times*, which used "germ warfare" the first two days, but changed to "biological weapons," "yellow rain," and "toxins" the next two days. Robert Trounson, assistant foreign editor of the *Los Angeles Times*, explained to the news council that "there was considerable discussion among our staff here as to whether Secretary

Haig was talking about biological or chemical weapons in his September 13 speech. . . . 'Germ warfare' would never have been used in *The Times* had it been immediately clear that the toxins Haig referred to were indeed chemical, rather than biological weapons."

Failure to understand the procedures followed by the California Supreme Court in arriving at its decisions contributed to an erroneous and misleading article in the *Los Angeles Times*. The 1978 article by William Endicott, chief of the *Times*'s San Francisco bureau, and Robert Fairbanks, Sacramento bureau chief, quoted unnamed sources to the effect that the state's highest court was delaying the announcement of a controversial decision to help its chief justice win a confirmation vote at the polls the day the story appeared. The decision reportedly was to overturn a law requiring judges to give prison terms to persons who used a gun while committing a crime, a law strongly supported by law and order proponents. The story charged that the chief justice, Rose Bird, had voted with the majority to strike down the new law. Bird won her confirmation vote the day the article appeared but by only 51.7 percent, the slimmest margin a California Supreme Court justice had ever received. The head of the Law and Order Campaign Committee contended that if the *Times* story had come out "just one day earlier, Rose Bird would not be chief justice today."[14]

Betty Medsger, former *Washington Post* and Philadelphia *Bulletin* reporter, dug into the background of the Endicott-Fairbanks article and found that the reporters did not understand that no decision on the controversial law had been made at the time they wrote their piece. In the California Supreme Court, as in many appellate courts, the justices customarily take a preliminary vote shortly after hearing the case, Medsger reported. "Then the majority and minority opinions are written," she said. "Many weeks or months may pass before the opinions are completed, for each justice is juggling many cases simultaneously, trying to convince fellow justices to change their minds." Medsger reported that the two *Times* reporters told her that neither of them understood at the time how the court worked. Endicott explained that it would have been impossible the day the story was written to find out how the court worked "because Rose Bird runs such a closed court." Medsger, however, said she had no trouble finding out how a case proceeds from hearing to decision simply by calling some court aides not in Bird's office.

In this case, the *Times* reporters were lucky. The preliminary vote to overturn the controversial law turned out to be the decision that was handed down six weeks after the *Times* article was published. However, seven weeks after the "final" decision, the court, "in a rare action," agreed to rehear the case, and on the reconsideration one justice switched his vote and the law was upheld.

The *Times* article, because it suggested ethical misconduct by the court, spurred an unprecedented investigation of the court by the Commission on Judicial Performance, an investigation that took nearly a year and cost the taxpayers more than half a million dollars. But the story that started it all, by the admission of Fairbanks, who wrote it, "was based on mere speculation from unnamed sources and on the reporters' lack of understanding of how the supreme court works," Medsger said.

If that kind of reporter ignorance can mar a newspaper with the high standards of the *Los Angeles Times*, think what must be happening out in the "boonies" in reporting courts and the legal process. The *Times* claimed in 1980 that it had more reporters covering the legal system than any other newspaper in the country — seven covering various courts full time, several others who cover suburban courts as parts of other beats, and one full-time specialist on legal affairs. That claim was made in a lengthy report by media reporter-critic David Shaw on the quality of reporting about the legal system by U.S. news organizations. His conclusion was that such reporting is improving but "media coverage of the nation's legal system is still largely inadequate."[15]

At least some of the blame for inadequate coverage of this important institution has to be placed on lack of knowledge by the reporters covering it. Although an impressive number of top legal system reporters have legal training and even law degrees, the average reporter on the beat has none. Shaw, who interviewed almost one hundred attorneys, judges, legal scholars, journalists, and journalism professors, found that most favored some legal training for reporters assigned to this area. Such training "enables a reporter to speak the same, often arcane language as the people he covers, and it also enables him to invite confidences not easily given to non-lawyers — and to provide historical perspective to his daily reportage," Shaw concludes. Several lawyers told Shaw they were "astounded by the number of reporters who accepted what they said — or did not say — without either question or challenge, either out of laziness, ignorance, or a fear of being perceived as ignorant."

Another area in which news sources often complain about journalists' lack of knowledge is business and economics. Although the larger newspapers and network television news departments have beefed up their coverage of business and economics in recent years, "media coverage is often simplistic, careless and cursory," A. Kent MacDougall wrote in the *Los Angeles Times*. But he pointed out that "deliberate distortion" was rare.[16] One of the examples MacDougall used in his prize-winning series on how the media cover business concerned a business story that was interpreted three different ways by three top dailies. It happened when the General Accounting Office (GAO), the investigatory arm of Congress, reported on its investigation into whether American oil producers had deliberately worsened the oil shortage. The *New York Times* headlined its story, "G.A.O. Study Asserts That Oil Companies Worsened Shortage," and reported that American oil companies had aggravated the petroleum shortage in the spring of 1979 by cutting production of crude oil within the United States while imports from Iran were disrupted. But the *Wall Street Journal's* headline read, "GAO Says Oil Firms Aren't to Be Blamed for Recent Shortage," and its story said GAO had concluded that "there isn't any evidence that the major oil companies created the U.S. oil shortage that occurred after the closing of Iran's oil fields." The *Los Angeles Times* ignored GAO's judgment on oil company culpability; its story emphasized GAO's criticism of Department of Energy actions. Who was right? It was not the *New York Times,* which ran a lengthy correction two days later, saying it had misinterpreted the GAO report.[17]

One explanation for errors in business reporting can be surmised from the experiences of Cortland Anderson, who worked as a newspaper journalist and in corporate public relations before becoming director of the School of Journalism at Ohio University. Anderson commented that when he was public relations chief at the New York Telephone Company, "we had to educate reporters seemingly thrown in at the last minute to cover specific complicated rate stories." He recalls how John de Butts, then chairman of American Telephone and Telegraph, terminated an interview with a reporter from "a highly respected publication specializing in business news" when de Butts "discovered the reporter did not know the difference between stocks and bonds." Anderson tells of another case in which a reporter was gathering information from him (as vice-president of the Washington Post Company) to prepare for an interview with Katharine Graham, chairman of the Washington Post Company, for a story on the company's state of business. "In a discussion preceding that interview," Anderson said, "my concern rose and my confidence fell when I learned that this reporter did not understand the implications of a company repurchasing its own stock. That was a process in which the company was deeply involved at the time — a vital part of the story."[18]

Some of the ignorance problems in processing news could be avoided by more preparation — journalists doing their homework before asking questions. Robert Scheer of the *Los Angeles Times* sees library research as the first line of ethical reporting. He believes reporters have to make themselves authorities on the subjects they write about (interview, 25 Nov. 1980). The ethical question, he says, is "whether you're really going to put out, or whether you're going to surrender to the cynicism and the mentality of shit and just shove it into the paper." Scheer's primary standard is: "I want to be able to pick up the piece two or three years later and say 'God, this holds up!' "

Inadequate Education. Education is a cure for ignorance. Why don't the news executives of this country staff their newsrooms with people who have advanced formal education in all the important areas of knowledge? Some editors try to do that, to a degree. Sprinkled through the news staffs of the larger, better newspapers and the TV network news departments are people who have had advanced formal education in legal matters, political science, business and economics, science, medicine, and other fields. But by and large the typical journalist has only a bachelor's degree, usually with a major in journalism, and very little expertise outside the skills of writing and editing.

There are several explanations for the dearth of specialists in American newsrooms. One is that the news business is mostly a business for generalists, reporters and editors who can handle any type of story on any given day. When editors and news directors hire, they usually are not interested in specialists; they want people who can do everything, at least well enough to get by. A second explanation has to do with the abysmally low beginning salaries in news work (discussed in Chapter 2). Although salaries for experienced journalists are quite high, the low pay at the entrance level discourages apprentices from carrying their formal educations beyond the minimum — which is now a bachelor's degree or close to it. There is a third reason: The streak of antiintellectualism that has been part of the history of American journalism from its beginning has not dissipated. There are still news bosses out there who place little or no value on formal education; only what is learned in the newsroom has worth.

Ignorance and incompetence will continue to pollute the news process unless news media owners and executives recruit and retain better educated and smarter journalists. They should insist that journalism schools turn out graduates with background knowledge in one or more areas in addition to their journalistic skills plus a solid underpinning of instruction in the ethics, law, and history of journalism. And when they hire they should look for people with expertise not already represented on their staffs. This might mean five to seven years of formal education with a master's degree or two before aspirants would be allowed to step into their first jobs. And that, of course, would require higher salaries up and down the line.

There is also a need for more informal education: seminars and workshops, not just in newsroom practices, but in background subjects, such as those dealt with in the conferences organized by the Washington Journalism Center. Most of the informal education going on now is in the "nuts and bolts" of news work. That is useful, but it will take more than that to abolish ignorant errors and misinterpretations from news reports.

Very few journalists are encouraged by their managements to take sabbaticals for advanced study, as is commonly done for faculty in the better universities. And only a relative handful are able to win spots in the few programs, such as the Nieman program at Harvard, that allow journalists to pull out of the front lines for a few months and pursue some special interest of study. More journalists need to be able to do what Walter Lippmann did in the twenties when he was editorial writer and then editorial page editor of the *New York World* — negotiate a contract that allowed him to spend summers in Europe at the paper's expense boning up on his specialty, foreign affairs.[19]

Having made these arguments for more formal and informal education in American journalism, I must add a personal observation as one who has worked many years in both journalism and higher education: Higher education cannot solve all human problems. There are too many Ph.D.'s in our universities who cannot write a clear sentence, too many professors whose vision of the world is as narrow as that of a pet goldfish, too many administrators deficient in humanity and ethics to encourage a faith that more formal education among journalists would necessarily improve journalism. But there is greater competence in the average university than in the average newsroom — a lot more in most cases — and most campuses with reasonably equipped libraries and faculties offer a would-be journalist the opportunity to develop the kind of knowledge needed to combat the ignorance that mars American journalism. Would-be journalists and the universities should be encouraged by the news business to do just that.

CORRECTING THE RECORD

As we have seen in the specific cases covered so far in this chapter, many news organizations admit and correct their errors. That has been the obvious trend in the country for the past two decades. Not all errors get corrected, of course. Sometimes they slip by unnoticed; nobody complains. And some editors get stubborn and simply decline to correct errors that are dubious in their minds or not completely the fault of the newspaper or broadcast station.

Some of the corrections are bewildering to news consumers not intimate with or who have forgotten the news item that erred. They seem to have been written just to get the complaining parties off the editor's back. This kind of correction, for example: "A report on a College Township Industrial Development Authority meeting in yesterday's *Times* incorrectly attributed a statement to Ben Malone. The statement was made by Ben Niebel."[20]

The *New York Times* is one of the newspapers that started a few years ago putting all its corrections in a set place in the paper. This does not satisfy critics who believe corrections should be run in about the same place as the error, but it is a giant step forward from the day when the *Times* and most newspapers simply refused to acknowledge, let alone correct, most errors. I had firsthand experience with the self-righteousness of those earlier *Times* editors in the early sixties when, as director of the School of Journalism at Penn State University, I tried to get that paper to correct an error. The erroneous item in its column on the advertising business said that Penn State was changing the name of all its advertising courses to "paid propaganda" (it was apparently based on the fact that the late Howard Gossage was about to become a visiting lecturer in the school's advertising sequence and planned to teach a special, one-time course entitled, "The Nature of Paid Propaganda"). Phone calls and letters protesting the reported change flooded the school the day of publication. Most came from advertising leaders and practitioners, many of them alumni. Phone calls and letters to the advertising columnist and Turner Catledge, then *Times* managing editor, brought no correction. The letters of protest to the school continued for almost a year as other newspapers and magazines would pick up the item and, because it was from the *Times,* republish it without checking with the university. To the *Times* apparently this was a small error not worth the bother, but it caused great grief and annoyance to the people at Penn State who had to correct the record as best they could without the help of the paper that caused all the trouble in the first place.

The *Times* is better today — not perfect, but better. Recently it corrected a seven-year-old error with a front-page article that said the former U.S. ambassador to Chile, Edward Korry, knew nothing of covert CIA efforts to overthrow Chilean President Salvador Allende Gossens. The 2,300-word corrective was written by former *Times* reporter Seymour Hersh, who also wrote the earlier stories that implied Korry played a major role in an aborted CIA coup against Allende. Other reporters wrote similar stories but Hersh admits he "led the way in trashing" Korry. Hersh discovered he had been wrong about Korry while doing research in the fall of 1980 for a book on Henry Kissinger. When he told *Times* executive editor A. M. Rosenthal that some of the things he had written for the *Times* about Korry were wrong, Rosenthal asked Hersh to write the corrective. "My God, if we were wrong in any way I want to correct it," Rosenthal said. Hersh's article was published on 9 February 1981, seven years after Hersh's first story (apparently based on a Senate subcommittee source) implied that Korry had been involved in the CIA plot. Korry's eight-year diplomatic career was ruined as a result of the story even though no charges of wrongdoing were ever filed against him, and it was not until 1979 that he was able to land a job as visiting professor of international relations at Connecticut College.[21]

One of the more charming *New York Times* corrections appeared recently at the bottom of Flora Lewis's "Foreign Affairs" column on the opposite editorial page. It read:

> NOTE: I've just eaten a large plate of crow. I am now satisfied that the document on El Salvador discussed in my column last Friday, which I believed was an official paper, was indeed spurious, as the State Department later said. Many of the facts checked out, but it wasn't a Government paper. I'm abashed.[22]

Before moving on to errors corrected by other news media, it should be said that it is easy to find examples of slips by the *New York Times* because it is the country's most visible and written about newspaper. Errors and the way they are corrected or not corrected in that newspaper provide fodder for many *Times* watchers who make beer money free-lancing pratfall pieces to journalism reviews and other publications.

Another constantly watched paper, the *Washington Post,* ran a front-page apology to former president Carter and his wife, Rosalynn, after the Carters threatened to sue the *Post* for libel. The Carters were disturbed about an item in the *Post*'s gossip column, "Ear," which said the Carters had bugged Blair House to eavesdrop on Ronald and Nancy Reagan when the Reagans stayed there prior to President Reagan's inaugural. The column, written by Diana McLellan (who has since been lured to the *Washington Times)*, offered a "hot new twist" on the "tired old tale" of how Mrs. Reagan had reportedly said she wished the Carters would vacate the White House before inauguration day to give her time to redecorate the living quarters before moving in. "Now word's around among Rosalynn's close pals about exactly why the Carters were so sure Nancy wanted them out," McLellan wrote. "They're saying Blair House, where Nancy was lodging — and chatting up First Decorator Ted Graber — was bugged. And at least one tattler in the Carter tribe has described listening in to the tape itself."

McLellan apparently got her "hot new twist" from free-lancer Dotson Rader, who claimed that there were tape recordings of Mrs. Reagan making such a statement to her decorator, Ted Graber, at Blair House. Somehow in the conversation between McLellan and Rader, "tapes" became "bugs." After the item was published, and the Carters threatened to sue, Benjamin C. Bradlee, *Post* executive editor, went up to Princeton, New Jersey, to talk to Rader and was astounded to learn that Rader had not meant to suggest that Blair House was bugged but only that there were tapes of Mrs. Reagan's discussion with her decorator. Bradlee said the writer did not see any difference between bugged or taped, but Bradlee saw a big difference: A tape could have been made by a reporter, or anyone else, with a tape recorder. Bugging means that microphones are hidden around the place to record conversations surreptitiously.

Bradlee returned to Washington and the *Post* soon retracted the "Ear" item and apologized to the Carters.[23]

The Carters then announced they would not sue the *Post,* but the former president lectured the *Post* in a statement which said in part:

> This incident and the newspaper policy which caused it have been of considerable concern to us. Fortunately, because of my previous position, I had access to the public news media and could draw attention to my problem. Many victims of similarly false allegations do not enjoy this opportunity, but suffer just as severely.
>
> The decision by the publishers of a nationally and internationally influential newspaper like the *Post* to print a regular column which is widely known to be based on rumor and gossip adds unwarranted credence to its false reports. Even an instant and enthusiastic effort by newspaper editors to correct errors can never be completely successful in erasing the damage caused by unfounded gossip.[24]

Threatening to sue as the Carters did does not always result in an apology or retraction, but it usually gets editors to pay attention to your complaint. In the old days, threatened litigaton was about the only way you could get a newspaper to admit it had erred. It is much less difficult today to get news organizations to acknowledge and correct their mistakes, but the reluctance to do so still hangs on. There is apparently a belief that the public will not trust a news medium that errs — and perhaps that fear is justified in the short run — but if admitting errors and apologizing for them is seen as a sign of maturity in people, why would it not be similarly so for news organizations?

Sometimes a news maker is better off not demanding a retraction or apology. The correction simply calls attention to the original error for people who missed it. There is also the risk that you will get the kind of apology that George Papadakis did when he took offense at the *Signal Hill* (California) *Tribune* for calling him a "Greek orator" in an editorial. Papadakis, who was a council member in that city, said the reference to him was a "racial slur." This was too much for editor Ken Mills. "The *Tribune* apologizes, George," Mills wrote. "What we meant to call you is a loquacious asshole, a bore without peer. ... We've reported your councilmanic doings accurately and without malice. So stuff it." Mills explained to the AP that he used "Greek orator" to mean that Papadakis was articulate.[25]

SIGNS OF TROUBLE

Although there are signs of an improved and more ethical journalism wherever you look, there are also plenty of signs that say the opposite. Unfortunately, incompetence and irresponsibility remain a problem in a field still trying to work out its standards.

Even hopeful observers lose hope when they hear tales of ineptitude and insensitivity like this one. A reporter for the AP stumbled on a report that Congressman Edward I. Koch, then Democratic candidate for mayor of New York, had some years before been found in a car with another man engaging in what police call sodomy. No charges had been filed, so the report went, and the matter was hushed up by politicians. Two reporters were assigned by the AP to check this out, and eventually they came up with a vague story full of qualifications that suggested Koch was gay. One of the reporters was instructed to take copies of the story to Koch and his opponent, Mario Cuomo, Liberal Party candidate for mayor, to get their comments. The reporter gave one copy to Koch and left the other with one of Cuomo's aides.

Koch called the AP and demanded that the story not run because it was a lie and he threatened legal action. Cuomo said something to the effect that he intended to continue to campaign "on the issues." The AP decided to hold its story. But soon calls started coming in from people identifying themselves as editors of various New York City news organizations, saying that they had copies of the story and asking when it was going to be put on the wire. The AP determined that these callers were phony: no one by the names the callers gave worked at the news organizations they said they represented. Somebody was trying to pressure the AP into running a story it had spiked. Then copies of the story actually started turning up in newspaper, TV, and radio newsrooms around town, and AP was able to confirm that the copies had been made from the copy of the story given to Cuomo's people.

So the AP, by its clumsy handling of a story that was based on flimsy facts and was of questionable news value, handed ammunition to one side against the other in an important local election. Inexcusable. After the election, which Koch, of course, won, the *New York Post* did a front-page story on rumormongering in that campaign, and specifically mentioned AP's role. When you are justifiably attacked by the *New York Post* for an ethical lapse, you've hit bottom.[26]

The incompetence exhibited by that AP incident is probably much less common in that news organization than it is in many newsrooms around the country. As we have seen in other cases involving the AP in this book, that organization has high standards and lives up to them most of the time. But no news organization, including the AP, has been able to completely rid itself of people who are at least occasionally incompetent and irresponsible.

Art Nauman, ombudsman of the *Sacramento Bee,* who calls incompetence the "great soft underbelly of American journalism," says that good

Newspaper Guild contracts have turned some newsrooms into "homes for mediocre people." (Interview, 2 Nov. 1981.) He recalls how he spent the first two or three months after becoming *Bee* city editor evaluating the staff he had inherited and coming up with a recommendation that six to eight people be dismissed. "My supervising editor said, 'Fine, you're right; I identified those same people long ago, but maybe you'd better sit down and read the Guild contract and then talk to personnel,'" Nauman reports. The personnel manager was also agreeable, instructing him to start keeping a notebook on each one of the incompetent staffers, keeping track of when they came to work, when they went home, when they took coffee breaks, saving samples of their stories, and on and on. "Well, we didn't get rid of them," Nauman admits. "I don't think in my ten years at the *Bee* that I've seen a single reporter fired purely for incompetence. It's very difficult to weed out the deadwood."

Gene Foreman, managing editor of the *Philadelphia Inquirer,* has had a similar experience (interview, 28 May 1981). When the *Inquirer* tried to fire a reporter for incompetence, the Guild fought it and won. "Now we have a reporter that we're not able to use on assignments," Foreman says sadly. "The Guild does not see it as one of its functions to police the profession."

But incompetence is a problem in non-Guild newsrooms as well. Robert P. McHugh, former executive of non-Guild newsrooms in Columbia, South Carolina, and Gulfport/Biloxi, Mississippi, observes that the problem is not with the obviously incompetent people who commit big errors and move on, but with the marginal people who do not quite do anything bad enough to get them fired, but who also do not do anything very well (interview, 16 Feb. 1981). "That's how you end up with deadheads on your staff," McHugh adds.

Charles Puffenbarger, assistant financial editor of the *Washington Post* who has taught journalism at two universities, sees lots of room for improvement in news staffs (interview, 23 Sept. 1981). "There aren't enough journalism-school-educated people who think like journalists," Puffenbarger holds. "Too many journalists want to go out and play cowboys and Indians without realizing that their arrows and bullets are going to hurt somebody or be directed at the wrong people. Media institutions need to do more educating in ethics."

Some journalists see a sign of trouble ahead in journalism's increasing reliance on lawyers. Because we live in a time when so many Americans are ready to sue at the drop of a hat, news media executives, hoping to avoid suits for libel and invasion of privacy, have turned more and more to lawyers for advice before stories are published or broadcast. Some of the larger news organizations, such as the *Washington Post,* have their lawyers right in the house, so to speak, easily accessible for quick decisions on any questionable material. Others have lawyers on retainers, ready to counsel at the ring of a telephone. This is great for the law business but is it good for the news business?

Lyle Denniston of the Baltimore *Sun* does not think so (interview, 5 June 1981). "Our lawyers have scared the bejesus out of us," says Denniston, who has covered the U.S. Supreme Court off and on for more than thirty years and who wrote the book, *The Reporter and The Law*.

> Having lawyers in newsrooms is as great a threat to the First Amendment as having reporters in jail. It is wrong to have someone sitting there constantly warning us about legal consequences. We consult lawyers too soon and pay too much attention to them: the editorial process is almost a stepchild of the legal system....The same thing has happened to us that has happened to others in whom the law has got its hook: we are now acting as if law were the primary consideration in our business.

Puffenbarger is another who objects to lawyers in the newsroom (interview, 23 Sept. 1981). "We have a lot of lawyer involvement in stories here, lawyers reading stories and suggesting changes," he claims. "I don't think we should have lawyers keeping us out of trouble — although they should help get us out of trouble — because we're supposed to be in trouble. Instead we play it safe."

Some lawyers, of course, believe in the First Amendment as strongly as most journalists do. And their counsel may seldom if ever deter aggressive reporting or prevent news organizations from taking legal risks with worthwhile stories (*Post* lawyers, for example, passed the "Ear" item described earlier in this chapter that brought the threat of a libel suit from former president Carter). But in smaller news operations, where aggressive reporting is less common, lawyers seem to play it safer in their advice to their news media clients; some stories never see the light of day as a result.

The Isolated Elite. Walking into the offices of the larger newspapers and broadcast stations today is like visiting your cousin in prison. Because of bomb threats and other problems with "crazies," virtually all urban news organizations have hired security guards to protect them. Unfortunately, they also protect them from people who may have news and information but who never get into the fortress. Once while waiting in the lobby of a big TV station for the person with whom I had an appointment to come out and claim me, I listened to an elderly woman trying to explain how a drowning the day before was similar to some previous and suspicious one she had witnessed. The guard patiently discouraged the woman from pursuing the matter and escorted her to the door, apparently judging her, on the basis of his vast news experience, to be just another crazy.

Newspapers and broadcast stations in areas that are less urban can achieve the same isolation from their audiences by locating themselves out in the country where land is usually cheaper. The old-fashioned newspaper office on Main Street is disappearing, for all sorts of economic reasons. Valuable contacts between people and journalists are also being lost.

In addition to the physical isolation provided by security guards and suburban industrial park locations, journalists also are isolated by their elitism. Journalists are not like most people, sociologist John Johnstone and two colleagues at the University of Illinois reported in 1976 after the first nationwide study of people who do news work. They found that journalists were better educated and better off economically and socially than most people, and tended to come from the same ethnic group — white Anglo-Saxon Protestants (WASPs). By the measures of age, sex, geographic origin, parents' occupations, political and religious leanings, journalists were found to be very unlike the rest of the population.[27]

More recently Everette E. Dennis and a colleague from the University of Minnesota found the same elitism among the more than one hundred newspaper and television reporters they surveyed in the Minneapolis-St. Paul area. Dennis urged that reporters pursue an orderly process of "staying in touch" with the community and the audience because:

> Like Johnstone, we found that reporters were quite unlike the average citizen, both in their demographic characteristics and in their views on a variety of public issues. At a time when confidence in various American institutions was by no means high, reporters demonstrated a deeper distrust and cynicism than did the public. Our study showed that reporters were well-off financially and highly educated. Their lifestyles were different, too. They were more likely to be single, to live in urban apartments and shun suburbs. Further conversations with many of these same reporters demonstrated the disturbing degree to which they were out of touch with the mainstream of community life and how little they really knew about it from personal experience. They had little direct knowledge of how people unlike themselves worked, lived or played.[28]

Some of the errors and misinterpretations that journalists make must stem from their inability to understand people and experiences with which they are unfamiliar. There may have been a time when most editors and reporters were very much like most other people: At least there has been a strong belief that journalists were in the mainstream and could represent the average American because they were average Americans. But modern research seems to say that journalists are enough different from many other citizens that they are going to have to make special efforts to overcome their ignorance and misunderstanding of other people.

The Scoop Mentality. "Scoop" is an old-fashioned word for beating the competition. And even though competition between separately owned newspapers and journalistic competition in general is falling victim to increasing group and conglomerate ownership of news media, scoops live on. Only today they are usually called "beats" or "exclusives." The passion for beating the other guy, even if that means going on the air or to print before the story is completely checked out, has caused some of journalism's greatest "boo-boos." For example, Washington, D.C., residents heard from their radio and television sets one hot summer night that their mayor, Marion S. Barry, Jr., had been shot. Virtually all of the city's stations broadcast the report, and the UPI put out a bulletin quoting the broadcast reports. But the mayor had not been shot. The false report came from someone who called the television stations, claiming he was calling from the mayor's command center, which handles all city emergencies. The caller provided a telephone number and answered questions when TV reporters called the number, but the number turned out to be a public telephone booth. In their haste to get the news on the air, the TV reporters never thought to look up the correct command center number, which had been provided earlier to every newsroom in town.

The AP Washington bureau did not get taken in on the hoax, despite pressures from members to match the TV and UPI report. Actually, the AP put out a story forty-eight minutes after the first TV station aired its "scoop" saying that the report was false. When AP heard the original report on WRC-TV, its Washington night crew started checking police, the mayor's command center, the mayor's press secretary, and city officials, but no one would confirm the report. People they called simply told AP what they had heard on TV. Finally, AP talked to a police officer who said Barry had not been shot, although there was an accidental shooting of an officer earlier that evening near the mayor's home. Then the mayor's command center confirmed that the mayor had not been shot.[29]

Those D.C. broadcast journalists who rushed the false report to the air must have short memories. Only three months earlier the broadcast networks made the terrible mistake of telling the world that President Reagan's press secretary, James Brady, had died in the attempted assassination of the president. Brady, of course, had not died. In those hectic moments after the shootings and the immediate capture of the accused assassin, NBC reported that Reagan had had open heart surgery; he had not. There is a difference, of course, between a newscaster bursting onto the air with a bulletin that the mayor has been shot and one who passes along a false report in the midst of many factual ones as he or she sits in front of a camera or microphone for hours as the assassination-attempt story is developing. What the networks do when a story as big as that breaks is let the viewers and listeners come into their newsrooms to witness the story being pieced together.

The networks apparently learned from their mistakes. At least they were very careful in the fall of 1981 not to report President Anwar Sadat as dead until he had been officially declared so. First reports after the assassination attempt on the Egyptian president suggested that he was safe. But Dan Rather was in front of his CBS camera in New York when correspondent Scotti Williston phoned in from Cairo and reported that Sadat was dead. Rather was visibly shocked. He questioned Williston about her sources and how reliable her information was. She said her sources were reliable and she believed them. That first report held up, but Rather and other network anchors were very careful to label their reports of Sadat's death as unofficial until the Egyptian government confirmed them hours later.

Competition has many advantages. So does the discipline, bred out of competition, of trying to get the news out to the public as soon as possible: Let historians take care of history; journalism's job is to get the news out. But if that discipline is skewed by a passion to be first and not tempered by the checking that accuracy requires, then the public is apt to get false and misleading reports.

Pack Journalism. While most news organizations seem to have a hard time sparing a few reporters to dig into many subjects of public concern, the news media as a whole send as many as fifteen thousand staffers to cover a national political party convention, as many as four hundred to a presidential press conference, as many as two thousand to a super bowl, hundreds to a big court trial or to the scene of a major tragedy — so many that journalists frequently become part of the story.

But the principal objection to ganging up on big stories — pack or herd journalism, as it's called — is not in the misuse of human power. It is the tendency for all the reporters in the pack "to get hooked on the same line," as Charles B. Seib, retired ombudsman of the *Washington Post,* puts it (interview, 9 Nov. 1981). "One interpretation becomes everybody's interpretation," declares Louis D. Boccardi, executive editor and vice-president of the Associated Press (interview, 8 Oct. 1981). "And soon you see the attributions disappearing and that single interpretation becomes almost a fact."

So when you have scores or hundreds of different reporters covering the same story, instead of getting scores or hundreds of quite different stories, you tend to get pretty much the same story from all of them. Part of the reason for this lack of diversity lies in the way that sponsors or public officials try to organize (sometimes even orchestrate) the coverage of many big stories. They set up special press rooms, arrange transportation, and schedule news conferences, interviews, and photographic opportunities. Reporters are thrown together, whether they like it or not, and forced to base their stories more or less on the same information made available to all. "Reporters covering a major event get all glued together," comments Nancy J. Woodhull, managing editor for news of *USA Today* (interview, 16 Oct. 1981).

But Woodhull broke out of the pack when she was sent to Texas on her first big assignment for the *Detroit Free Press* to cover the Bobby Riggs-Billie Jean King tennis match. "I didn't really know any of the other people covering it," Woodhull recalls. "So I just went out on my own and got a story no one else had. . . . When I met up with other reporters the next day, I found that their editors had been bugging them about this story by a Nancy Woodhull from Detroit. They spent the next day and a half trying to disprove my story. Then when it held up, a couple of the biggies invited me to dinner to try to find out what I was working on next."

Richard P. Cunningham, associate director of the National News Council, broke out of the pack when he was covering Martin Luther King in Selma, Alabama, for the *Minneapolis Tribune* (interview, 5 Oct. 1981). He dug up a story on his own that King, who was under a federal court order not to march on that day, had struck a deal with the Justice Department that he would stop the march at an agreed-upon point. When he was dictating his story, Cunningham recalls, his news editor came on the phone to express his concern that nobody else was reporting what Cunningham was saying. "I saw the map, I saw the deal being cut," Cunningham said to reassure him. Later at supper, Cunningham told Claude Sitton and John Herbers of the *New York Times* about his story. They left the table immediately, checked out Cunningham's story, called the new information to the *Times,* and then rejoined Cunningham for supper. When he was dictating additional material to his paper later that same evening, Cunningham says his news editor broke in again to tell him, "Dick, you're OK. The *New York Times* just filed a new lead." In other words, Cunningham explains, "it wasn't OK until the *New York Times* did it."

The *Sacramento Bee*'s Nauman participated in the herd when he was chief of the state capital bureau for that paper (interview, 2 Nov. 1981). "Government knows how to play the herd like a violin," Nauman observes.

A press conference would be called. I'd better be there because if I'm not, our competitor will be and I'll get a call from my desk "Why didn't you have that story?" What I'd like to say is that I decided not to cover the press conference because it's nothing but a self-serving piece of crap and the wire services will cover it anyway. And I'll be able to work on that hard-hitting investigative story on transportation that you've always wanted. But I know that won't fly. The editor back home just isn't going to see it that way.

Leslie H. Whitten, novelist who was senior investigator for the Jack Anderson column for twelve years, has observed pack journalism at work in Washington for years and calls it "a bullshit way of doing things." He believes that most of the reporters in town all work on the same story — Bobby Baker, Watergate, Koreagate, now the economy (interview, 2 Sept. 1981). "Lots of Washington reporters are nothing but titsucks for the administration," Whitten charges. "They follow, they pick up handouts, or they jump into a big story long after everyone else has been in it . . . rather than going their individual ways. The beauty of Jack Anderson's column is that he's Peck's bad boy, an outsider, who's always been willing to tackle the tough stories."

The pack journalism of Washington also concerns Jonathan Friendly, news media reporter for the *New York Times* (interview, 7 Oct. 1981). "It's silly to have a thousand reporters accredited to cover the president and only three covering the Justice Department full time, and nobody routinely plugging away at Interior, or the Nuclear Regulatory Commission, or the Food and Drug Administration," Friendly holds. "The perception that we must all go after the same big story bothers me a lot. It's event journalism."

Political and sports reporters seem to run into pack problems more than other kinds of reporters: So many of the events they cover are staged to a degree and it is easy for them to become pawns of the stage managers. They can become very dependent on the people they cover. "They end up using you," says Robert Scheer, *Los Angeles Times* reporter (interview, 25 Nov. 1981). "You can't say, 'Wait a minute, is this true, and why are you giving this to me now?' You end up being a conduit."

Quote swapping is an offshoot of pack journalism. A number of sports reporters covering a game swarm the winning and losing team locker rooms and then trade quotes and information with other reporters to get a fuller picture. A political reporter covering a closed meeting of the House Judiciary Committee in Washington can grab only one committee member or at the most two as they break for lunch. James Naughton, associate managing editor of the *Philadelphia Inquirer* who was in that situation when he reported for the *New York Times,* maintains: "It became a case of 'I'll give you a Father Drinan if you'll give me a Pete Rodino.' So there are some circumstances in which it is done and usually by people who have enough confidence in one another's integrity that they don't get burned. But I still don't like it." (Interview, 16 Sept. 1981.)

But David Broder, one of the most respected reporters in the business, does not see any serious problems with quote swapping (interview, May 1981). Broder, political reporter-columnist for the *Washington Post,* believes "it's a useful device sometimes, such as a situation not uncommon when you're waiting outside a Senate hearing room or the White House for some meeting to break up. Reporters pick up targets of opportunity and then get back together and exchange quotes."

Jack Landau, director of the Reporters Committee for Freedom of the Press, sees some good in pack coverage: "It was advantageous to have twenty-five different reporters all with different contacts working on the Bobby Baker case," concludes Landau, who broke that case as a reporter for the *Washington Post* (interview, 24 Sept. 1981). He also recalls press conferences at the Justice Department or at regulatory agencies where reporters with many intellects and backgrounds were able to pose questions a single reporter might never think of and to prevent the entire pack from being snowed. "Good reporters also pick up on one another's questions," Landau believes. "There's something to be said for that kind of reporting."

The television networks feel they have no choice but to put up with pack reporting because they have to cover the big stories. They are in the same boat as the two major wire services. "It's easier for the print guys to break out of the pack, do their own stories, and let the wire services cover the principal stuff," comments Brit Hume, Capitol Hill correspondent for ABC News (interview, 4 Nov. 1981). "But the TV networks assign the top stories each day to the correspondents they want most to have on the air. It's difficult to get away from the major story of the day to which you've been assigned."

None of the journalists interviewed for this study had any solution to the pack journalism problem. No one in the business likes pool reporting — allowing only a handful of reporters to observe an important event and then having them brief the other reporters who weren't there. Editors want the right to decide which stories their reporters should cover each day. It is unfortunate that so many editors choose the same stories to the point that the sheer number of reporters and photographers covering certain stories gets in the way of competent reporting. And it is difficult for observers to understand why so many of the nation's best reporters are so often tied up on the same story when so much significant material is being ignored or handled by less able reporters.

Another kind of pack problem is the tendency of much of American journalism to let the *New York Times* and the *Washington Post* set the agenda — decide what journalists should be attending to. When the *Times* and/or the *Post* decide a certain story is important, it automatically becomes important in virtually every news medium in the country. Such sheeplike behavior destroys one of the advantages that is supposed to accrue from freedom — variety, diversity, differences. It also helps explain why some news is overcovered and some is never developed at all.

IS THIS AN ETHICAL PROBLEM?

Except for correcting the record, the codes and policy statements on ethics in journalism do not usually address the issues discussed in this chapter. Matters of incompetence and irresponsibility are not, for the most part, seen as ethical or moral problems by journalists. But maybe they should be.

Because of incompetence ("I don't know") or irresponsibility ("I don't care"), some journalists fail to recognize a question of right or wrong until it is in the paper or on the air. They do not even get to the ethical level. But the effects of their ignorance-carelessness can be just as immoral as the effects of pornography or a particularly nasty piece in the *National Enquirer.* If citizens make decisions based on false or misleading information, isn't the incompetence or irresponsibility that created the false or misleading information immoral?

But why split hairs? The important thing is not how to label or classify sins but to recognize they exist and then work on banishing them. One thing that needs to be done is to improve the education of journalists. Although better educated than the average citizen, journalists still exhibit ignorance and misunderstanding in their news reports and analyses. Another need is for more instruction in ethics, in both classrooms and newsrooms.

And journalists should not overlook the incompetent and irresponsible journalism that comes from some, not all, of the folklore of the business. There is peer pressure in newsrooms just as there is in any group endeavor. In some newsrooms at least, the peer pressure works toward a journalism of haste, recklessness, and shallowness. Such pressure comes from the pacesetters in those newsrooms — the editors and reporters who by their behavior set the standards, good or bad. While the top editor may be off at conventions perfecting codes of ethics, the newsroom pacesetters continue to practice a kind of journalism that may not be precisely unethical but that falls far short of the accurate, fair, thoughtful, and comprehensive report the public needs. And then there are the more serious cases of newspapers and broadcast stations that make virtually no effort to truly inform their publics, media whose

owners and managers are ignorant of or who ignore their principal
responsibilities.

Codes on Corrections. Although media codes of ethics virtually ignore
the causes of their errors, most of them advise journalists what to do
about correcting them. All of the codes of national journalistic organizations say that errors should be corrected promptly.

The codes of the three commercial broadcast networks all deal with
different parts of the error-and-correction problem. NBC News dwells on
the detection of errors. "Any assertion that a broadcast report by NBC
News personnel includes any significant error of fact must be investigated, objectively, promptly and thoroughly," by an appropriate NBC
News official, the NBC code holds. It also calls on its employees to report
errors they detect. Significant fact errors "must be corrected promptly in
an appropriate broadcast," NBC maintains. "The correction must be
open, specific and unequivocal."

CBS News is concerned about making it clear that "we are
broadcasting a correction." Its code states:

> It is not sufficient to report that the statement included in the
> original broadcast has been denied. The accuracy of the denial must
> be specifically confirmed. It is not sufficient merely to include the
> accurate information in the correcting broadcast. The fact that it is a
> correction must be specifically noted. It is not sufficient merely to
> broadcast a letter from a viewer or listener which asserts that we
> were in error. The accuracy of the assertion must be specifically
> admitted.

ABC News, after stating that "significant errors of fact must be
corrected in a clear and timely manner," sees "another cause for
corrective action." Its code notes that "sometimes the error is not one of
fact but of balance, when we leave out something important or give too
much prominence to the wrong thing. That, too, calls for a report to
redress the balance."

The advice on corrections in newspaper codes is usually brief and
comes out to something like "mistakes should be corrected promptly and
candidly," which is what the *Chicago Sun-Times* code requires. But the
Philadelphia Inquirer guideline is detailed and specific. "We promptly
and forthrightly correct our published errors," the *Inquirer* code states.
"An allegation of factual error in our news columns should be treated
with the utmost seriousness and should be referred to the appropriate
assigning editor immediately." Then the code describes two forms of
corrections. The more common form is a separate item under the
standing headline, "Clearing the record," which is placed on the second
page of the first section if the error being corrected was in general news,

or on the page on which the error occurred if it was in special sections such as sports, business, the arts, and obituaries. An exception is noted for page one errors, which are to be corrected on page one with a regular headline. The second form of correction is a parenthetical paragraph inserted into a new article on the same subject as the article in which the error occurred.

When the *Inquirer* publishes one of its standard "Clearing the record" corrections, it includes this policy statement: "It is the intention of The Inquirer that its news reports be fair and correct in every respect. If you have a question or comment about news coverage, write to the Public Service Editor. . . ." Then it gives an address, phone number, and office hours for that editor.

The *Inquirer* guideline on corrections continues:

> B. All corrections are approved by the managing editor or, in his absence, by the assistant managing editor in charge. The assigning editor should always determine the reason for the error; this could result in a refinement of procedure to prevent our making the same kind of mistake again.
>
> C. When a factual error results in a possibility of libel, the newspaper's attorneys must be consulted in the phrasing of the correction.
>
> D. Here are some guidelines for writing corrections:
>
> 1. State the facts as simply as possible. Unless needed for clarity, the error should not be repeated.
>
> 2. Tell when the error was published. Examples: "yesterday's Inquirer," "the May 2 issue of The Inquirer," or (if the error was corrected in later editions) "in an early edition of Friday's Inquirer."
>
> 3. Do not write, "The Inquirer regrets the error." In exceptional cases, we will include an apology, but generally we prefer to regard this as implicit.
>
> 4. A "Clearing the record" notice may also be used to clarify published facts that, while technically not in error, may have been confusing or misleading.

It is encouraging that journalists seem more willing these days to correct their errors. The posture of infallibility that dominated the journalism of an earlier day was ridiculous and harmful to everybody. The time has come, though, for journalists to reduce errors through a more competent and responsible style of journalism.

Toward Ethical Journalism

"Are you grading today, dear, or judging the ethics of journalists?"

THE PICTURE THIS STUDY PAINTS of the state of ethics in the news business in the United States is one of large numbers of obviously intelligent people honestly disagreeing about most ethical standards, goals, and procedures. There is agreement on the goal of accurate and fair reporting and the standard of separating information, opinion, and advertising, but that is about it. Other ethical principles may be adhered to religiously by some or many journalists but ignored by some or many others.

There is even disagreement about what constitutes an ethical or moral issue in the field. Many journalists would not consider all of the quandaries laid out in this study as matters of ethics or morality. Some think of ethics as merely a matter of avoiding freebies and conflicts of interest. The variety of visions about what is or is not an ethical problem has handicapped journalists as they have tried to come to grips with their ethics.

The codes of ethics adopted by national organizations of journalists

have a nice ring to them, particularly when read to musical accompani-
ment by Henry Mancini. But they are of limited help in the day-to-day
ethical decisions that journalists have to make. They are statements of
ideals and aspirations, which is about the best that can be expected from
a field that puts as much stock in freedom and individuality as U.S.
journalism does. As such, the national codes have been useful in getting
many journalists to think about the objectives of journalism. But what is
needed, it seems to me, is more down-to-earth advice for journalists
trying to figure out wrongs and rights in their work lives, the kind of
advice found in the more detailed written operating standards of CBS,
NBC, and ABC, and of newspapers like the *Philadelphia Inquirer* and the
Washington Post. Journalists working for such news organizations have
few excuses for ethical lapses.

Many news organizations, however, have declined to lay down
written codes of ethics for their staffs, sometimes out of fear that such
codes will be picked up by outsiders, particularly judges, and applied as
standards for all journalists. That fear has been encouraged by the recent
history of judicial aggression against the press. But it seems a shame that
a fear of something that might never happen (or if it did happen, might
not be so bad or might be successfully combatted) has prevented fine
newspapers like the *Los Angeles Times* and the *New York Times* from
taking the lead in establishing ethical standards as they have in setting
other journalistic standards.

Some editors and news directors shun written ethical standards
because they believe that ethical behavior is best learned from others,
from models in the newsroom. It is true that many newsrooms have
editors and reporters who are good models for learning how to be ethical
journalists. But there are also plenty of bad models, and the folkore of
journalism in this country teaches unethical as well as ethical practices.
Younger journalists need to know in clearly stated terms what their news
organizations and journalism in general regard as ethical and unethical.
Tough, clear, written standards in every U.S. newsroom would seem to be
a step in that direction.

Journalists and the public need to acknowledge that the business
nature of American journalism affects its ethics. The need for news media
to find audiences they can sell to advertisers limits the freedom of editors
to determine content. Almost all U.S. cities today have but one daily
newspaper or two owned by the same company: the disappearing
competition between separately owned papers demands new responsibilities of journalists and calls into question some of the possibly unethical
methods that grew out of competition. Business necessities may bring
new delivery systems to newspapers in the future — through television
sets hooked up to home printers, for example — and that certainly will

demand a rethinking of ethical principles. Likewise, the ethics and standards of television journalists will need to be examined and reexamined as television news continues to be virtually the only source of news for increasing numbers of Americans and as television reaches more and more into the lower economic and social classes of our cities once served by but now being abandoned by many mass circulation newspapers. So the things that news media have to do to survive as businesses are bound to affect not only their technology and procedures, but their ethics as well.

In recognizing the business tugs and pulls that work on journalism, the public should not assume that journalists have lost control of the news process. They certainly have not. Journalists, even those working for corporate giants, seem to have amazing freedom. The philosophy of not interfering in the newsrooms they own seems to dominate the thinking of all but a few news media managers and proprietors, particularly those at the top of the larger organizations. The business environment in which our news media operate has to be a fact of life for editors and broadcast news directors, but it is not a fact that seriously restricts their ability to determine the ethics and quality of news work in their domains.

AN ASSESSMENT

It was impossible to do the research for this book without forming an impression of the people who do the work of journalism in this country. Most of the some 150 journalists interviewed and the scores whose books and articles were studied came across as highly intelligent and interesting people, very much wrapped up in their jobs. Some pomposity and arrogance popped up, but much less than you would find in a comparable exposure to university professors (and no doubt with other groups with which I am less familiar).

The candid opinions and experiences of the journalists interviewed and studied for this book have been melded into an assessment of how journalists are doing, ethically. I realize, of course, that it is presumptuous for a single observer to make such an assessment (a safer but sillier way would be to survey some "scientifically selected sample" of people with questions designed to bring responses that can be squeezed into a computer). But it would also be unfair to you, the reader, *not* to assess the ethics of journalism in a report on its status. In making this evaluation, I have divided the principal ethical problems of U.S. journalism into six categories: conflicts of interest, freebies, journalists' methods, privacy, compassion, and competence. The reader needs to know that occasionally the teacher in me cannot resist using the A, B, C, D, F letter grades common in college classrooms to express a judgment. I also refer to an "ethical sin scale" I have developed in my own teaching of ethics: The scale runs from "ten" (reserved for saints and saintly conduct) to "one" (given to reporters who lie, cheat, rifle garbage cans, and misspell *accommodate*).

Conflicts of Interest. Conflicts of interest have been a major target of journalism's recent reformers. But there is disagreement about what constitutes a conflict of interest and whether conflicts should be avoided by all who own or work for the news media or just by those who work in news departments.

The prevailing belief in the field is that editors, directors, reporters, photographers, and newscasters — the people involved in news work — have to avoid outside activities and associations that might unduly influence their ability to process the news impartially. Political activity or partisanship of any sort seems to head the list of taboos, but then the list gets fuzzy. Some would even prohibit affiliation with a political party (registering as a Democrat or Republican) or with a conventional church. Others see memberships in local groups as acceptable, even desirable, but draw the line at holding office or directing publicity.

Conflicts are not always a matter of associations and memberships: Reporters who get too cozy or entangle themselves in confidentiality deals with news sources can get caught up in a conflict of interest. So can those who cooperate with the CIA and law enforcement at all levels. This is not to say that a conflict is created every time a reporter gets on a first-name basis with a source, or goes off the record, or trades information with a cop, but the threat is there. Similarly, journalists who take money from outside interests for free-lance material, speeches, or other services risk conflicts of interest.

Different standards seem to be applied to media owners and to executives not directly involved in news. Some media owners still adhere to the Warren G. Harding model and openly seek and hold partisan political office. More commonly, the outside involvements of media proprietors and business managers are in the business and civic arena, rather than the political one (although the line between business and civic projects and politics is often hard to draw). In smaller and medium-sized communities, local news media are usually among the most important businesses in town. A majority of media owners in such communities seem to feel a responsibility to be involved, in varying degrees, in the kinds of community projects that interest business proprietors. Such activities and involvements undoubtedly contribute to the image of the news media being tied up with and generally representative of business interests.

A double standard between the news department and the owners, publishers, and business managers does not exist in all news organizations. On newspapers like the *Washington Post*, top executives take the view that their outside involvements can create conflicts of interest, real or apparent, that threaten the newspaper's credibility just as much as do the conflicts arising from the activities of news people. If anything, the behavior of the top brass is probably more visible than that of most of the news staffers.

Adding to this confused picture of how journalists deal with conflicts of interest is the spouse problem — what to do about spouses of journalists and news executives who, by their occupations or activities, seem to create a possible conflict of interest for the spouse-journalist and his or her news organization. Most news executives feel that about all a news organization can decently do when such conflicts occur is to move the journalist whose spouse is the problem to an assignment that will minimize the conflict. They hope the public will get used to the idea that in this day and age spouses have a right to their own careers and activities that may create conflicts of interest, real or imagined, beyond the power of the affected news medium to correct.

Journalists and news media owners need to do more thinking about real and apparent conflicts of interest. There is a lot of talk in the field about the appearance of a conflict being as damaging to news media credibility as a real conflict. In other words the offending extrajournalistic activity really does not influence the journalist involved in any damaging way, but it looks bad to the public. Yet in most news organizations anything that appears to be a conflict is prohibited just as if it were a real conflict. Perhaps journalists need to consider disclosing and explaining conflicts of interest rather than prohibiting them when it is the appearance not the reality that is bothersome. The public may not be as intolerant of minor conflicts as journalists seem to assume. After all, conflicts of interest are all about us; no one — not even journalists — can avoid all of them. The avoidance of all conflicts of interest that arise in daily life is another way of saying that you are avoiding life itself in that you are removing yourself from the mainstreams of human action and thought. Do we really want journalists who are so aloof from the rest of us that they inevitably fail to understand the rest of us? There are real conflicts for journalists — working on the side for a news source, for example — but there are lots of activities now seen as "apparent conflicts" that need to be reevaluated.

Freebies. Along with conflicts of interest, freebies have gotten the major attention in the comparatively recent effort to improve the ethics of U.S. journalism. And the progress in banning freebies from news work has been noteworthy as journalists increasingly turn their backs on gifts, free meals and drinks, free or cut-rate transportation and lodging, special price discounts on consumer goods, and press perquisites offered by present or potential news sources. The larger news organizations in particular deserve an A for their mostly successful efforts to remove the "For Sale" sign from journalism.

But would-be seducers of journalists are still out there and they still find acceptance in some newsrooms, particularly those in smaller newspapers and broadcast stations. In many cases, owners and operators of smaller media encourage their reporters and editors to take freebies by keeping their news departments on such miserly budgets that some important news cannot be covered unless a free ticket, free ride, or free lodging is provided. It is difficult to believe, in view of the generally good health that media operations enjoy in the U.S. economy, that smaller news operations cannot pay their own way to the essential news events, at least. When managements encourage the acceptance of freebies for their staffs to cover news, it is no wonder that individual staff members have a hard time drawing lines between accepting freebie A to cover an out-of-town football game, freebie B to take the family on a free trip to an amusement park, and freebie C to get a better price on a new car.

It should be said that there has been some silliness in journalism's drive to eliminate freebies. There is a difference between accepting a meal from a news source who insists that lunch in his office is the only time he has to spare for you and accepting a junket from a Hollywood film studio interested in promoting a new movie. Nor does letting a news source buy you a drink once in a while constitute a major ethical sin. Journalists have to be trusted to decide when a freebie is apt to compromise them and when rejecting one would do more harm than good in their primary mission of getting and understanding the news.

Journalists' Methods. Some of the methods journalists use to get news and present it fall at or near the bottom of my ethical sin scale. Lying to people, by faking or manufacturing news and plagiarizing, are such flagrant violations of the accuracy standard and so out of place in modern journalism that they should not have to be discussed in a book on journalism ethics. Yet they emerged as two of journalism's thorniest ethical problems in the early 1980s. This is not to suggest that our newsrooms are full of liars. But the fact that some writers have recently admitted they made up news stories has stirred up fear in the field that there must have been others who got away with it and still others waiting in the wings to pass off fiction as fact.

Hyping news by the use of exciting language, whether the facts justify it or not, and by taking little shortcuts with the facts, is a more

common problem in their field than journalists like to admit. And the
hyping is done not just by the reporters trying to make their stories sound
better than they are but by editors trying to sell those stories for the front
page, or even for prizes.

The various uses of deception and misrepresentation by journalists
have raised some bewildering ethical questions. On the surface, deceiving somebody by misrepresenting who you are, passively or actively,
seems unethical. Yet some very honorable journalists argue that the only
way to get close to the truth about certain vital situations is to get on the
inside and watch what is going on, like a fly on the ceiling, or even
participate enough to get a feel for what is going on. That is usually
called undercover reporting and some leaders in the field oppose its use
except in extraordinary circumstances. But there are just as many if not
more editors who see nothing wrong with using undercover reporting if
the conventional methods of observation, interviewing, and library
research do not work on some important investigation.

Most undercover reporting requires reporters to pretend they are
somebody other than reporters: auto workers, welders, common laborers,
seamstresses, tavern owners, dance instructors, accident victims, convicted wife killers, vagrants, burglars, or nursing home aides, to mention
a few of the roles reporters have played in recent newspaper undercover
reporting projects. Often when reporters go undercover they do so with
the knowledge of some official in the subject area being investigated: for
example, the Illinois Department of Law Enforcement was brought in on
the deal by the *Chicago Sun-Times* when it bought and operated a tavern
to expose shakedowns by city inspectors. Letting some official or agency
know what your reporters are doing surreptitiously may make things
safer for the reporters and may make editors feel more ethical about it,
but such cooperation is not always possible and it does not change the fact
that people still are deceived by reporters posing as others.

Reporters also misrepresent themselves in everyday reporting. It is
not too serious ethically when they merely pass as members of the public
— at a large public meeting or checking on retail prices, for example. But
it is no more than a "two" on the ethical sin scale when reporters lead
news sources to believe that they are cops, coroners, or other law
enforcement officials to get people to tell them things they might not tell
reporters.

Bribing a news source to get a story would be a sure "one" on my sin
scale, but that is academic because bribery is not regarded as one of
journalism's contemporary tools. Yet checkbook journalism — paying for
some notorious person's exclusive story — still exists in this country. Isn't
that close to bribery?

Eavesdropping is occasionally resorted to by a reporter who has been barred from some important meeting or event. Eavesdropping with the naked ear is the usual way that reporters try to learn what is going on behind the closed door or wall, and that is probably more undignified than it is unethical. But using electronic listening devices or phone taps is an absolute "no-no" to all of the journalists interviewed for this book.

The ambush interview when used by television journalists can sometimes make the ambushed person appear to be guilty without a fair trial. That may make good theater, but it is unfair. Responsible journalists should reserve that technique for public officials and miscreants who obviously need to be called to account. The ambush interview is also a method that print journalists use, but it is less of an ethical problem when the interviewees are not being photographed as they stumble incoherently or run away from hard questions.

Most news photographers hold that taking pictures of people in public places is fair game regardless of whether the people realize their pictures are being taken. But a published photograph can still be unfairly embarrassing or humiliating to the subjects even if they are in public places. The use of hidden cameras can raise more serious ethical questions. Hiding the camera may be justified if the story being exposed is important and in the interest of the public, such as surreptitiously photographing police officers accepting bribes, but responsible photographers avoid visual eavesdropping in less obviously vital news situations.

It is probably unfair to mention stealing or rifling garbage cans in this list of dubious methods because they occur so rarely, but a few reporters have done such things. And when you add stealing and garbage rifling to the more commonly employed methods of hidden cameras, ambush interviews, eavesdropping, buying exclusive interviews, misrepresentation, deception, hyping, plagiarizing, and lying, you get a picture that falls short of an ethical profession.

Privacy. American news media, by and large, have shown sensitivity about protecting the identity of rape victims and juveniles involved in lesser crimes. The changing attitude of journalists and society toward less protection does not detract from the commendable restraint that journalists have often shown in cases in which publicity might have done more harm than good.

But the news media generally have been less restrained about invading the privacy of many public persons and their families. Public officials, particularly at the upper levels, give up some of their privacy when they enter the goldfish bowl of government service, but they don't give up all of it. Journalists have not always recognized the right to and need for some privacy by even the highest ranking public officials — and particularly members of their families. The publicity given to the troubles of David Kennedy, Randy Agnew, and Senator Scott's forty-one-year-old daughter in recent years struck an awful lot of people as unfair. And newspapers and magazines could put the cork on that disgraceful photographer who hounds Jackie Onassis and her children simply by not running any more photos and recognizing that family's right to decent privacy.

Celebrities who lead public lives and depend on publicity for their livelihood invite invasions of their privacy, but the news media have also invaded the privacy of relatives of celebrities who are not public persons seeking publicity. What justification was there for the play given to the shooting death of Mary Tyler Moore's son, many people asked, some angrily.

Another bad practice is the way journalists invade the privacy of ordinary people caught up in the news involuntarily. Barging into private property after a tragedy has occurred or a crime has been committed is inexcusable. So is taking advantage of people who are unsophisticated about dealing with journalists and who may unknowingly, even trustingly, permit invasions of their privacy. Most journalists are not insensitive oafs, but some still act as if they had some God-given right to roll over other people in the name of the public's right to know.

Another troubling tendency in the privacy area is for journalists to rely on law and court decisions to guide their conduct. That cop-out too often results in a newsroom decision based not on what is right or wrong, but on "How far can we go and still win a lawsuit?" Journalists need to think through the ethics of privacy and come up with guidelines that are clearer and more responsible than those derived from the complexities of privacy law.

Compassion. Many journalists will quarrel with compassion as a category of ethical problems in the news business. They either do not see it as a big ethical issue or they fear that the softness implied by that emotion might deter the primary mission of journalism — to get the news out.

But it is treated here as one of the important categories of ethical problems because, in a way, a scarcity of compassion is at the base of many of the troubles journalists have with methods, privacy, and other ethical areas. Failure to feel sympathy for or empathize with the people involved in news — sources and subjects alike — produces a sterile sort of journalism that is superficial at best and grossly misleading at worst.

The lack of compasison displayed by some journalists has also created the impression in the public's mind that journalists and the news media (newspapers, in particular) are arrogant and uncaring. That is the impression many people got of the *Washington Post* when its executives appeared not to care about the life or death of "Jimmy," the eight-year-old heroin addict in Janet Cooke's moving article (assumed then to be true and not the fabrication it later turned out to be).

There seems to be something in the way many journalists interpret their role as neutral observers that makes them come across as cold and uncaring. This impression is conveyed, not just in the few clearcut cases in which journalists turn their backs on human victims in the name of doing their jobs, but in their often uncivil and snobbish treatment of news sources, both on and off camera. The great journalists are people who excel at getting the news out but who also never forget their humanity. Being humble and compassionate in dealing with other human beings involved in the news should be seen as virtues in a news professional.

Journalists have also lost public esteem when they have shunned their responsibilities as citizens and asked for special privileges. There are times, of course, when journalists may have to be uncooperative with government by not testifying about legitimate secret sources, but journalists should argue for that special treatment only in extreme cases, working harder than most do now to get more sources on the record. Constantly insisting that courts and other arms of government exempt them from the responsibilities that all citizens are supposed to bear makes journalists appear to be seeking privileges. That impression coupled with the image of being uncaring in their attitudes toward other people has certainly handicapped journalists in their primary job of getting the news out.

Competence. All the ethics codes and discussions will be for naught if the competence level of journalists is not sufficient to support quality journalism up and down the line. Competence may be the number one ethical problem in the field.

It may be asking too much of journalists that they improve on their knowledge and skills: after all, they already have more formal education than the average person. But journalists are our educators, teaching most of us most of what we know about the world outside of our immediate experiences. Don't we expect our teachers to know more than their students?

Every newsroom in the country has incompetent people. Errors and misinterpretations continue to be a major problem in every news medium we have. There is a great concern among thoughtful journalists about the lack of effective training for news executives: too many editors and broadcast news directors get promoted to those higher-paying positions because they were good reporters. Not many reporters, no matter how good they are, can stop reporting news one day and become good editors the next. Some never become good editors.

Several things would seem to be needed to improve competence in journalism. Despite the occasional whimpers from small-minded publishers and broadcast owners that they want colleges to send them more technicians, the obvious need in all newsrooms is for more depth of education, not less. And something has got to be done about those disgraceful beginning salaries that not only discourage potential journalists from getting more education for news work, but also discourage potential journalists, period. Perhaps news executives could find the money to pay more to beginners by paying less to or culling out the incompetents who now occupy a chair or a video display terminal or two in every newsroom in the country. At the same time, greater efforts need to be made to retain competents who now leave news work for public relations, education, politics and government, and other more lucrative and challenging careers. This flight from news work by competent journalists has left most newsrooms with an overpopulation of people under thirty-five, when a balance of ages and experiences would be more desirable. News organizations ought to run more in-house training programs for their news staffs, and send more staffers to good educational programs around the country. And the programs should not be just on the rudiments of cropping photos or laying out pages, but on substantive matters as well.

Finally, news organizations need to do more research on many questions, but particularly to find out how their journalists differ from or are like most members of the general public and what misconceptions and ignorances their journalists may have about people in their communities and society.

Any thoughtful journalist could come up with a similar or different list of suggestions for improving competence in this essential calling. The sins of incompetence are visible to all thoughtful journalists. It is programs of correction that are scarce.

(Although they do not easily fit into any of the six categories discussed in this section, the ethical problems presented for journalists by shocking material in news are nevertheless important. The present policy in most newsrooms of protecting the public from many of the shocking photographs and words that often crop up in the news usually results in a distorted picture. We do not need more sensational *National Enquirers* or *New York Posts*, but news executives should test their assumptions about what shocks the public and how much shock the public is willing to accept if the information is essential. More research might lead to more truthful portrayals of certain news now heavily blue penciled because of fears that people will be shocked.)

ETHICS THRIVES ON QUALITY

It may seem to the casual reader that some of the better known and most respected news operations in the country have more ethical problems than the lesser known ones. So many examples of questionable behavior in this book came from our most respected media. Part of the explanation for the abundance of ethical violations or marginal practices by the better news organizations lies in their visibility, the attention they get from media watchers. But the other explanation lies in their quality: because they seek out the news aggressively, they take more risks and get into more trouble. News organizations that play it safe and do little more than report what news comes in over the transom or from the wire services do not get into too many conventional ethical problems. But they commit the biggest ethical sin of all: failure to fulfill the primary responsibility of reporting the news fairly, accurately, aggressively, and as comprehensively as possible.

In my judgment, the most ethical journalists in the business are found in quality news operations, large and small. But there are many journalists out there who never get a chance to learn and practice either good or ethical journalism because they work for sleazy news operations that cover the news superficially, cater to the power elements in their communities, and avoid controversy.

If, as it seems, quality and ethics go hand in hand, then journalism will have to get better in many ways to become an ethical calling. As long as there are Thomson newspaper chains and radio stations with one-person news departments and media owners who see themselves as being socially responsible because they never let their news operations rock any boats, U.S. journalism as a whole may never get an A for ethics. But all except the substandard operations can earn top grades if the leaders in the news business want improved ethical practices in the first place and are willing to engage in honest dialogue to get them. The dialogue will have to include all levels of journalism — owners and managers, reporters, editors, photographers, news producers, and directors from both large and small media. And it also ought to include educators in journalism and communications and members of the general public.

And then after the talk, talk, talk has gone far enough, news executives will have to start making the changes that seem called for to bring greater quality and better ethics to the practice of journalism. The dialogue should continue, of course, because so many of the ethical quandaries journalists face do not lend themselves to quick solution by following rule a and principle b. Many times the only solution is the best answer that civilized people reasoning together can come up with at that moment. Civil discourse, that's what's needed.

In their striving for more ethical practices, journalists are well advised to avoid seeking special privileges for themselves and the news media. Freedom of the press and of speech belong to everybody in the American system, not just journalists. And journalists do not stop being citizens or human beings when they go to work. Ethical principles that segregate journalists as a class from the rest of society ill serve either journalism or society. What is needed is a set of principles based on a journalism that serves the public by aggressively seeking and reporting the closest possible truth about events and conditions of concern to people, a journalism that collects and deals with information honestly and fairly and treats the people involved with compassion, a journalism that conscientiously interprets and explains the news so that it makes sense to people. That's all.

NOTES

A list of the interviewed persons quoted in this work appears on pages 317– 318.

CHAPTER ONE

1. George Bernard Shaw, *Pygmalion and Other Plays* (New York: Dodd, Mead, 1967), 45.

2. Paul Janensch, "Journalistic Ethics ... Public Discussion and Private Soul-searching," Louisville *Courier-Journal,* 4 Oct. 1981.

3. *A Free and Responsible Press: Report of the Commission on Freedom of the Press,* Robert M. Hutchins, ch. (Chicago: Univ. of Chicago Press, 1947); Fred S. Siebert, Theodore Peterson, Wilbur Schramm, *Four Theories of the Press* (Urbana: Univ. of Illinois Press, 1956), 74-78.

4. Ibid.

5. Clifford G. Christians, "Fifty Years of Scholarship in Media Ethics," *Journal of Communication* 27, no. 4(Autumn 1977):23.

6. John L. Hulteng, *The Messenger's Motives: Ethical Problems of the News Media* (Englewood Cliffs, N.J.: Prentice-Hall, 1976), 13.

7. Harold L. Cross, *The People's Right to Know* (New York: Columbia Univ. Press, 1953).

8. Walter Lippmann, *Public Opinion* (New York: Macmillan, 1922; Free Press Paperback, 1965), 226.

9. *Problems of Journalism: Proceedings of the ASNE 1923* (Washington, D.C.: ASNE, 1923), 39-52, 118-25.

10. *Problems of Journalism 1924,* 67-80.

11. Nelson A. Crawford, *The Ethics of Journalism* (New York: Knopf, 1924); Leon Nelson Flint, *The Conscience of the Newspaper* (New York: Appleton, 1925); William Futhey Gibbons, *Newspaper Ethics: A Discussion of Good Practices for Journalists* (Ann Arbor, Mich.: Edwards, 1926); Albert F. Henning, *Ethics and Practices in Journalism* (New York: Long and Smith, 1932).

12. Christians, "Fifty Years," 19-29.

13. Charles B. Seib, "Ethics: Many Questions, Few Right or Wrong Answers," *Presstime* 3, no. 2(Feb. 1981):4-9.

14. Estimate provided by David J. Eisen, director of research and information, the Newspaper Guild, Washington, D.C., Apr. 1981.

15. Memorandum to Guild officials from Richard J. Ramsey, executive secretary, contracts committee, the Newspaper Guild, Apr. 13, 1976.

16. Norman E. Isaacs, "Journalism Ethics -- 1975-2,000," lecture at Washington and Lee University; reprinted in *Social Responsibility: Journalism, Law, Medicine* (Lexington, Va.: Washington and Lee University, 1975).

17. Daniel J. Leab, *A Union of Individuals: The Formation of the American Newspaper Guild, 1933-1936* (New York: Columbia Univ. Press, 1970).

18. Charles Perlik, remarks prepared for panel discussion at Region 5 convention, SPJ-SDX, Muncie, Ind., 9 Apr. 1976.

19. Charles Long, "Editors Note," *Quill* 64, no. 4(Apr. 1976):2.

20. John W. C. Johnstone, Edward J. Slawski, and William W. Bowman, *The News People: A Sociological Portrait of American Journalists and Their Work* (Urbana: Univ. of Illinois Press, 1977), 195.

21. *Free and Responsible Press,* Hutchins, ch., 19.

22. Jerry Walker, "The Commission Alleges: 'Press Fails to Meet Needs of Society' " *Editor & Publisher,* 29 Mar. 1947, 7, 60, 61.

23. *A Free and Responsive Press: The Twentieth Century Fund Task Force Report for a National News Council* (New York: Twentieth Century Fund, 1973), 3.

24. Figures taken from *After "Jimmy's World": Tightening Up in Editing* (New York: Report by the National News Council, 1981). The media contributors listed were: Allentown (Pa.) *Call-Chronicle;* American Association of Schools and Departments of Journalism; *Anniston* (Ala.) *Star;* Bellevue (Wash.) *Daily Journal-American; Bennington* (Vt.) *Banner; Bergen* (N.J.) *Record; Berkshire* (Mass.) *Eagle;* Bingham Enterprises of Kentucky; Brattleboro (Vt.) *Reformer;* Capital Cities Communications; CBS; *Charleston* (W. Va.) *Gazette; Chicago Sun-Times;* Copley Press; *Daily Pantagraph; Delta Democrat Times; Denver Post; Des Moines Register & Tribune; Florida Times-Union* and *Jacksonville Journal; Free Lance Star* (Fredericksburg, Va.); Gannett Foundation; Harte-Hanks Communications; *Home News* (New Brunswick, N.J.); *Honolulu Advertiser; Longmont* (Colo.) *Times-Call;* Longview (Wash.) *Daily News; Loveland* (Colo.) *Reporter-Herald; Manhattan* (Kans.) *Mercury; Milwaukee Journal* and *Sentinel; Minneapolis Star* and *Tribune; Northern Virginia Sun;* Philip L. Graham Fund; Port Angeles (Wash.) *Daily News;* Press Enterprise Co. (Riverside, Calif.); Readers Digest Foundation; Salt Lake City *Tribune;* San Mateo (Calif.) *Times;* Stauffer Communications; St. Louis Post-Dispatch Foundation; *St.Petersburg Times;* Texas Press Association; Torrington (Conn.) *Register;* Southbridge (Mass.) *News;* Western Communications; and Wometco Enterprises.

25. Janet Cooke was a reporter for the *Washington Post* who admitted in 1981 that she had made up a story that had just won her a Pulitzer Prize for feature writing. The *Post* returned the prize and fired her. A more detailed report of this episode appears in Chapters 7 and 10.

26. Robert Haiman, talk prepared for convention of the ASNE, 22 Apr. 1981.

27. Ibid.

28. *Problems of Journalism 1981,* 65.

29. Paul Janensch, *"You Need an Ombudsman...,"* Report of the Professional *Standards Committee,* APME, 1981.

30. Published regularly in the masthead, *Columbia Journalism Review.*

CHAPTER TWO

1. "Journalistic Ethics: Some Probings by a Media Keeper," *Nieman Reports,* Winter/Spring 1978, 9-10.

2. A. Kent MacDougall, "In Reporting Profits, There Are Many Bottom Lines," *Los Angeles Times,* 7 Feb. 1980.

3. "Independent Dailies Growing Fewer, All Sources Agree," *Presstime* 4, no. 5(May 1982):59; Margaret Genovese, "Hot Newspaper Market Cools Down," *Presstime* 3, no. 5(May 1981):4-7.

4. "Sale to Times Mirror of TV Units Backed," *New York Times,* 28 Mar. 1980, D3.

5. Peter A. Falco, *Merrill Lynch Investment News,* 26 Aug. 1981.

6. Genovese, "Hot Newspaper Market," 4-7.

7. J. Hart Clinton, "Fate of Independents Is Cause for Alarm," *Presstime* 3, no. 5(May 1981):23.

8. Christopher H. Sterling and Timothy R. Haight, *The Mass Media: Aspen Institute Guide to Communication Industry Trends* (New York: Praeger, 1978), 83.

9. "Independent Dailies."

10. Clark Newsom, "For Competing Dailies, Disappearing Act Goes On," *Presstime* 3, no. 5(May 1981):8-9.

11. *Facts About Newspapers '82* (Reston, Va.: American Newspaper Publishers Association, 1982), 14.

12. Ibid., 9.

13. Harrison E. Salisbury, *Without Fear or Favor* (New York: Ballantine Books, 1980), 560-61.

14. Eugene Patterson, remarks to First Amendment Congress quoted in *Editor & Publisher,* 26 Jan. 1980, 15.

15. "Majority of Dailies Fill Ad Positioning Requests," *Editor & Publisher,* 1 Mar. 1980, 11, 50.

16. "Over 300 Daily Papers Prepared to Accept RJR's Camel Scoreboard," *Editor & Publisher,* 5 Sept. 1981, 21; "Camel Scoreboard Ads Now Appearing in 75 Newspapers," *Presstime* 4, no. 5(May 1982):37.

17. "What E. B. White Told Xerox," *Columbia Journalism Review* 15, no. 3(Sept./Oct. 1976):52-54.

18. Ibid.

19. Howard Bray, *The Pillars of the Post* (New York: Norton, 1980), 203.

20. Jonathan Friendly, "Trenton Times Journalists Quit over New Policies," *New York Times,* 21 Feb. 1982, 39.

21. "Allbritton Admits Error in Using Press Release," *Editor & Publisher,* 20 Mar. 1982, 16.

22. Express News Corporation, employer, v. San Antonio Typographical Union #172 a/w International Typographical Union AFL-CIO, petitioner, before the NLRB, Case 23 — RC — 4219; decided 6 Apr. 1976.

23. John Seigenthaler, remarks prepared for talk at Southern Illinois Univ., Carbondale, Ill., 5 Mar. 1981.

24. "Honesty and Ethical Standards," *Gallup Report* 192 (Princeton, N.J., Sept. 1981).

25. James W. Carey, "A Plea for the University Tradition," presidential address to the Association for Education in Journalism, Seattle, Wash., 13 Aug. 1978.

26. Jack McKinney, "A Matter of Ethics: Learning Write from Wrong," *Philadelphia Daily News,* 11 Dec. 1981.

27. Warren W. Schwed, "Big City Editors Earn over $50,000 a Year," *Editor & Publisher,* 4 July 1981, 9-10.

28. Vernon A. Stone, "Moderate Gains in News Salaries," *RTNDA Communicator,* Dec. 1981, 16-19.

CHAPTER THREE

1. Bill Gloede, "Journalists Examine Ethical Questions," *Editor & Publisher,* 24 Nov. 1979, 14.

2. Frank Wright, remarks to national convention, SPJ-SDX, New York City, 17 Nov. 1979.

3. Determination of the Minnesota Press Council No. 36, Minnesotans against the Downtown Dome v. The Minneapolis *Tribune,* 1979; Determination of the Minnesota Press Council No. 37, Minnesotans against the Downtown Dome v. The Minneapolis *Star,* 1979. (Shortly after these decisions, the council changed its name to the Minnesota News Council.)

4. Ronald Steel, *Walter Lippmann and the American Century* (Boston: Little, Brown, 1980), 107, 168, 246-47, 384-85, 537-38.

5. Francis Russell, *The Shadow of Blooming Grove* (New York: McGraw-Hill, 1968), 559.

6. Howard Bray, *The Pillars of the Post* (New York: Norton, 1980), 17-23, 161.

7. Current Biography: Who's News and Why 1947, s. v. Knowland, William F.; *Los Angeles Times,* 25 Feb., 3 Sept. 1974.

8. William Allen White, *The Autobiography of William Allen White* (New York: Macmillan, 1946), 630-31.

9. Paul Hutchinson, "What Makes Public Opinion?" *Survey Graphic* 28(June 1939):376.

10. *In The Public Interest — II: A Report by the National News Council, 1975-1978* (New York: National News Council, 1979), 393-414.

11. Walt Harrington, "The Hospital Memoirs, Chapter Eleven, The Watchdog's Bite," Allentown *Call-Chronicle,* 16 Jan. 1979.

12. *Washington Post,* 18, Sept. 1979; 16 Mar. 1981.

13. "The Reporter," *Philadelphia Magazine,* Apr. 1967, 42-45, 92.

14. "Nightlife Columnist Reassigned," *Philadelphia Inquirer,* 14 Sept. 1978.

15. Richard B. Tuttle, "Invitation Led to Dispute," 1980 report of the APME Professional Standards Committee, 9-10.

16. Ibid.

17. "Editor Seeking Political Post Embroils Duluth Papers in Legal Battle," *New York Times,* 17 Nov. 1978, A16.

18. "Reporter Fired for Mixing Work with Politics," *Editor & Publisher,* 17 May 1980, 21.

19. Patterson to author, 10 Mar. 1982.

20. Celeste Huenergard, "No More Cheerleading on the Sports Pages," *Editor & Publisher,* 16 June 1979, 11.

21. John Consoli, "Pro Baseball Eyes Solution to Official Scorer Problem," *Editor & Publisher,* 3 Nov. 1979, 20; "Baseball Scoring: A Dying Art," 1980 report, APME Professional Standards Committee.

22. Ibid.

23. Al McCready, "Being Married to the Mayor," *APME News,* June 1981, 15-16.
24. Jack Anderson, "Why Mike Wallace Axed a Probe," *Centre Daily Times,* State College, Pa., 27 Feb. 1981; Tony Schwartz, "'60 Minutes' Will Go Ahead with Report on Haiti," *New York Times,* 3 Mar. 1981, C20.
25. See Nelson A. Crawford, *The Ethics of Journalism* (New York: Knopf, 1924).

CHAPTER FOUR

1. Rick Alm, "Merchants Woo Writers with 'Freebie' Feasts," *Kansas City Star* and *Times,* 17 Feb. 1980; Bill Norton, "Some Outdoor Writers Accept Gifts, Discounts," Ibid.
2. Quoted by George E. Osgood, Jr., in "Ethics and the One-Reporter, Rural Bureau" (Master's paper, Pennsylvania State University, July 1981), 22-23.
3. Ibid., 25.
4. Jay Mathews, "All the President's Men," *Columbia Journalism Review* 20, no. 4(Nov./Dec. 1981):5-7.
5. Tom Hritz, "Bottled Gratitude Dies with the Rule," *Pittsburgh Post-Gazette,* 24 Dec. 1980.
6. "The Selling of the Super Bowl," *Time,* 28 Jan. 1980, 68.
7. Richard Benedetto, "The Winter of the 'Freebie Olympics,' " *1980 Report of the Professional Standards Commitee,* APME, Phoenix, Ariz.
8. Marian Burros, "The Proof Is in the Promotion," *Washington Post,* 23 Oct. 1980.
9. "Convention Reporters Filled Up," *Editor & Publisher,* 11 Oct. 1980.
10. David Halvorsen, "Managing Editors and Critics Are in Agreement on Quality," *Modern Living Report,* 1980, APME.
11. Perri Foster-Pegg, "Integrity: Not for Sale at Any Price," *Trenton Times,* 10 July 1981; Foster-Pegg to author, 27 July 1981.
12. *Report of the 1979 Ethics Committee,* ASNE.
13. Memorandum to active and associate members, SATW, 2 Sept. 1981.
14. Judy Flander, "Battlestar Los Angeles: The Networks Meet the Press," *Washington Journalism Review* 1, no. 8(Sept./Oct. 1979):57, 58, 60.
15. Sylvia Lawler, "Chasen's in Walnut Grove?" Allentown (Pa.) *Morning Call,* 27 June 1980.
16. *Report of the 1979 Ethics Committee,* ASNE.
17. Aljean Harmetz, "Film Junkets for Journalists Raising Divisive Questions," *New York Times,* 19 Mar. 1978, 54.
18. *Report of the 1979 Professional Standards Committee,* APME.

CHAPTER FIVE

1. "Inquirer Conflict in Cianfrani Case," *Philadelphia Inquirer,* 27 Aug. 1977, 1.; "Reporter Linked to a Senator's Gifts," *New York Times,* 28 Aug. 1977, 4. (Laura Foreman worked for the *Philadelphia Inquirer* from September 1973 until January 1977; she was in the Washington bureau of the *New York Times* from January until September 1977.)
2. Richard Cohen, "For Notorious Woman, 'It Just Ain't Fair,' " *Washington Post* 2 Oct. 1977.
3. Eleanor Randolph, "Conflict of Interest: A Growing Problem for Couples," *Esquire* 89, no. 2(Feb. 1978):55-59, 124-29.
4. Ibid.
5. Donald L. Barlett and James B. Steele, "The Full Story of Cianfrani and the Reporter," *Philadelphia Inquirer,* 16 Oct. 1977; Jack Tobias, "It's Okay to F—— Elephants, Just Don't Cover the Circus" (Term paper, Pennsylvania State University, Oct. 1980).
6. Laura Foreman, "My Side of the Story," *Washington Monthly* 10, no. 3(May 1978):49-54.
7. "Cianfrani, Ex-reporter Are Married," *Philadelphia Inquirer,* 16 July 1979.
8. Jack W. Germond and Jules Witcover, *Blue Smoke and Mirrors* (New York: Viking, 1981), 55-75.
9. Ibid., 77-78.
10. "Greider-Stockman Meetings Were No Secret at the Post," *Editor & Publisher,* 28 Nov. 1981, 36; "Apologetic Stockman Stays," *New York Times,* 13 Nov. 1981, 1, D16.

11. "High Court Refuses Farber Case Review," *New York Times,* 28 Nov. 1978, 1; "Jail Threat Ends for Reporter Farr," *Editor & Publisher,* 26 Dec. 1981, 9.

12. William A. Rusher, "The Press Rampant," *Columbia Journalism Review* 19, no. 4(Nov./Dec. 1979):17-19.

13. James Carey, "A Plea for the University Tradition," presidential address to the Association for Education in Journalism, Seattle, Wash., 13 Aug. 1978; Renata Adler, "Reflections on Political Scandal," *New York Review of Books,* 8 Dec. 1977, 20-23.

14. Clark Mollenhoff, "A Lack of Clear Standards for Sound Corroboration," *Bulletin of the American Society of Newspaper Editors,* May/June 1981, 34, 35.

15. "Confidential Sources," *Freedom of Information Annual Report 1979,* APME, 4-5.

16. "Who Is 'Deep Throat'? Ben Bradlee Replies," *New York Times,* 7 May 1981.

17. Ron Javers, "Poor Penn-manship," *Washington Journalism Review* 3, no. 7(Sept. 1981):16.

18. Carl Bernstein and Bob Woodward, *All the President's Men* (New York: Simon and Schuster, 1974), 71.

19. AP Log, 21 Apr. 1981.

20. Benjamin C. Bradlee, "Standards and Ethics," in *Washington Post Deskbook on Style,* ed. Robert A. Webb (New York: McGraw-Hill, 1978).

CHAPTER SIX

1. Ben H. Bagdikian, "No. 50061, Inside Maximum Security," *Washington Post,* 31 Jan. 1972.

2. Bagdikian to author, 14. Nov. 1981.

3. David Shaw, "Deception — Honest Tool of Reporting?" *Los Angeles Times,* 20 Sept. 1979.

4. Bradlee to author, 8 Mar. 1982.

5. Steve Robinson, "Pulitzers: Was the Mirage a Deception?" *Columbia Journalism Review* 18, no. 2(July/Aug. 1979):14-16.

6. Lina Mainiero, ed., *American Women Writers from Colonial Times to the Present: A Critical Reference Guide* (New York: Frederick Ungar, 1979)1:381-83.

7. Silas Bent, *Newspaper Crusaders: A Neglected Story* (New York: Whittlesey House, 1939), 198.

8. Doug Struck, "Inside Crownsville," Annapolis *Evening Capital,* 6-25 Oct. 1975.

9. Bent, *Newspaper Crusaders,* 47.

10. Frank Luther Mott, *News Stories of 1934* (Iowa City, Ia.: Clio Press, 1935), 258-60, 264-71.

11. Robinson, "Pulitzers," 14-16.

12. Dennis Holden, "Examiner Prize Lost in the Shuffle," *Washington Journalism Review* 4, no. 5(June 1982):26.

13. Virginia Dodge Fielder, "Chicago Sun-Times Study of Investigative Reporting," research report, 20 Mar. 1980.

14. "Undercover," research report of the Times Publishing Co., St. Petersburg, Fla., and the Department of Mass Communications, University of South Florida, Summer 1981.

15. Holden, "Examiner Prize," 26.

16. Shaw, "Deception."

17. John Seigenthaler, text of talk at Southern Illinois Univ., Carbondale, 5 Mar. 1981.

18. *In the Public Interest — II, Report by the National News Council, 1975-1978* (New York: National News Council, 1979), 146-50.

19. *"1 2 3 4 5," 1979 Report of the Professional Standards Committee,* APME, 2-10; Michael Cordts, remarks to the national convention, SPJ-SDX, New York, N.Y., Nov. 1979.

20. Beth Nissen, "An Inside View," *Wall Street Journal,* 28 July 1978.

21. Michael Salwen, "Getting the Story by Hook or by Crook," *Quill* 69, no. 1(Jan. 1981):12-14.

22. David Anderson and Peter Benjaminson, *Investigative Reporting* (Bloomington: Indiana Univ. Press, 1976), 109.

23. Shaw, "Deception."

24. *Investigative Reporting,* 6-7.

25. Clark R. Mollenhoff, *Investigative Reporting: From Courthouse to White House* (New York: Macmillan, 1981), 359.

CHAPTER SEVEN

1. AP Los Angeles Bureau, 21 Sept. 1981.
2. David Shaw, "AP Reporter Resigns Over Erroneous 'Banzai Run' Feature," *Los Angeles Times,* 29 Sept. 1981.
3. Ibid.
4. Nelson A. Crawford, *The Ethics of Journalism* (New York: Knopf, 1924), 39-40; Haynes Johnson, "A Wound That Will Be Long in Healing and Never Forgotten," *Washington Post,* 19 Apr. 1981.
5. Remarks by Sal Micciche, "Ombudsmanship and The Jimmy Story," *Problems of Journalism,* Proceedings of the ASNE, 1981, 60.
6. Janet Cooke, "Jimmy's World," *Washington Post,* 28 Sept. 1980.
7. *After "Jimmy's World,"* report by National News Council (New York: 1981), 16-22.
8. William Green, "The Confession," *Washington Post,* 19 Apr. 1981.
9. NBC "Today" Show, 1 and 2 Feb. 1982; AP, "She knew she'd be caught after winning Pulitzer," *Leesburg* (Fla.) *Commercial,* 2 Feb. 1982.
10. Michael Daly, "On the Streets of Belfast, the Children's War," New York *Daily News,* 6 May 1981.
11. Mitchell Stephens, "More 'Jimmy' Fallout," *Washington Journalism Review* 3, no. 6(July/Aug. 1981):13.
12. *After "Jimmy's World,"* 82.
13. Teresa Carpenter, "From Heroism to Madness: The Odyssey of the Man Who Shot Al Lowenstein," *Village Voice,* 12 May 1980.
14. Paul L. Montgomery, "Deception Denied by Reporter for Voice," *New York Times,* 11 May 1981, D12.
15. Carpenter, "From Heroism to Madness."
16. Paul Blustein, "Some Journalists Fear Flashy Reporters Let Color Overwhelm Fact," *Wall Street Journal,* 14 May 1981.
17. David J. Blum, "A Kafkaesque Tale of Health Faddists Eating Cockroaches," *Wall Street Journal,* 28 Sept. 1981.
18. James M. Markham, "Writer Admits He Fabricated an Article in Times Magazine," *New York Times,* 22 Feb. 1982, A1, A4.
19. Ron Lovell, "Wrong Way Stretch: Scoops Vanish, Credibility Remains — as One Reporter Learned after Re-creating Quotes," *Quill* 69, no. 7(July/Aug. 1981):19-20.
20. Rich Stim, "Was Randy Mantooth Ever in the Service?" *Columbia Journalism Review* 19, no. 4(Nov./Dec. 1980):38-40.
21. Clark DeLeon, "The Scene," *Philadelphia Inquirer,* 1 May 1981.
22. Ken Auletta, "Bribe, Seduce, Lie, Steal: Anything to Get the Story?" *More* 7, no. 3(Mar. 1977):14-20.
23. James C. Thomson, Jr., "Journalistic Ethics: Some Probings by a Media Keeper," *Nieman Reports* 31, no. 4/32, no. 1(Winter/Spring 1978):7-14.
24. Gallup Poll, "Investigative Reporting Has Broad Public Support," news release, 17 Dec. 1981.
25. Ann Zimmerman, "By Any Other Name . . ." *Washington Journalism Review* 1, no. 9(Nov./Dec. 1979):32-39.
26. "Long Ears in Louisville," *Time,* 14 Oct. 1974.
27. From the *Best of Gannett 1980* (Rochester, N.Y.: Gannett Co., 1981), 44-45.
28. Philip Gaskell, "The Moment of . . . What?" *Journalism Studies Review,* no. 6, July 1981, 24-25.
29. Thomas Collins of *Newsday,* "News Photographers under Fire," Orlando (Fla.) *Sentinel-Star,* 12 Dec. 1981.
30. Anthony Lewis, "Hire and Salary," *New York Times,* 26 Jan. 1978, A29; Tom Wolfe, *The Right Stuff* (New York: Farrar-Straus-Giroux, 1979), 277-96, 352-79.
31. Fred Friendly, interviewed on "Watching the Watchdog" documentary, WBBM-TV Chicago, 20 Apr. 1981.
32. "60 Minutes," CBS, 27 Sept. 1981.
33. Robert A. Webb, ed., *The Washington Post Deskbook on Style* (New York: McGraw-Hill, 1978), 4.
34. Clark R. Mollenhoff, *Investigative Reporting: From Courthouse to White House* (New York: Macmillan, 1981), 357-60.

CHAPTER EIGHT

1. Lewis Regelman is the man who tried to help save the woman's life and then took photographs as fire fighters and an ambulance crew worked on her before taking her to the hospital. He gave permission to reproduce his photographs and asked that he be credited only in this way.

2. Lil Junas, "Tragedy, Violence Photos Dominate in News Prizes," *Editor & Publisher*, 23 Feb. 1980, 17, 26; updated by Junas for this book.

3. Charles B. Seib, "Impact Photos And Reader Sensibilities," *Washington Post*, 3 Aug. 1975.

4. Remarks by Stanley Forman, Region One Conference, SPJ-SDX, Rochester, N.Y., Apr. 1976.

5. Jim Gordon, "Judgment Days for Words and Pictures," *News Photographer*, July 1980, 25-29.

6. Edwin Guthman, "On the Photos of Carter's Fall: The Inquirer Goofed," *Philadelphia Inquirer*, 1 Feb. 1981.

7. Joseph M. Ungaro, "Would You Publish This?" Undated APME photo-letter, 1976.

8. Kathleen Pavelko, "Wet T-shirt Photo: The Way the Contest Really Was," *Daily Collegian*, University Park, Pa., 11 Apr. 1977.

9. Mitchell Stephens and Eliot Frankel, "All the Obscenity That's Fit to Print," *Washington Journalism Review* 3, no. 3(Apr. 1981):15-19; Nicholas Von Hoffman, "Nine Justices for Seven Dirty Words," *More* 8, no. 6(June 1978):12-15.

10. Russell Baker, "Anti-Anglo-Saxonism," *New York Times*, 11 July 1978, A17.

11. David Shaw, *Journalism Today* (New York: Harper & Row, Harper's College Press, 1977), 208-9; "Editor's Notes," *Quill* 63, no. 5(May 1975):2.

12. Charles Alexander, "A Word — About Telling the Whole Truth," *Quill* 63, no. 5(May 1975):29-30.

13. John McCormally, letter to the editor, "Over Reacted?" *Editor & Publisher*, 26 Apr. 1975, 7.

14. John Dean, "Rituals of the Herd," *Rolling Stone*, 7 Oct. 1976.

15. Tony Schwartz, "The Insider," *New Times*, 15 Oct. 1976, 27.

16. "Most Papers Bleeped Out Butz's Punch Line," *Editor & Publisher*, 16 Oct. 1976, 13.

17. Ibid.

18. Ibid.

19. Shaw, *Journalism Today*, 211.

20. Charles B. Seib, "Media Influence," *Washington Post*, 7 Oct. 1976.

21. Stephens and Frankel, *All the Obscenity*, 15-19.

22. "Somebody Sanitized, but Not the Union," *Excerpts*, mimeo or xeroxed, ONO, 2, no. 5(Aug. 1981):1.

23. Lou Boccardi, *Prose & Cons*, no. 4, 15 Sept. 1981.

24. Stephens and Frankel, *All the Obscenity*, 15-19.

25. Boccardi, *Prose & Cons*.

26. Jim Martz, "Now, Tigers' Ford Has Time to Go Fishing," *Miami Herald*, 3 Jan. 1982.

27. John Laurence, "In Politics a Joke Is No Laughing Matter," *Washington Journalism Review* 2, no. 5 (June 1980):16-18.

28. Robert Scheer, "The Ruling Class: With a Friend Like Me. . . .", *New Times*, 7, no. 8,(15 Oct. 1976):16-18.

29. Tom Masland, "Greeks Call Mob Link Ethnic Slur," *Philadelphia Inquirer*, 5 July 1981.

30. "Colleagues Bid Judge Resign Over Slur at Homosexuals," *New York Times*, 10 Oct. 1980; Charles Maher, "Federal Judge under Fire for Use of Word 'Faggots,' " *Los Angeles Times*, 8 Oct. 1980.

31. Robert A. Webb, ed., *Washington Post Deskbook on Style* (New York: McGraw-Hill, 1978), 5, 38.

32. Ibid., 44-45.

CHAPTER NINE

1. Charles B. Seib, "How the Papers Covered the Cinema Follies Fire," *Washington Post,* 30 Oct. 1977.

2. George Beveridge, "Identifying the Movie-fire Victims," *Washington Star,* 31 Oct. 1977.

3. Seib, "How the Papers Covered."

4. Beveridge, "Identifying the Movie-fire Victims."

5. Seib, "How the Papers Covered."

6. Beveridge, "Identifying the Movie-fire Victims."

7. Seib, "How the Papers Covered."

8. David Burnham, "Poll Finds Increasing Concern over Threats to Privacy," *New York Times,* 4 May 1979, A19.

9. This very brief description of libel and privacy was drawn from Wayne Overbeck and Rick D. Pullen, *Major Principles of Media Law* (New York: Holt, Rinehart and Winston, 1982), 70-129, 344-45; Paul J. Levine, "Invasion of Privacy and the News Media," in *Reporter's Handbook* (Tallahassee: Florida Bar Association, Florida Press Association and Florida Association of Broadcasters, 1981); Christopher H. Little, "Newspaper Law and Fairness," in Robert A. Webb, ed., *The Washington Post Deskbook on Style* (New York: McGraw-Hill, 1978).

10. Ellen Karasik, "Sen. Scott's Daughter Is Arrested," *Philadelphia Inquirer,* 31 July 1975.

11. "Gannett Daily Fined $10,000 in Invasion of Privacy Case," *Editor & Publisher,* 10 Oct. 1981, 32.

12. Reece Hirsch, "It's a Small Town After All," *Byline,* Spring 1980, 31-33.

13. William Cooney, "Ex-Marine Probably Saved Ford," *San Francisco Chronicle,* 23 Sept. 1975.

14. Harry F. Rosenthal, untitled news story, AP wire, 13 Apr. 1976.

15. Daryl Lembke, "Hero in Ford Shooting Active among S.F. Gays," *Los Angeles Times,* 25 Sept. 1975.

16. Pat Murphy, "Ford Hero's Mother Has Misgivings," *Detroit News,* 26 Sept. 1975.

17. Daryl Lembke, "Ford Note Thanks S.F. Man Who Deflected Gun," *Los Angeles Times,* 26 Sept. 1975.

18. R. W. Hollis, "Sipple," research report, School of Journalism, Pennsylvania State Univ., University Park, Pa.

19. Ibid.

20. "Court Dismisses Suit by Homosexual Who Saved Ford's Life," *News Media and The Law* 4, no. 4(Oct./Nov. 1980):28-29.

21. "Sex Change Held Not Newsworthy," *News Media and The Law* 4, no. 4(Oct./Nov. 1980): 27-28.

22. Overbeck and Pullen, *Major Principles,* 116-17.

23. Complaint 195, Jan Reynolds and Judy Gibson against Winfield, Kans., Daily Courier, National News Council, filed 22 Sept. 1981.

24. Ibid.

25. Ibid.

26. Susan Seliger, "Twice Invaded," *Washington Journalism Review* 1, no. 3(Apr./May 1978):50-52.

27. Craig Ammerman, "When Being Professional Hurts Others Badly," Philadelphia *Bulletin,* 10 May 1981.

28. Julia Cass, "Smoke Bomb Puts Student on Probation," *Philadelphia Inquirer,* 6 Aug. 1981.

29. Jonathan Friendly, "9-year-old Suspect Poses Ethical Issue," *New York Times,* 8. Mar. 1981, 39.

30. I. William Hill, "Top Court Rules Out Prior Restraint Law," *Editor & Publisher,* 30 June 1979.

31. Michael T. Malloy, "Journalistic Ethics," *National Observer,* 26 July 1975.

32. Frank Sutherland, "Jerry Thompson: Before and After the Klan Series," *Gannetteer,* Apr. 1981, 10-11.

33. Ramon Coronado, "Broken Goblet, Broken Table: The Media Cover a Hostage Family," and "How Far Should the Media Go to Get a Story?" in Editorially Speaking section, *Gannetteer,* May 1981, 2, 4.

34. Robert Giles, "Some Guidelines for Newspeople," *Gannetteer,* May 1981, 12.

CHAPTER TEN

1. H. L. Stevenson, "Bill Murphy and the Bridge Jumper," *Editor & Publisher,* 12 Nov. 1977, 34.

2. Jim Gordon, "Judgment Days for Words and Pictures," *News Photographer,* July 1980, 25-29.

3. "A Public Photo, but Boy's Mother Grieves Privately," *Philadelphia Inquirer,* 6 July 1980.

4. Michael Guilfoil, "Editors Defend Play of Page 1 News Photo," *Editor & Publisher,* 3 Oct. 1981, 16, 25.

5. Bob Greene, "By Any Other Name," *Esquire,* 96, no. 3(Sept. 1981):23, 24.

6. Charles B. Seib, "Could a Little Caring Have Prevented Hoax?" *Presstime* 3, no. 6(June 1981):35.

7. Thomas J. Bray, "What If the 'Jimmy' Story Had Been True?" *Wall Street Journal,* 17 Apr. 1981.

8. John Troan, "The Lesson in the Janet Cooke Case," *Pittsburgh Press,* 3 May 1981.

9. *After "Jimmy's World": Tightening Up in Editing* (New York: National News Council, 1981), 61.

10. Phillip Knightley, *The First Casualty: From the Crimea to Vietnam — The War Correspondent as Hero, Propagandist, and Myth Maker* (New York: Harvest Book, Harcourt Brace Jovanovich, 1975), 376.

11. Michael Schudson, *Discovering the News: A Social History of American Newspapers* (New York: Basic Books, 1978), 171-72.

12. Bill Boyarsky, "Motives Sought in Suicide of Oakland Publisher Knowland," *Los Angeles Times,* 25 Feb. 1974.

13. Joe Shoquist, "When Not to Print the News," 1974 report, Professional Standards Committee, APME.

14. Paul Poorman, "Kidnapped!" *Bulletin of the ASNE,* Nov./Dec. 1975, 10-12.

15. Deirdre Carmody, "Some News Groups Knew of 6 in Hiding," *New York Times,* 31 Jan. 1980, A10.

16. *Covering Crime: How Much Press-Police Cooperation? How Little?* (New York: National News Council, 1981), 20-21.

17. Christopher H. Little, "Newspaper Law and Fairness," in Robert A. Webb, ed., *The Washington Post Deskbook on Style* (New York: McGraw-Hill, 1978), 24-25.

18. David Shaw, "Newsmen Generally Criticize Lopez Decision to Testify in Bonin Case," *Los Angeles Times,* 18 Dec. 1981.

19. Ibid.

20. Tom Zito, "Witness to a Shooting on a New York Street," *Washington Post,* 22 Sept. 1981.

21. "IRE Leader Feels Reporters Should Surrender Notes," *Editor & Publisher,* 3 Mar. 1979.

22. "Son of Sam" is the label New York police gave to the killer of six people in New York City in 1976-77. After an intense manhunt, police captured and charged David Berkowitz, who in 1978 was sentenced to twenty-five years to life for each killing and up to twenty-five years for seven other attempted murders and assaults; Stephen Salisbury, ".44-Caliber Journalism" *Nation* 228, no. 20(May 26, 1979):591-93.

23. Arnold H. Ismach and Everette E. Dennis, "Congdon Case: Did Press Make It a Show?" *Minneapolis Star* Saturday Magazine, 1 Oct. 1977.

24. Charles W. Bailey, "Point of View," Minneapolis Tribune, 9 Oct. 1977.

25. Flora Johnson, "The Persecution of Frank Walus," *Student Lawyer* 9, no. 9(May 1981):21-23, 46-52.

26. Benjamin C. Bradlee, "Standards and Ethics," in Robert A. Webb, ed., *The Washington Post Deskbook on Style* (New York: McGraw-Hill, 1978), 3.

27. Christopher H. Little, "Newspaper Law and Fairness," ibid., 16-18.

CHAPTER ELEVEN

1. Gary A. Hogge, M.D., "You Can Fight City Hall: Even When It's a Newspaper," *Medical Economics,* 21 July 1980, 69-72.

2. National News Council Report, "Random Check Left Out Doctor at Top of Fee Listing," *Columbia Journalism Review* 19, no. 2(July/Aug. 1980):86-87.

3. Hogge, "You Can Fight," 69-72.

4. George Gallup, Jr., "Americans Favor Tougher Controls on the Press," *Editor & Publisher,* 19 Jan. 1980, 7.

5. "Movers and Shakers," *Washington Journalism Review* 3, no. 9(Nov. 1981):7.

6. *After "Jimmy's World": Tightening Up in Editing* (New York: National News Council, 1981), 114.

7. Ibid., 124-25.

8. Drake to Professor R. Thomas Berner, Pennsylvania State University, 30 Nov. 1981, excerpted with the letter writer's permission.

9. *After "Jimmy's World",* 124-25.

10. "Associated Press Moves Erroneous Hinckley Photo," *Editor & Publisher,* 11 Apr. 1981, 48.

11. H. L. Mencken, *Prejudices: Sixth Series* (New York: Knopf, 1927), 15.

12. Nelson A. Crawford, *The Ethics of Journalism* (New York: Knopf, 1924), 74.

13. Complaint 194, Robert Gulack against New York Daily News, National News Council, New York, N.Y., 14 Sept. 1981.

14. Betty Medsger, "Trial by Newspaper," *New West,* 19 Nov. 1979, 126-35.

15. David Shaw, "Legal Issues: Press Still Falls Short," *Los Angeles Times,* 11 Nov. 1980.

16. A. Kent MacDougall, "Flaws in Press Coverage Plus Business Sensitivity Stir Bitter Debate," *Los Angeles Times,* 3 Feb. 1980.

17. A. Kent MacDougal, "When Press Errs on Business, It's Usually Muddled, Not Malicious, *Los Angeles Times,* 4 Feb. 1980.

18. Cortland Anderson, remarks to APME Convention, Toronto, 21 Oct. 1981.

19. Ronald Steel, *Walter Lippmann and the American Century* (Boston: Little, Brown, 1980), 200.

20. "Corrections," *Centre Daily Times,* State College, Pa., 14 Mar. 1981.

21. "The 2,300-word Times Correction," *Time,* 23 Feb. 1981, p. 84; Andrew Radolf, "New York Times Clears Ex-envoy's Name," *Editor & Publisher,* 28 Feb. 1981, 42-43.

22. Flora Lewis, "The Meanest Way," *New York Times,* 9 Mar. 1981, A23.

23. Phil Gailey, "The Trail of the Rumor on Blair House's 'Bug,' " *New York Times,* 18 Nov. 1981, A24; Gailey, "Carters Threaten to Sue for Libel," *New York Times,* 9 Oct. 1981, A25; Paul Taylor, "Post Apologizes to Carter for Gossip Column Item," *Washington Post,* 23 Oct. 1981.

24. "Text of Carter Statement on Paper's Apology," *New York Times,* 25. Oct. 1981, A27.

25. "So There: Editor's Apology in No Uncertain Terms," AP unpublished file copy, 22 Dec. 1980.

26. The author cannot identify the reliable source for this tale without harming him or her.

27. John W. C. Johnstone, Edward J. Slawski, William W. Bowman, *The News People: A Sociological Portrait of American Journalists and Their Work* (Urbana: Univ. of Illinois Press, 1977).

28. Everette E. Dennis, "Touchstones: The Reporter's Reality," *Nieman Reports* 34, no. 3(Autumn 1980):40-43.

29. "Mayor Not Shot . . . and That Was the News," *AP Log,* 6 July 1981.

INTERVIEWS

Interviewees are identified by the job titles they held at the time of the interview.

AMMERMAN, CRAIG, executive editor, Philadelphia *Bulletin,* 27 May 1981.
ARTHUR, WILLIAM B., executive director, National News Council, 5 Oct. 1981.
BEAUPRE, LARRY, managing editor, Rochester (N.Y.) *Times-Union,* 15 Oct. 1981.
BEHRINGER, FRED, vice-president and executive editor, Montgomery Publishing Co., Ft. Washington, Pa., 26 May 1981.
BELLUNE, JERRY, editor of editorial page, Philadelphia *Bulletin,* 3 Nov. 1981.
BENISON, DIANE, managing editor, Worcester (Mass.) *Evening Gazette,* 19 Oct. 1981.
BLACK, DON, director of photography, Salem (Oreg.) *Statesman-Journal,* 10 Nov. 1981.
BOCCARDI, LOUIS D., executive editor and vice-president, Associated Press, 8 Oct. 1981.
BORCOVER, ALFRED S., editor, travel section, *Chicago Tribune,* 10 Sept. 1981.
BRADLEE, BENJAMIN C., executive editor, *Washington Post,* 5 June 1981.
BRODER, DAVID, political reporter-columnist, *Washington Post,* May 1981.
BUKRO, CASEY, environment editor, *Chicago Tribune,* 10 Sept. 1981.
BULL, JOHN, assistant to the managing editor, *Philadelphia Inquirer,* 27 May 1981.
BUTTERFIELD, BRUCE D., reporter, Providence (R.I.) *Journal-Bulletin,* 18 Nov. 1981.
CASALE, ANTHONY, executive city editor, Rochester (N.Y.) *Times-Union,* 16 Oct. 1981.
CHANDLER, OTIS, editor in chief, Times Mirror Co., Los Angeles, 25 Nov. 1980.
CONY, ED, vice-president for news, Dow-Jones & Co., 20 Oct. 1981.
COWLES, JOHN, JR., president, Minneapolis Star and Tribune Company, 15 Mar. 1982.
CUNNINGHAM, RICHARD P., associate director, National News Council, 5 Oct. 1981.
CURRIE, PHIL, director of news staff development, Gannett Company, 22 Oct. 1981.
DAVIES, MICHAEL J., editor, *Kansas City Star* and *Times,* 23 Oct. 1981.
DEIBLER, WILLIAM E., managing editor, *Pittsburgh Post-Gazette,* 22 Oct. 1981.
DENNISTON, LYLE, Supreme Court reporter, *Washington Star,* 5 June 1981.
DONNA, JAMES, chief of New York bureau, Associated Press, 8 Oct. 1981
DORNFELD, STEVE, Washington correspondent, Knight-Ridder Newspapers, 3 Apr. 1981.
DUNLAP, JAMES A., editor, Sharon (Pa.) *Herald,* 28 Oct. 1981.
DUSCHA, JULIUS, director, Washington Journalism Center, 5 June 1981.
EISEN, DAVID J., director research and information, the Newspaper Guild, 17 Apr. 1981.
FEINSILBER, MIKE, Washington reporter, Associated Press, 23 Sept. 1981.
FINDLEY, ELLEN R., special projects reporter, Baton Rouge (La.) *Morning Advocate,* 15 Feb. 1981.
FOREMAN, GENE, managing editor, *Philadelphia Inquirer,* 28 May 1981.
FRIENDLY, JONATHAN, news media reporter, New York Times, 7 Oct. 1981.
FULLER, CHET, reporter, *Atlanta Journal,* May 1981.
GAY, BOB, free-lance news photographer, 16 Nov. 1981.
GILES, ROBERT, editor, Rochester (N.Y.) *Times-Union* and *Democrat & Chronicle,* 15 Oct. 1981.
GRAHAM, DONALD, publisher, *Washington Post,* 4 June 1981.
GREEN, WILLIAM, ombudsman, *Washington Post,* 3 June 1981.
GREENE, ROBERT W., assistant managing editor, *Newsday,* Long Island, N.Y., 6 Oct. 1981.
HASKIN, DONALD, associate editor, *Philadelphia Daily News,* 27 May 1981.
HEALY, BRIAN, Washington producer, CBS Morning News, 25 Sept. 1981.
HOGE, JAMES, editor in chief, *Chicago Sun-Times,* May 1981.
HUME, BRIT, Capitol Hill correspondent, ABC News, 4 Nov. 1981.
ISAACS, NORMAN L., chairman, National News Council, 7 Oct. 1981.
ISAACS, STEPHEN D., editor and senior vice-president, *Minneapolis Star,* 12 Nov. 1981.
JANENSCH, PAUL, executive editor, *Louisville Times* and *Courier-Journal,* 19 Oct. 1981.
JOHNSON, HAYNES, reporter-columnist, *Washington Post,* 4 June 1981.
JONES, DAVID R., national editor, *New York Times,* 7 Oct. 1981.
KELLY, TOM, director of photography, Pottstown (Pa.) *Mercury,* 8 Jan. 1982.

KIMBALL, JOSEPH, reporter, *Minneapolis Tribune,* 26 Mar. 1982.
KURTIS, BILL, chief anchor, WBBM-TV, Chicago, 8 Sept. 1981.
LANDAU, JACK, director, Reporters Committee for Freedom of the Press, 24 Sept. 1981.
LANGFORD, GEORGE, sports editor, *Chicago Tribune,* 8 Sept. 1981.
LAWLER, SYLVIA, TV reporter-critic, Allentown (Pa.) *Call-Chronicle,* 18 Nov. 1981.
LEWIS, CLAUDE, associate editor, Philadelphia *Bulletin,* 17 Sept. 1981.
LOVELADY, STEVE, associate executive editor, *Philadelphia Inquirer,* 16 Sept. 1981.
LUDLOW, LYNN, reporter, *San Francisco Examiner,* 29 Nov. 1980.
LYON, BILL, sports reporter, columnist, *Philadelphia Inquirer,* 28 May 1981.
MATTHEWS, CURT, Washington correspondent, Baltimore *Sun,* 3 June 1981.
McHUGH, ROBERT, executive editor, Gulfport/Biloxi (Miss.) *Sun* and *Daily Herald,* 16 Feb.
     1981.
MILLER, IRA, sports reporter, *San Francisco Chronicle,* 2 Dec. 1980.
MILLER, NORMAN C., Washington bureau chief, *Wall Street Journal,* 29 Oct. 1981.
MONAGHAN, NANCY, day metro editor, Rochester (N.Y.) *Democrat & Chronicle,* 16 Oct. 1981.
MURPHY, WILLIAM T., JR., photographer, *Oregon Journal,* 27 Mar. 1982.
NAUGHTON, JAMES, associate managing editor, *Philadelphia Inquirer,* 16 Sept. 1981.
NAUMAN, ART, ombudsman, *Sacramento Bee,* 2 Nov. 1981.
NELSON, JACK, Washington bureau chief, *Los Angeles Times,* 2 June 1981.
O'DONNELL, LAURENCE, managing editor, *Wall Street Journal,* 22 Feb. 1982.
O'NEILL, MICHAEL J., editor and executive vice-president, New York *Daily News,* 8 Oct. 1981.
OTWELL, RALPH, editor and executive vice-president, *Chicago Sun-Times,* 9 Sept. 1981.
PERLIK, CHARLES A., JR., president, the Newspaper Guild, 18 Apr. 1981.
PETERSON, THEODORE, professor, College of Communications, Univ. of Illinois-Urbana, 3 Sept.
     1981.
POORMAN, PAUL A., editor and vice-president, *Akron Beacon Journal,* 8 Apr. 1981.
PRATO, LOU, news director, WDTN-TV, Dayton, Ohio; treasurer RTNDA, 9 Nov. 1981.
PUFFENBARGER, CHARLES, assistant financial editor, *Washington Post,* 23 Sept. 1981.
RAMSEY, RICHARD J., executive secretary, Contracts Committee, the Newspaper Guild, 17
     Apr. 1981.
ROBERTS, EUGENE L., executive editor, *Philadelphia Inquirer,* 28 May 1981 and 15 Sept. 1981.
ROSENTHAL, ABRAHAM M., executive editor, *New York Times,* 7 Oct. 1981.
SAUL, ANNE M., managing editor, Cocoa (Fla.) *Today,* 21 Oct. 1981.
SCHEER, ROBERT, reporter, *Los Angeles Times,* 25 Nov. 1980.
SCHWARTZ, JERRY, reporter, Associated Press, New York bureau, 13 Nov. 1981.
SEATON, DAVE, publisher, Winfield (Kans.) *Courier,* 5 Mar. 1982.
SEIB, CHARLES, retired ombudsman, *Washington Post,* 9 Nov. 1981.
SEVERSON, JACK, regional reporter, *Philadelphia Inquirer,* 18 Sept. 1981.
SHAW, DAVID, media reporter-critic, *Los Angeles Times,* 25 Nov. 1980.
SHOQUIST, JOSEPH W., managing editor, *Milwaukee Journal,* 19 Oct. 1981.
SITTON, CLAUDE, editorial director and vice-president, News and Observer Publishing Co.,
     Raleigh, N.C., 4 Nov. 1981.
SMALL, WILLIAM J., president, NBC News, 5 Oct. 1981.
STARR, RICK, sports editor, *Valley News Dispatch,* New Kensington, Pa., 14 Nov. 1981.
TAIT, ELAINE, food editor, *Philadelphia Inquirer,* 12 Nov. 1981.
THOMAS, WILLIAM F., editor and executive vice-president, *Los Angeles Times,* 2 Nov. 1981.
TUTTLE, RICHARD B., executive editor, Elmira (N.Y.) *Star-Gazette,* 14 Oct. 1981.
URBAN, ROBERT J., editor, Pottstown (Pa.) *Mercury,* 26 May 1981.
WALL, JAMES, editor, *Christian Century,* 9 Sept. 1981.
WHEELER, LINDA, photographer, reporter and editor, *Washington Post,* 24 Sept. 1981.
WHITE, RAY, editor, *Washington Journalism Review,* 1 June 1981.
WHITTEN, LESLIE H., investigative reporter turned novelist, 2 Sept. 1981.
WOLIN, MERLE LINDA, Latin affairs reporter, *Los Angeles Herald Examiner,* 16 Nov. 1981.
WOODHULL, NANCY, managing editor, Rochester (N.Y.) *Democrat & Chronicle,* 16 Oct. 1981.
ZEKMAN, PAMELA, director, investigative team, WBBM-TV, Chicago, 8 Sept. 1981.

BIBLIOGRAPHICAL ESSAY

MINING WRITTEN SOURCES for knowledge and insights about journalistic ethics in the United States is interesting business — if you like looking for needles in haystacks. There are few direct sources: Books, magazine or journal articles, or reports devoted entirely to this subject are scarce. You have to glean what you can from written works that deal with news media ethics secondarily or even peripherally — examining all that had been written by or about Lincoln Steffens, for example, as one of my graduate students did, to try to discover how the famous muckraker felt about and coped with his ethical problems.

Many of the sources for this book, of course, were working journalists and news media observers. I taped interviews with about 150 such sources, about 100 of whom are quoted in the book. I tried to include in this book the best of what I learned from those interviews, but it was impossible to use more than a fraction of the oral gems collected. The tapes will be turned over to the Pennsylvania State University library in due time so that they will be useful, I hope, to students of ethics as applied to U.S. journalism.

Of the few current books that do deal solely with journalistic ethics, I found three to be particularly useful: John L. Hulteng's *The Messenger's Motives: Ethical Problems of the News Media* (Englewood Cliffs, N.J.: Prentice-Hall, 1976) and *Playing It Straight* (Chester, Connecticut: Globe Pequot, 1981); and Bruce M. Swain's *Reporters' Ethics* (Ames: Iowa State University Press, 1978). (*Playing It Straight* is a 90-page interpretation and discussion of the Statement of Principles of the ASNE, which published the book.) These three books provide contemporary examples and assessments of how U.S. journalists define and deal with their ethical quandaries.

Other current books are helpful even though they cover matters besides the ethics of journalism: Sissela Bok's *Lying: Moral Choice in Public and Private Life* (New York: Vintage Books, 1979) is a thoughtful examination by a thoughtful ethicist of liars and lying in several fields, including journalism and advertising. *Investigative Reporting* by David Anderson and Peter Benjaminson (Bloomington: Indiana University Press, 1976), and *Investigative Reporting: From Courthouse to White House* by Clark R. Mollenhoff (New York: Macmillan, 1981) contain

319

interesting advice by their experienced journalist-authors on walking the ethical tightropes posed by the kind of reporting that often sends big shots to jail. Similar insights and experiences are offered in *All the President's Men*, by Carl Bernstein and Bob Woodward (New York: Simon and Schuster, 1974), the two *Washington Post* reporters who openly admit to ethical transgressions in their investigation of the Watergate scandal that helped bring down President Nixon. Some valuable material on journalistic ethics can be strained from Howard Bray's *The Pillars of the Post* (New York: W. W. Norton, 1980) and Harrison E. Salisbury's *Without Fear or Favor* (New York: Ballantine, 1980), two excellent histories of the *Washington Post* and of the *New York Times*. Besides Salisbury, two other *Times*men have contributed to an understanding of this subject — Tom Wicker through his *On Press* (New York: Viking, 1978) and James Reston through *The Artillery of the Press* (New York: Harper & Row, 1966). I found useful extractions on journalists and their ethics in Jack W. Germond and Jules Witcover's account of the 1980 presidential campaign, *Blue Smoke and Mirrors* (New York: Viking, 1981); in Phillip Knightley's study of war correspondents, *The First Casualty: From the Crimea to Vietnam — The War Correspondent as Hero, Propagandist, and Myth Maker* (New York: Harvest, 1976); and in Anthony Smith's description of what the computer is doing to newspapers and journalistic practice, *Goodbye Gutenberg* (New York: Oxford, 1980).

Two readers and the third edition of an old friend need to be acknowledged. The readers — *Ethics, Morality and the Media*, compiled and edited by Lee Thayer (New York: Hastings, 1980) and *Questioning Media Ethics*, edited by Bernard Rubin (New York: Praeger, 1978) — contain some useful essays. Particularly stimulating to me were Thayer's introductory essay, and commentaries in his collection by Ben Bagdikian, Harry Ashmore, and Sander Vanocur. In Rubin, the most valuable chapters for someone interested in journalism ethics were contributed by Rubin himself and by James C. Thomson, Jr., curator of the Nieman Foundation at Harvard. The old friend is *Responsibility in Mass Communication*; I used its first edition by Wilbur Schramm in an introductory mass media and society course when I first got into teaching years ago. The third edition (New York: Harper & Row, 1980) credits two coauthors, William L. Rivers and Clifford G. Christians, who have strengthened an already sound book with new material, much of which is relevant to the study of news media ethics.

The standard histories of American journalism seldom deal directly with ethical problems in journalism, but the following works are useful for those interested in tracing the roots of rights and wrongs in the field: Perhaps the most valuable of the few early books on journalistic ethics is Nelson Crawford's *The Ethics of Journalism* (New York: Knopf, 1924).

Crawford argued for the firm establishment of objectivity as the basis of news reporting and called for a broad-based organization of journalists to make journalism a true profession and to develop licensing standards. In doing so he described ethical problems in the field early in this century. His book also contains a collection of many of the early codes of ethics and rules adopted by organizations of journalists and newspapers, including the one adopted by the Kansas Editorial Association in 1910, which Crawford believed was the earliest code of ethics put forth by any association of U.S. journalists. Michael Schudson's stimulating reinterpretation of how news evolved in this country in his *Discovering the News: A Social History of American Newspapers* (New York: Basic Books, 1978) contains a refreshing discussion of objectivity in reporting. Daniel J. Leab describes the beginnings of the Newspaper Guild in *A Union of Individuals: The Formation of the American Newspaper Guild, 1933-1936* (New York: Columbia University Press, 1970).

To get at the history of ideas that might bear on ethical practices in journalism, the following works are valuable: the report of the Commission on Freedom of the Press, headed by Robert M. Hutchins, *A Free and Responsible Press* (University of Chicago Press, 1947); one of the spin-off studies from the commission's investigation written by a commission member, William E. Hocking, Harvard professor of philosophy, *Freedom of the Press, A Framework of Principle* (University of Chicago Press, 1947); the classic interpretation of the main ideas that have shaped the four basic press systems in the world, *Four Theories of the Press*, by Fred S. Siebert, Theodore Peterson, and Wilbur Schramm (Urbana: University of Illinois Press, 1956); Harold L. Cross's *The People's Right to Know* (New York: Columbia University Press, 1953); and Walter Lippmann's still-worthy-after-all-these-years *Public Opinion* (New York: Harcourt, Brace, 1922). (Additional insights into Lippmann's thinking can be found in Ronald Steel's fine biography, *Walter Lippmann and the American Century* [Boston: Little, Brown, 1980].)

A Free and Responsive Press, published by the Twentieth Century Fund in 1973, contains the report of the task force that led to the formation of the National News Council later that same year and a background paper by Alfred Balk discussing the press council experiment here and abroad. Other useful background on U.S. press councils can be found in *Backtalk* by William L. Rivers, William B. Blankenburg, Kenneth Starck, and Earl Reeves (San Francisco: Canfield, 1972), an account of four local press councils established in Riverside, California; Bend, Oregon; St. Louis, Missouri; and Cairo, Illinois. These councils were set up by university researchers supported by the Mellett Fund for a Free and Responsible Press, a small foundation established in 1966 with a bequest from Lowell Mellett, the first editor of the Washington *Daily*

News. (I have been a director of the fund since its founding and am, at this writing, its president.)

Since it started in 1973, the National News Council has been an important source of current information for those interested in journalistic ethics and standards. The New York-based council has issued a number of publications describing its findings in cases it has investigated, and plans to issue more in the future. See especially: *In the Public Interest — II*, a meaty report on the cases investigated by the council between 1975 and 1978; *Covering Crime: How Much Press-Police Cooperation? How Little?*, a 1981 report by council associate director A. H. Raskin; and *After "Jimmy's World": Tightening Up in Editing*, another 1981 report, written by William B. Arthur, the council's executive director, and by the two associate directors, Raskin and Richard P. Cunningham, who describe the council's findings in its investigations of the *Washington Post* hoax "Jimmy's World" and the New York *Village Voice* article on the murderer of Congressman Allard Lowenstein.

At least two professional associations of journalists publish materials that shed light on ethics and standards. Since its founding in 1923, the ASNE has published the proceedings of its annual meeting under the title *Problems of Journalism: Proceedings of the ASNE 1923*, etc. This volume usually contains the full report of ASNE's standing Ethics Committee. The APME also publishes its proceedings under the title *APME Red Book 1982*, etc. It also contains at least a partial report of the APME Professional Standards Committee; the full report in printed form is distributed at APME's annual conventions.

Among journals, the *Columbia Journalism Review* and the *Washington Journalism Review* have paid frequent attention to ethical problems. *Quill*, the magazine of the SPJ, and *Feed/Back*, a West Coast journalism review published in San Francisco, often contain articles and items dealing with the ethics of journalism. So does *Nieman Reports*, published by the Nieman Foundation of Harvard University. Ethical matters also are frequently examined in the monthly ASNE *Bulletin* and the "Editorially Speaking" section of the monthly *Gannetteer.*

Finally, the ethics codes and policies of national associations of journalists and of individual news organizations are useful in understanding ethical standards in the field. Particularly helpful are the codes of the ASNE, APME, the RTNDA, and the SPJ. The most valuable of the more detailed and specific ethics policies of individual news organizations are those adopted by the *Philadelphia Inquirer*, the *Washington Post* (published in *The Washington Post Deskbook on Style*. [New York: McGraw-Hill, 1978]), and the news departments of the three commercial broadcast networks, ABC, CBS, and NBC.

INDEX